D0461362

Ethics and international affairs: Extent and limits

Edited by Jean-Marc Coicaud and Daniel Warner

 **United Nations University Press**

TOKYO · NEW YORK · PARIS

United Nations University Press
The United Nations University, 53-70, Jingumae 5-chome,
Shibuya-ku, Tokyo, 150-8925, Japan
Tel: +81-3-3499-2811   Fax: +81-3-3406-7345
E-mail: sales@hq.unu.edu
http://www.unu.edu

United Nations University Office in North America
2 United Nations Plaza, Room DC2-1462-70, New York, NY 10017, USA
Tel: +1-212-963-6387   Fax: +1-212-371-9454
E-mail: unuona@igc.apc.org

United Nations University Press is the publishing division of the United Nations University.

Cover design by Andrew Corbett

Printed in the United States of America

UNUP-1052
ISBN 92-808-1052-9

Library of Congress Cataloging-in-Publication Data

Ethics and international affairs : extent and limits / edited by Jean-Marc Coicaud and Daniel Warner.
    p.   cm.
    Includes bibliographical references and index.
    ISBN 92-808-1052-9
    1. International relations-Moral and ethical aspects.   I. Coicaud, Jean-Marc.   II. Warner, Daniel.
JZ1306   .E873   2001
172′.4—dc21   00-012897

Contents

Acknowledgements

This book is the product of a two-year research project conducted under the auspices of the Peace and Governance Programme of the United Nations University (Tokyo). It was made possible by a grant from the . Trust Fund for Interest on the Contribution to the United Nations Special Account. In the course of the project, the editors and authors benefited from the hospitality offered by the Graduate Institute of International Studies (Geneva) and the New School for Social Research (New York), with the support of Sondra Farganis, for the holding of two workshops. At the first workshop, in Geneva, Andrew Clapham, Ibrahim Fall, Pierre-Michel Fontaine, Françoise Héritier, Peider Koenz, Gangapersaud B. Ramcharan, Pierre de Senarclens, and Fernando Tesón helped to focus on a number of key areas and issues. In Tokyo, Yoshie Sawada was instrumental in giving administrative support for the implementation of the project. The editors and authors wish here to thank these institutions and people for their support, as well as the anonymous reviewers of the manuscript for their very useful comments and, in the office of the United Nations University Press, Manfred Boemeke, Janet Boileau, and the copy editor, Cherry Ekins, for their help for bringing this book to life.

Jean-Marc Coicaud and Daniel Warner

1

Introduction: Reflections on the extent and limits of contemporary international ethics

Jean-Marc Coicaud and Daniel Warner

To introduce what is at stake in ethics and contemporary international affairs requires us to focus on three sets of issues. First, since nowhere in the rest of the book is ethics defined and discussed in general terms, a few thoughts are needed to clarify what is meant in a broad sense. Second, the authors will reflect upon some of the major elements shaping the interplay between ethics and contemporary international affairs. Touching upon these two sets of issues will lay the ground for the examination, throughout the book, of the ethical dimensions of the current international context. Finally, this chapter will offer a brief overview of the main themes addressed and areas covered by the authors.

Some considerations on ethics in general

Ethics is concerned with being as close as possible to realizing the idea, the positive idea, of what it is to be a human being. It is about approaching as closely as possible a sense of what is essentially *human* in our nature. In thinking and acting in an ethical manner, the individual makes himself a witness to what positively distinguishes humans: the quest for dignity. As such, ethics is a search for a reconciled presence – a reconciled presence to oneself, presence to others, presence to the world. This is also to say that ethics is not about the self in isolation. Ethics,

1

fundamentally, has a social quality. It aims at integrating the existence and the fate of others into our vision of ourselves, into our thoughts and actions. It is about feeling that our individual lives extend to the lives of others. Ethics forces each of us to feel that our identity is also defined by our relations to others. It is the experience that, somehow, we owe something to others and that our ability to handle what we owe to others decides in some sense who we are. In fact, this social dimension of ethics tells us that virtues, which we can generally think about as the substance of ethical behaviour, are social virtues. Think, for instance, about justice, or responsibility, or solidarity. The essence of these virtues is a recognition of what we owe to others and is dedicated to ensuring that others receive their fair share.

On ethics, reciprocity, and responsibility

It follows from this that ethics has also to be understood as the experience and organization of reciprocity. It has to be understood as the organization of rights and duties. Nothing is more common, indeed, than to think of an ethical attitude as one that presupposes the existence of others' rights. This recognition engenders a duty – the duty to respect others' rights. By the same token, in respecting others' rights, by making it one's own duty, one secures one's own rights and others' sense that they are similarly duty bound to protect them. It is this constant exchange of rights and duties among people that accounts for the sense of reciprocity among them, a system of ethical interactions. The importance that every discourse on ethics attributes to respect and tolerance is a clear illustration of the special place of reciprocity.

From the organization of reciprocity, the exchange of rights and duties, which in the end is part of the social cement required for people to live together, derives a sense of responsibility and solidarity. Ethical and dutiful action is bound up with the projection of responsibility and solidarity. Incidentally, while these two notions – responsibility and solidarity – constitute the cornerstones of ethics in any society, it is interesting to note that they have acquired a prime importance in contemporary ethics as shaped by democratic ethics. There are two simple reasons for this. On the one hand, responsibility echoes the modern conception of the individual; that is, the idea that each person has the power to deliberate freely and autonomously about whom he or she wants to be. On the other hand, because they are so dependent upon the will of the individual, responsibility and solidarity constantly run the risk of being undermined by self-centredness and self-interest.

Ethics, values, and law

The sense of reconciled presence and the experience of reciprocity that primarily comprise ethics lead each of us to try to embody a concept of decency. Ethics is about trying to be decent. As such, ethics is charged with values. It is the expression of a preference for certain values over others. When it comes to ethics, values play three key roles. First, values define what is good and, consequently, what is bad. They define what is right and, consequently, what is wrong. Obviously, the good defined by these values is premised upon the respectful interaction of people. That is why justice is the ultimate ethical value. Justice focuses on finding and constantly fine-tuning what is good, what is right. This constant search for justice explains the evolution of rights. It explains, for instance, the fact that acts not forbidden by law yesterday may today be viewed as crimes.

Second, in defining what is good and bad, what is right and wrong, values participate in the ethical mapping of the world in which we live. They contribute to the establishment of distinctions and hierarchies between, on the one hand, principles to abide by and ideals to aspire to, and on the other hand, courses of action to avoid. They are part of the process that articulates what is commendable and what is condemnable. They help point the arrow towards what we should be striving for, what we should be and what we should do. To understand how the power of ethics to discriminate between what is good and what is bad differs from morality – because ethics and morality, although highly related, are not strictly identical – a precise definition is needed. Morality is primarily, if not exclusively, an evaluation of what is good and what is bad in absolute terms. It is a praise of what is good and a condemnation of what is bad, conducted in absolute terms. Ethics is different. Ethics approaches and organizes what is good and what is bad by keeping sight of the imperative of reciprocity among people, of the need to facilitate their lives together. This is why morality can sometimes be intolerant in its absolute judgements, while ethics tends to value tolerance, to look for ways to accommodate, reconcile, and bring together different people and their various points of view.

Values play a third role in ethics, especially the positive values, those that ethics favours and cherishes the most: justice, love, friendship, tolerance, compassion, empathy, generosity, integrity, sincerity, courage. Here ethics boils down to the fact that positive values, values that bring people together, not only allow people to relate to themselves, to others, and to their environment in a reconciled manner. They are also the good exchanged in the relationship. Take, for instance, the value of justice. Justice puts two individuals in contact on an equitable footing *and* is a good that they exchange. Similarly, love is a value that brings two individuals closer *and* is a good that is exchanged between them. Another effect of positive values on people – the effect of justice, of love – is that they fuel a desire for and the possibility of more – more justice, more love. The more people experience love, the more people value love. The more people experience justice, the more they value justice. In brief, experiencing positive values has an inspirational and fulfilling effect on people, an effect that enhances the desire for and the possibility of a more ethical world geared towards opening up to others and sharing.

The sense of justice and reciprocity that animates ethics cannot, however, be implemented in a vacuum or on its own. The positive effect that the experience of justice has on people is not enough to ensure that individuals will abide by the rule of ethics naturally. After all, human beings are imperfect, and they have to be helped to become and remain ethical. If we were assured that people would behave ethically naturally, if we were certain that compassion and respect for others would be the exclusive guiding principles of people's thoughts and actions, law would not be needed. In the absence of such certainty, laws are required to make a minimum of ethics a daily reality. Law, whether private or public, whether national or international, ensures that a minimum sense of responsibility and reciprocity, a minimum sense of ethics, regulates the relationships among individuals and among states.

From ethics to international affairs

Ultimately, the ethical dimension of responsibility is linked with the notion of choice, and with the central place, and the moral burden, that it has come to hold in modern life. From the start, ethics is about deliberating and eventually choosing among a variety of options. This requires a choice between what is morally right and what is morally wrong. The difficulty and the challenge of modern culture, and more specifically of contemporary culture, are that there have never been more options for our moral judgements and our ethical choice than today, at least in highly developed societies. In addition, if it is the power to influence the world, to change and improve it, that creates the possibility of an ethical choice, if it is this power that makes an issue of whether to feel responsible, whether to exercise responsibility, it results that the responsibility for ethical behaviour falls first to the powerful rather than to the powerless.[1] Think of the destitute individual in India who struggles daily to stay alive. Can this individual do anything to improve the ethical character of international relations, of world order? The answer is, largely, no. But wealthy and powerful individuals and countries can certainly help. It is then up to them to use their power ethically or otherwise.

A telling and perturbing illustration of this state of affairs is the fact that most of the theorization on ethics, on the conditions of an ethical exercise of power, is a by-product of situations of power hegemony. This is the case for the ethics of politics at the national level, but also for the ethics of politics at the international level. For example, in international law scholars such as Vittoria, Grotius, Pufendorf, and Vatel were reflecting upon and theorizing international ethics and international affairs at a time when Europe was dominating the world and was confronted with the ethical and unethical dimensions of its international power. Nowadays, a great number of the works dealings with international ethics come from the USA, and American scholars are all too often led to think that international ethics is first and foremost about analysing whether US hegemony could ever be internationally ethical.[2] While this matter is certainly of great importance, there is more than this to ethics and contemporary international affairs.

International ethics and the contemporary context

The 1990s brought about a renewal of activity at the international level. Local, national, regional, and international actors seized the opportunity offered by the period – especially in the first half of the 1990s – to call for changes envisioned and designed to improve the distribution of power and responsibilities in some of the most critical areas of international politics. Human rights, humanitarian intervention, refugees, international economic justice, and the environment came to the fore. The spirit of the times advocated greater respect and better implementation of certain norms in the name of a more "ethical" politics.

Acting ethically at the international level seemed a real possibility in the 1990s. Minimally, the end of the Cold War created space that did not exist before, for the clear reason that confrontation between the superpowers superseded other considerations. Along with the end of the Cold War, the growing importance attributed to the democratization of the international system also favoured a more ethical approach to international problems. As a result, progress was achieved in the last decade – a progress that worked in favour of the awareness, conceptualization, and implementation of a different agenda in international affairs. Human rights, international criminal justice, and environmental issues have now become central features of public discourse. In itself, this is no small achievement.

But the initial sense of opportunity and optimism proved to be presumptuous. Indeed, at the beginning of 2000, 10 years into the post-Cold War era, we are still very far away from having the new agenda supersede traditional notions of power and security. In fact, one of the lessons of the 1990s is that traditional forces seem to accompany the intrinsic thin socialization of international affairs. Another lesson is that when ideals and principles of democratic culture acquire a greater influence on international deliberations and actions, the situation certainly gets better and ethical concerns are more central to the attention of public opinion and decision-makers. However, deliberations, decisions, and actions are still framed in traditional choices. While recognizing the importance of the international realm, decision-makers tend to minimize a commitment to it, often reverting to simplistic notions of national interest. Ethics has not become a global political reality.

Nothing illustrates this state of affairs better than the ways in which Western decision-makers have handled humanitarian crises in the past decade and the ambiguous results they produced. As the political culture of the 1990s became increasingly a mixture of responsibilities on both the national and international levels, it turned out to be difficult for political leaders to stay away from crises. Nationally and internationally under pressure, they had to attempt to find solutions. But with the demands for ethical action came a number of tensions and dilemmas. As political leaders served the international community and those who fall under its aegis, they were also responsive to the demands of domestic constituencies. Such demands, while pressing for international action, remained wary of a full international commitment, especially if it involved great risks. Hence, international affairs were marked by the half-hearted measures which epitomized, in one way or another, the humanitarian and military interventions in the 1990s. In a time when issues of national interest are less and less able to justify the sacrifice of soldiers' lives, it was almost inevitable that, although engaged in the extension of international solidarity, the democratic powers would search ever further for ethical fulfilment without full ethical commitment.

The duality of international ethics

The half-hearted measures adopted under the auspices of the major Western democratic powers and the United Nations in the situations of humanitarian crises in the 1990s are part of a particularly dramatic context. But they are certainly not an isolated phenomenon. Rather, they are an illustration of the general dual character of contemporary international ethics. The same dual character can also be found, although often in a less emotional fashion, in other areas of application of international ethics, such as environment, economic justice, etc. In the context of its duality, contemporary international ethics is both extended and limited. It is both activist and passive, progressive and conservative. The duality of contemporary international ethics is largely the tip of the iceberg, the manifestation of the structural characteristics, at the same time compatible and in competition, of contemporary democratic culture in its national and international dimensions. As such, it also lies between the democratic and ethical obligations attached to the existence of the international community and the demands of the nation-state.

The extent and limitations of international ethics have to be understood in light of the structure of the international realm and of the constraints it imposes on ethical considerations. A central feature of this structure, and of the obstacle it constitutes for institutionalizing ethics at the international level for socializing international relations, lies in the limits of the experience of identification with others and of the extension of the sense of community. Already a challenge at the national level, where fragmentation and multiculturalism are increasingly evident, the experience of identification and the extension of the sense of community beyond borders appear even more difficult in the international realm. The internationalization of democratic culture attenuates the effects of this difficulty, since its aim is precisely to extend a sense of reciprocity and solidarity universally, constituting as such one of the most advanced contributions yet to international ethics. But it does not get rid of them. One could even argue that it makes ethical choices more agonizing. In periods of extreme necessity, the imperative of survival tends to constitute in itself an overall justification. However, in times of relative peace, things are different. When one has the power to act ethically or not at the international level, deliberations on what acting ethically means, and on how much is required or on how far one should go to satisfy the demands of ethics, end up being at the centre of the debates and do not offer an easy way out. Another example of the difficulty of fulfilling the requirements of identification beyond borders is the fact that although rational constructions of extended spaces like the European Union are appealing, emotional attachments to smaller and smaller political units are very strong.[3]

Continuum and divide

The extent and limitations of contemporary international ethics, of international ethics in a time when democratic culture has come to constitute the ideological frame of reference, have to be understood in connection with two elements. They have to be understood in connection with both the continuum and the gap that exist among the individual, national, and international levels when it comes to deliberation, decision, and action in ethical terms.

The continuum accounts for the extension of ethics beyond borders towards the universalization of ethics. This continuum that bridges the individual, national, and international levels is based on democratic ideals and their diffusion, and tends to make the individual the prime beneficiary of international ethics. Under this light, international ethics, the extension of a sense of solidarity and responsibility beyond borders, is first and foremost a projection and an externalization, at the international level, of some of the core political and legal democratic values, such as the universality of equality and freedom, and individuals' rights. Hence, powerful Western democratic nations are eager to be involved in international affairs, to act and intervene in the defence of human rights, to contribute to the diffusion of democratic ideals. It is not only their economic and military power that make such course of action possible, but also key elements of their democratic political culture. This should not come as a surprise, since the democratic message and the ethics of international law contained in current international law and international organizations, especially the United Nations, are mainly a creation of the major democratic powers.

The importance of this continuum does not exclude the existence of a gap between the individual, national, and international levels. This gap accounts primarily for the limitations of international ethics, and takes place within the framework of a "we" versus "them" divide – a divide that the sense of transborder solidarity that Western democratic countries and a number of international organizations convey and promote never eliminates entirely. The existence and the effects on international ethics of such a divide echo the fact that the extension of identification and solidarity works in a concentric manner. Humanity beyond borders is itself one of the widest of the circles. It does not generate the level of commitment that the national circle still tends to produce, especially in stable, developed countries that are economically, socially, and politically integrated; hence the tendency to evaluate the ethics of international responsibility on the basis of national considerations. Hence, also, an evaluation of the costs and benefits of the sense of international responsibility and intervention which is designed to ensure that the costs will not be higher than the benefits. "We" tend to be responsible internationally when it is in "our" interest.

The guiding principle of the cost-benefit assessment is the existence of an implicit hierarchy between the recognition and allocation of rights and the public good at the domestic level (benefiting both the individuals and the national collectivity, if not the state), and the recognition and allocation of rights and the public good at the international level. Here, the ethics of the national competes with and often prevails over the ethics of the international. Such a hierarchy is, after all, rather natural in the present international environment, which is still inhabited by a strong nation-state tropism. Western democratic countries recognize that it is part of their responsibility as essential actors in international democratic life to act beyond their own borders in order to enhance a sense of international solidarity and responsibility. However, they continuously deploy the extension and implementation of international responsibility within a hierarchical world view which rarely, if ever, jeopardizes the domestic level for the sake of priorities attributed to the international level. Developing countries themselves tend to be the adepts of the "we" versus "them" divide – sometimes in the name of international ethics itself. The diffidence with which a number of them consider, for instance, human rights issues, and the fact that they often consider them to be used by the West as a tool against the exercise of their national sovereignty, are not always and only based on bad faith. They can also express a legitimate concern for respect for local cultures and diversity. The growing awareness of the ideological charge of certain categories and aspects of universal rights serves here as a proof. And so does the growing recognition of the need to contextualize and multiculturalize the universality of rights to preserve the validity of their claims.[4]

The combination of the continuum and divide which shape international affairs thus explains the fact that the extent and limits of contemporary international ethics are best cast in the ethical dilemmas through which deliberations and actions tend to take place in the international realm. By way of example, three of these dilemmas can be seen in the dramatic context of the humanitarian crises of the 1990s. A first dilemma has been how to extend international solidarity while preserving as much as possible the lives of the national and United Nations personnel involved. The balance between these two goals has proved to be difficult to strike – for instance in Somalia, Bosnia, Kosovo, and Sierra Leone – and has often led to modalities of intervention more designed to avoid casualties for the intervening powers than to attend and protect the population on the ground. Another dilemma of contemporary international ethics that political decision-makers of the 1990s had to face again and again was to strike the right balance between protecting human rights and continuing to uphold the principle of national sovereignty as one of the cornerstones of the international system. Finally, and more generally, there is the ethical dilemma of weighing the political and normative appropriateness of being either too conservative or too progressive in handling the humanitarian and war crises at the international level.

The normative evolution of international ethics

The limitations undermining the extent of ethics in international affairs could lead some to adopt a cynical and pessimistic view on the present and future state of international ethics. While there is certainly no reason to be overjoyed by the current situation and naively optimistic for the years to come, it would be a mistake to follow the path of cynicism and pessimism. It would be a mistake for it would mean overlooking the historical dimension of ethics and the changes it brings about over time as individuals become more aware of their rights and more empowered. The system of norms which shapes international law and gives normative guidance to the international system, the evolution it goes through, and the incremental progress it displays in the end serve here, in spite of the unavoidable momentary setbacks – which can sometimes be very long, to the point of appearing as the permanent state of affairs – as a reason for adopting a more balanced view.

A number of major principles constitute the fundamentals and structural standards of international law and the international system. They establish the overall legitimacy of the international system, in terms of both values and modalities of action. They also spell out for state actors the main rules of the game of international life and, as such, a certain ethics *of* international affairs and *in* international affairs. These principles include the sovereign equality of states; the self-determination of peoples; a prohibition on the threat or use of force; the peaceful settlement of disputes; non-intervention in the internal affairs of other states; respect for human rights; international cooperation; and good faith. Once these principles are analysed as a whole, it quickly becomes apparent that there are relations of compatibility and competition among them. It happens that the juxtaposition of the sense of compatibility and competition among them echoes the various demands that the international system as regulated by international law is asked to recognize and negotiate with. An example of the compatibility among these principles is the possible complementarity between the respect for human rights and that for self-determination for peoples. Both deal, at least in principle, with people's rights.[5] On the other hand, more and more observers recognize the growing competition or problematic coherence between the respect for human rights and that for non-intervention in the internal affairs of states.

The relationships of compatibility and competition among the norms of the international system are by no means fixed. They are the products of a historical and political evolution, and hence evolve with the international system. Ultimately, the more-or-less explicit and entrenched hierarchy that emerges from the compatibility-competition relationships among the normative principles of the international system indicates its evolving priorities. Increasingly, the international system and the norms which give guidance and validity – political, social, and ethical guidance and validity – have changed with the values that people, ordinary people, support and identify with. They have evolved with the values and the implementation of the values that individuals have more and more seen as essential to their sense of human dignity. Hence, since the beginning of the 1990s, the ethics of international affairs has tended to give more importance to principles that focus on democratic culture, that are part of a commitment to democratization. Concerns for human rights and humanitarian issues have become a trademark of international discourse in the 1990s.

Reasons for cautious optimism for the future

In addressing the democratic dilemmas of international action without transcending them, international ethics is today merely reflecting and crystallizing the plurality of motivations, imperatives, and ultimately legitimacies and loyalties which inhabit contemporary political life. The actual ethics of international affairs is incorporating and projecting the orders and disorders of the contemporary world. It is echoing both the resistance to change and the demands for change. As such, it is participating, although hesitantly, in the improvement of international life. This situation, along with the ambiguities and tensions it entails, may appear not fully satisfactory to anyone eager to see implemented an international landscape displaying a sense of total reconciliation and justice. However, one has to recognize that the fact that international action is taking place within the constraints of dilemmas also represents a positive step. Compared to a world in which these dilemmas would be disregarded altogether, and in which considerations of national interest and raw power alone would be the sole criteria of deliberation and action at the international level, compared to a world in which absolute priority would be given to the national dimension, it constitutes progress in the negotiation of political life.

Scanning the book

The research project leading to this book began as an exploration of new ethical issues in international affairs in the 1990s. In the end, most of the chapters brought together by the project reflect upon what is the *motto* of the time – of today and most likely of the near future – when it comes to ethics and international affairs; that is, the extent and the limits of contemporary international ethics. In this context, the book achieves three main goals.

First, it takes stock of the extent and limits of the sense of international responsibility in some of the most crucial contemporary challenges on which international attention and action have focused in the past 10 years. As such, human rights, humanitarian intervention, environmental issues, specific gender considerations, especially in time of war, international economic justice, matters of war and peace, and refugees are at the centre of the book. Second, the book searches for explanations for the juxtaposition of the extent and limitations of international responsibility (see for instance Chapter 4, Hassner). It is in this context that the juxtaposition of a continuum and of a divide between the individual, national, and international levels constitutes one of the main themes of the book. Third and finally, the book explores ways to overcome these limitations. Here, as the voices brought together in the book do not necessarily agree on what should be done to enhance international ethics, the authors offer a number of directions not systematically convergent. While some insist on the necessity of revisiting the very interpretation and conceptualization of the categories of international ethics (Chapter 2, Kratochwil, and Chapter 5, Campbell, each in his own way), others focus on the necessity to push for a better implementation of the international norms available, if not of their constant improvement along the way (Chapter 6, Donnelly, Chapter 7, Young, Chapter 8, Hutchings, and Chapter 9, Gibney).

As a result, there is no universal definition of ethics in this book, and no attempt by the authors to refer to one clear and simple tradition within international ethics. Rather, each of the authors tries to come to terms with what ethics means today in a specific context, and to develop an understanding of the ethical from that specific context. The coherence of the book is in that searching and the articulation of the dilemmas encountered. In the end, indeed, none of the authors claims that we can eliminate the dilemmas of international ethics. International ethics involves the very tensions created by the juxtaposition of the continuum and the "we" versus "them" divide. The ethical/political exists in the very negotiation of the dilemmas. As international order is not about stability, but about socialized instability, international ethics is not about achieving fully just order. At the international level, like at the national level, aiming for a totally reconciled world, aiming for a world where the inequalities and tensions would disappear, is a dangerous utopia. This world would presuppose a form of universality that would be undemocratic, the very antithesis of what is looked for.

If ethics is about choosing and implementing values, then the best we can do when it comes to the ethics of international affairs is to aim for making the continuum between "we" and "them" ever stronger, so that reciprocity and solidarity play an integrating and socializing role, without ever hoping to eliminate the gap. After all, ethics is not about getting rid of the sense of alterity and difference. It is about humanizing the experience of the other, the sense of distance that it encompasses. It is about founding and affirming our humanity in making others part of our lives while recognizing their right to be different, their right not to be us. The problem is not in the "we" and "them". It is in the radicalization of the differentiation, instead of its celebration in a socialized way.

Notes

1. It is worth adding here that as soon as the powerless, or the victim, stops being entirely powerless or a victim, and finds himself/herself in a relative situation of power and influence, he/she becomes ethically accountable, accordingly to his/her relative position of power. See Warner, D., 1991, *An Ethics of Responsibility in International Relations.* Boulder and London: Lynne Rienner.
2. See for instance Brilmayer, L., 1994, *American Hegemony. Political Morality in a One-Superpower World.* New Haven and London: Yale University Press.
3. The fact that it seems to be a growing norm is all the more troubling. While rational constructions of extended spaces are likely to enhance democracy – the plurality and diversity they bring together invite them to do so – smaller and smaller political units tend to encourage the development of the negative and non-democratic aspects of communal values as a way to make their own case as separate entities. It also is problematic considering that the mushrooming of these small entities is sometimes taking place with the endorsement of the international community and in line with "international democratic cosmopolitanism".
4. As such, it provides an illustration of how international ethics, initially envisioned as a projection or externalization of democratic values aiming to be universal, ends up having to leave room for a number of specific contexts to sustain its claims of universality. This boomerang effect of universalism on the universality of democratic values is not new (for instance, the spread of universal democratic ideals originating in revolutionary France to continental Europe at the beginning of the nineteenth century shows that it contributed to the conceptualization and validation of the rights of each nation as a collectivity, thus favouring the rise of modern nationalism and the undermining of a cosmopolitan version of democratic universalism). Furthermore, it is an invitation to reflect upon the future of democratic universalism.
5. The connection between self-determination and human rights is, however, far from being mechanic and automatic. See Coicaud, J.-M., 2000, "Self-determination, Human Rights and Cosmopolitanism in the 1990s", *Peace Studies Newsletter*, No. 19, July, Peace Studies Association of Japan.

2

International law as an approach to international ethics: A plea for a jurisprudential diagnostics

Friedrich Kratochwil

The problem of ethics and law

To approach the problem of ethics in international relations from the perspective of international law seems at first blush a dubious undertaking. There is first the common-sense notion that law and morals are two distinct sets of norms that ought to be distinguished. Lawyers have vigorously tried to insist on this distinction[1] by showing that, different from morals, law is a sanctioning order, and philosophers have shown that in evaluating legal rules and norms we commonly use moral criteria or intuitions.[2] Consequently, the latter must not only be of a higher order of generality, but must also be satisfying requirements different from those of mere legality. Thus the authority of law in modern societies is largely held to be a matter of procedure, not of belief, or some ultimate common ground. The link between the separate realms of morality and law nevertheless often remains unclear and contested. Several options are now open: either to accept the "autonomous logic" of both spheres, or to grapple with the question of how law and morality interact. But whichever option one might be inclined to adopt, one thing seems clear: ethics appears to be the more abstract (even perhaps the more comprehensive) perspective, since it is charged with articulating the standards by which legal prescriptions can be evaluated. To that extent, attempts to use jurisprudential forms of argument or to assume that legal theories might be of use for deciding questions of ethics seem rather quaint. Thus, while

14

the author is aware that different conceptualizations of ethics and morals, of "professional" ethics and ethics conceived as the articulation of truly universal standards,[3] exist, it is this latter project of articulating abstract, binding standards which is the focus of the analytical school of ethics, and which this discussion attempts to address.

There is a second and even weightier reason to reject international law as an approach to international ethics. After all, even if we agree that ethics seems to be concerned with goodness and badness of action, with the virtuous, the deontic, or the utile (and their opposites), it is hard to deny the fact that the possibility for moral action has usually been held to be conditioned by the existence of a well-ordered society. Indeed, the crucial distinction between the "inside" and the "outside", between the domestic arena and international anarchy, has been one of the major themes in political theory from Plato to Machiavelli, Hobbes, Hegel, and Weber.[4] Not only did these theorists not believe that the international arena provided any opportunity for the realization of the "good life" and its ethical imperatives, they even doubted whether one could at all speak even of law among "persons of sovereign authority". To that extent an approach to international ethics via international law appears as a doubly impossible undertaking.

Third, even for the adherents of the powerful counter-tradition that ranges from the Stoics via the medieval proponents of natural law to the "cosmopolitans" of modernity, law was usually considered a less than perfect instrument for determining our obligations, as many legal entitlements are tied to membership in a community. Thus, there is in law itself always a tension between positive law and those transcendental standards, which – according to the natural law approach – provides positive prescriptions with the character of "true" law. If one argued within this tradition the focus of attention usually shifts quickly from the *lex lata* to the standards or the goals and purposes which law (*de lege ferenda*) had to incorporate. The study of actual legal institutions and their contribution to determining our obligations and solving our moral dilemmas – if they exist at all in international politics, such as the laws of war – appears to be highly problematic when viewed from this perspective. Many of the conventional doctrinal distinctions, such as the traditional differentiation of *guerre couverte*, of *guerre mortelle*,[5] and actual war, or just war, seem scholastic or even counterproductive for the overarching ethical project of, for example, abolishing war as a means of statecraft. The apparent incoherence of many particular prescriptions, such as the acceptance of numerous deaths as the result of collateral damage while forbidding the utilization of simple tear gas in combat, makes this point quite vividly.[6] Similarly, as Mark Gibney's contribution to this volume shows (Chapter 9), the legalistic definition of "refugee" at present seems to prevent rather than help to foster adequate responses to the humanitarian problems which we increasingly face when the internal order of states breaks down or large-scale violence displaces large numbers of people.

In short, when ethics is seen as part of the project of enlightenment where questions of the justifiability of principles are at issue, the analysis of existing institutions and their reaffirmation through existing political practices seems an odd way to begin one's reflections. Would it, therefore, not be more sensible, as the analytical approach to ethics indeed suggests, to define first the autonomy of ethics apart from any particularistic tradition or institutional understanding? In that case one could proceed to formulating the principles that satisfied this ethical point of view, and then apply these principles to the problems at hand. In this way one would be able to assess the institutions in terms of their conformity with the articulated yardsticks, and to propose the necessary remedies. Of course, if one proceeded in such a fashion the criteria would have to be abstract and universal, so as to avoid charges of ethnocentrism and/or relativity. But abstractness and universality by themselves do not seem to avoid charges of partiality, as the debate about Western values and the cultural imperialism of human rights shows. Even if we take such charges with a grain of salt, and accept that the human rights discourse of the last few decades has created a common rhetoric in which normative problems can be vetted, as Jack Donnelly shows (Chapter 6), there remain some problems. If, for example, the universalistic stance in the human rights discourse is limited only to the least common denominator distilled from the different traditions and customs, it might be virtually empty. After all, various traditions, singly and in conjunction, appear to have serious blind spots, most noticeably in respect to women, often denying them full moral agency, as feminists have correctly pointed out. In addition, as Kimberly Hutchings suggests (Chapter 8), the very categorical framework of "doing" ethics and granting or ascribing rights needs to be reflected upon, for which feminist theory provides some important pointers. Deriving obligatory standards from the mere practice of different cultures might prove too thin a reed to hang one's hat on, quite aside from the inherent dilemma that following such a procedure seems to involve us somehow in the questionable activity of deriving an "ought" from an "is". On the other hand, arguing for a more substantive version of rights might engender hostility, as such substantive prescriptions might be an intrinsic part of a particular way of life that militates against some deeply held cultural convictions.

Thus we face a dilemma: beginning with abstract principles rather than concrete practices and institutions leads not only to a devaluation of the "state" as an institution of Hegelian *Sittlichkeit*, but it also reinforces the tendency to conceive of ethics as an analytical enterprise, concerned with the elaboration of standards to which every rational being has to consent. But then, such an approach reduces ethical reflection to a largely cognitivist enterprise that can be tackled through the demonstration and application of the right principles to a specific "subsumed" situation. On the other hand, since abstract principles do not come with their own specification for application, we are often at a loss when a situation can be described from two different perspectives and can be subsumed under two different principles, or even when the same principle leads to entirely different prescriptions in a concrete case, depending on the level of generality one applies, as will be shown.

Nevertheless, after the demise of virtue as the yardstick for moral action[7] – since such a "virtue ethic" seems to presuppose the acceptance and validity of a more-or-less accepted way of life[8] – it seems that there remains for "ethics" only the task of articulating the standards which possess normative pull either on the basis of their universalizability or as indicators for the (un)desirable consequences. Consequently, it is understandable that modern analytical ethics largely concerns itself with the elaboration of a "moral" point of view from which principles and actions could be construed and particular norms could be evaluated. How this "moral point of view" could be constructed, whether we need an act- or rule-utilitarian calculator, Sidgewick's sympathetic observer, the Kantian categorical imperative, or the Rawlsian original position, remains, of course, contentious.

Contrary to this belief, it is the thesis here that the analytical enterprise has failed on its own terms and thus has forced us to look elsewhere for guidance. It has failed because it is not able to provide us with criteria that can simply be "applied" to a subject matter. On the other hand, an approach indebted to *legal analysis* seems more appropriate for resolving some of our real-world perplexities. While neither this nor any other approach to ethics is able to "solve" our moral dilemmas, the author maintains that an ethical reflection informed by a legal mode of reasoning is at least sensitive to the institutional settings, the factual circumstances, and the inevitable problems of conflicting values, all of which are mostly neglected when we focus on the elaboration of context-free criteria derived from idealized assumptions as the main task of the ethical enterprise. It is argued that a reorientation of ethical reflection from an analytic enterprise to a more casuistic mode of analysis seems required for both domestic and international affairs.

To that extent a legal approach might indeed be a useful beginning, even if a legal mode of reasoning and practical reasoning have different characteristics, and even if ethical reflections as part of practical reasoning exhibit certain specific features.[9] A more casuistic-oriented approach also seems necessary, as we can no longer engage in abstract philosophical discussions while ignoring the pressing moral problems of contemporary politics. These problems arise out of the increasingly dense interaction among various political orders, creating duties beyond borders, and, as importantly, from the decay of the state. In other words, both the new political practices we observe and the intellectual dissatisfaction with the modern project of ethics as an analytical enterprise make new conceptual departures necessary.

The last remarks should be sufficient to show the questionable nature of the realist tradition that limits ethics to the internal realm, particularly since states have frequently ceased to be functioning political orders with any claim to providing the essential preconditions for attaining the "good" life.[10] On the other hand, we must not assume that simply because of these changes, and the concomitant conceptual confusions with regard to ethics, no relevant distinctions between the domestic and international arena exist anymore and that, therefore, moral reflection nowadays has simply to coincide with notions of a universalistic cosmopolitan justice. The author defends the view that the problem of ethics and international relations has to be one of reflection and criticism *within* our present practices and institutions, and not one of constructing some brave new world based on blueprints conceived from outside of present politics and law, regardless of whether such a standpoint is conceived as that of God, of the ideal observer, of the felicific calculus, or of the good will in itself.

Precisely because the author has doubts about foundationalist constructs, characteristic of analytical ethics, the attempts to base an approach simply on human rights will also be resisted, even while recognizing the human rights discourse as a powerful political force and a serious new departure in the sense mentioned above. While this might seem a rather inconsistent rejection of the legal approach, much of the present human rights discourse can be accommodated only with great difficulty to the mode of legal analysis which the author has in mind, as too many different concerns and traditions have been subsumed under the concept of human rights. To the extent that the human rights discourse relies partly on some form of natural law, or on some intuitionist notions of human nature, it moves away from the legal mode of analysis and opens itself up to the same objections as the other foundational attempts criticized above. To put it bluntly: the point here is that neither a purely formal elaboration of ethical standards nor the aggregation of various *desiderata*, nowadays often discussed as "rights" (even if only as manifesto rights or as rights *de lege ferenda*), is particularly helpful. Instead, it is neither human rights nor foundational attempts such as a theory of "justice" that enhances our capacity to think critically about our practical choices and moral dilemmas, but rather a mode of arguing a "case" in which factual and normative concerns both "count" when we deliberate about the "right" choice in a particular situation. Such a deliberation is poorly captured by the notion that we subsume a fact pattern under a certain norm, which, in turn, has been justified by a different set of criteria and procedures, or that we concern ourselves with procedures to find universally applicable rules that are beyond debate.

These assertions might seem like heady claims. In order to make good on them, the argument will take the following steps. In the next section it will examine critically several leading modern analytical approaches, and show that both fail in terms of their own criteria. Moving from criticism to a more constructive mode, the chapter takes up the problem of ethical judgements, and shows how deeply political and institutional considerations are involved when we reason about right and wrong and the obligations we might have. In this fashion it will demonstrate that ethical reflection cannot be limited to the elaboration of fundamental principles and their subsequent application to some concrete problems of domestic or international politics. Rather, since principles need interpretation and since our interpretations are inevitably informed by substantive background understandings that decisively shape our expectations and moral projects, a more casuistic style of analysis is required for ethical reflection. Here legal reasoning, which constantly oscillates between the norms and the relevant facts which co-condition each other in their relevance for a particular situation, seems to provide a more apt model for our deliberations than the usual models of inference developed by either consequentialist or deontic theories. Section four attempts to engage in such a model of deliberation in regard to problems of humanitarian aid and intervention. A short summary concludes the chapter.

Rights, goods, and principles

In discussing the problem of an international ethics, let us begin with the following question: do we owe certain duties only to those with whom we have a special connection, be it through particular contractual obligations or through the ties that bind us to our family and fellow citizens,[11] or do we owe them to all human beings, *qua* their status as moral actors? Two difficulties arise in this context: if we assume that our obligations are limited, then we need, according to the project of "ethics" as a reflexive application of principles of action, some justification for endowing the (political) boundaries with significance. In the extreme case one might argue that it is precisely these boundaries that are determinative, and while misery abroad and perhaps some superrogatory considerations might move us, no "duty" in the relevant sense can be construed. If we, on the other hand, assume true universality, we obviously must treat this issue as an open question, and at the extreme have again to realize that we might have obligations that could crush us all and make a "normal" life – which is usually assumed to be the precondition for moral choices – impossible.

There are, of course, some customary criteria that we usually employ as beings of "limited generosity", as Hume has so aptly characterized us. So is it not surprising that we manage the problem practically by limiting our duties in terms of concentric circles. But this practical criterion, which gives preferences to those "near us", or to those who are, for whatever reasons, our "friends", over those further away,[12] is precisely a demarcation that needs justification. Besides, arguing that either the wider or the narrower circle automatically deserves precedence, as communitarians on the one hand and "cosmopolitans" on the other hand, shows the indeterminacy of the concentric circle approach by playing down the possibility of genuine dilemmas.[13] After all, at least in one interpretation, Antigone's predicament consists precisely in the fact that the wider society and its laws conflict with the moral obligations she feels for her kin. It is this loyalty which, for good reasons, the political authority (Creon) wants to weaken in order to pacify a city that, in the past, has suffered from political strife among the noble families. Thus, even Antigone's justification – the appeal to universality in order to buttress her claim of the special standing of family obligations – belies the ordering logic of the concentric circle approach in its universalistic version![14]

This chapter will next examine three more explicit proposals that attempt to wrestle with these issues. But, as we shall see, all three proposals are based on different models of the moral perspective, and human rights, utilitarianism, and Kantian deontology rather quickly become incoherent.

To begin with *rights* seems initially to have definite advantages. First, given that in modernity there no longer exists a shared ontologically grounded understanding of what *is* right, attributing subjective rights to actors (and even accepting that the exercise of such a right might entail doing the "wrong thing") fractionates conflict. It establishes autonomous domains where actors are free to act without basing this entitlement necessarily on some commonly shared notion of the good. Second, precisely because visions of the common good differ considerably, limiting oneself to morally significant constraints rather than to an algorithm, which is supposed to guarantee optimal results, is a prudent way of dealing with complexity. As we know, contrary to the requirements of (act) utilitarianism, the agents possess only limited capacities to compute their own utilities, quite aside from the necessary complete information concerning the alternatives and their impact. Focusing more narrowly on rights, therefore, relieves the actors from worrying about the impact of their actions in general, since only claims of specific right-holders need to be considered.

But resorting to rights also has significant liabilities. One concerns the specification of the duty-bearers that corresponds to my rights, the other concerns the political problem of delimiting the group of right-bearers that may make claims against me. Here, both the importance of groups and boundaries and the limitations of the rights talk come to the fore. As long as we talk only about what *is* right or wrong to do, as long as we consider only right action, our discussion need not specify who the potential or actual beneficiaries of the right action are, or would be. Such issues are either regulated by tradition, the *de facto* existing consensus, or some ontologically founded notion of the good. If we, however, shift the discussion from right action to the notion of subjectively claimable rights, my exercise of a right must entail someone else's obligation. At the very least, the notion of "rights" safeguarding the minimum conditions of liberty among equal actors entails the duty not to interfere with others' activity. This duty is usually easily performed by everybody, even *vis-à-vis* countless other right-holders. It is fulfilled by simply respecting the freedom of others, and does not require specific actions on the part of duty-bearers.

Things are different, however, when we move out of the zone of forbearances and enter that of positive actions that are required from us in order to implement the special duties that the right of others imposes upon us. Claims arising out of welfare rights come readily to mind. Here, a variety of responses are made. The classical libertarian argument *à la* Nozick[15] opposes transfers not only beyond the borders of the community but even within. To that extent, the claims beyond those safeguarding the "negative freedom" are unassignable to specific other agents, and thus cannot be "rights" by definition. Supporting the poor might be a laudable enterprise of generosity, but it is not a matter of a "right". The social consequence is that only family ties seem to be acknowledged as special entitlement, since membership in a community does not seem to bestow such a privilege. But even here, leaving one's property to one's heirs is conceptualized not as a right but as a privilege that belongs only to the owner, who is, after all, not obliged to leave his estate to his children, at least according to American law.

It is, of course, impossible to subject these complex arguments to an even-handed assessment in a short chapter like this, but some brief remarks concerning "positive" duties are in order. Consider in this context the first seemingly rather easy case for the "basic" right to food. After all, does not the guarantee of "liberty" become rather hollow when actual survival is not addressed or is neglected? In other words, if it is at all possible to make a good *prima-facie* case for the notion of "rights" going beyond the principles of negative freedom,[16] then "basic" rights, and within that category again the "right to food", occupy a central place.

There is, however, also a conceptual flaw that undermines the persuasiveness of this argument about substantive rights. Let us return to our paradigmatic case of the right to food. Nobody can possibly deny that hunger is one of the greatest moral "scandals" of our time, and that we certainly have at least some "imperfect" duties, in Kantian parlance, to alleviate the suffering of those who are in need of the most basic things. The question, nevertheless, remains whether such obligations are the result of subjective, even though "basic" subjective, rights. The usual strategy of demonstrating such a connection is to cast doubt on the traditional distinctions between positive and negative rights by pointing out that even negative rights need enforcement, and thus involve costs. To the extent that, thereby, the very distinction between negative and positive rights becomes problematic, one feels entitled *a fortiori* to claim for "positive", in particular "basic", rights a similar obligation *erga omnes* attendant to negative rights.[17] However, as even a sympathetic critic of this position points out:

While it is true that the enforcement of a right not to be tortured demands positive action, just as the enforcement of a right to food does, the difference between the two remains. Suppose we think there are both rights not to be tortured and rights to food. If, in the absence of enforcement, A tortures B, we are quite clear who has violated B's right; but if A does not provide B with food, nor even with an aliquot morsel of food, we are not sure whether A has violated B's rights. There nothing shows that it is *against* A that B's claim to food should be lodged, or enforced.[18]

The upshot of this argument is that many so-called "rights", even if "basic", are "manifesto" rights only; they figure prominently in our arguments *de lege ferenda* but do not possess the ability to allocate specific obligations, and are therefore of little help for the morally perplexed. It is thus not surprising that the most radical alternative to the indeterminacy of the rights discourse consists in leaving the logic of the discourse behind, while not eschewing its form. In other words, such a move entails shifting back to some notions of what "is right". The basic rights and basic needs argument avails itself, therefore, of the latter dimension of the concept of "right" in order to propagate new rights.

But such a move away from the problem of who has to act, to the question of how we are able to tell the "rightness" of actions, puts us back to the dilemma that we attempted to avoid by focusing on actor-specific rights and obligations. If we are ready to leave the rights discourse as it seems unsatisfactory, two types of criteria exist for informing us about the duties we "rightfully" incur: consequentialist and deonto-logical. An added advantage of such a move is that these criteria seem particularly apt for registering harms and benefits *irrespective of boundaries*, or of the existence of specific institutions or rights. Let us begin with a "strong" case for the usefulness of consequentialist criteria, for which Peter Singer's argument can serve as a good example.[19] Faced with the undeniable scandal of world hunger, Singer would oblige us to give away our possessions up to that point that marginal utility considerations come into play, when one unit more would cause me and/or my family as much harm as it would alleviate by giving it away. There is, of course, something very odd about this proposal, even though the utilitarian logic on which it is based seems convincing.

There is first the problem that the marginal utility argument, which is taken from the economic problem of production – the entrepreneur de-liberates about *his utility* in investing further – is suddenly applied here to some distributional issues among a group of people. This makes inter-personal utility comparisons necessary, which entrepreneurial decisions about production do not entail. The fact that we usually engage in such interpersonal comparisons, and that public authorities necessarily have to engage in them, does not solve, however, the problem that no general algorithm exists which allows us to make such calculations with any de-gree of confidence, quite aside from justifying such a scheme "politi-cally". But since the *moral* character of utilitarianism crucially depends on the accuracy of such calculations, which, in turn, presuppose adequate causal understanding of complex systems and knowledge of all relev-ant options, the "moral character" of such proposals can seriously be doubted.

Similar objections can be made to Pogge's proposal of a "resource dividend" which is supposed to finance economic development in the third world.[20] If anything has been learned in the past few decades, it is that simple resource transfers are more likely to spur corruption rather than development. Thus, it is not sufficient to show that even small taxes in the developed world could do a lot of good for the poor in the devel-oping world unless one is also able to show plausible routes to reach such a goal. In other words, as in the case of disarmament, it is simply not enough to pretend that showing a "better" way (the savings engendered by disarmament) solves the political and moral problems, exemplified by a "prisoner's dilemma" situation. One also has to design specific in-stitutions, and must see to it that they are in place, before the principled claims attain any plausibility.

Second, one of the severe shortcomings of such distributional schemes – and here, Rawls's principles, particularly the "difference principle", also have to be mentioned[21] – is that because they pay no attention to the *problem of production* and the necessary incentives for it, they can hardly claim to represent sensible criteria for acting, or even more so for choosing a set of institutions. The world as we know it is one of scarcity; consequently, we have to realize on pain of irresponsibility that the goods which our philosophers simply want to distribute do not just sit on the shelf awaiting their "just" distribution, but that they have to be produced first.

Third, how indeterminate the standards become, depending on which factual assumptions we make, can be gathered from the analysis of some other utilitarians. Since for an ever-increasing population redistribution is hardly the panacea, some utilitarians, utilizing the *same consequentialist* criteria but informed by Malthusian assumptions rather than liberal optimism, have come to radically opposite conclusions. They argue that redistribution is not going to alleviate poverty, but rather increase population, and thus maximize aggregate misery in the long run rather than increase utility.[22] Whatever the actual merits of either of these dubious arguments might be, they do cast serious doubt on the proposition that ethics can be conceived as the elaboration of set of principles which are able to generate solutions to our dilemmas. Using the same yardsticks, we end up with diametrically opposite recommendations!

But perhaps the same is not true if we entrust our reasoning to the other class of criteria, "deontic" ones, of which Kant's categorical imperative and the Rawlsian paradigm of a "choice behind the veil of ignorance" are good examples. However, as we shall see, similar difficulties appear which suggest that there is perhaps something fundamentally mistaken about the way in which this style of thinking proceeds. Consider in this context the Kantian version of the "golden rule" – that we ought to act in such a way as to be able to postulate that the maxims underlying our actions can be universally prescribed.[23] In other words, if everybody were to do a certain act x, for example, trample on the grass, it would lead to an undesirable state of affairs, and consequently one ought not to do x.

If stated in this form, the "generalization" argument is, however, subject to the simple retort that since not everybody is trampling on the grass, my doing so can hardly be said to lead to such a disaster. But should everybody act in this fashion, then certainly my doing so can hardly be blamed for bringing about this result, as my "contribution" to it was infinitesimally small. Similarly, my paying taxes certainly makes only a small contribution to maintaining the government, so I cannot be blamed for its potential breakdown if I decide to withhold my contribution. But if, on the other hand, everybody else also did not pay their taxes, not only would I then be demented to do so, but, in addition, my action in that case would even be of questionable "moral" character, at least according to utilitarian considerations, since my contribution would not bring about the desired result. Other examples lead to further puzzlement. Thus we do not hold bachelors morally blameworthy, although nobody could want the "stay single" rule as a general precept, since society – at least as we know it – would thereby soon come to an end. In short, if stated in this fashion, the double "so what?" argument seems to rebut rather effectively the notion that we can "solve" our practical problems through the application of this principle, at least in this version.

In order to avoid such perplexing conclusions, the Kantian version of the generalization argument inherent in the categorical imperative is said not to rely on the consequences of the actions of concrete actors but of *hypothetical* actors; in other words, it bases its assessment on "idealized assumptions". To that extent, my duty to do (or not do) x does not vary; I have to do x irrespective of whether others are doing their part or not. Nevertheless, even in this version several problems arise. First, we have to understand what type of "generality" (or universal validity) such a procedure generates. Second, we have to ask whether thereby the incoherence of the "so what?" situation is truly overcome, or whether it just reappears in a different disguise. If this were so – and it will be argued to that effect below – then we would have to investigate further through what measures our actual reasoning with categorical principles attains at least a *prima-facie* plausibility.

Let us begin with the first problem. Common to all generality arguments is obviously their "abstraction". But reasoning with idealized assumptions involves not only abstract notions, in that it leaves out certain predicates that are true of concrete agents and objects; rather it uses constructs that apply only to hypothetical agents which satisfy predicates that actual agents or agencies do not (fully) satisfy. Speaking strictly, idealized reasoning applies only in those ideal worlds inhabited (for example) by rational economic men with perfect information, fully transitive preferences, and unlimited capacities to calculate. By contrast, merely abstract reasoning applies to agents, whether or not they satisfy the predicates from which it abstracts. Since much liberal and socialist thought uses idealized models of the human agent, objections to idealized reasoning have a serious point.[24]

The effects of arguing with the ideal construct are twofold. First, it puts the weight for establishing the deontic force of an action-guiding principle increasingly on the *logical criterion* of non-contradiction, as several of the examples used by Kant in support of the "categorical imperative" show. Thus, one could not possibly postulate that stealing can serve as a maxim for actions, because if this were so "property" would soon cease to exist, and there would be nothing left to steal. Second, given its generality, the criterion often fails to serve as a meaningful yardstick for assessment. If we, for example, want to know whether agriculture is a good thing that we should engage in, the recommendation obviously cannot be based on a Kantian maxim, since if everybody engaged in agriculture no functioning society could exist. A functioning society is only possible when a division of labour exists, and when certain practices do not exceed certain thresholds. Given the importance of threshold effects, it is impossible to argue *in vacuo* and evaluate a practice solely in terms of what every hypothetical actor would do, given the intentions of the agent who "tests" their suitability as maxims. In other words, depending on whether or not one smuggles in some substantive knowledge of "how much is enough", the result changes dramatically, since the class of actions over which one generalizes thereby gets redefined.

This state of affairs has, however, some further absurd corollaries: since we have to generalize the maxim or actual subjective principle upon which an actor acts, "the generalization argument will confront him with sharply differing evaluations, depending upon how precisely, he formulates his subjective principle of action".[25] Furthermore, if we take the criterion of non-contradiction as part of the categorical imperative seriously, then it is not clear why we rely on "threshold effects" in assessing the consequences of a *pattern of actions* but do not allow for such an assessment in the case of *individual actions.*

The paradox is simply this: we are asked to believe that the rightness or wrongness of many of our actions depends on the probable consequences, not of what we know to be true, but of *what we know to be false.* For, in practically every case where we consider what would happen if everybody acted as we propose to act, we know as surely as we can know anything that it is not a priori, that by no means will everybody act in this way.[26]

Precisely because the purely formal criteria of generalization leave open the question of which classes of actions one has to generalize, a decision which crucially depends on "threshold effects", the maxims which are supposed to help us in deciding our practical questions and the possibly concomitant moral dilemmas cannot resolve our perplexity. In other words, "am I to guide my conduct by the trivial individual consequences, or by the collective significant aggregate consequences of everybody doing the same?"[27] The upshot of the argument is that a course of action seems to be classifiable as morally acceptable as well as immoral at the same time, depending how we apply the principle of generalization. If strictly and consistently applied, any form of generalization principle not only overwhelms the agents with moral obligations, but also abolishes virtually any zone of freedom and of discretion for the agent. Everything becomes prescribed: from not eating meat (as producing meat wastes valuable protein and is unavoidably connected with cruelty to animals)[28] to forgoing a concert (as the act or, even more so, the general practice of giving the money for the ticket away could result in doing more good somewhere else).

Ethical judgements and their justification

The upshot of this argument is that something more goes on in moral reasoning than the application of ethical principles whose validity has been established by the moral point of view. Having given up on evaluating choices from the constitutive point of "nowhere", be it God who makes us subjects of his law, or of the "sympathetic observer", the universal calculator, or of reason itself, there are three issues that need further clarification. While the author cannot claim to have resolved the issues, a further discussion might be useful for shedding some light on this matter.

The first issue concerns the actual procedures of "reasoning" by which we attempt to arrive at a reflective judgement concerning our actions and obligations. The second, connected, point deals with the peculiarity that not only cognitive problems are involved in our moral judgements, but that at least part of the "rightness" of our judgements depends upon an ability to marshal our "feelings of approbation and disapprobation", which, in turn, are largely part of moral training. Particularly in complex cases, we often reject solutions not because of the incorrectness of cognitions or inferences but because the result just "does not feel right". The feeling of absurdity attendant to holding the bachelor worthy of blame, is, after all, not based on a simple logical error.

Finally, it seems that some closer link has to be established between our actions and obligations than is provided by the assertion of universal rights or principles. In other words, we have to examine the procedures by which we attribute praise or blame: our practice of praising and blaming itself. While the standard argument of traditional philosophy is that we blame a person when s/he as a free agent has caused harm to others, a closer investigation shows that such an argument is untenable. Not only do we hold persons responsible for actions that are not the result of a free choice, but our understanding of causal chains is crucially influenced by some (often vague) scientific understandings, and even more importantly by our notions of social roles and by the bounds of a community. Thus, contrary to our normal assumptions, it is neither the metaphysical principle of "free will", nor the identification of causal chains linking our actions to some harm, but rather our practice of blaming and praising which provides the best account of what is involved. This practice connects the question of right and wrong not only with punishment or rewards, but with the notion of duty and responsibility. Let us examine our practice of blaming, therefore, in greater detail.

According to the standard account of modern analytic philosophy, "moral" responsibility is not part of the customs and habits of a concrete society but has to occur independent of our social practices, including that of blaming. Furthermore, the independence on the part of the blamer is paralleled by the assumed independence of the free agent who can be blamed because he did "bad" things although he had a free choice. Thus, Joel Feinberg provides us with a concise version of both criteria when, in distinguishing moral blameworthiness from legal responsibility, he writes:

A stubborn feeling persists even after legal responsibility has been decided that there is still a problem – albeit not a legal problem – left over: namely, is the defendant really responsible (as opposed to "responsible in law") for the harm? This conception of a "real" theoretical responsibility as distinct from a practical responsibility "relative" to the purposes and values of a particular legal system, is expressed very commonly in the terminology of "morality" – moral obligation, moral guilt, moral responsibility.

Like all matters of record, moral responsibility must be read off the facts or deduced from there: there can be no irreducible element of discretion for any judge. Just as it is "forever to the credit" of a hero or a saint that he performed some noble act, so a man can be "forever to blame" for his faults.[29]

Before we get unduly impressed by these megalomaniacally sounding phrases, we should realize that again an "idealized" construct is here invoked in order to approach the problem. It is not difficult to fathom that this "idealized construct" is largely a remnant of the Judeo-Christian tradition where God (since his "death" busily played by various philosophers on duty) served as the outside blamer. It is he who keeps the score of the sins of the people who are not abiding by his commands.

Fortunately, this modern version of responsibility, which consists of the "Christian concept of sin, minus the authority of God",[30] suffers from grave conceptual defects. There is first the assertion of the metaphysical notion of "free will". Second, despite the argument that the ideal blamer has to stand outside his society, and that, furthermore, our blame has to be construed independently of any policy, purposes, or conventions of a particular society, even the most superficial examination shows that such a point of view cannot be sustained. Inevitably, it seems, we have to fall back on our understandings of social roles, particularly when we trace the harm done back to the actor whom we blame. Both notions, "free will" and causal connection, singly and in conjunction, make the concept of blameworthiness as an aspect of moral agency incoherent.

Let us begin with the notion of "free will" as the constitutive condition for us to hold someone responsible or blameworthy. In other words, aside from possessing knowledge of circumstances and the foresight of the likely consequences, the blameworthy person must have acted voluntarily, and/or the action must have been within his power, as "ought" implies "can". However, it is clear that we hold people responsible even when it is patently obvious that the action was not (or no longer) in their power.[31] The driver who falls asleep on the wheel and therefore goes through a red light, or who drives his car off the road injuring other persons in the car, cannot claim to be free of blame because his actions were at that time not in his power. Similarly, claims of ignorance, beginning with the applicable moral principle itself and ranging through to the lack of knowledge of the consequences of an action, are hardly taken as excuses, even if they are true. It might very well be that a person is ignorant of what is right and appropriate in a given case, a situation that Aristotle[32] discusses and dismisses as an exculpatory principle (unless we are convinced that we are dealing with a truly "insane" person). It might also be true that a person might not have known that the gun with which he was gesticulating was loaded. If it goes off, and injures or kills someone, we do not think that the person holding the gun is simply free of blame. Furthermore, the mother who, as a drug addict, has "no choice" and makes her children steal in order to maintain her habit ought certainly to be blamed, even if we disagree as to the precise nature of the responsibility we impute.

In all of these cases (with the exception of the one indicating general ignorance of morality itself), our attention turns either to the time before the person lost his capacity to act voluntarily – we blame him for getting himself in a state in which he could not act freely – or to a counterfactual exercise of what s/he could, or should, have known. But as soon as we engage in such assessments, we necessarily have to fall back on the "encumbered" notions shaped by our practices and understandings in particular societies. Even more important (and debilitating for the argument of a clear-cut criterion, such as "free will"), we, as members of that society, might fundamentally disagree about the appropriate standards for the "reasonable man" for the "due care" or "necessary knowledge" that one can presuppose. In such cases, we need some decisions, administered usually by courts, which end the potentially interminable moral debate. Nevertheless, whatever the merits of the various moral arguments which we make, all of them are part and parcel of much more complex understandings of what a society should be, and of the life projects we want and should be able to pursue within these bounds.

Things are not better when we deal with the second criterion, the causal chain that establishes the crucial link between the harm and the agent. Given the fact that, for example, exposure to violence makes resort to violence much more likely, who is to blame when children become increasingly violent? Candidates are the television stations that inundate us every year with thousands of acts of abuse, of killing, maiming, and generally of harming others; the regulatory agencies that have "failed" in their mission; or the parents, who should have supervised their children better. While there is probably enough blame to spread around, in arguing about the proper attribution we implicitly lengthen or shorten the causal chain. Such a step, in turn, involves our conceptions of what role we consider appropriate for individuals and various social institutions in particular contexts. Thus, when a businessman gives a "pink slip" to several of his employees (in other words, gives them notice), he is directly causing appreciable harm to at least those who have no other realistic opportunities to find employment. Nevertheless, we do not hold him directly responsible despite the shortness and immediacy of the causal chain. We simply accept with regret that it is not the fault of the businessman, since it is after all not his business to run a welfare agency. If the employees have a claim to be indemnified at all, it is from us, society at large (which has no immediate causal connection with the harm caused!). Here, membership and communal boundaries establish both the attribution of harm and the entitlement. As the discussion above concerning the "right to food" showed, no such entitlement can be construed simply on the basis of the fact that certain practices generate harm beyond our community.

To that extent, even the harmful effects of complex institutions, such as markets, are by themselves insufficient to establish a claim to relief, quite aside from the fact that in making such assessments we utilize a variety of interacting standards that go far beyond the one of causally connecting harm with an actor's specific action. Thus, we might for example regret that a traditional farmer loses out to a modern agri-business firm when the fields he rented for food production are now used to grow flowers for export, to take Henry Shue's example.[33] But, although we might even be able to demonstrate considerable harm, we usually do accept it as part of our economic system that does not guarantee us the immutability of a certain position in society, or of a particular job, or even of a way of life. At best, we are inclined to abate some of the dislocations caused by the operation of such systems by means of taxes for our members and through some voluntary arrangements internationally. As Marion Smiley put it:

While we might think of ourselves as merely figuring out who is in the best position to prevent harm, we inevitably fall back on a variety of social and political considerations – considerations ranging in this case from our judgements of relative harm to our valuation of private property. Likewise, while we may think of ourselves as falling back on a neutral conception of an individual's ability to prevent harm in our discovery of causal responsibility, we in fact, incorporate into both our conceptions of an individual's ability to prevent harm and our judgements of causal responsibility a strong sense of when individuals can be expected to sacrifice their own projects for the sake of others' well-being.

What this suggests is that even if we wanted to place the value of preventing harm at the center of our theory of moral agency, we would have to explore the social and political considerations that ground our judgements of causal responsibility in practice. Likewise we would have to understand the prevention of harm in this context as a socially and politically charged enterprise to the extent that it incorporates into itself the social and political values of its operators.[34]

Thus, contrary to the original argument about responsibility consisting of the establishment of a causal chain of harm plus "free will", we usually dispense with the notion of free will rather quickly. Our assessment of liability is largely constituted by certain rules that establish the practice of blaming. Furthermore, even the causal connection between harm to others and our actions by itself seems insufficient for the attribution of blame, because we are usually not sure to what extent an actor should have taken the sufferings caused to others into account before acting, particularly if the causal chain reaches beyond the confines of our community.

In a way we are all, whether we like it or not, "communitarians", because the attempts to define an Archimedian point of view outside of our practices and experiences are "nowhere". It should come as no surprise that they can only lead "nowhere"[35] if we persist in basing our political and moral life on the prescriptions that are derived from these principles. This does not mean that our argument about the possibility of duties beyond borders is mistaken or useless. Our practices *do* change, because we do alter our judgements about causal responsibility on the basis of new insights concerning causation, on the basis of historical shifts in power in which traditional modes of understanding no longer have any pull, and on the basis of different conceptions of who "we" are. It is in this context that Daniel Warner's attempt to engage in a new discourse on "responsibility" deserves further attention.[36] Rather than founding such a reflection on subjectively freely chosen "ultimate values", as Weber proposed in his *Verantwortungsethik*, Warner searches for the relevant audience to which one has to respond. The contested nature of the boundaries of communities also shows us that there is no ultimate foundation in the notions of nations or states. These notions, too, might change, even though at present they provide for individual identification with the larger group, and as such establish the more specific expectations, roles, and duties we invoke when we deliberate about our choices and attribute praise or blame.

Nevertheless, this discussion also suggests that institutions remain of paramount importance in our ethical deliberations. They not only inform our practices but also provide the templates for our interpretation of the principles and norms that we utilize when we reflect on our practical choices. Here again, legal theory or jurisprudence provides us with further vital clues as to the importance of a shared life world underlying the interpretation of norms. That such problems arise not only in the case of general principles but even at lower levels of abstraction can be seen from the puzzles which would arise in the case of interpreting a seemingly unequivocal prohibition, if we considered the problem of interpretation to be only a semantic issue. According to this theory a rule has a definite meaning if its terms clearly correspond to the factual circumstances selected as relevant by the rule. That matters are considerably more complicated can be seen from the following examples.

Consider first the seemingly unequivocal prohibition: "No dogs on the escalator". Imagine now someone coming with his beagle Fido and claiming that the prohibition does not apply to him since he has only one dog! If we tell him that "dogs" here means dog generically, we would again be surprised if he came next day with his pet cougar on a leash (certainly no dog, generic or otherwise) and claimed to be exempt from the prohibition. Assume further that our prankster is also known to the police as a potentially seditious person, and is therefore followed by the police basset-hound Pluto wherever he goes. Thus, one day Pluto stands right next to him when, at the top of the escalator, a policeman stops the culprit and wants to give him a ticket. This time the prankster might actually convince the policeman, showing that Pluto is not his dog. But the same excuse will obviously fail when he shows up with Fifi, even if this dog does not belong to him but to his friend.

These remarks have important implications for issues of interpretation and for ethical reflection. They show first of all that the meaning of a term (and thus in the case of norms or principles which are supposed to provide guidance) is neither a matter of definitional exactitude, nor generality, nor is it even a purely cognitive matter. Rather it is a problem of *practice* deeply embedded in our institutions and role conceptions that serve as a background for making our judgements. As Rob Walker has persuasively argued:

To raise questions about ethics and international relations is to raise questions that invoke the difficulty of speaking about politics in the late twentieth century, about what concepts like political community, obligation, freedom, autonomy, democracy, or security can mean in the context of contemporary re-articulations of political space and time.

It is, therefore, necessary to be extremely cautious about the celebration of any revival of interest in ethics and international relations. A busier intersection is no indication of an escape from the routines through which attempts to speak of ethics are either marginalized or trivialized. These routines emerge from the way claims about ethical possibility are already constitutive of theories of international relations. Thus, rather than focus directly on attempts to speak ethics to international relations, as if speaking truth to power, it is more helpful to interrogate those sites within the theory of international relations in which ethical claims are either encouraged or discouraged.[37]

The upshot of the argument is that the reflexivity which is proper for ethical reflection has to be directed at the practices themselves, as abstract principles do little explaining or guiding, as we have seen. Above all, we have to pay attention to two things: first, the political discourses that provide the openings for voicing such concerns and for debating their merits. Precisely because politics has always to do with "projects" and not only with the ascertainment of what is or which regularities can be observed, it cannot be divorced from normative concerns; and the more-or-less established division of labour of letting political scientists deal with the "is" while philosophers shall concern themselves with the "oughts" is as pernicious as it is senseless. It leads not only to moral obtuseness but also to a conception of ethics that is divorced from practical political action and the historical "sites" which provide meaning and the opportunity for action and intervention.

Second, what these considerations suggest is that we are probably better served by a revival of a casuistic method in reflecting upon our actions and practices than by the analytical modes examined above.[38] In other words, what we primarily need is an appropriate heuristics for helping us in our perplexities rather than abstract principles from which we can elegantly and parsimoniously derive our more particular action-guiding prescriptions, ranging from nuclear war to animal rights.

The sketch in the next section considering the options in humanitarian emergencies or the application of sanctions shows that charting a viable and responsible course of action depends less on principles than on the proper knowledge of the circumstances and the completeness (rather than the rigour) of the analysis.

Diagnosing dilemmas: The cases of humanitarian aid and sanctions

These considerations show their relevance when we confront emergencies and reason about our duties and obligations in alleviating the suffering of those who have been visited by disasters. Providing relief for the suffering, be it in specialized circumstances as in the case of war, or in natural or man-made disasters when thousands are put to flight and need food and shelter, seems rather uncontroversial. Nevertheless, significant differences obtain that not only distinguish victims of war from those of internal violence and natural disasters, but also suggest different approaches to aid and pose different dilemmas.[39]

First of all, man-made disasters are different from natural ones, as games against nature differ from those of strategic interaction. This not only has implications for the criteria of rationality when we assess our choices, but even more importantly our strategies have to rely on social rather than natural or brute facts. Thus helping victims in a war, as in caring for the sick and the prisoners of war, necessitates elaborate regimes which, in turn, presuppose functioning military and political structures. The state, often maligned and considered part of the problem, is nevertheless also part of the solution. A mixture of common agreement on the desirability of humane treatment of non-combatants, be they civilians or prisoners, of reciprocity and surveillance, is usually able to prevent further deliberate atrocities. Even those who are able to flee the theatres of combat could traditionally invoke the status of a "refugee" and thus were able to claim certain rights and entitlements for relief.[40]

Second, the eclipse of the state and the latent or actual dangers of a disintegrating consensus on the inviolability of humanitarian aid comes clearly to the fore when the man-made disasters stem from a civil war. Here civilian casualties result quite frequently, not only from the devastations visited upon the civilian population by armed conflict, but the civilian population is often also the explicit target of the perpetrated violent actions. Thus the protection of civilians and their exemption from the hostilities often runs counter to the strategy chosen by one or all of the parties to the conflict. Here both "peace-keeping" and humanitarian interventions[41] can hardly operate in an environment that is conducive to the accomplishment of humanitarian missions.[42] The bitter experiences of the Congo, and more so of Lebanon, Somalia, and Bosnia, demonstrated this clearly. Under such circumstances the peace-keepers and humanitarian personnel quickly become pawns in the struggle for control as the civilian population is targeted for violent and extortionary action. While the peace-keepers are at least sometimes in a position to defend themselves, the civilians and those working for NGOs are practically at the mercy of armed gangs. They have to negotiate for their safety and for the delivery of relief, and accept various charges as the state can no longer provide the necessary security.

Humanitarian aid, even such seemingly uncontroversial measures as distributing food, no longer enjoys the protection afforded by the consensus on humanitarian aid. Starving the enemy becomes a deliberate political strategy, and Somalia has shown its brutal effectiveness. The injection of resources into the conflict might then have perverse effects, as Janice Stein points out.[43] The availability of emergency food and medical care relieves the political leaders from pressure to provide even minimal subsistence, and creates opportunities for hold-ups and robberies in order to satisfy the demands of the marauding combatants. In addition, the civilian masses displaced by the effects of internal wars increasingly find it difficult to get recognized as refugees, as states have become reluctant to shoulder responsibility for the mass emigrations engendered by domestic instability or genocidal activities. Besides, as relief has become increasingly "privatized" because non-governmental organizations (NGOs) have taken on a variety of roles for which traditionally states had responsibility (from education to public health and political reconciliation), many states are pointing to this makeshift private solution and absolve themselves from the traditional burdens of caring for others.[44]

The moral dilemmas that arise in this context stem less from the well-worn topics of the permissibility or prohibition of intervention, or from the grand distributive schemes propagated by our philosopher-kings, or from the conflicts engendered by sovereignty and its bar to intervention. They stem increasingly from our inability to identify the levers, any levers, that might help in the alleviation of pain and suffering. If "ought" implies "can" then much more thinking has to go into the "can" part of the equation instead of fiddling with various oughts. In this context it is not only tragic but irresponsible when, for example, large numbers of Rwandan refugees die from the lack of even minimal sanitary measures because the main focus in the refugee camps is on the dispensing of food.[45] Thus, our present practices are not something we can be satisfied with, nor is the smug (even if correct) statement that not much can be done humane and acceptable.

Nevertheless, there are certain dilemmas we had better face, instead of relying on some romantic notions of what has appropriately been called band-aid liberalism and the politically dubious theories that see in the ever-increasing density of relief networks and non-state actors the harbingers of world political change with emancipatory potential, as the hard shell of the state is being pierced. Similarly, in order to avoid paternalism and also prevent the population of humanitarian relief from becoming dependent on hand-outs – both eminently desirable and sensible goals – strategies of linking relief and development have been proposed. Local partnerships with NGOs, the empowerment of communities, and the development of grass roots are important steps in the transition to self-sustained development and conflict resolution. But, aside from the fact that the estimates about the time needed to realize such a transition seem wildly optimistic, given the physical and social destruction of countries like Liberia, Rwanda, Sudan, or even Bosnia, there is an implicit image of a vibrant civil society that in good Lockean fashion sets the parameters for the state and can challenge its exercise of power.[46] The bitter truth, though, is that in many cases neither a vibrant civil society in the fashion of Pufendorf, Locke, or Hegel exists, nor can we find autonomous state structures on which we could rely or which we could reform. Worse still, where such structures existed they seem to have been pretty much cast asunder by the violence and concomitant scores which the internal wars have created.

The relief-to-development-to-democracy approach creates pressures to reclassify emergencies so that the multifunctional approach can begin to work. Premature relabelling led to the "normalizing" of emergencies and the raising of thresholds of civilian violence before an emergency can be declared. More generically, developmentalist approaches to relief seriously underestimate the difficulty of implementing development programmes in the context of the acute violence and extreme insecurity that are characteristic of protracted humanitarian emergencies. They do so in part because they ignore the politics of those who benefit from the prolonged emergencies.[47]

The real problem seems again to lie more in the lack of political understanding than in some normative controversies. For example, there seems precious little thought given to the problem of how one can isolate rogue leaders from the population, particularly as an outsider. Our responses move, therefore, from phantasmagoric strategies of "bombing the hell out of them", to attempting to assassinate them, to problematic hopes about the strength of community-building, to blanket sanctions.

In the latter case the hopes placed in this strategy rely on a largely mistaken analogy, as Saddam Hussein has clearly demonstrated. Taking again in good liberal fashion the individual as the paradigm, we imagine the workings of sanctions as largely analogous to the noose, or an arm-twist which sooner or later leaves the individual no choice but to give in. Unfortunately, in the case of sanctions against a state or a population, the leadership can usually exempt itself from the hardship sanctions create and has, in addition, the opportunity of draping itself in the national flag. Parading its determination not to give in becomes widely accepted as an admired case of standing up to the bully. In other words, sanctions become counterproductive. While this point might be readily conceded, there is usually an implicit assumption that if things get really bad for everybody, people will somehow rebel – Locke's famous appeal to heaven – and throw the scoundrels out. The experiences with the bombing of Germany and Viet Nam should have convinced us that such hopes are usually idle indeed, and that internal resistance has probably the lesser legitimacy the more severe the forceful action by outsiders becomes. Here the experiences of Kosovo added an element of the surreal to this *problematique*, since force was used against civilian targets while the people for whose protection the operation was allegedly designed remained unprotected. All the while, the perpetrators of this disaster, although properly indicted, remained in power.

It is time to think more creatively about sanctions that hurt the rogue but not the people. Freezing the personal assets of rogue leaders abroad might actually hurt much more than placing an embargo on the entire country, and also make the enforcement measure correspond much more closely to the model from which it was derived. Nevertheless, genuine dilemmas will remain, precisely because we pursue competing and often conflicting values with our political projects. Consider in this context the dilemma of providing food and shelter to refugees who were also perpetrators of genocidal activities. According to the notion of humanitarian relief – whether it is aid to prisoners, medical care to soldiers, or the provision of food and shelter to refugees – these actions are morally legitimate, irrespective of the status of the person. A human life is worth saving even if the person himself might have acted in an inhuman fashion. Doctors – this is our understanding of their "role" – have no choice; they must tend to the needy even if they are culprits.

But we also want to have justice served, by making people pay for what they did. Can we condone then without further ado the feeding and clothing of war criminals if they are refugees?[48] Has such a person the same status as a suppliant in the temples or churches of yesteryear, and can he claim such a status without even any attrition or expiation that was usually required by such an institution? Should we encourage the self-administration of refugee camps even if this involves making common cause with the leaders with dirty hands, who can again use the civilian population as their pawn? Is it therefore sensible to let doctors run refugee camps? Or do we also want to have those other interests served even if this means relying on paternalistic measures instead of self-help at best, and on armed authority at worst? Is this at all feasible, and does it cross the line of humanitarianism? These are indeed troubling questions.

Consider also the problem of war-torn societies that engage in often heartbreaking exercises of reconciliation, as in Cambodia, South Africa, or Bosnia, which always entail having to embrace again those who have perpetrated crimes against humanity. Can we and should we back these attempts, or should we demand greater accountability? One thing we also seriously have to face is the possibility that humanitarian aid may have to be suspended in certain cases, despite the dismal consequences for the victims. If the security of the humanitarian personnel is not guaranteed and warring factions misuse the safe havens and resources of humanitarian aid, this might be the only credible threat and, unfortunately, if threats have failed, the last available option.

The moral dilemmas are so stark in those cases as we have only weak institutional structures which would mediate the dilemmas – as expiation in traditional societies, or re-education (in the case of Germany) – and no promising alternatives to the accommodations to the often atrocious facts and the compromises that might be required for a political settlement. While such thoughts might be revolting at first blush, there is also some hope. After all, in the memorial year of the Peace of Westphalia which ended the until then probably bloodiest and most atrocious civil and international war, this hope might not be entirely without foundation. Nevertheless, and this is important to remember, the ensuing development of political institutions mediating the relations among persons of "sovereign authority" depended on the virtually shared recognition among the warring parties, which the inscription in the town hall at Munster captures: "PAX OPTIMA RERUM".

Summary

This chapter discussed the *problematique* of ethics and international relations. It did so by criticizing the predominant approaches of ethics conceived as an analytical discipline concerned with the elaboration and justification of principles that can then be applied to issues of international politics. In examining several approaches, consequentialist as well as deontological, and in demonstrating that these approaches fail in terms of their own criteria, it was submitted that this failure calls into question the whole enterprise of "ethics" as an analytical discipline. The author argued instead for a more context-bound reflection that shows similarities to practical reasoning and casuistry. To that extent it was argued that "law" provides a useful first cut not because it informs us authoritatively about what we have to do when we face complex situations which often entail tragic choices and moral dilemmas, but because legal reasoning, going systematically from facts to norms and norms to facts, provides us with a better diagnostics than attempts to base our choices upon either generalization arguments, the felicific calculus, or the deontological criteria determining the good will in a Kantian fashion. Precisely because institutions do matter and many moral choices have less to do with the clarification of principles than with the complexities of the situation, the unclear causal connections and repercussions of our actions, and the "many hands" problems, we need to reflect critically on our decisions from within our political and social context and not from the viewpoint outside of not only our particular society but politics and society alike. Particularly at a time when the boundaries that once marked the "internal" side of politics have come under pressure, the traditional conceptual divisions and maxims for action have become problematic. To that extent the realist notion that the pursuit of the good life was possible only on the "inside", while on the "outside" the opportunity for ethical choices hardly arises, is not only belied by the increasing interdependencies that create new social facts and problems but also by the crisis or even the collapse of the state in many areas. For this reason the author argued for a more problem-solving perspective rather than for the further clarification of principles which were at the centre of attention in the enterprise, called "ethics" in modernity.

Notes

1. See the insistence on the distinction between law as a sanctioning order and morality in Kelsen, H., 1996, *International Law*, 2nd revised edn, ed. Tucker, R. New York: Holt, Rinehart, and Winston; see also Hart, H. L. A., 1983, "Positivism and the Separation of Law and Morals", in Hart, H. L. A., ed., *Essays in Jurisprudence and Philosophy*. Oxford: Clarendon.
2. See Strauss, L., 1953, *Natural Rights and History*. Chicago: University of Chicago Press; Fuller, L., 1969, *Morality of Law*, 2nd edn. New Haven: Yale University Press. For a modern version of natural law, deriving prescriptions from the intuition of certain self-evident goods and deriving the strength and moral authority of law from its contribution to a flourishing "community" allowing for the enjoyment of these human goods, see Finnis, J., 1980, *Natural Law and Natural Rights*. Oxford: Oxford University Press.
3. See the remarks in Toscano's contribution to this volume (Chapter 3) concerning the "professional" ethics of diplomats.
4. For a fundamental discussion see Walker, R. B. J., 1993, *Inside Outside: International Relations as Political Theory*. Cambridge: Cambridge University Press.
5. See the discussion by Nardin, T. and Mapel, D., eds, 1970, *Traditions of International Ethics*. Cambridge: Cambridge University Press.
6. See the controversy on the laws of war in Wasserstrom, R., ed., 1970, *War and Morality*. Belmont, CA: Wadsworth.
7. For a collection of essays concerned with a revival of virtue ethics see Crisp, R. and Slote, M., eds, 1997, *Virtue Ethics*. New York: Oxford University Press.
8. For a new attempt that emphasizes the role of moral worth without tying a virtue ethics to a "traditional" way of life see Watson, G., 1997, "The Primacy of Character", in Statman, D., ed., *Virtue Ethics. A Critical Reader*. Edinburgh: Edinburgh University Press.
9. On the distinction between practical and legal reasoning, see Kratochwil, F., 1989, *Rules, Norms and Decisions: On the Conditions of Practical and Legal Reasoning in International Relations and Domestic Affairs*. Cambridge: Cambridge University Press, especially Chapters 7 and 8.
10. See on the problem of collapsed states Zartman, W., 1995, *Collapsed States: The Disintegration and Restoration of Legitimate Authority*. Boulder: Lynne Rienner.
11. For a discussion of some of the controversy surrounding "special" obligations see Goodin, R., 1998, "What is So Special About Our Fellow Countrymen?", *Ethics*, Vol. 98, pp. 663–686; Miller, D., 1998, "The Ethical Significance of Nationality", *Ethics*, Vol. 98, pp. 647–662.

12. See Julia Kristeva's proposal based on exactly the reversal of this ranking because of the alleged precedence of cosmopolitan considerations, in Kristeva, J., 1991, *Strangers to Ourselves*. New York: Columbia University Press.
13. See Julia Kristeva, who in her "Open Letter to Harlem Desire" quotes Montesquieu's *Mes Pensées* in order to solve the dilemmas that arise from multiple memberships in communities: "If I knew something useful to myself, and detrimental to my family, I would reject it from my mind. If I knew something useful to my family, but not to my homeland, I would try to forget it. If I knew something useful to my homeland and detrimental to Europe, or else useful to Europe and detrimental to mankind, I would consider it a crime." Kristeva, J., 1990, *Nations Without Nationalism*. New York: Columbia University Press, p. 63.
14. For an elaboration of this point see Kratochwil, F., 1996, "Citizenship: On the Border of Order", in Lapid, Y. and Kratochwil, F., eds, *The Return of Culture and Identity in IR Theory*. Boulder: Lynne Rienner.
15. Nozick, R., 1974, *Anarchy State and Utopia*. New York: Basic Books.
16. On the concept of negative liberty, see Berlin, I., 1969, "Two Concepts of Liberty", in Berlin, I., *Four Essays on Liberty*. Oxford: Oxford University Press; for a further discussion see MacCallum, G. Jr, 1972, "Negative and Positive Freedom", in Lasslett, P., Runciman, W. G., and Skinner, Q., eds, *Politics and Society*. Oxford: Basil Blackwell.
17. See Shue, H., 1980, *Basic Rights: Subsistence, Affluence and US Foreign Policy*. Princeton: Princeton University Press, p. 53.
18. O'Neill, O., 1991, "Transnational Justice", in Held, D., ed., *Political Theory Today*. Stanford: Stanford University Press, p. 296.
19. Singer, P., 1972, "Famine, Affluence and Morality", *Philosophy and Public Affairs*, Vol. 1, No. 3, pp. 229–243.
20. See Pogge, T., 1995, "Eine globale Rohstoffdividende", *Analyse und Kritik*, Vol. 17, pp. 183–208.
21. Rawls, J., 1971, *A Theory of Justice*. Cambridge, MA: Harvard University Press.
22. See Hardin, G., 1977, "Lifeboat Ethics: The Case against Helping the Poor", in Aiken, W. and La Follette, H., eds, *World Hunger and Moral Obligation*. Englewood Cliffs, NJ: Prentice Hall, pp. 1–10. For a similar though more moderate position, arguing only against indiscriminate food assistance, see Fletcher, J., 1977, "Give if it Helps, But Not if it Hurts", *ibid.*, pp. 103–114.
23. For a general discussion of claims based on universalizable principles see Wimmer, R., 1980, *Universalisierung in der Ethik*. Frankfurt: Suhrkamp; Singer, M. G., 1971, *Generalization in Ethics*. New York: Atheneum.
24. O'Neill, note 18 above, p. 281.
25. Fishkin, J., 1982, *The Limits of Obligation*. New Haven: Yale University Press, p. 137.
26. Broad, C. D., 1915–16, "On the Functions of False Hypotheses in Ethics", *International Journal of Ethics*, Vol. 26, pp. 377–397, quoted at p. 387ff.
27. Fishkin, note 25 above, p. 143.
28. See the arguments by Rachels, J., 1977, "Vegetarianism and the Other Weight Problem", in Aiken and La Follette, note 22 above, pp. 80–93.
29. Feinberg, J., 1970, *Doing and Deserving: Essays in the Theory of Responsibility*. Princeton: Princeton University Press, p. 30.
30. Smiley, M., 1992, *Moral Responsibility and the Boundaries of Community*. Chicago: University of Chicago Press, p. 9.
31. See the fundamental discussion by Hart in his two articles, "Acts of Will and Responsibility" and "Intention and Punishment", in Hart, H. L. A., 1968, *Punishment and Responsibility in the Philosophy of Law*. Oxford: Clarendon Press.
32. Aristotle, 1953, *Nicomachian Ethics*, transl. Thompson, J. A. K. Harmondsworth: Penguin, Bk III, p. 80. "Then there are acts done through ignorance. For a man who has

been led into some action by ignorance and yet has no regrets, while he cannot be said to have been a voluntary agent – he did not know what he was doing – nevertheless, cannot be said to have acted involuntarily, since he feels no compunction."

33. Shue, note 17 above, Chapter 2. Shue has, however, modified his position considerably in later essays which stress the importance of intervening institutions; see Shue, H., 1988, "Mediating Duties", *Ethics*, Vol. 98, pp. 687–704.

34. Smiley, note 30 above, p. 115.

35. See Thomas Nagel's remarks in Nagel, T., 1986, *The View From Nowhere*. Oxford: Oxford University Press.

36. See Warner, D., 1991, *An Ethic of Responsibility in International Relations*. Boulder: Lynne Rienner.

37. Walker, note 4 above, p. 79.

38. For an argument concerning the revival of causistry see Jonsen, A. and Toulmin, S., 1988, *The Abuse of Causistry: A History of Moral Reasoning*. Berkeley: University of California Press.

39. On the problems of man-made disasters and the need for "early warning", see Jones, B. and Stein, J., 1999, *NGOs and Early Warning*. New York: Columbia University Press.

40. For the problematic increase in refugees from some 17 million in 1991 to over 27 million under the responsibility of the UNHCR alone (not counting internally displaced persons and those who have just fled their war-torn homeland), see UNHCR, 1995, *The State of the World's Refugees in 1995: In Search of Solutions*. New York: Oxford University Press.

41. For this *problematique* see the collection of essays in Warner, D., ed., 1995, *New Dimensions of Peacekeeping*. Dordrecht and Boston: Martinus Nijhoff.

42. For a discussion of the problems of humanitarian aid after the lessons of Somalia see the collection of essays in Clarke, W. and Herbst, J., eds, 1997, *Learning From Somalia: The Lessons of Armed Humanitarian Intervention*. Boulder: Westview Press.

43. Stein, J., 1998, "Mean Times", mimeo.

44. See Duffield, M., 1998, "NGO Relief in War Zones: Toward an Analysis of the New Aid Paradigm", in Weiss, T., ed., *Beyond UN Subcontracting: Task Sharing with Regional Security Arrangements and Service Providing NGOs*. New York: St Martin's Press.

45. Thus it is alleged that as many as 80,000 people may have died in Rwandan refugee camps due to insufficient attention to basic hygienic needs; see Burton, J. *et al.,* 1996, *Joint Evaluation of Emergency Assistance in Rwanda*. Copenhagen: DANIDA, quoted in Stein, note 43 above, p. 16.

46. Stein, note 43 above, p. 25.

47. Thus Duffield reports that Rwandan "troops" who were implicated in genocidal activities managed to turn NGO-operated refugee camps under UN auspices into political and resource bases for further genocidal warfare both within Zaire and in western Rwanda. See Duffield, M., 1994, "The Political Economy of Internal War and Hunger", in Zvi, A., ed., *Rethinking International Responses to Complex Emergencies*. London: Zed Books.

3

The ethics of modern diplomacy

Roberto Toscano

Introduction

The crisis over Kosovo, in the spring of 1999, brought the ethical discourse to the forefront of international debate. Political and military leaders have started referring to moral considerations not only, as was traditionally done, to illustrate the foundations of their political options, but also to justify specific strategies, in particular the recourse to military force to attain morally relevant results. Intellectuals and columnists debate the concept of "ethical war" in the pages of the world's press. Although the issue relates to the use of military force, it is more than ever evident, in the case of the conflict over Kosovo, that diplomatic and military means are concomitant and intertwined, rather than being sequentially linked in a continuum. That if we dare to rephrase von Clausewitz, military action – like diplomacy – is one of the means of politics. Thus the issue is at the same time one of "ethics and war" and "ethics and diplomacy".

Yet, paradoxically, whereas the debate on ethics and war, while being controversial, is relatively "easy" and clear cut, the issue of ethics and diplomacy has been less thoroughly explored and in particular has been overlooked, if not openly discarded as irrelevant, by practitioners in the field. This writer can testify that it is especially difficult for a professional diplomat to address the issue of "ethics and diplomacy". More precisely, one can do so only by deciding to go against the current, to challenge the conventional wisdom of one's peers, the majority of whom, if asked to react to the idea of such an endeavour, would probably respond as one of the author's colleagues actually did: "Ethics and diplomacy? But it is an oxymoron!" A difficult task, indeed, but an unavoidable one if one is not satisfied with the simple technicalities of a profession, if one wants to ask "what for" and not only "how".

It is not enough, evidently, to reject the idea that diplomacy can be declared "off limits" for an ethical discourse. What is necessary, if one wants to challenge this predominant view, is to try to understand the reasons for its widespread acceptance, to identify the specific difficulties faced by the extension of an ethical discourse to the field of diplomacy, and finally to see whether and how such a discourse can be phrased in the actual conditions that characterize contemporary international relations.

Why look for specificities? In a way one could stop this exercise from even starting by accepting an apparently indisputable truth: diplomacy is just an aspect of politics, it is but practical politics applied to international relations. So, why reopen the ancient debate on politics and ethics? Nothing new can be said there: Machiavelli and his critics, in particular, have said it all long ago. The terms of the question are clear: what is left is only declaring our own ethical preference.

This reductionist view has the misleading charm of apparent common sense, but its clay feet become quickly evident. The legitimacy, or – better – the need, of addressing the issue of ethics and diplomacy with a degree of autonomy *vis-à-vis* the "ethics and politics" debate is proved by a few simple questions. If diplomacy is but politics beyond national borders, why is it that Machiavelli dominates in diplomacy – at least on the level of unspoken assumptions[1] – but not in internal political discourse? Why does the brilliant Florentine cross international frontiers so freely, whereas the ethical discourse tends to be stopped at border crossings? Why does the same Machiavellian recipe for ethics-free political action produce horror (in the same citizens who implicitly accept it without qualms as an obvious foundation for diplomacy) once it is brought back to its original birthplace, the internal body politic?

So, after all, there might be a real need to understand and explain the separate issue of ethics in the conduct of international relations.[2]

First, however, it should be stated from the outset, for the benefit of unambiguous understanding of the text, which is the working definition of both terms (ethics and diplomacy) that will be used.

Ethics and morality

A warning to the reader: in this chapter, "ethical" and "moral" will be used (for practical purposes and following a widespread though perhaps objectionable practice) in an interchangeable way. This does not mean to imply that the author is convinced that no distinction can be drawn between the two concepts. Ethics, in fact, answers the question "How should I live?", whereas the moral question is "What must I do?". Ethics is germane to wisdom and borders with love, morality deals with obligation and borders with law. Morality commands, ethics recommends. One may think that ethics is superior to morals, but moral rules are in any case socially indispensable so that, recognizing duty, people will live as if they loved their fellow humans. Paraphrasing St Augustine's "Love, and do what you want", one could say "Love, or do what you must".[3]

In both cases, however, we will expressly avoid a "foundational" discussion: why one should live in a certain way and not in another, or why one must do something instead of something else, falls beyond the scope of what intends to be a modest attempt at exploring a particular field of "applied ethics" and not elaborating a study in moral philosophy.

Here, however, the author – though not stating his own preferences as to the possible foundations (or lack of them) of ethics – will clearly state his belief that both questions ("How should I live?" and "What must I do?") are incomplete, not because they do not include the "Why?", but because they lack the definition of a relationship/obligation toward "the Other".[4] Confessing a humanist bias, this author, in other words, wants to state from the outset his conviction that both ethics and morals are inconceivable outside human relationships, that both questions, therefore, are incomplete, and should read respectively: "How should I live with others?" and "What must I do unto others?".

Diplomacy and international relations

As for the definition of diplomacy, preferences should be stated from the outset. This author finds that – especially for the purpose of a discussion on ethics and diplomacy – the most satisfactory definition can be found in Der Derian: "the mediation of estranged peoples organized in states which interact in a system". Der Derian then defines "diplomatic culture" as "the mediation of estrangement by symbolic power and social constraints".[5]

All the necessary elements are thus present in this two-stage definition: the "otherness" ("estranged peoples"); the focus on relationship ("mediation"); the reference to the fact that the protagonists are "states which interact in a system"; and the combination of "symbolic power" and "social constraints", referring to the mix (present at all levels of politics) between material power and symbolic hegemony.

Diplomacy is of course about politics on the international level, but its specific profile is linked with the "mediation" Der Derian speaks about.

It identifies at the same time a profession, some would say an art (or at least a set of peculiar skills), and its focus is on the role and choices of practitioners. One might therefore maintain that international relations – in so far as it is a discipline dealing with historical events and the actual working of functional systems – does not lend itself to a reading conducted on the basis of ethical premises. It would, however, be much less justified to dismiss the possibility of ethical scrutiny if our focus is not international relations but diplomacy, which means choice and action by what one, again following Der Derian, could venture to define as "professional mediators of international otherness".

Diplomacy and ethics: An impossible coexistence?

Realism versus ethics – From Nicolo' Machiavelli to George Kennan

If realism can be considered a very powerful school of thought in international relations at the academic level, once we turn to practitioners in the field it is without doubt the predominant, if not in practice the exclusive, one.[6] Most practitioners share what has been aptly defined as "skepticism concerning the relevance of moral categories to the relations among states"[7] to the point of considering all contrary opinion as a symptom of soft-headedness,[8] to be dismissed intellectually and rejected as unprofessional and dangerous to the defence of national interest. The famous "my country, right or wrong" (uttered by an American patriot who would certainly have been surprised to be qualified as "Machiavellian") is the unspoken but quasi-universal foundation of the role and professionalism of diplomats the world over, who would also – in most cases – reject any intellectual or moral link with Machiavelli, and yet would accept as a matter of fact the need to have recourse, when necessary in the defence of their state, to deceit and/or the threat or actual use of violence.

One of the most brilliant diplomats of the twentieth century, George Kennan, has consistently espoused in his many and very influential writings the same view: that there are national interests consisting mainly in security, political independence, and well-being of the population; and that such needs have no intrinsic moral quality, and cannot be subject to moral scrutiny or judgement.[9] As Hobbes said:

[T]he law of nations, and the law of nature, is the same thing. And every sovereign hath the same right, in procuring the safety of his people, that any particular man can have, in procuring his own safety.[10]

But should we accept the claims of realists when they say that their approach to international relations is objective and value-free? The author would say exactly the opposite, starting from a critical appraisal of the nature of Machiavelli's challenge to morals – to individual morals. Isaiah Berlin maintains that, in spite of the conventional wisdom on Machiavelli's "amoralism", his whole political theory is firmly grounded on a strong moral option that privileges over all other considerations the security and strength of the *res publica* (today we would say the state).[11] Or, as Stuart Hampshire has written, "Machiavelli himself is an advocate of one specific concept of the good".[12] Contemporary realists follow in the footsteps of their most eminent maestro, with the added peculiarity that they, differently from Machiavelli – whose intent was to give practical advice to the "Prince" – pretend to clothe their own options in "objective", "scientific" garb.

Facing this claim, it becomes necessary to draw attention to the ideological nature of realism, which appears to be the far-from-objective rationalization of a specific moral and political option in favour of the nation-state, its power, and its right to pursue political ends without being subject to ordinary moral scrutiny. Realism in international theory should be more correctly called "state realism".

To realize how far from being universal and non-controversial "state realism" is, it is useful to stop for a moment to consider other causes for moral justification that have been historically devised by humanity with the aim of justifying behaviour, even anti-social and violent behaviour. We might still have a preference for the state, but we will have to admit that there are other possible "realisms". The state has never been, and is not today, the only "legitimizer". Sophocles's *Antigone* is an early, and very powerful, testimony of the drama of conflicting ethical stands, with Creon representing the *raison d'état* and Antigone finding her legitimation in the adherence to another ethical paradigm, centred on duty to the family and religious piety. Creon appears to be a true realist. For him – to quote Paul Ricoeur – "the only good is that which serves the *polis*, the only evil that which harms it".[13] Ricoeur, however, acutely points out that both Creon and Antigone are one-sided, partial, and sectarian. They are the stubborn and substantially inhuman holders of non-compatible ethical stands. Thus in no way could we say that Creon is "realist" while Antigone is "moral".

Of course, family and religion have a good name, and when confronted with *Antigone* most contemporary viewers are willing to follow Sophocles in his attempt to let both sides (the state versus religion and family) be heard without caricature or bias. Things become more difficult when we are confronted with another kind of "realism": revolutionary realism. Both in practice and in theory revolutionaries (in our era mostly of the

Marxist-Leninist persuasion) have systematically challenged common (for them "bourgeois") morality on the basis of a different brand of realism. We owe to Leon Trotsky the most articulate apology for this stand.[14] It is remarkable to see how much his arguments follow the reasoning of the "realist" school: it is enough to substitute "revolution" for "nation-state".

As a matter of fact, if we want to be consistent realists, we could not avoid adding, together with family[15] and revolutionary party, also fundamentalist religion, race, class, and even criminal groups.[16] Contemporary reality gives abundant evidence of the fact that "state realism" gives voice to only one of the manifold claims to such exemption. And yet today, for historical and cultural reasons – as well as for the ideological hegemony of the nation-state – few would be as bold as Thomas Hobbes was in the following description, in which claims of "ethical exceptionality" of the state versus other human groups are in practice dismissed:

And in all places, where men have lived by small families, to rob and spoil one another, has been a trade, and so far from being reputed against the law of nature, that the greater spoils they gained, the greater was their honour ... And as small families did then, so now do cities and Kingdoms which are but greater families (for their own security) enlarge their dominions, upon all pretences of danger, and fear of invasion, or assistance that may be given to invaders, and endeavour as much as they can, to subdue, or weaken their neighbours, by open force, and secret arts, for want of other caution, justly; and are remembered for it in after ages with honour.[17]

It would be one more ideological fallacy, on the other hand, to attribute the difficulty that ethical considerations face in crossing borders to the strength and dominance of the realist school of international relations. Beyond the prestige and intellectual appeal of thinkers/practitioners from Machiavelli to Kennan, from Hobbes to Kissinger, the real reason for the strong appeal of realism lies in the fact that it appears to coincide with (and to supply an adequate rationalization to) actual features and actual problems characterizing relations among nations; those very features and problems that make it so difficult for ethics and diplomacy to be rendered at least compatible.

The menace of war

Every being tends to persevere in its existence, with an "urge to be" (Spinoza's *conatus essendi*[18]) that overrides any moral precept; war threatens the existence of humans as individuals and as communities; *ergo*, to the extent that diplomacy unfolds under the menace of war, survival takes precedence over ethics. There is nothing specific in this process, since it is but the extension to the international sphere and the generalization of the principle (both legal and moral) of self-defence Since self-defence is a universally recognized cause of exemption from moral judgement, positing nation-states as existing in a constant state of actual or potential self-defence against aggression (war) cannot but rule out any relevance of ethics for diplomacy. The "potential", here, is an essential qualification, since otherwise one could only suggest the need for a sort of "suspension of ethics" in open war or in its imminence, and not a blanket exclusion of ethics from diplomacy.

In describing the Islamic concept of *jihad*, commentators insist on the fact that the state of war it describes does not have to be open and actual: it is instead a sort of normal, natural, permanent condition which may be interrupted by temporary truces, but which never stops supplying the only real paradigm of the relations between the House of Islam (*dar al-Islam*) and the House of War (*dar al-Harb*), meaning the non-Moslem world.[19] We find a similar concept in Hobbes: "[T]he nature of war, consisteth not in actual fighting; but in the known disposition thereto, during all the time there is no assurance to the contrary."[20]

But when can there be "assurance to the contrary" in the real world of international relations? How can states – and their respective diplomacies, pursuing national interests in the real world thus described – exit from the conceptual mode of war, a mode that appears to rule out ethics? The problem is that nation-states have shown, historically, the tendency to give to the concept of self-defence against aggression a very wide interpretation. Again, let us go back to Machiavelli. Examining in Chapter 3 of *The Prince* the imperial policy of Rome, he considers it "justified ... by the nature of the international environment: the Romans were compelled to conquer to forestall threats to their security ... *They conquered the world out of self-defence.*" (emphasis added).[21] Thus Machiavelli justifies on the basis of the absolute primacy of self-defence and security both imperial expansion and pre-emptive attack. Even realists will agree that things become more complicated here. One example only: it is difficult to question the fact that the Soviet Union was historically guided, in its diplomacy, by a true "obsession for security" – the product of both the awareness of internal weakness[22] and of events like post-1917 international intervention and Hitler's 1941 attack (with Napoleon's invasion in the distant, but still psychologically important, past). And yet, who would refrain from a political and moral judgement of events such as Hungary 1956, Czechoslovakia 1968, and Afghanistan 1979? How is it possible to accept at face value the all-purpose, self-declared (and self-serving) security rationale for that "ethical exemption" that traditionally, facing a theoretically always looming danger of war, diplomacy claims for itself?

The dogma of national interest

The panoply of arguments utilized by those who maintain the necessarily "extra-ethical" nature of diplomacy is, however, not limited to self-defence and the overwhelming imperatives of security. Actually, self-defence and security are but the most dramatic, most cogent items within a wider category: that of national interest.[23] According to this dogma (the common catechism of diplomats of nations belonging to all geographical areas, cultures, and political orientation), ethics is inevitably subjective, whereas national interest is objective; thus the former is debatable, the latter is not; the former is abstract, the latter concrete. Ethical preference is divisive, national interest unites.

Once again we are apparently facing a claim of "ethical exemption" on the basis of a realistic, objective approach: "the process of government is a practical exercise, and not a moral one".[24] But once more it is not too difficult to detect, behind this apparent realism, a different moralism, one that consists in ethical partiality in favour of the state. National-interest doctrine, in other words, is but a doctrine of "higher allegiance", overriding – whenever necessary – not only the specific interests of individuals, but their common morality. We are not facing, indeed, amoral realism, but rather what one could call "statist ethics".

The idol of sovereignty

This chapter is not the right context in which to examine the concept of sovereignty, one of the main pillars of the contemporary system of international relations. And yet any discourse on ethics and diplomacy cannot avoid touching upon sovereignty. Once more, we are led back to Hobbes, and in general to prevailing doctrine on the nature of state power. "Ethical exemption" claimed by diplomacy is not only based upon the overriding right to act in self-preservation, or the wider concept of national interest, but also upon the nature of the sovereign state, an entity that "recognizes no superior" (superiorem non recognoscens, as the Romans stated). Though today few would formulate it in openly Hobbesian terms, this doctrine is still very strong as an implicit assumption underlying contemporary interstate relations. And it is a doctrine that has not only legal but also moral repercussions.[25]

The fact is that diplomacy has been traditionally conducted on the basis of the assumption that no one has the legitimization to question on moral grounds the international behaviour of states; an assumption that has been (and is being) challenged,[26] but which is still very strong, especially among practitioners.

The fetish of territoriality

One more reason for the problems that diplomacy has with ethics is the fact that the object of interstate relations is often territory. But what is it, exactly, that makes territorial issues and disputes so incompatible with an ethical approach? Ethics is recognizing the relevance of the other, admitting that the other's demands might be justified and at least should be seriously considered; territorial issues tend to be of a "zero-sum game" nature. Territory means resources, population, and strategic control. Territory constitutes the very body of the state, so that every loss is perceived as a mutilation, every gain as vital growth (or, more often, recovery of previously detached limbs).

This organic explanation, however, would not adequately explain the enormous attachment to territory displayed by most if not all nation-states. We must shift from geography (and geopolitics) to symbols. Why otherwise, if not for symbolic and ideological reasons, would it be that even uninhabited, barren, economically useless territory frequently becomes the object of ferocious, ethically deaf, diplomatic and military contention? It is ideology – nationalist ideology – that works systematically in order to transform real estate into sacred soil, that (to go back to the organic metaphor) is able to present the insignificant paring of a fingernail as the painful mutilation of an arm. Honour, history, and identity are brought to bear on what from a rational point of view might be seen as minor, or in any case negotiable, territorial issues. The result is that the space for reasonableness and morally defensible diplomacy is annulled. Once more, morality is presented as a treacherous weakness incompatible with the preservation of the integrity and honour of the nation.

The terminology used above to describe the main facets of the ethical "unfriendliness" of diplomacy is purposefully judgemental and biased: the idol of sovereignty, the dogma of national interest, the fetish of territoriality. Does this mean that the author denies the importance of sovereignty, the validity of the principle of the national interest, the reality of the territorial dimension? Quite the opposite. The attack is not, and could not be, on aspects and principles that do characterize, for very good intrinsic reasons, international relations – and that should be thoroughly considered in the theory and practice of diplomacy.

What is to be criticized is not their recognition, but their absolutization. The common fallacy (an intellectual fallacy inevitably turning into a moral one) in all these cases is the idolatric raising of a particular concern into an all-powerful, unconditionally overriding consideration. Indeed it can be said, following the Jewish tradition, that at the root of evil there lies the absolutization of particular aspects – even true, valid, positive aspects – of human reality.[27] The same concept can be found in a

Christian thinker, Pascal, when he defines "tyranny" as the pretence of affirming the value of a specific category (be it strength, beauty, knowledge, or piety) "outside its order".[28] The result has been described as follows by a contemporary writer in ethics:

Conscientious wickedness is rarely a case of pursuing an end unaware of the attendant consequences as evils; it is more often the case of a single-minded pursuit of an objective which can be reasonably seen as good, but at the cost of a callous insensitivity to evil done by the way.[29]

Thus, defence of territory is legitimate, sovereignty is the necessary keystone of the international system, and national interest is the obvious point of reference for foreign policy. What is to be questioned, also because it expels ethics from the realm of diplomacy, is the raising of territoriality, sovereignty, and national interest to the absolute (which, one should remember, etymologically means unfettered, loose) status of an idol not subject to ethical scrutiny.

Ethics and diplomacy at the end of the twentieth century

The elements the author tried to identify in the previous section are of a permanent, intrinsic nature. But we live in history, we live in a society that undergoes rapid and radical transformations. An analysis of the ethics-in-diplomacy theme must therefore be conducted with reference also to the peculiarities of our epoch.

Ethics and diplomacy in a globalized world

Globalization is a limited, imperfect, and probably oversold paradigm, but one that, if handled with care, can function as a useful tool for understanding the times in which we are living. The author will suggest just a few points for reflection on the specific implications of globalization for the ethics (or non-ethics) of diplomacy.

If ethics means choice of morally relevant action, how can diplomacy allow for an ethical dimension in the presence of a theory/ideology that posits the impossibility of choice facing the "iron laws" of the globalized economy?[30] Paradoxically, neo-liberals tend to go the same way as their arch opponents, the Marxists: if reality is determined by "objective laws", then all political action, including diplomacy, must be shaped accordingly, so that any talk of ethics is simply inane. What sense can there be, to make one example, in assessing from an ethical point of view the impact of internationally sponsored (one might say imposed) stabilization plans, if we are convinced that there is no possible alternative choice? *Force majeure*, as everybody knows, entails an exclusion of both legal and moral responsibility, so that there is a possibility that globalization will turn into a functional equivalent of the Cold War[31] as a tool for rationalizing the exclusion of ethics from diplomacy. As a matter of fact, the intellectual positions of the realist school of international relations have always been remarkably similar – in their focus on necessity – to those that characterize Marxist economic determinism,[32] another ethics-unfriendly doctrine. Following the end of the Cold War, realism in international affairs and (neo-liberal) economic determinism tend to coincide.

What is the impact on the possibility of an ethical dimension of diplomacy of the fact that today people who are still enormously different are put, as never before, in direct contact? If the face of the other is so radically different, what will happen to its concrete recognition, the basis of ethics? Of course this is an individual dilemma: for instance, many Europeans are confronted for the first time with the presence of radically different human beings in the streets of their cities, and their reaction, in many cases, leaves a lot to be desired from the point of view of ethics. But it also involves diplomacy: the diplomacy of migrations. The challenge is serious, often putting under stress not only the logistics involved with the absorption of an irregular and sometimes massive influx, but also the avowed progressive and humanistic beliefs of many governments. We are dealing here not with land or resources, not with trade or cultural programmes; we are dealing with real people, among them many women and children, suffering people escaping from situations of horror (be it war or persecution) or from conditions of difficult economic survival, if not downright hunger. If this branch of diplomacy is not ethically relevant, one cannot imagine which other branch could be. And yet here, too, the constraints of a globalized world – and its disconcerting combination of difference and proximity – heighten defensive attitudes and barriers, and raise the Moloch of necessity over choice, including moral choice. At times one gets the impression that governments (often fully supported by public opinion) are trying to compensate – through a rigid, often ostentatious, attitude of control and exclusion at the borders – for their growing loss of power, so characteristic of globalization, over vital items such as capital flows, exchange rates, localization, and conditions of investment. This, too, contributes to aggravating the insensitivity of "migration diplomacy" – an important branch of contemporary diplomacy – to ethical considerations.

Universality challenged

Ethics in diplomacy could be defined as the relevance of moral concerns in determining the policies applied by nation-states in their reciprocal relations, with a view to the repercussions of diplomatic action on the lives of concrete individuals. But which moral concerns? The question would have appeared merely rhetorical up until not very long ago (say, the middle of the twentieth century and decolonization), in so far as the marked cultural (and even religious) homogeneity of most international actors determined an implicit coincidence, at least in theory, on fundamental ethical values. It is interesting to note, however, that homogeneity was broken only in fact, but not in theory, at a very recent date, basically coinciding with the end of the Cold War. For about 50 years, a less homogeneous composition of the international community did not have any visible impact on the articulation of ethical values. In part this was due to the persistent cultural hegemony that colonial powers continued to exert over their former colonies even after independence; in part, also, to the fact that the main ideological challenge to the hegemony of Western powers came from Soviet communism, a system that was in its practice the antithesis of Western liberal democracy, but which in its doctrine purported to uphold the same values of human dignity, freedom, non-alienation, and democracy. The gap between theory and practice was of course monumental, often grotesque, and yet this ideological camouflage had as a consequence the fact that a real East–West confrontation on ethical issues never took place. This, of course, had major consequences in a world in which most weaker, non-European, non-developed countries had to find a niche and an alignment in the great schism dividing the more developed, or in any case more powerful, world.

The outbreak of an open ideological confrontation in recent years is due to several factors. One is of course the end of the East–West confrontation – a confrontation that for about half a century not only imposed discipline in political behaviour, but also strongly discouraged the formulation of alternative values. Second, we can point to the strengthening of political (often radical) Islam, a religion which focuses on morals rather than on theology, on "how to live" rather than on "what to believe", and which therefore identifies the confrontation on moral values as being one of the most promising grounds for proving vitality and building consensus. Thirdly, in many Asian countries economic success has stimulated a renewed pride in ethical traditions that are presented as alternative to, and sometimes contradictory with, the hitherto unchallenged moral canon of the West.

Since these aggressive alternatives to Western "ethical hegemony" have already been voiced, especially in the field of human rights (a theme that is dealt with separately by Jack Donnelly in Chapter 6 of this volume), the writer will refrain from advancing deeper into the subject. Yet it has to be pointed out, in the framework of a discussion on ethics and diplomacy, that ethical relativism in the field of human rights not only has a direct impact on the diplomacy of human rights as such, but it also raises supplementary doubts – confronted as we are today with ethical options that are divergent not only in practice, but also in theory – as to whether ethics and diplomacy are at all compatible.

Ethics and diplomacy: The case for compatibility

In the previous sections the author has attempted to identify the reasons, both intrinsic and historically contingent, that make the coexistence of ethics and diplomacy a most problematic endeavour. In setting out the arguments for the sceptical view the chapter tried to subject them to criticism. But is it possible to conceive "ethics and diplomacy" instead of "ethics *versus* diplomacy", and, in a more concrete focus, "how is it possible to look for compatibility"?

The purpose of this chapter is in fact that of challenging the common-sense, conventional-wisdom "oxymoron dogma" predominant among practitioners of diplomacy – not that of claiming a coincidence of ethics and diplomacy. The idea of a total coincidence of ethics with diplomacy, as with any other branch of politics, is the very essence of fundamental-ism, or, better, *intégrisme*,[33] since by eliminating all autonomy of the political sphere, it ends up subsuming politics (and inevitably also political institutions and mechanisms) into an moral sphere that demands the rigorous application of rules – not subject to critical scrutiny or political option – that in most cases are interpreted and applied by an oligarchy of priests/ideologues. From Giovanni Gentile's "ethical state" in fascist Italy to present-day fundamentalisms (not only Islamic, but also Christian or Jewish), the coincidence of ethics and politics makes for bad politics and questionable ethics. Compatibility means instead that, though not co-inciding, politics (in this case diplomacy) and ethics can be linked in a way that is not mutually exclusive. Although there will be tensions, contradictions, and conflicts between them, there is nothing that prevents them from maintaining a sort of permanent dialogue; especially, subjecting diplomacy to ethical scrutiny is neither conceptually absurd nor practically unfeasible.

Ethics and the diplomat

Up until this point the subject of the discussion has been "diplomacy"; we will now turn to the diplomat to address the issue of the ethics of the public servant. According to a universally held view, the essence of the moral duty of a public servant consists in the obligation to perform the tasks that the state assigns to each without letting personal interest or personal opinion interfere. This obligation is dictated by a self-evident consideration: if each individual official were to act according to personal taste and preference, the correct functioning of any governmental structure would be rendered impossible. One way of proving that this is indeed so is to take an empirical look at those systems which have not reached this stage of "depersonalization" of the role of a civil servant: they are backward systems, disorderly systems, unjust systems, endemically conflictive systems.

This is certainly true in the field of international relations. Let us imagine foreign policy conducted according to the personal inclinations (political and/or moral) of individual diplomats and the chaos and unpredictability that would follow. The state needs reliable representatives who will not let personal inclination interfere with instructions received – instructions that originate in the constitutionally competent organs and are formulated and conveyed through the bureaucratic, hierarchically ordained machinery of the ministerial department competent for foreign affairs. It is so, and it can only be so.

Yet we cannot stop here. If we did we would deprive the single individual as diplomat of the possibility of ethically relevant action. There would be no choice. Obedience would have to be of the no-questions-asked type, whatever the policy and whatever its consequences.[34] But this is not so, and has never been so even in practice. It is by now widely accepted that for all kinds of public servants (and this includes diplomats), obedience to bureaucratic orders is not a cause of exemption from moral – and legal – responsibility. This is especially evident in the case of major crimes. The road that was opened in Nuremberg[35] has now taken us to Rome, where in July 1998 the approval of the statutes of the permanent International Criminal Court would not have been possible without a wide global consensus on the moral/legal responsibility of individuals who serve their state in different capacities but who, by so doing, are in no way exempt from ethical scrutiny and legal sanction.

It would be untenable to maintain that diplomats are exempt from such scrutiny (and sanctions), and that the mandate of the International Criminal Court covers only the actual physical purveyors of violence. It would indeed be a bizarre limitation, especially in a world in which the distinction between military action and diplomacy is more and more blurred in the framework of complex conflictive situations; all the more so since the mandate of the court includes (though for the time being still wanting a definition) the crime of aggression, one in which diplomats can play as big a role as soldiers.[36]

How can we square the contradictory needs of impersonal bureaucratic discipline and persistent moral responsibility? The fact is that we cannot. The fact is that there must be a limit, a certain threshold beyond which the duty of allegiance and obedience is overruled, annulled by the moral outrage of certain acts in which the individual "servant of the state" is instructed to participate. The ethics of the public servant (with its corollary of obedience, of non-personalization of behaviour and choices) can take us only so far. A morally sane human being should be capable of determining when that limit is reached, when one must be able to breach one's allegiance and say "no" to the crossing of that threshold.

It is necessary to recall that decisions to rebel against orders that are legitimate as to the line of command but that become illegitimate by their moral unacceptability are definitely not unheard of in the annals of diplomacy. Several historians of the Holocaust have stressed the role (sometimes merely passive, often active) of Italians, officially allied with the Germans, in saving thousands of Jews from detention and deportation to death camps.[37] Among those Italians were many military officers, but also several diplomats. Though the policy of the highest levels of fascist Italy, starting from Mussolini himself, was often wavering, contradictory, and ambiguous, there is no doubt that on many occasions Italian diplomats, in particular in the Balkans, proceeded totally on their own to perform acts of political indiscipline and to infringe very basic bureaucratic rules, for instance by giving Italian passports to Jews whose only link with Italy was having visited it once: a rather serious breach of the ethics of an official and one that would make any self-respecting consular officer cringe.[38] In an unforgettable interview (included in Joseph Rochlitz's documentary *The Righteous Enemy*), the former Italian consul in Salonica, Guelfo Zamboni, replied in a half-surprised, half-amused tone to the interviewer, amazed at this most unusual concession of passports to aliens: "Well, they were in danger of death, weren't they? So, what was I supposed to do, let them be deported and exterminated?"[39]

The threshold at which personal assessment of moral duties becomes destructive of the ethics of the public servant is not a clearly defined line. Each – but that of course is no news in ethical discourse – has to draw that line and act accordingly. Certainly, if we were to allow the possibility for each diplomat to turn personal disagreement and mental reservation on any given issue into undisciplined behaviour and active rebellion we would revert to that individualistic free-for-all that is the antithesis of a functioning *polis*, even the most open and pluralistic one. And yet, there is always, even in cases that are not as monumentally horrendous as the Holocaust, a path for a dignified stand in the presence of radical moral disagreement with specific policies. In those cases one can avoid taking the extreme, always-questionable step of breaking loyalty by opting out – by resignation. Of course, in non-democratic regimes such an act can entail consequences that may be as dire as those provoked by open rebellion, but outside those regimes resigning means losing income, prestige, and career, but not life or freedom. Thus it becomes more feasible. But where has it happened more frequently, in the past decades? It seems not without significance to note that it is in the USA that many diplomats have resigned (over policy issues from Viet Nam to Bosnia), a country whose citizens give a special relevance to debate on ethical issues and at the same time are frequently haunted by the awareness of the responsibility that their government's actions or omissions entail in terms of human consequences around the world. To be able to raise ethical issues in diplomacy you indeed need both: moral sensitivity, and the perception of the impact on human beings outside your borders of the power wielded by your country in the international arena.

If there is this sort of "ethical switch" that can interrupt allegiance to the state in the case of moral dissent, wouldn't it be safer for a state, any state, to privilege staunch nationalists as their diplomats, at least in the highest-ranking positions? Wouldn't they be more reliable in all conditions and facing any sort of problem, any sort of dilemma? The fallacy of this sort of reasoning lies in forgetting what a government official is supposed to be. It is true that public servants are not justified in sacrificing their loyalty to the state and their disciplined behaviour within their administrations to the vagaries of personal taste, nor to political inclinations, local partiality, or special interests. However, by the same token it is not necessary, and even counterproductive, that they should be militants of the nation-state, true believers in king and country. They can be such as citizens, but no one demands that they be such as officials. The confusion between the two roles (citizen and official) is typically totalitarian, and amounts to saying that the only good lawyers are those who believe that their clients are innocent – and possibly love them, too.

Going back to diplomats, we indeed see that if we cast them as lawyers, and not as crusaders for the cause of their own nation-state, we will have solved part of our ethical dilemmas. Diplomats involved in a negotiation or dispute, no more than lawyers in court, do not have to believe in the righteousness of the cause they are defending. That is the essence of professionalism, a much more reliable foundation for good performance and loyalty than is belief. But the diplomat, as well as the lawyer, may decide at a certain point that there are some causes that are just too morally uncomfortable to defend, and opt out. It is of course easier to abandon litigation than to resign from government service, but conceptually there do not seem to be radical moral differences between the two instances. Both are rare, but both are possible.

The ethical dimension of diplomacy, however, should not be seen only in negative terms – as a limit to bureaucratic allegiance, as a moral safety valve allowing us to escape complicity with morally outrageous actions. The assumption one should challenge, in this context, is that of a *"status quo* diplomatic system".[40] Actually, *status quo* leaves very limited room for ethical discourse, since it confronts the individual actor with the stark alternative between playing by the existing rules or becoming a sort of conscientious objector and dropping out of the "regular" game. In real history – and real diplomacy – we are instead confronted with a moving framework of rules, with diplomats themselves playing a relevant role in the evolutionary process. Here ethics "gains space", in so far as individual practitioners of diplomacy, even those who stick to the strictest allegiance to existing norms, are allowed to bring their own ethical inspiration to bear in shaping new international rules.[41]

Ethics and international law

If, as is widely accepted (with the exception of *intégristes* of various persuasions), ethics and law are different dimensions and do not necessarily coincide, then the same can of course be said for international ethics and international law. Ethics is indeed different from law, but how could one conceive the very possibility of ethical action in a totally lawless world? Anarchy and ethics are hardly compatible, so much so that those who deny the possibility of international ethics are logically obliged to describe the world as substantially anarchic, with individual states having the right to operate, for their own defence and for the pursuit of their interests, in a Hobbesian state of nature. According to Kenneth Waltz, for instance:

There is no way to get from here – a world of sovereign states operating in a state of nature – to there – a world of permanent peace, where morality and law reign in relations between sovereign entities.[42]

It is of course true that in the total absence of law, ethical action amounts to the self-sacrificial option of saints and martyrs: in the international field, it would spell extinction. And yet, contrary to what Waltz maintains, a non-ideological analysis of the actual state of the world reveals that we are neither "here" nor "there". As a matter of fact, both "state of nature" and "reign of peace and morality" are opposed, but equally unreal, descriptions. Saying that "we are neither here nor there" means, of course, that we are in part "here" and in part "there". We have a legal framework that is real but fragile, developed but decentralized in its enforcement, and always threatened by actors who normally accept it, but who can at any moment upset the table and stop playing by the rules they have adhered to until then.

But that is exactly why projecting on to the international sphere the ethical discourse that was traditionally developed within the legally regulated domestic body politic is a difficult task. Difficult, but not impossible, since in the very behaviour of states the two dimensions are not inexorably contradictory. It would be enough to consider the following, hardly questionable, factual consideration:

Commonly states will internalize the norms and principles embodied in regimes created out of pure self-interest, such that those norms and principles take on a moral hue over time ... Gradually the moral authority of internalized norms permits them to survive in the absence of external enforcement.[43]

But the distinction between international law and international ethics cannot be pushed too far and transformed into a rigid dichotomy, not least because of the very nature of international law. It has been correctly remarked that the inadequacies and weaknesses of international law (if compared to the better-structured, systematically enforceable domestic norms) render it more similar to the field of ethics.[44] But this similarity goes beyond the relative "softness" of international law and has to do with its very structure and language. This is what has been defined by Dorothy V. Jones as "the declaratory tradition".[45] Jones writes:

It is precisely in this declaratory strand that the states have spelled out what international law means to them, and what they think it ought to be and, in so doing, have opened themselves to the possibility that there will be attempts to hold them to their word.

We are here confronted with an apparent paradox. International relations, as we have seen, seem rather impervious to ethical talk. And yet, in a bizarre compensation, present-day international texts (not only declarations, but also treaties, covenants, and bilateral and multilateral agreements of all sorts) indulge in the extensive spelling out of moral principles. For an ethics-unfriendly environment, as diplomacy should allegedly be, it is a remarkable fact indeed. One could talk here of "the diplomacy of the preamble", since it is usually in the preambular part of international agreements that these moral *consideranda* are inscribed. Pure rhetoric and hypocrisy? Definitely, if we were to subject to critical scrutiny the motivations of the subjects formulating those ethical avowals, we might reach this conclusion. Yet, even if we want to consider preambles as just receptacles of hardly believable moralistic rhetoric, those who follow international relations know that rhetoric (including rhetoric about ethics) is also a component of politics.

Machiavelli never thought that force alone was a determinant of power, but on the contrary gave strong consideration to a psychological component, *fame*, which in our time we would define as prestige or image. And it is interesting that we find basically the same concept in one of the most eminent of contemporary realists, Henry Kissinger.[46] In other words, power is also "soft power",[47] and – as the rise and fall of the Soviet Union seems to confirm – it would be a very precarious super-power indeed that were to rely exclusively on military, or even economic, strength and not on the capacity to exert its hegemony in the realm of values. But saying "values" means saying "ethics", so that one can conclude that ethics turns out to be a component in, and not an alternative to, real power.[48]

We need, however, to take one step further, and to see what are the consequences – for the relationship between international law and international ethics – of this "declaratory approach". Here we have to move beyond the preambles, and see that even the normative part of international law shows an intrinsic connection with the ethical discourse.

Let us examine those principles that, as most will agree, can be considered as the fundamental pillars of international law:
• the sovereign equality of states
• the territorial integrity and political independence of states
• self-determination
• non-intervention in the internal affairs of states
• peaceful settlement of disputes
• no threat or use of force
• fulfilment in good faith of international obligations
• cooperation with other states
• respect for human rights and fundamental freedoms.[49]

It is enough to read through this list to realize how artificial is the dichotomy of law/ethics in international relations. All these principles are as much legal as they are ethical, or, perhaps better, they are ethical principles on the way to being "hardened" into legal ones. If one thinks that this smacks of evolutionist positivism, then what could be alternatively suggested is that these principles are like synapses at which a constant exchange between ethics and law takes place. Whatever our approach, however, in the light of these principles it seems difficult to deny the legitimacy of the ethical discourse in international law – as well as in diplomacy, whose task is to work with and on those principles to pursue political ends.

The positing of those principles, furthermore, opens up a whole set of contradictions and dilemmas that appear to be more moral than legal, since their solution can be found not by a very problematic process of interpretation or reference to jurisprudence, but by applying criteria of an ethical nature. The main obstacle to solving the dilemmas that constantly arise in real-life international situations is that those principles have no objective ranking: is self-determination – to take one of the more frequent quandaries – to prevail over territorial integrity, or vice versa?

The author maintains that in practice the only way of solving this conceptual legal gridlock is by having recourse to ethical considerations. It is also maintained that this is exactly what the international community has been doing in practice. One can recall several cases. Michael Walzer has written:

Nonintervention gives way to proportionality only in cases of massacre or politically induced famine and epidemic, when the costs are unbearable. Then we are justified in acting or, more strongly, we ought to act (like the Vietnamese in Pol Pot's Cambodia, or the Tanzanians in Idi Amin's Uganda, or the Indians in what was then East Pakistan) without regard to the idea of sovereignty.[50]

Of course, writing in the spring of 1999, we should add to this list NATO intervention against Serbia over Kosovo, a case of ethically motivated disregard of the principles of sovereignty and non-intervention. Indeed, the international community by and large condoned (in all these cases – and in others like the Syrian intervention putting an end to the Lebanese civil war) evident violations of the principle of non-intervention because the costs of the *status quo* were considered – as Walzer writes – unbearable. But "unbearable" does not sound like a legal term; rather, it is a moral one.

But let us take other cases of contradiction over fundamental principles. The way a regime treats its own citizens is, according to traditional doctrine, "its own business", and the principle of non-intervention in domestic affairs (not only a general principle of international law, but one that is also enshrined in the UN Charter)[51] should prevent any outside meddling. Yet, from apartheid in South Africa to repression against Kurds in north Iraq, the international community has shown that it can, on some occasions, overcome that impediment and overrule that prohibition even in the presence of a hostile attitude on the part of the state concerned. Of course that has been done, as a rule, by recourse to Chapter VII, the enforcement chapter, that is indicated in the UN Charter itself as the only exception to the prohibition of interference in the domestic affairs of any country.[52]

NATO intervention against Serbia over repression and ethnic cleansing in Kosovo has shown that, even apart from Chapter VII of the UN Charter, the growth of an ethically based sensitivity to human rights the world over is exerting such pressures on diplomacy that, with increasing frequency, "principle 9" of the list is ominously knocking at the door of the once scarcely challenged "principle 4". Intervention in Kosovo has been extremely controversial, especially as far as legal legitimization is concerned, but who would maintain that respect for the principle of non-interference in 1994 Rwanda should have ruled out trying to save, forcibly if necessary, hundreds of thousands from genocide?[53] And who has the moral courage to maintain, today, that the principle of non-interference rules out international action to stop the outrage of Taleban treatment of Afghan women? (Incidentally, what are the moral differences between the situation of Afghan women under the Talebans and that of South African blacks under apartheid, to which the international community did respond forcefully setting aside the taboo of non-intervention?)

The same is happening to "principle 3", self-determination, once very high – given its compensatory function towards the injustices and crimes of colonialism – in the moral ranking of the international community, but now (especially after the consequences of its application to former Yugoslavia) being more and more subject to a scrutiny that is not, cannot be, of a legal nature (the principle still stands, and international law could not do without it), but rather is moral. We have all become consequentialists, since we are asking ourselves what will be the repercussions on real people of the application of that abstract principle? The widespread reluctance to accept the idea of the independence of Kosovo – an apparently unjustifiable exception to the previous indiscriminate approval in the region of self-determination for anyone who would bother to ask for it – is also of this nature, should also be of this nature, and is not only the product of balance-of-power considerations.

Given the impossibility of an objective, non-contentious prioritization of principles, it is ethical orientation (together, to be sure, with political preference, usually formulated – however – in moral terms) that determines the actual ranking of principles; a ranking that is not fixed but which, as we have seen, shifts together with changes in culture and moral sensitivities the world over.

A space for ethics: Between anarchy and total power

In the attempt to look for an ethically compatible diplomacy one must necessarily try to clarify what are the systemic conditions that make such an option possible – how, to put it differently, the space for ethical action can be identified, or created, in the structure of the international system.

The author has already hinted at the fact that if it were true that the relations between states are of a purely anarchic nature, no talk of ethics in diplomacy would be possible: *bellum omnium contra omnes* is the "point zero" of ethics. But if there is a point zero of ethics in the total dispersion of anomic power, there is also a vanishing point located at the total concentration of power. Moral behaviour is practically impossible with anarchy, but it hardly thrives better in conditions of totalitarian power, where lack of limit and control breeds injustice,[54] and where individual moral choice not only constitutes a deadly risk but is often annulled by the hammering in of an official message that fills all spaces and leaves no room for alternative views or contradiction. Choice itself, of any kind, is not conceivable in conditions of absolute, totally centralized power: and choice is the very core of ethics.

If we apply this to the international sphere, we realize that a space for ethical diplomacy requires, to go back to the critical quote from Kenneth Waltz's formula, that the international system continues to be "neither here nor there". The world could definitely use some more and some better legal "vertebration", especially in the phase of enforcement and not only standard-setting. And yet, it is false that, since anarchy is bad, world government is good. Kant himself, though putting peace and coexistence first, had serious doubts (also of an ethical nature) on the possibility of a world government.[55] Apart from the tautological consideration that world government would eliminate diplomacy (ethical or otherwise), it can be said in more general terms that the space for ethics is only created when the individual can actually choose – the space between total anarchy and total rule.

It is important to address the question of power, its levels, and distribution in relation to the possibility of a space for ethical action. In classic political theory (domestic), Montesquieu's doctrine is still valid in identifying a mechanism of repartition of powers that impedes tyranny – and is perfectly functional for the creation of a space for ethically relevant individual choice and also for ethically compatible politics. What should we aim for in the international field? World government, we have seen, is not the answer. But a system based exclusively on individual sovereign states runs the constant risk of oscillating between lapses into anarchy and attempts to impose imperial rule: the space for ethics is threatened in both cases.

If it is true that both absolute anarchy and absolute power destroy the space for ethics, then what we need is a sort of "vertical Montesquieu". Similarly to the positive ethical impact of the horizontal, intra-state division of power spelled out by that great political thinker, a vertical division, both supranational and subnational, would help create that "space for ethics" (including ethics in diplomacy) by making power more efficient and more diffuse. Indeed, we have seen that the denial of the possibility of ethical behaviour in diplomacy is closely linked to the doctrine of the exclusive, sovereign, and absolute power of the nation-state.

State-centrism, in many cases becoming "statolatry", is one of the main enemies of ethics (both within and without borders). Of course the state – though being a historically contingent form – is, and will remain for the foreseeable future, the main form in which man lives in society. Yet it is by applying some "vertical Montesquieu" that all ethics-incompatible idolatry of this specific political form will be overcome. Power should be vertically distributed along a line that starts with subnational units (local communities with a degree of autonomy and self-administration), in some cases followed by federal units, continues to the level of the state, reaches the regional level of both political and economic integration, and finally attains the level of world governance (not government) that is guaranteed by the functioning of international organizations, sectorial or universal in character.

Vital local power is a reality the world over. More and more, centralized states are looking for forms of federal or non-federal decentralization of power capable of reabsorbing tensions and addressing diversity without sliding into disintegration: The United Nations, in spite of all its problems, is much more than a forum for debate, and operates functioning institutions in fields as varied as security, development, and human rights: it is a vital part of world governance. Regional arrangements are moving from mere trade to politics. The case of the European Union is the most advanced and the most significant, so much so that the power of its member states – whether they like it or not, whether they realize it or not – is already drastically curtailed. What is even more relevant to our subject, EU partners have developed among themselves a new kind of diplomatic relations in which – though divergences of interest are still a reality – ethical behaviour is no less taken for granted than among actors within a national body politic; a type of diplomacy where "Machiavellians" are not only disapproved but – given the intrinsically cooperative nature of the system – cannot possibly manage to get very far in the pursuit of their diplomatic goals.

It is indeed by strengthening and continuing this growing vertical distribution of power in the international system that we will ensure a space for ethically compatible diplomatic action, because the institutional counterweights of a multi-layered system of governance – as well as the multiplicity of allegiances as opposed to the idolatric recognition of only one power (whatever that power may be) – are the best guarantees that the diplomat (as well as the judge, the soldier, or even the common citizen) will be able to resist the pressure to violate ethical norms because of a mistaken concept of duty and loyalty. This multi-layered system of power is not, and will never be, in a position of equilibrium. On the contrary, it will remain in constant tension, in need of continuous institutional adjustments, the theatre of frequent political reassessments. And yet, it is in this very tension that resides the best hope for a dignified and moral life for free and sociable individuals. As an Italian philosopher has written:

The European archipelago exists insofar as it faces a double danger: being resolved into a hierarchically ordained space/being dissolved into inhospitable, idiotic units, incapable of looking for one another, of calling one another, into parts that have no longer anything to partake.[56]

A space for ethics: Between self-preservation and self-denial

The previous section considered, in the search for compatibility between ethics and diplomacy, both legal norms and institutional arrangements, and tried to see how a space for ethics could be identified in their framework. It is time now, still in search of that controversial space, to focus on a more specifically ethical approach. Again, realists try to formulate the issue in starkly alternative terms: either a nation-state fights systematically (and regardless of moral principles) for self-preservation or, in that acceptance of the needs and reasons of others that is the essence of ethics, embarks on a path of self-denial leading to its gradual weakening – eventually to the point of extinction. The implications for the discourse on diplomacy are clear. Who are the diplomats who would consciously embark, on account of moral concerns, on a path leading to the weakening and possibly the extinction of their own country? If we phrase the question in these terms, ethics and diplomacy indeed look incompatible.

An answer to this dilemma – an artificial one, actually a case of intellectual blackmail – can be found in ethical theory at large, with no reference to the specific case of the nation-state. Self-preservation and survival are by no means the exclusive need of nation-states: they are first and foremost a primary urge/right of individuals. But who would maintain, in ethical theory, that self-preservation destroys the possible space for ethical behaviour? Concern – even love – for the other does not have to be contradictory with survival: on the contrary, survival is the evident precondition of ethical action. One of the most compelling enunciations of this concept is found in Vladimir Jankelevitch. According to this eminent French moral thinker, the territory of ethics can be located in the space between absolute love – self-denial to the point of self-destruction – and absolute being, by definition totally indifferent to ethics. Jankelevitch writes: "A being totally deprived of love is not even a being; a love without a being is not even a love."[57] As a consequence, a space for ethical behaviour can only be found by pursuing all the love that is compatible with the preservation of being.

Let us try to apply this principle to international relations, and specifically to diplomatic action. Nation-states can be actually threatened with extinction, so it would be preposterous to state that the only possible "ethically compatible" diplomacy is one of pacifism. Ethics demands that diplomacy be peaceful, yes – in the sense that there is a moral duty to try to avoid violent conflict – but not pacifist, if we interpret this term in its most consistent meaning: the refusal to have recourse to armed force in all instances, even defensive ones. Chamberlain and Churchill are of course the archetypes of two different approaches to diplomacy, and more specifically to diplomacy in the face of a threat of aggression. And yet, if we take Great Britain as the historical subject, we see that morally, facing the Nazi challenge, the country demonstrated that it was willing, in order to avoid violent conflict, to go to the brink of self-denial, only to draw later the conclusion that there was no alternative to violent self-defence and self-affirmation. What is important to stress is that Chamberlain was deeply wrong *in fact* (wrong assessment of the adversary, of the possibility to stipulate solid agreements with him, of the fact that appeasement with Adolf Hitler could mean peace), but he was not wrong *in principle*. It is important to state this, especially since bellicose "realists" the world over have been using Chamberlain, ever since 1938, as a handy symbol to deny the legitimacy of the morally justified and politically rational search for alternatives to violent conflict. Cries of "Chamberlain!" resound whenever, from the Middle East to the Balkans, there are attempts to find an alternative to war.

Another important clarification concerns the very definition of survival. As mentioned above, the tendency of nation-states to declare as "vital" marginal chunks of real estate, or even symbols, is quite widespread – and yet it would be absurd if we were to take those claims at face value. Up to a certain point, a threat to survival entails subjective elements of appreciation, but the idea (the mainstay of nationalist agitation) that a barren rock in contested waters is vital for the survival of a country – and therefore diplomacy aimed at its preservation or acquisition for the homeland should not be subject to moral scrutiny – is too preposterous to be taken seriously.

The issue of survival, for nation-states, is often bound with that of identity – one additional problem for ethics, indeed, given the non-rational, non-negotiable nature of this deep psychological need. If we shift from survival (a debatable but substantive concept) to the more dubious concept of identity, moral discourse becomes even more complicated. In fact, one can rationally prove, in many if not most cases, that yielding – on the basis of both legal and moral considerations – to the claims and rights of others does not have to mean for a nation-state to go inexorably down the path to self-destruction.

But one cannot "prove" that even a minor event, psychologically charged with historical symbolism, will not irreparably mutilate (to use the language of nationalists) the very soul of the nation. Here, again, as in the case of survival, one should try to "deconstruct" nationalist claims and see what identity really means. National identity – a most complex, many-faceted phenomenon – cannot be tied, if not ideologically, artificially, to a single specific item, be it a piece of land or a flag or a geographic denomination. In other words, national identity does not have to be idolatric. History knows of nations that have grown, shrunk, shifted in territory, and still maintain their own identity. To phrase it in philosophical terms, identity is about remaining *ipse* (a self that is preserved through time), not about staying *idem* (unchanged).[58] The sleight of hand of nationalist agitators consists in turning all modifications of *idem* (an inevitable phenomenon, both for individuals and for nation-states) into a threat to identity *ipse*, thereby mobilizing – regardless of any ethical consideration or limit – the violent defences of the allegedly threatened nation.

Ethical diplomacy: Proposals for an agenda

Facing war

In trying to identify an agenda for ethically compatible diplomacy one must necessarily start from the issue of war: definitely the most problematic, most highly charged of ethical questions in the international sphere. In moral terms, there is no doubt that "diplomacy for peace" is better than "diplomacy for war". But is any peace morally better than any war?

We have already seen that self-defence (a concept, to be sure, that should not be stretched to preposterous limits) gives individuals and nation-states unquestionable legitimization, not only legal but also moral, for the use of violence. One should note that Article 51 of the UN Charter reiterates this fundamental principle (*ad abundantiam*, one may note, since even without that article, self-defence would remain a valid principle, both legal and moral). But there is another case in which legality and morality show their interconnectedness. Recourse to military action (and this includes the diplomacy that is necessarily associated with it) can be morally defensible in so far as it is justified by international norms. This refers to enforcement action under Chapter VII: a kind of military and diplomatic action that has a coercive nature, and yet can be considered morally admissible.

Two considerations are in order at this point. The first is that at the present stage of international relations it has become extremely difficult to separate diplomatic and military means, so that the flat category of "war", with all its ethical implications, has become too unsophisticated for our present conceptual needs. What we have been seeing in the second half of the twentieth century is the intertwining of the military and the diplomatic dimensions, be it in enforcement of Chapter VII of the UN

Charter, peace-keeping, humanitarian action, and even – though for the moment, as an exception – in human rights (the Kurds in northern Iraq). With reference to contemporary international relations, the famous Clausewitzian dictum according to which war is the continuation of *politik* by other means should be revised both as concerns "war" and "other means", and should read: "Military action is one of the means of international politics." If this is so, then the fundamental ethical question in international relations is not about how to use diplomacy in order to prevent recourse to military means, but how to use diplomacy *and* military means in order to pursue ethically compatible political ends.

The second issue has to do with *jus in bello*, the rules and limits concerning the means used in warfare. In the first place one should remark that, with all the justified horror one feels facing the prospect of war, it would be not only a conceptual but also a moral fallacy to insist on putting war outside the law (and outside the field of ethics) in all cases. Putting war outside the law would mean, in practical terms, banishing the law from war. It would mean accepting the Hobbesian "state of nature" to which neither legal nor moral norms are applicable.

Moral debate on NATO intervention in Kosovo has indeed touched upon not only the justification for military action, but also the strategy adopted, in particular the consequences of the bombing of militarily relevant targets located in urban areas and the so-called "collateral damages" to civilians. And even people who have no doubt about NATO's right to conduct military action against Belgrade have expressed moral reservations as to the specific strategies, for example stressing that from a moral point of view land operations directed against enemy troops would have been less troubling than bombing from a distance that is safe for the pilots, but less so, in spite of all earnest and technologically supported efforts at precision, for the civilians living in the targeted areas.

This, however, does not concern military means only. In diplomacy, too, legitimacy as to *jus ad bellum* does not necessarily entail an exemption from moral scrutiny as to the application of *jus in bello*. The most interesting example has to do with sanctions. The fact that they have been legitimately imposed under the UN Charter does not mean that they cannot be judged according to ethical standards. Here legality and ethics can part company, in the sense that the standards of international ethics must be stricter, and more concrete, than those of international legality. From an ethical point of view, it is not sufficient to determine whether sanctions have been legally declared: the question to be asked is what are their consequences for human beings, for their suffering and survival, and for the possibilities of reconstruction and normalization of a given society. Very clearly we are dealing here with the "ethics of responsibility", and since responsibility is personal, no amount of reference to the impersonal legal nature of the sanctions nor to the moral responsibility of other subjects (who might well be much more guilty than we are in determining the continuation of the sanction regime) will suffice to exempt us from the dilemma of moral choice.

"Ethical" diplomacy, however, is not only concerned with how to conduct legitimate military action. Its task can be more ambitious. It is diplomacy, indeed, that has worked through the years both for a definition of *jus in bello* and for a restriction of *jus ad bellum*. In both cases a moral inspiration has been more than evident, both in the motivation for diplomatic initiatives and in the very language utilized in the drafting of relevant international norms.

An ethically compatible diplomacy should thus not limit itself to "denouncing", "rejecting", or "outlawing" war – but rather should embark upon a patient, professionally conducted exercise aiming at the following objectives.

- Continue working on the definition of restrictive rules as to the admissible means of war. The ban of anti-personnel mines with the Treaty of Ottawa is an excellent example of the possible results of ethically motivated yet fully professional diplomacy, and a case in which national interest and ethical considerations have found (at least for most countries) an area of compatibility.
- In more general terms, though the triumph of universal and permanent peace seems utopian, diplomacy should pursue the morally urgent goal of banning a certain kind of conflict: that which aims not at the simple defeat, but at the extermination of the adversary. They are two radically different types of conflict, especially from a moral point of view.

The Greeks – starting with Plato – had the distinction so clear that they used two different words for war: *polemos*, meaning total war against the totally "other" (the non-Greek, the barbarian), and *stasis*, meaning violent but limited conflict between enemies who share a common culture, and who know that after the confrontation they will eventually return to coexistence and even cooperation.[59] Here is one more reason why "war" seems today an indiscriminate, inept term to describe present-day conflicts, in particular since it posits a conflict between the subjects of international law, nation-states. The reality is quite different, since most conflicts are today of an internal, non-international nature (though they do have international implications): diplomacy has had to adapt to these conflicts inside borders, and actually to revise its *modus operandi* and many of its principles. And, of course, it has had to face – witness the cases of Bosnia and Kosovo – a new set of ethical dilemmas.

The problem is that, whereas "classic" international war can be of the *stasis* type (witness, for a recent example, the Anglo-Argentine war over the Falklands/Malvinas), internal conflicts, with their charge of fear and hatred, tend to turn into all-out *polemos*. What can diplomacy do in the presence of such ethically devastating transformation of the nature of conflict? It can do much. In the first place, it can further perfect the normative banning of the most repulsive and indiscriminate modes of conflict: genocide, ethnic cleansing, and systematic rape as an instrument of war. Then it can work towards better instruments for enforcement: the 1998 Rome Conference for the institution of a permanent International Criminal Court is a very relevant case of ethically inspired diplomacy. More generally, it can continue to work gradually towards a reappraisal of traditional priorities as to the fundamental principles of international law, in the sense that the threat that *polemos*-type conflicts entail to the life and dignity of human beings should be enough to justify – even in the absence of a "threat to international peace and security" according to the UN Charter – the relativization and overruling of the principle of non-interference.

Thus, from an ethical point of view, the task of diplomacy is not that of rejecting the reality of war: ethics, as this chapter has tried to stress, does not mean utopian pacifism. At the same time diplomacy cannot limit itself to coexistence with war while trying to limit the means employed in its conduction or ban its most inhuman forms. It can, and must, set its sights much higher, though in a gradual, politically credible way. The goal must be not that of "excommunicating" war, but of depriving it of political oxygen; not to deny the reality of contrast, even tough confrontation, between nation-states, but to supply alternative, non-violent paths to the solution of controversies.

An ethic of responsibility

Anyone who is interested in ethics will be familiar with Max Weber's famous distinction between an ethic of ultimate ends and an ethic of responsibility.[60] There is no doubt that, in so far as diplomacy is a branch of politics, when we speak of "ethical diplomacy" we are necessarily referring to an ethic of responsibility. Politics is in fact choice between alternative actions in view of their desired or feared consequences in a society. It would indeed be difficult, in the field of international relations, to imagine an ethic of ultimate ends – except, of course, in the framework of "fundamentalist" approaches that recognize no autonomous space for politics *vis-à-vis* religious inspiration and duty.

As Daniel Warner writes at the very outset of his book, however, one should not push too far the distinction between the two kinds of ethics, given the fact that Weber himself, writing about Luther, considers his typically non-consequentialist *Ich kann nicht anders* not as an alternative to, but as an extreme but logical development of, an ethic of responsibility.[61] This remark is extremely important for the discussion of ethics in diplomacy. "Responsibility" can in fact be interpreted in different ways. One is still self-referential, non-dialogic, ready to be converted into non-negotiable "ultimate-end" ethics. And, as the "self" can be presented as a collective entity, responsibility may actually turn into individual abdication from personal evaluation and judgement, and into passive delegation of power (and of justification) to "higher authorities": "the ethic of ultimate ends leaves the consequences with the Lord, and the ethic of responsibility leaves the result with the leader and his perception of how the consequences relate to his cause".[62]

But there can be another interpretation of the concept of responsibility. If we set aside the debate on ultimate ends (ends that are by definition non-negotiable, at times not even explicable to those who do not share the same ideological premises), and if we try instead to give an ethical appraisal to diplomacy on the basis of the criterion of moral responsibility, our task is complex but possible. Consequences of action (or, one should add, of lack of action) are not, though subject to interpretation and even controversy concerning actual facts, totally impossible to assess. Who would deny, for instance, that the consequences of international passivity towards the mounting crisis in Rwanda (1994) were such as to involve ethical responsibility on the part of those who could have acted and did not? Who would today criticize from a moral standpoint international diplomacy aimed at the termination of apartheid and the introduction of non-racial democracy in South Africa? Speaking of responsibility, of measurable consequences of specific actions, renders ethical discourse more concrete, less ideological, easier to be shared by a wide and diverse set of international subjects.

Central to the concept of responsibility is that of imputation (or "accountability", according to the prevalent English usage). It is a concept that is shared by both the legal and the ethical dimension, in so far as both law and ethics need the identification of a point of reference in the individual human being. Both in criminal law and in moral discourse, responsibility is always personal, so that it is impossible to attribute it to a collective body, be it the state, an association, or a corporate entity. Imputation, in other words, identifies responsibility, and the trail always leads to an individual subject. More specifically, imputation is opposed to causality, in that it defines – on the basis of the assumption of the freedom of the individual – a break in the causal chain.[63] Both law and ethics are based on this assumption, without which neither legality nor morality would be conceivable, since every consequence-generating human action could theoretically be presented (and justified) as being, in its turn, the effect of some preceding cause.

It is especially important to insist on this fundamental assumption in the context of a discussion on ethics and diplomacy. Individual diplomatic officials have the tendency (as do all public officials) to present themselves in the image of a simple element inserted in a chain of command that operates according to the principle of causality, excluding thereby any possibility for ethical evaluation and moral responsibility. But of course they, no more than other human beings, have no right to be exempt from the principle of accountability and find refuge in the comfortable haven of irresponsible causality.

Imputation is thus a concept that is shared by law and ethics. But after having coincided on this specific point, law and ethics must now again part company; it must now be repeated once more that law and ethics are related, linked by reciprocal influence, but do not coincide. And indeed, the ethic of responsibility in international relations comes to the forefront whenever one leaves the strictly legal field.

We definitely do not need to talk of ethics in the presence of patent violations of international law, as the Iraqi invasion of Kuwait or cases of international terrorism. But take, for instance, the case of conventional arms sales. They are absolutely legal, except in cases when the buyer is under a sanctions regime. But since the selling state knows to what use those weapons are being put (ethnic wars, repression of their own population by dictatorial regimes, at times even the arming of groups that are on the borderline between political and criminal activity), ethics does become an issue. There may be no international legal responsibility deriving from the sale of arms that end up in the hands of opposed factions in East-Central Africa or in Sudan, but there is a huge moral responsibility.

Also, there is no legal prohibition to the carrying out of underground nuclear experiments by countries that have not accepted any treaty limitation to such sovereign prerogative. And yet such totally legal action can be (and is) subject to critical moral scrutiny, and criticism, in the light of the damage it can cause to the reduction, through non-proliferation, of the danger of nuclear confrontation – a goal that most countries, and most people, find morally defensible.

Since we are trying to address the subject of ethics and diplomacy with a contemporary focus, it is important to draw attention to a specific feature of our time that has a definite bearing on ethical responsibility. Today – given the accelerated development of all kinds of communications – we all know more about the international consequences of our acts. Thanks to television, in particular, we are practically forced to see what once we could try to avoid knowing: today there is very little sand left in which to stick our heads. We are daily confronted, in other terms, with very graphic summons to our responsibility even towards people living – and suffering – far away from us. More knowledge/more responsibility: and that is also true for diplomacy. The face of the other, who may be suffering or even killed because of our international actions or omissions, often looks straight at us from the TV screen.

Conclusion: Beyond responsibility

Paradoxically, at the end of this examination of the issue of ethics and diplomacy, we come to the conclusion not only that the widespread dogma of a sort of "moral exemption" of diplomacy is untenable, but that the ethical rules applicable to political action in the international sphere might actually be seen as extending beyond the classical definition of responsibility. The interconnectedness of the whole world, a product of economic globalization and communications technology, has increased to a once unthinkable level. Many of the things that are done, or not done, within a certain society have almost immediate repercussions at a distance of thousands of kilometres. In a way, we are now in a situation that has been described in the framework of "chaos theory", a theory that took its first steps when in 1979 a metereologist, Edward Lorenz, delivered at a scientific congress a paper entitled: "Predictability: Does the Flap of a Butterfly's Wings in Brazil Set Off a Tornado in Texas?"[64] In our present globalized world one can apply this paradigm well beyond metereology (and beyond physics in general), and extend it to human society. If we consider, for instance, the volatility of international financial markets, we realize that individual decisions taken in one country can rapidly and sometimes catastrophically impact on many others.

But who would declare the Brazilian butterfly guilty for the disaster in Texas? If there is no predictability (chaos is by definition non-predictable), how can there be responsibility? The author would like to suggest that today the fact of global interconnectedness demands, in international relations, ethical standards that go beyond a strict, legalistic concept of responsibility. The butterfly does not *know* about the consequence of the flapping of its wings; but the butterfly cannot *rule out* that consequence. We move here from responsibility to a related but more restrictive concept, that of precaution.

The "precautionary principle" has been developed, especially in Germany and France, with reference to environmental laws and the legal protection of public health.[65] According to such "precautionary doctrine", it is possible to consider responsible "not only those who have not taken preventive measures required by a known or predictable risk, but also those who, in case of uncertainty or doubt, did not take precautionary measures".[66]

In the field of diplomacy the "precautionary" extension of the principle of responsibility should be considered particularly relevant. The world is interconnected, but the "wiring" of this complex system is so complicated and intricate that it is extremely difficult, if not impossible, to reconstruct a precise causal path for each individual action or omission. Indeed, the precautionary principle intrinsically deals with the problem of decisions in a situation of uncertainty, a rather adequate description of the quandaries of contemporary diplomacy. Moreover, if we go back to the original area in which the precautionary concept was first developed, that of the environment, we find that natural environment and "political" environment have a lot in common as to the duties they impose on each inhabitant. There is a sort of "international pollution" (harmful to others in terms of security or in economic terms) that we should always consider from a moral point of view.

A French author has written that the precautionary principle seems peculiarly fitting for the field of international law because "in international law the practice of recommendation – in part with recourse to general concepts with a strong ethical connotation – is all the more important as that of prescription is limited".[67] It is true that the constant exchange between international law and ethics creates a space where precautionary approaches can usefully be applied. Yet one would tend to maintain that international law at large (leaving aside the specific area of environmental protection)[68] should, for the sake of both political realism and legal guarantees, remain centred on the strict principle of accountability. But whereas it would be excessive, and in any case premature, to extend systematically the precautionary principle to the whole body of international law, if we shift to a moral discourse then this more demanding criterion is not only possible, but also necessary.

Morally, diplomacy should be held responsible, even outside a strict criterion of imputability, for that "international pollution" that is often the consequence of an insufficient precaution. One example will suffice. Even if we rule out specific breaches of international law or accountability for specific conflicts, would not a diplomatic approach consisting in an indiscriminate support of all separatist causes be responsible, according to the precautionary principle, for the "pollution" of the international political environment brought about by the proliferation of ethnic conflicts? Should we not, when acting in the diplomatic field, keep in mind worst-case hypotheses?

Our moral goal should be one of "zero damage" to others, including those living beyond our borders. Uncertain knowledge of the results of our acts is no excuse:

In the framework of traditional responsibility doctrine, an uncertain knowledge waives responsibility. If we apply the precautionary principle, the result is totally different: uncertain knowledge not only is no excuse, but must be seen as an incitement to prudence.[69]

A strict goal, indeed, and one that can never be fully attained, but can reasonably be pursued if – as advocated by philosophers from Spinoza to Hans Jonas – we are capable of following the precepts of the virtue of prudence.

Precaution, prudence, worst-case hypotheses, zero damage: are we not running the risk of implying that the only ethically compatible diplomacy is one of scrupulous abstention and negative self-restraint? The question is a serious one, since it would be practically disastrous, and morally questionable, if for the sake of an ethically irreproachable profile, diplomats the world over, facing tangled issues, crises, and conflicts, were to inscribe in their banners the famous Roman saying: *in dubio abstine* (when in doubt, abstain).

It is important here to clarify once more that, when speaking of all kinds of political action (diplomacy included), ethical scrutiny should be applied both to action and to omission. The "moral cost" of action, measured by its repercussions, should be considered in parallel with the costs of inaction. Responsibility and precaution should apply in both cases. This line of reasoning is particularly valid if applied to those international subjects which wield more power. In this case it quickly becomes evident not only that their responsibility must be considered as directly proportional to power, but also that their non-action can have as much international impact as their action. And since we are talking about moral and not legal duty, there is no reason why we should consider action differently from omission.

If we move, however, from the negative to the positive, if we posit not only a moral duty to abstain from causing harm, but also the duty to act in order to prevent it or put an end to it, should we not be widening our concept of responsibility to include solidarity? Is it not true that the first and most fundamental ethical precept can be derived *a contrario* from Cain's sinister disclaimer of responsibility? But if we are indeed our brothers' keepers, then no "zero damage", and no abstention from harming others, will suffice to fulfil our moral duty.

This remains true in the specific field of diplomacy, where the dimension of solidarity appears today to be the only one capable of supplying the moral, and also the operational, tools to cope with a chaotic, destructured yet thoroughly interconnected world. Because we are all "butterflies"; some with wide, strong wings, others tiny and apparently insignificant, but still capable of starting devastating processes. Thus knowing one another across borders, caring for one another's problems, recognizing one another's rights – and developing and applying a compatible diplomacy – is not only morally commendable, but it is the sign of a higher realism:
- because conflict, wherever it happens, does not threaten only contiguous areas, but poisons the very blood of the international body politic;

- because beggar-thy-neighbour economic and commercial strategies are demonstrably self-defeating in a globalized world economy;
- because human rights violations generate conflicts that disrupt normal international life;
- because huge (and sometimes growing) differentials of development induce – together with the effect of conflicts – massive and irregular movements of destitute people who usually end up knocking on some-one else's door.

If this is the reality, and if moral considerations coincide with self-interest in inducing us to address it on the basis of solidarity, then ethical diplomacy is thus not to be put in contrast with *realpolitik*; it is not utopia but rationality.

The author would like to suggest that in the field of international relations moral principles may also be interpreted under the same "functional" optic that is applied within each domestic framework, where nobody denies that ethics is an indispensable foundation for society. Moving beyond the narrow vision of the national interest – the exact equivalent of individual interest in domestic theory – we should finally be able to see, abandoning the strong state-centric ideology that still dominates the international discourse, that there is a sort of "evolutionist advantage" for those states that are capable of harmonizing the pursuit of legitimate national interest with ethical criteria.

It is indeed bizarre that in international theory the prevailing "realist" school has continued maintaining to this very day that the best diplomacy is one that is practically deaf to all moral considerations and that only pursues self-interest. This approach, even leaving aside all moral consid-erations, appears incredibly dogmatic and short-sighted. Not only, in fact, does it not consider the fact of reciprocity in unethical diplomacy, a factor not to be underestimated which puts each, alternatively, on the receiving end of immoral international behaviour; but even if we want to stick to the primitive "law" of survival in a tough, evil world (which would mean, incidentally, that the worst guy determines the ethical level of all), we should still consider the systemic level.

Immoral diplomacy affects and undermines the very foundation of international norms, thereby weakening an international system which even the most powerful states need as the necessary framework for the pursuit of their fundamental interests in terms of security and prosperity. Thus this ethics-incompatible diplomacy ends up being harmful to the very national interests it purports to defend, so that perhaps one could suggest, answering the diplomat quoted at the beginning of this chapter, that the true oxymoron is "unethical diplomacy".

But as it is usually the case, theory is challenged by events rather than by contrary theory. The writer would like to conclude by referring to the

1999 conflict over Kosovo: a conflict that will certainly entail deep and lasting consequences for international relations in Europe and beyond. One can advance the hypothesis that the consequences for the issue of ethics and diplomacy will be as deep if not deeper. Because of this conflict, ethical considerations have been elevated more explicitly than ever before to the status of a decisive factor in the conduct of foreign policy up to and including the decision to have recourse to military force. One must point out, on the other hand, that there is still a lot of (understandable) reluctance on the part of those responsible for foreign policy in each country to define moral considerations not only as decisive, but as overriding all other concerns. Moral argument, if formulated in absolute terms, risks of course binding those who handle it without sufficient care in ways that can be dangerous if applied consistently, or leave them exposed to criticism of "double standards" if not.

Thus it is important to note that ethical motivations for the intervention against Serbia are not formulated in absolute terms outside a wider context. Repeatedly, allied leaders (starting with President Clinton)[70] have referred to a double motivation for intervention over Kosovo: the moral urge not to allow Serb atrocities, and the "realist" goal of preventing geopolitical destabilization and widening conflict in the Balkans.

Definitely, the issue is far from being easily addressed, because firstly NATO action has been from its very inception subjected to scrutiny on the basis of ethics-of-responsibility criteria (What are the results? What are the costs in human terms?),[71] and secondly because combining "ethical" and "realist" motivations for military (and diplomatic) action brings about a sort of "overdetermination" that can be very problematic to assess in its exact mix of components and in its credibility.

On 22 April 1999, in Chicago, Prime Minister Blair was the one to put the question in its most explicit terms, when, referring to the "simplicity" of the Cold War, he said: "Now our actions are guided by a more subtle blend of mutual self-interest and moral purpose." A "subtle blend", indeed, and one that will engage – even tax – our moral temper and our political skills for many years to come, especially until we are able to perfect international institutions capable of channelling our moral impulses through mechanisms that are more effective and less arbitrary than the present ones.

In any case, something that Tony Blair went on to say in the same speech is definitely not controversial: "In the end values and interests merge. If we can establish and spread the values of liberty, the rule of law, human rights and an open society then that is in our national interest too. The spread of our values makes us safer."[72]

The ethical justification for the war over Kosovo has been strongly challenged, not only by pacifists but also by "realists" denouncing the dangerous and erratic nature of ethics as a guiding principle of diplomacy (and of war). Yet, beyond the merits of the present debate, it can be said that after the conflict over Kosovo the discussion of "ethics *in* (rather than *and*) diplomacy" will remain open, and will be considered not only by politicians, but also by the traditionally reluctant practitioners, as a legitimate, inescapable, and even indispensable one.

Notes

1. On the level of propaganda, on the contrary, the enemy tends to be negatively described in Machiavellian terms. See for instance President Reagan's assertion, referring to Soviet leaders: "they reserve the right unto themselves to commit any crime, to lie, to cheat". Quoted in Der Derian, J., 1987, *On Diplomacy*. Oxford and Cambridge, MA: Blackwell, p. 1.
2. Actually, "that a discipline within which normative issues arise so often, should fail to take normative theory seriously is a paradox that calls for critical investigation". Frost, M., 1996, *Ethics in International Relations. A Constitutive Theory*. Cambridge: Cambridge University Press, p. 5.
3. Comte-Sponville, A., 1994, *Valeur et vérité. Etudes ciniques*. Paris: Presses Universitaires de France. See in particular the chapter "Morale ou éthique?", pp. 183–205.
4. For a detailed discussion on this point, with special reference to the philosophy of Emmanuel Levinas, see Toscano, R., 1998, "The Face of the Other: Ethics and Interethnic Conflict", in Weiner, E. (ed.) *The Handbook of Interethnic Coexistence*. New York: Continuum. For English readers, a good way of approaching Levinas's vast body of works is Hand, S., ed., 1989, *The Levinas Reader*. Cambridge, MA: Blackwell.
5. Der Derian, note 1 above, p. 42.
6. It has rightly been remarked that realism enjoys "an institutionally entrenched position". Frost, note 2 above, p. 21.
7. Forde, S., 1993, "Classical Realism", in Nardin, T. and Mapel, D. R., eds, *Traditions of International Ethics*. Cambridge: Cambridge University Press, p. 62.
8. For a detailed listing of realist arguments against normative (ethical) approaches to international relations see Frost, note 2 above, p. 41ff.
9. See in particular Kennan, G., 1985–86, "Morality and Foreign Policy", *Foreign Affairs*, Winter, p. 206.
10. Hobbes, T., 1996, *Leviathan*. Oxford: Oxford University Press, Part 2, XXX, 30, p. 235.
11. Berlin, I., 1980, "The Originality of Machiavelli", in *Against the Current. Essays in the History of Ideas*. London: Hogarth Press, pp. 25–79.
12. Hampshire, S., 1989, *Innocence and Experience*. Cambridge, MA: Harvard University Press. p. 165. Terry Nardin also rejects the "extra-moral" claim of realism, bringing it back into the area of moral debate: "As a moral argument, realism amounts to a claim that the reasons for overriding the constraints of ordinary morality in emergency situations are themselves moral. There is, in other words, a higher law that legitimizes bowing to the necessities of national survival, one that requires that these ordinary constraints be set aside when the state is threatened with catastrophe." Nardin, T., 1993, "Ethical Traditions in International Affairs", in Nardin and Mapel, note 7 above, pp. 15–16.
13. Ricoeur, P., 1990, *Soi-même comme un autre*. Paris: Seuil, p. 284.

14. Trotsky, L., 1997, *Their Morals and Ours. The Class Foundation of Moral Practice*. New York: Pathfinder.

15. Banfield's description of "amoral familism" in the culture of a southern Italian village clearly identifies, rather than an absence of morality as such, a pattern of different moral allegiance, so that the very definition turns out, after all, to be a misnomer. See Banfield, E. C., 1958, *The Moral Basis of a Backward Society*. Chicago: Free Press.

16. To go the the most extreme case, here are two amazing but authentic rationalizations by Mafia killers. Giovanni Brusca, who admits among other crimes to having killed the 14-year-old son of a *mafioso* turned police informer, justified himself as follows: "I never killed for personal reasons, but only for Cosa Nostra." (*ANSA*, 30 July 1997). Gaspare Mutolo, another *mafioso*, who admits to having killed with his own hands at least 20 people, explains: "For someone who is a member of the Mafia, it is natural to go and kill. Those who do it act out of duty, of solidarity, a spirit of community." (*La Repubblica*, 31 May 1996).

17. Hobbes, note 10 above, Part 2, XVII, 2, pp. 111–112. This author agrees with Frost (note 2 above, p. 163) when he writes: "My contention is that the questions about the justification of unconventional forms of violence are in the same class as questions about the justification of war."

18. Spinoza. *Ethics*. Part III (Of the Origin and Nature of Feelings), Propositions VI, VII, VIII, and IX. Here we are not just facing a variant of possible ethical options, but something much more radical. In fact, whereas ethics is by definition exclusively human, *conatus essendi* (the striving for the preservation of being) is, according to Spinoza, a property of "things" in general. In other words, if *conatus essendi* – naturalistic laws on a par with the laws of thermodynamics – is the only or the absolutely overwhelming guiding principle for action (both individual and group), this evidently makes all ethics – and also legality – inconceivable.

19. Lewis, B., 1988, *The Political Language of Islam*. Chicago: University of Chicago Press, p. 73.

20. Hobbes, note 10 above, Part 1, III, 8.

21. Forde, note 7 above, p. 65. Machiavelli, an advocate of preventive strikes, writes: "war is not removed, but postponed to the advantage of others" (*The Prince*, III, 8).

22. In a 1952 dispatch from Moscow, George Kennan wrote: "Russian political leaders have usually operated against a background of uncertainty and anxiety with respect to domestic political and economic conditions which heightened their congenital sense of insecurity and caused them to wish for a larger margin of numerical safety in armed strength than would be thought necessary elsewhere." Kennan, G. F., 1972, *Memoirs 1950–1963*. New York: Pantheon Books, p. 335. See also Mastny, V., 1979, *Russia's Road to the Cold War*. New York: Columbia University Press.

23. For a brief but substantial discussion of the theme of national interest and its ethical implications, see Donnelly, J., 1993, "Twentieth-century Realism", in Nardin and Mapel, note 7 above, pp. 91–93.

24. Quoted in Donnelly, *ibid.*, p. 93.

25. It seems interesting to note that the concept of sovereignty has been utilized by thinkers, from Nietzsche to Bataille, who have radically challenged moral constraints imposed on the individual: like the sovereign state, the sovereign individual is self-referential and recognizes no limitation in the pursuit of self-appointed ends.

26. "To say that a state is sovereign does not commit us to saying that it is wrong or pointless to discuss what norms it ought to follow in its dealings with other states. Any suggestion that it is probably rests on some confusion about the relationship between power and moral norms." Frost, note 2 above, p. 91.

27. Halbertal, M. and Margalit, A., 1992, *Idolatry*. Cambridge, MA: Harvard University

Press; Halperin, J. and Levitte, G., eds, 1985, *Idoles, Actes du XXIV colloque des intellectuels juifs de langue francaise*. Paris: Denoel. See in particular Riveline, C. ("Les differentes formes de l'idolatrie dans la Bible et aujourd'hui"), who writes that "idolatry is not the worship of a false value. Idolatry is a disproportionate importance given to one of the components of truth" (p. 26).

28. Pascal, 1954, "Pensées, 244", in *Oeuvres complètes*. Paris: Gallimard, p. 1153.
29. Lynch, C., 1994, "Kant, the Republican Peace, and Moral Guidance in International Law", *Ethics and International Affairs*, Vol. 8, p. 39.
30. True believers in globalization have fallen in love with a certain "TINA" (acronym for "there is no alternative"). According to a pamphlet published by Royal Dutch Shell, globalization has created a world without alternatives, the world of TINA. See Royal Dutch Shell, 1997, *Global Scenarios 1995–2000*. Geneva: Royal Dutch Shell.
31. "Cold War politics was such that there seemed little point in studying international ethics." Frost, note 2 above, p. 5.
32. *Ibid.*, p. 53ff.
33. Though "fundamentalism" is the most common definition of the phenomenon in the English language, at times it seems better to use the hardly translatable French expression, *intégrisme*. Fundamentalism, in fact, etymologically refers to a strict adherence to the fundamental, traditional tenets of a religious doctrine, whereas the peculiar essence of the contemporary "fundamentalist" phenomenon consists in the denial of every and each sphere of individual and social autonomy with reference to a global, integral religious/moral precept that allows no separate "domain of discourse", no distinct "sphere" or "order".
34. From Eichmann to Papon, there exists a disturbing coincidence, whatever the specific culture and ideology within which each individual operates, among this kind of *fonctionnaires* who ask no questions (especially of a moral nature) but just perform whatever is required of them.
35. It is important to recall that at the Nuremberg trial the argument of "superior orders" claimed by the lawyers of the Nazi defendants was rejected by the court as a cause for non-responsibility, and retained only as a mitigating circumstance. See Best, G., 1994, *War and Law Since 1945*. Oxford: Oxford University Press; see in particular pp. 188–206. Most relevant to this discussion is the case of Ernst von Weizsaecker, state secretary of the German Foreign Ministry from 1938 to 1943. On trial at Nuremberg, von Weizsaecker was eventually acquitted on the first count of his indictment ("crimes against peace"), but convicted on the second ("crimes against humanity") because, according to the court, his silence on the policy of extermination of the Jews amounted to "consent to the commission of murder". Walzer, M., 1977, *Just and Unjust Wars*. New York: Basic Books, pp. 292–296.
36. In assessing "how the theory of political duty applies to foreign policy", Rawls, in a chapter titled "The Justification of Conscientious Refusal", writes: "Given the often predatory aims of state power, and the tendency of men to defer to their government's decision to wage war, a general willingness to resist the state's claims is all the more necessary." Rawls, J., 1983, *A Theory of Justice*. Oxford: Oxford University Press, pp. 377–382.
37. Arendt, H., 1963, *Eichmann in Jerusalem. A Report on the Banality of Evil*. New York: Viking; Zuccotti, S., 1987, *The Italians and the Holocaust*. New York: Basic Books.
38. See in particular Steinberg, J., 1991, *All or Nothing. The Axis and the Holocaust 1941–43*. London and New York: Routledge.
39. The heroic role of the Swedish diplomat Raul Wallemberg in Hungary is well known. But – and allow this author, a diplomat, to interject a passionate "luckily" – there are many other stories of diplomats who, facing the monster of the Holocaust, put ethics

first; for instance Chiune Sugihara, Japanese consul in Lithuania during the Second World War. As is true also in the case of Italian diplomats in the Balkans, there are legitimate historical debates on the real nature of the instructions that individual diplomats may have received in those complicated times, and doubts have been voiced on the real nature and motivations of Sugihara's action in favour of the Jews. In any case, one hears a ring of truthfulness from the Japanese diplomat when he writes, with typical diplomatic understatement: "People in Tokyo were not unified ... So, I made up my mind not to wait for their reply. I knew that somebody would surely complain to me in the future. But I myself thought this would be the right thing to do. There is nothing wrong with saving many people's lives." Quoted in Sayle, M., 1997, "Sugihara's List", *New York Review of Books*, 4 December, p. 46. This author, second secretary at the Italian embassy in Santiago at the time of the 1973 coup, can testify to the fact that, even before instructions could be received from capitals, many diplomats thought that "there was nothing wrong with saving many people's lives" and took the initiative to give refuge in their embassies to Chilean citizens pursued by the *golpistas*.

40. Der Derian, note 1 above, p. 2.
41. It is interesting to note that George Soros applies this sort of distinction when explaining his own behaviour as an operator in the international financial system, playing by the existing rules out of self-interest while advocating, on the basis also of ethical considerations, a change of those very rules: "I think one should distinguish between competing by a given set of rules and the process of making and improving those rules. When it comes to making the rules, I'm guided by the common interest. And when it comes to competing, I'm guided by my self-interest." Soros, G. and Madrick, J., 1999, "The International Crisis: An Overview", *New York Review of Books*, 14 January, p. 40.
42. Quoted in Lynch, note 29 above.
43. Welch, D. A., 1994, "Can We Think Systematically About Ethics and Statecraft?", *Ethics and International Affairs*, Vol. 8, p. 35.
44. Nardin and Mapel, note 7 above, p. 13.
45. Jones, D. V., 1993, "The Declaratory Tradition in Modern International Law", in *ibid.*, p. 42ff.
46. Quoted in Donnelly, note 23 above, p. 94.
47. Nye, J. S., 1990, *Bound To Lead. The Changing Nature of American Power.* New York: Basic Books. Nye rejects the very distinction between values and interests in foreign policy, stating that "values are simply intangible interests". "Being Tough To Be Kind", *Financial Times*, 27 May 1999.
48. Martin Wight writes: "Powers have qualitative differences as well as quantitative, and their attraction and influence is not exactly correlated to mass and weight. For men possess not only territories, raw materials and weapons, but also beliefs and opinions. It is true that beliefs do not prevail in international politics unless they are associated with power. But it is equally true that power varies very much in effectiveness according to the strength of the beliefs that inspire its use." Quoted in Der Derian, note 1 above, p. 4.
49. Jones, note 45 above, p. 44–45.
50. Walzer, note 35 above, xvii.
51. Article 2.7 of the UN Charter reads: "Nothing in the present Charter shall authorize the United Nations to intervene in matters which are essentially within the domestic jurisdiction of any state or shall require the members to submit such matters to settlement under the present Charter."
52. Article 2.7, in fact, goes on to say: "... but this principle shall not prejudice the application of enforcement measures under Chapter VII".
53. Since we are speaking of Africa, we can note that the principle of non-intervention has never been considered by European countries as an impediment to military action

carried out periodically to rescue nationals (and not only nationals) in cases of internal chaos and military confrontation.

54. "No human nature is capable of governing alone things human without being filled with injustice and *hubris.*" Plato, *The Laws*, IV, 713 c–e.

55. Kant, I., 1971, *Zum Ewigen Frieden*, English translation in Reiss, H., ed., *Kant's Political Writings.* Cambridge: Cambridge University Press.

56. Cacciari, M., 1998, *L'Arcipelago.* Milan: Adelphi, p. 21.

57. Jankelevitch, V., 1981, *Le paradoxe de la morale.* Paris: Seuil, pp. 88–90. For a more detailed analysis of this point, see Toscano, note 4 above, in particular pp. 76–77.

58. Ricoeur, note 13 above, p. 368.

59. On the nature and classification of present-day conflicts, see Toscano, R., 1998, "An Answer to War: Conflicts and Intervention in Contemporary International Relations", in Weiner, note 4 above, p. 263.

60. For a thorough examination of this issue, see Warner, D., 1991, *An Ethic of Responsibility in International Relations.* Boulder and London: Lynne Rienner. It is very interesting – but outside the scope of the present chapter – to examine the cultural and religious roots of this ethical approach, which is definitely the product of Protestant moral debate between Luther's *"Ich kann nicht anders"* (I cannot otherwise) and Kant's concept of *Zurechnung* (imputation of acts and their consequences). See also Ricoeur, P., 1995, *Le Juste.* Paris: Editions Esprit, in particular the chapter "Le concept de responsabilité", pp. 41–70.

61. Warner, note 60 above, p. 14.

62. *Ibid.*

63. "Imputation of man does not take place because he is free, but he is free because of imputation." Hans Kelsen, quoted in Ricoeur, note 60 above, p. 50.

64. On chaos theory, see Kellert, S. H., 1993, *In the Wake of Chaos. Unpredictable Order in a Dynamical System.* Chicago: University of Chicago Press.

65. Godard, O., ed., 1997, *Le principe de précaution dans la conduite des affaires humaines.* Paris: Editions de la Maison des sciences de l'homme.

66. *Ibid.*, p. 20. It should be pointed out, here, that we are not dealing only with doctrine, but also with actual legislation. For instance, a French law on the protection of the environment (Art. 1 of Law 95–101 of 2 February 1995) states: "the absence of certainties ... must not delay the adoption of measures aiming at the prevention of a risk of serious and irreversible damage". Quoted in Martin, G. J., 1997, "Précaution et évolution du Droit", in Godard, *ibid.*, p. 331.

67. Gilbert, C., 1997, "La précaution dans l'"empire du milieu'", in Godard, *ibid.*, p. 323.

68. In the field of international environmental norms, the precautionary principle has been incorporated in texts from the Treaty of Maastricht (Art. 130) to the Rio Declaration (Principle 15). See Martin, note 66 above, p. 335.

69. Ewald, F., 1997, "Le retour du malin génie. Esquisse d'une philosophie de la précaution", in Godard, note 65 above, p. 115.

70. "It is not only the morally right thing for America, it is the right thing for our security interests in the long run." President Clinton's speech on Kosovo to veterans of foreign wars, 13 May 1999. The text can be found in: http://www.usia. gov/cgi-bin/washfile/display.pl?p=/products/washfile/topic/intrel&f=9905121/05/99

71. "After what was done a half-century ago to another European minority, the Jews, this intervention may even be held to have been a necessary decision by West Europeans and Americans. Morality, however, is qualified by the question of efficacy. Has NATO accomplished anything that has helped the Kosovars? [...] The only moral justification for NATO's initial intervention was the protection and the rescue of civilians. To have subsequently killed from a great distance, while assuring NATO safety at the cost of

civilian suffering, has been dishonoring." Pfaff, W., 1999, "Overlooking Kosovo's People Hurts NATO's Case", *International Herald Tribune*, 13 May. "NATO was not wrong in principle to intervene. But to be justified, in practice, its intervention had to have a good chance of improving the outcome." Wolf, M., 1999, "The Road to Hell", *Financial Times*, 7 April. "NATO's intervention is undoubtedly a just cause. But in order to judge the morality of a war, one also has to take into account two other considerations: Are the values destroyed in the war less important than the values defended? Is there, as the Christian just-war doctrine also requires, a reasonable chance of success?" Hoffmann, S., 1999, "What Is To Be Done?", *New York Review of Books*, 20 May.

72. The full text of Tony Blair's speech can be found at http://www.fco.gov.uk/news/ speechtext.asp?2316

4

Violence and ethics: Beyond the reason of state paradigm

Pierre Hassner

To write about violence and ethics for a volume dedicated to the new challenges for the ethics of international relations in our time means trying to establish a position at the intersection of several series of difficulties, or at least open questions.

The first concerns the collective enterprise as such. Can there be new dimensions of ethics or only new issues? If one takes ethics seriously, either in its deontological or its consequentialist version, does it not rely on a universally valid law or calculus? If, on the other hand, it is historically determined, is it not condemned either to lapse into cultural relativism or to rely on a less than credible global philosophy of history?

The second problem is also common to the whole project. Can one really speak in the same breath of ethics and of international relations, or does one produce what Roberto Toscano's colleague calls, in the case of the ethics of diplomacy, an oxymoron?[1] On the one hand, if there is such a thing as one morality, can it accommodate the plurality of communities and national interests? On the other hand, if one starts from this plurality, in the absence of a common authority and of common institutions, can one ever reach an international ethics (in the sense of the Hegelian *Sittlichkeit* as distinct from *Moralität*) as a community of mores and practices? Or is one condemned, as the debate between Goodin and Miller[2] would seem to indicate, never to reach the concreteness of the particular if one starts from the abstractness of the universal, and vice versa?

More specifically, are not international relations essentially based on the violation not only of the Sermon on the Mount but of the Decalogue, since they cannot exclude either lying and killing for one's country, or such selfish passions as avarice or envy? Or do international relations have their own morality, based on the primacy of national interest, on ambition, or, simply and ultimately, on the survival of the community? We are led, then, to the classical oppositions between conscience, individual or universal, and national interest or reason of state, between idealism and realism, between Kant and Machiavelli, or between the two Weberian ethics of conviction and responsibility. Both Rousseau and Kant have pointed out that this clash was particularly severe when it came to relations between states, and that it risked jeopardizing the very idea of a just and peaceful order.[3]

In an important piece of work on theories of justice and international relations, James Fishkin[4] has shown the impossibility of applying what he calls the SIC (systematic impartial consequentialism) paradigm to international relations. Furthermore, he points out that this teaches us a lesson about ethics in general, that "the ethics of international relations, more clearly than that of domestic justice, unveils the necessity of moral conflict, of balancing incommensurable considerations, and hence the impossibility of satisfying absolutist expectations".

The quandary is made worse still by the peculiar character of our time, and by the peculiar character of this chapter's subject. The impossibility of a rigorously satisfying moral theory has been, throughout history, mitigated by collective beliefs and attitudes, by what Montesquieu called "*les moeurs*" and Hegel *Sittlichkeit* (as opposed to *Moralität*), whether based on religion or simply on tradition or trust in a common understanding of good and evil. The solidity of this common moral universe has been shaken in modern times by the debunking critique of radical doctrines, and replaced by the belief in scientific progress or in militant ideologies which would provide a historical, future-oriented standard instead of a permanent one.

Today, we cannot believe either in a common, stable universe (whether physical, metaphysical, or ethical) or in futuristic utopias which would guide our behaviour. The fashion for ethics indicates this plight of individuals and citizens, in search of standards they could trust, and even the dilemma of professional organizations and states which set up "ethics committees" but are at a loss about the criteria which should govern both the choice of their members and their decisions.

This search is even more problematic when it comes to violence. No relationship is more paradoxical than that between force, in particular war, and morality. There is no society that does not threaten, and sometimes use, force against domestic and foreign enemies and which does not honour the heroism and sacrifice of those who have given their lives fighting for it. Yet there is no society where taking human life does not raise a moral problem, where war does not need a special justification, whether based on religion, on the right or duty of revenge, or on the necessities of survival.

Precisely, violence (as distinct from force) can be seen as lacking this justification, as emanating from individual or collective passions rather than from some legitimate authority or purpose. Here we encounter the distinction, and at the same time the connection, between moral and legal legitimation. To the extent that, in modern times, violence based on divine inspiration or on righteous wrath is not considered legitimate, institutional authority prevails over good cause or intention as a justification. The conventional distinction between force and violence is based on that between violence exercised by the state, either against unlawful citizens through the police or against other states through the army, and violence exercised by individuals or social groups. As against this conservative distinction, revolutionary movements use an opposition between the present violent order based on the state and social injustice and the future peaceful order based on the free development of the individual. The violence of the state is illegitimate, whereas violence against the state in order to bring about a non-violent society is morally justified.[5]

It is fair to say that both these opposite justifications are today decisively weakened, at least in the West. "The moral standing of states", to use Michael Walzer's[6] expression, is severely weakened, and even more so the legitimacy of war for gain or prestige. On the other hand, while revolution has seemed briefly to take the place of war as a legitimation of violence,[7] the results of murderous utopias sometimes pursued in the name of peace were so horrendous in the twentieth century as to delegitimize the very idea of revolution. Without subscribing to the idea of the end of history, it does seem that today, in the West, liberal democracy and capitalism based on possessive individualism appear as the only legitimate order, and that the corresponding ethics is the Hobbesian or Lockean one in which the search for security and prosperity are the dominant values and violence is justified only in defence of life and property.

Eric Hobsbawm has argued, in a round-table discussion concerning the NATO intervention in Kosovo, that it was:

the first war fought under conditions of, you might say, consumer sovereignty. We are back to the situation which Thomas Hobbes assumed to be normal: that whatever the Leviathan can do, he cannot force people to run the risk of death. For several centuries politics was based on the opposite assumption. This return to Hobbes may only be true of America, but the Kosovo war was waged by politicians who believed that their people would not stand casualties.[8]

However, the historical dialectic of ethics does not stop there. The currently victorious, bourgeois morality is permanently haunted by its own prosaic selfishness; the ghosts of an ethic of compassion and solidarity and an ethic of manliness, nobility, and heroism are never fully exorcised, even though we all know they have respectively given rise to communism and fascism, which in turn have produced the decisive ethical experience of the twentieth century, that of ultimate evil through the totalitarian denial of common humanity, or the derecognition of man by man. Wounded dignity and moral indignation can still be the sources of righteous violence and overcome the barriers raised by the love of comfort and the fear of death. For the bourgeois ethic itself, war may be delegitimized, but police actions against crime are not.

It is time for the writer to make his prejudices explicit: contemporary efforts in ethical theory, whether of the specialized and fragmented or of the abstract and general sort, whether constructivist, structuralist, or post-structuralist, are unlikely to carry us much beyond the dialogues, implicitly alluded to above, between Kant and Machiavelli, Aristotle and Hegel, Rousseau and Nietzsche. Yet the author does believe that the permanent dilemmas brought forth by these dialogues take fundamentally new forms because of basic changes in historical context. A century which, on the one hand, delegitimizes war, an activity which has been central to the life of political communities throughout history, but which at the same time has reached unknown extremes in genocide and in endangering mankind's physical and spiritual survival, certainly gives a new twist and perhaps a new dimension to the permanent problems of ethics, including the most fundamental of all, that of what Kant has called radical evil.[9]

From permanent dilemmas to new paradoxes

The particular and the universal

Perhaps the deepest human tension is "between one's own and the good", a tension which, as Leo Strauss[10] put it, "may well lead to a break, be it only the breaking of a heart". Its political expression is the relation between fatherland and regime, which, internationally, is translated in the tension between particular states and universalistic ideologies or institutions. The division between schools of thought in international relations as proposed by Martin Wight[11] and Hedley Bull[12] (the realist, the rationalist, and the revolutionary), and the one between ethical positions as defined by Charles Beitz[13] (moral scepticism, morality of states, and cosmopolitanism) are largely convergent. At both levels, one can say that while the tyrannies and wars of the twentieth century give strong support to Machiavellianism or moral scepticism, that while the attempts at institutionalized cooperation between states, including in the area of arms control and even, to some extent, of crisis management, confirm that the "rationalist" attempts at appealing to a society of states based on reciprocal restraint are not entirely misplaced, it is no less true that the point of view which has considerably gained is the one labelled "revolutionary" or "cosmopolitan".

This is so first because the two ideologies which survived the Second World War – liberalism and Marxism – were both universalistic. Second, because globalization under the guise of economic interdependence, of instant communication, and of global dangers, gives it a basis in actual historical trends. Thirdly, and perhaps most importantly, because television has brought an awareness of distant horrors (continentwide famines, ecological catastrophes, and genocide) which have created a new kind of victimhood: "victims who have no social relations capable of mobilizing their salvation and who, as a result, make an ethic of universal moral obligation among strangers a necessity for the planet".[14]

This awareness leads to a kind of "species politics", that of voluntary organizations which instead of old ideologies of national interests base their commitment on the borderless fight against suffering: this is the morality of extreme urgency, theorized by Bernard Kouchner and André Glucksmann out of the practice of the "French doctors" such as Médicins Sans Frontières and Médicins du Monde.

Beyond this relatively restricted "international civil society" based on environmentalist and pacifist movements practising the politics of the planet earth and humanitarian movements practising the fight against inhumanity, there is a global awareness of distant suffering and crime which leads to sporadic movements of compassion or indignation.

In turn, governments challenged to "do something" by public opinion have embarked on the road of "humanitarian intervention" justified by moral or world-order goals, and based on a mandate or at least a *post factum* legitimation by the United Nations in the name of "the international community". Hence the use of force tends to be justified (at least as much as by national security or survival) by universalistic goals in conflicts which touch the respective nations only in an indirect way. The French legal and political thinker Antoine Garapon has suggested this means a fundamental reordering of international ethics, law, and politics:

The war in Kosovo accelerates a new representation of the world, based on crime and justice, a new access to politics which no longer involves being assimilated into a collective body but identifying with somebody else's suffering ... Through this last conflict of the century, sovereignty, around which both domestic and international politics were revolving, is faced with the possible criminalization of its action, and is, therefore, liable to be judged in the name of a value which, from now on, is superior to it: human dignity.[15]

All these cosmopolitan advances, however, can be challenged from a particularistic point of view, which either can be seen to be hidden behind universalistic appearances and proclamations, or is being brought forth as a reaction to the realities as well as the myths of globalization.

First, the proclaimed universalism of liberalism and Marxism is based on power relations: in an empire or an alliance, the particular interests of the leading power tend to be presented and seen by itself as universal. Second, globalization produces conflicts and inequalities as well as cooperation: its homogenizing drive produces a reassertion of particularism and the search for identity. Its dynamics create a destabilization through opening that makes self-closure unattainable in the long run but increases its appeal in the short run. Thirdly, the global village created by television cannot escape the differentiation produced by regional, cultural, and political divisions.

The "ethics of extreme urgency" very quickly runs into classical political problems."Borderlessness", the refusal to choose among victims and to bow in front of states refusing access to them, is fully valid in principle; in practical terms, it cannot avoid condemning some states, compromising with some others, seeking or accepting the help of third ones, at the risk of being manipulated by them, as humanitarian concerns can serve as alibis for both political and military action and inaction. Hence the quarrels which have plagued the world of humanitarian organizations, between the position of strict neutrality adhered to by the Red Cross, state humanitarianism as a step towards the international rule of law as advocated by Bernard Kouchner, and the strict separation of humanitarianism and politics with, in case of doubt, a priority to military intervention in the name of politics (to put an end to conflicts instead of alleviating them) or of justice (to punish the aggressors instead of treating them as victims) – a position advocated by many of the original French doctors like Rony Brauman and Alain Destexhe.[16]

For wider public opinion, global solidarity is a fugitive, contingent, and selective phenomenon. We may be more sensitive to anonymous suffering than before, but we are certainly more sensitive the more we are able to identify with the victims, and this identification, more often than not, depends on particular commonalities. Michael Ignatieff expresses both sides of the coin particularly well. After the passage already quoted on new conditions and universal moral obligations, he adds:

Doubtless such an ethic of obligation will always have a secondary claim on our moral will, subsidiary to the attentions we lavish on a brother, a sister, a fellow-citizen, a co-believer or a co-worker. But without this weak and inconsistent ethic, this impersonal commitment to strangers, the universal victim will find no one beyond the wire to feed him. It is this weak moral language, and the new experience of universal victimhood it is trying to address, of which television has become the privileged modern medium.[17]

When it comes to governments, these ambiguities and inconsistencies are even more unavoidable and more troubling. Some are directly related to the feelings of their respective populations – for instance, the difference in the value accorded to human lives according to whether they belong to their nationals, to their allies, to the populations of adversaries, or to distant populations one is supposed to protect. It would be wrong to assert, following a *boutade* of Stanley Hoffmann, that current American military doctrine is less concerned with the immunity of non-combatants than with the immunity of American combatants. The truth is that it aims at winning with as little killing as possible of civilian populations and even of enemy combatants. But it is also true that it is much more concerned with protecting American lives, including those of combatants, than foreign ones, including those of civilian populations or allied troops. This was particularly clear during the war in Kosovo, which seemed to imply, in the American perception, three categories of lives. The first imperative was no American casualties. The second, to avoid civilian casualties on the Serb side, but not to the extent of endangering American lives (hence only military or economic targets were sought, but from an altitude which, while safer for the pilots, made accidents inevitable). The third category were the Albanian victims of ethnic cleansing, whose plight was increased by the bombing and made inevitable, over a period of 11 weeks, by the refusal to initiate any ground invasion.[18]

Even more important ambiguities and consistencies are specific to the states as such. One is sovereignty. Each state pays lip service to the "international community" and the United Nations, but none is ready to relinquish its own ultimate authority to decide on war and peace. Of course, the contradiction is widest in the case of the USA, which acts as a sheriff in the name of the international community and universal principles, and which supported the creation of the International Criminal Tribunal on Former Yugoslavia, but refuses to obey the International Court of Justice in the Hague, and, even more strikingly, to join the nations which decided, in Rome in 1998, to create an International Criminal Court.

But the most basic and most unavoidable tension between the universal and the particular concerns the targets and motives for military intervention. The end of the Cold War has brought both a broadening and a fragmentation of potential targets. If there is no clear and present danger to the survival of great powers, they (and in particular the only remaining superpower) are free either to renounce the use of force or to put it in the service of less directly obvious and selfish goals, of what Wolfers[19] called "milieu goals", concerning world order or the fight against the proliferation of weapons of mass destruction. Curiously, humanitarian causes have been classified by successive US Secretaries of State or of Defense, such as Perry and Christopher, as important but not vital: important enough to justify intervention, but not important enough to make it imperative or to justify accepting major costs or running major risks, such as losing American lives. Hence the danger of acting symbolically and falling short of what is needed for success.

But this, then, raises the obvious question of choice: how to select among the many cases of human suffering, of political oppression, or of reckless behaviour those to be acted upon? Obviously the number of victims or the character of the threat to world order will be one criterion. But even more obviously considerations of feasibility, of cost and risk, as well as considerations linked to other particular interests, domestic or international, economic or strategic, will sometimes weigh decisively. Very often the official justification will be lofty and universalistic, and critics will delight in unmasking particular motives from the electoral to the geopolitical. Both sides are usually right, with the result that the ethical motivation appears particularly vulnerable to the question of double standards: why Bosnia and not Chechnya? Why Somalia rather than Sudan? Why Iraqi violations rather than Israeli ones?

The no-less-inevitable answer is: better acting in some cases than in no cases at all. Doing "something" everywhere may mean not doing enough anywhere. Selectivity, even though based on extra-ethical criteria, at least saves *some* victims and punishes *some* criminals. In addition it may deter others by showing that there is no guarantee of impunity.

This is not likely to convince those victims of injustice who are not among the select largely because they have only the justice of their case working for them, to the exclusion of such criteria as domestic pressures or precious resources. But for the external spectator trying to form an objective judgement, the classical question arises of whether to judge according to intentions or to consequences. After all, the genocidal Cambodian regime of Pol Pot or the criminal "rogue" one of Amin Dada were overthrown not by "world public opinion", or by "the international community", but by Vietnamese and Tanzanian troops acting, one may safely suspect, out of national interest narrowly conceived rather than for the protection of human rights. Yet, when universal motives are failing, should one not welcome particularistic motives if they achieve universally positive results? Should one not combat a bigger evil with a smaller one, or at least cheer when out of the clash of two evils a morally good outcome emerges?

Obviously there is no universally valid or satisfactory answer to these questions. Normally they are the object of prudential judgements which cannot be decided in the abstract. Yet there are some cases where the answer does seem obvious in advance, because they involve some evil so massive that it must be resisted at any cost, or some means so destructive that they cannot be accepted under any circumstances. These are extreme situations that may perhaps give us the at least partially firm standards we are looking for.

The normal and the extreme

Here too a certain shift seems to have occurred in the twentieth century, this time from the primacy of the normal to that of the extreme. This can be illustrated by replaying, so to speak, an imaginary dialogue between two important contemporary thinkers, Leo Strauss and Dieter Henrich, one of whom emphasizes the Aristotelian primacy of the normal case as a standard while the other points out the need of a new ethic for what Hobsbawm has called "the age of the extremes".[20]

According to Strauss:[21]

The common good consists normally in what is required by commutative and distributive justice. But the common good also comprises, of course, the mere existence, the mere survival, and the mere independence of the political community in question. Let us call an extreme situation a situation in which the very existence or independence of a society is at stake. In extreme situations there may be conflicts between what the self-preservation of society requires and the requirements of commutative and distributive justice. In such situations, and only in such situations, it can justly be said that the public safety is the highest law ... By saying that in extreme situations the public safety is the highest law, one implies that the public safety is not the highest law in normal situations; in normal situations the highest laws are the common rules of justice. Justice has two different principles or sets of principles: the requirements of public safety, or what is necessary in extreme situations to preserve the mere existence or independence of society on the one hand, and the rules of justice in the more precise sense in the other. And there is no principle that defines clearly in what type of cases the public safety, and in what type of cases the precise rules of justice, have precedence. For it is not possible to define precisely what constitutes an extreme situation in contradistinction to a normal situation. What cannot be decided in advance by universal rules, what can be decided in the critical moment by the most competent and most conscientious statesman on the spot, can be made visible as just, in retrospect, to all; the objective discrimination between extreme actions which were just and extreme actions which were unjust is one of the noblest tasks of the historian.

Are we not, then, back to Machiavelli? The whole point, Strauss would say, is that we are not.

It is important that the difference between the Aristotelian view of natural right and Machiavellianism be clearly understood. Machiavelli denies natural right, because he takes his bearings by the extreme situations in which the demands of justice are reduced to the requirements of necessity, and not by the normal situations in which the demands of justice in the strict sense are the highest law. Furthermore, he does not have to overcome reluctance as regards the deviations from what is normally right. On the contrary, he seems to derive no small enjoyment from contemplating these deviations, and he is not concerned with the punctilious investigation of whether any particular deviation is really necessary or not. The true statesman in the Aristotelian sense, on the other hand, takes his bearings by the normal situation and by what is normally right and he reluctantly deviates from what is normally right only in order to save the cause of justice and humanity itself. No legal expression of this difference can be found. Its political importance is obvious. The two opposite extremes, which at present are called "cynicism" and "idealism" combine in order to blur this difference. And as everybody can see, they have not been unsuccessful.[22]

This intemporal analysis is certainly not without relevance for our time, as the example of Churchill (the model, according to Strauss, of the true statesman in the Aristotelian sense) would indicate. And yet, one may wonder whether the analysis is not a little too "normal", including its definition of the extreme, for the experience of the twentieth century, as this century has had to face such extreme extremities that they end up by calling into question the normality of the normal. This seems to be the position of Dieter Henrich, one of the main students of German idealism, who, rather than returning to Aristotle, starts from Hegel and looks into the future to ask what the nuclear era changes in the relation between ethics and history.

Henrich[23] distinguishes three levels of ethics. The first is that of the categorical imperative or of abstract universality. The second is that of concrete ethics which results from the subject's reflexive awareness of his or her identity and particular situation. The third is that of "world orientation" for, according to Henrich, any ethics, including Kantian morality, presupposes a certain state of the world that guarantees the possibility of its application. It is this historical or cosmic context which is put into question by nuclear weapons, in so far as they imply the possibility of mankind's self-destruction. This possibility entails a double temptation: on the theoretical level, that of nihilism or of radical ethical scepticism;

on the practical level, that of collective suicide (for which that of the Jones sect may serve as a warning signal). The problem, then, is to found an ethics which may, from now on, dispense with the postulate of historical progress as well as with that of a permanent cosmos, and whose validity should be compatible with the essential precariousness of the human condition.

Henrich's analysis, at least in the cited work, is centred on the nuclear bomb. It does not bring it together, as Karl Jaspers[24] had done, with totalitarianism, the former threatening humanity with physical death and the latter with spiritual death. And yet there is a compelling parallel between his reflection and the much-discussed question of ethics after Auschwitz.[25] In both cases the question is whether an experience of evil or of the extreme case, more radical or tragic than the political one indicated by Strauss following Aristotle, does not impose another vision of international politics: a vision for which nothing should be "normal as before", a vision like that of Jan Patocka, for whom the twentieth century as war leaves only one basis for reconstruction, that of what he calls "the community of the shaken", in which an "ethics of dissidence" would provide an escape from the unacceptable dilemmas of universalism and particularism, of absolutism and relativism, of formalism and substantialism.[26]

One could articulate the extreme historical experience of the twentieth century with the permanent nature of ethical problems through a formulation such as Paul Ricoeur's,[27] for whom the victims of the Holocaust are, for us, the representatives of all the victims of history, or through a mental conversion like that of the great Protestant theologian Karl Barth, who went from opposition to nuclear war to opposition against war as such: in that case, Auschwitz and nuclear war would reveal the true nature of collective violence, whether inflicted by governments upon their own people or upon other nations. One should beware, however, of falling into the trap denounced by Strauss[28] of obliterating the very distinction between the extreme and the normal. What the twentieth century has taught us is "what man can do to man",[29] or, more precisely, the possibility of the derecognition of man by man, of the breaking of the common bond constituted by the mutual recognition of human dignity. This does not make this recognition meaningless, but shows us that it is never irreversible, and that our vision of man must include the possibility of something that remains ethically incomprehensible.

From a practical point of view, the consideration of the extreme case, as seen in the light of the twentieth century, shows us that there are absolute limits, more than Strauss seems to indicate. However much, as has been noted, the dilemmas of universal principles and particular situations, the morality of action and abstention, are normally impossible to decide in advance, there are *some* cases where the question is not whether one should act but *how*; and there are *some* means which are simply not permissible. Nobody could maintain that in the name of sovereignty, of non-interference in internal affairs, of the respect of cultural differences, or of the risks for one's own nationals entailed by any forcible action, Hitler should have been left free to proceed with the destruction of the Jews. On the other hand, nobody could advocate retrospectively the nuclear destruction of Germany, of Russia, or of the planet in order to eliminate the totalitarian crimes of Hitler or Stalin. But the fact of knowing that some ends and some means are intrinsically evil, that in some cases we may have to inflict considerable evil in order to stop an absolute one, that some choices are tragic, should not lead us to fall into apocalyptic thinking which denies any normality in the name of the extreme case. It should rather induce us to do everything we can to preserve the chances of peace and moderation, while always keeping in mind what the twentieth century has taught us, namely the fragility of humanity, in both meanings of the term.

Permanent dimensions and new patterns

Examining the dialectics of the universal and the particular, as well as of the normal and the extreme case, may shed at least some light upon the basic dialectics of ethics, that of ends and means, and of international relations, that of actors and structures.

On the one hand, the problem of ends and means is basically permanent, but it is affected by ideological and technological changes whose effects are complex and contradictory. On the other hand, the dialectics between actors and structures are undergoing fundamental changes, due to the decline in the moral authority of the state, the increasing role of transnational forces and alternative communities, and the emergence, however fragmentary and discontinuous, of a feeling of planetary responsibility. In turn, these structural changes constitute an even more serious challenge to the feeling of identity and self-confidence of a deeply divided moral actor in a deeply divided moral universe.

In turn, this leads within individuals, within societies, within the international world, to the struggle of at least two moral codes and attitudes concerning violence, and to the struggle between two processes that the author terms "the embourgeoisement of the barbarian and the barbarization of the bourgeois".

Let us start with the narrowest and most specific problem, that of the ethics of war, which has been heavily dependent on social and historical factors. The late Ernst Gellner, in his last book, was proposing "a new law of three stages":

at first, violence was contingent and optional. At a second stage, violence became pervasive, mandatory and normative. Military skills became central to the dominant ethos. In the third stage, which we are at present entering, violence becomes once again optional, counter-productive and probably fatal.[30]

The crux of the argument is that agricultural societies were static and needed to be warlike to defend a fixed economic product, while with prolonged economic growth the balance went away from coercers towards producers and traders. But if growth stops, the coercers may come back into power, and the evolution of technology may lead to their mutual neutralization or, on the contrary, to an advantage for a nuclear first strike or an increased blackmailing or destructive power for more dispersed groups of more fanatical individuals.

An even broader view would see war first as a man's main activity, both natural and ritualized, and in continuity with hunting and slavery. In a second stage, it becomes exceptional but legitimate as a last resort between constituted communities – *ultima ratio regum*. Finally it becomes at the same time delegitimized and out of control.

From the point of view of its relation to justice, the interplay between *jus ad bellum*, concerning the legitimacy of its ends, of the reasons for going to war, and *jus in bello*, concerning the means used during war itself, is a good guide to its historical evolution. Both *jus ad bellum* and *in bello* are, of course, present in the medieval, Augustinian notion, but one should note an incipient tension between them, since the most just war from the point of view of *jus ad bellum*, the crusade against infidels, is free from the restrictions imposed by *jus in bello*. Until our time, the latter has always had a selective, élitist character, as it applies to adversaries with whom one recognizes having something in common, whereas everything is permitted towards "the others": infidels, barbarians, or "non-civilized" peoples.

With the decline of religion and the emergence of the modern state, *jus ad bellum*, ultimately based on the judgement of the Church, disappears, while *jus in bello* among states which reciprocally recognize each other's legitimacy takes centre stage.[31] But after the French Revolution, popular and ideological passions do away with the conventions and restraints of the eighteenth century's *"guerre en dentelles"*. During the second half of the nineteenth century and the beginning of the twentieth, the emergent humanitarianism of the Red Cross and the peace congresses at The Hague and Geneva tries to reintroduce principles of restraint in war, such as the immunity of non-combatants, the status of war prisoners, or the banning of certain weapons. But the deadly evolution of technologies as well as of bellicose passions (both foreshadowed by the American Civil

War) in the two world wars of the twentieth century seem to do away with any restraint and open the way to any excesses.

Here one encounters again the dialectics of the normal and the extreme. The potentially suicidal character of nuclear war and the genocidal character of total war as practised in the twentieth century seem to delegitimize war as such, at least in the eyes of Western individualistic societies. But, first, versions of the just war are reborn under the form of wars of national liberation or of fundamentalist resistance against the triumphant modern or capitalist culture. Second, the observation that war becames either a crime or a crusade cuts both ways: by becoming a crime it calls for a crusade to eliminate it. The horizontal model pitting state against state tends to be replaced by the vertical model pitting the police against criminals or against the breakdown of law and order. According to Garapon,[32] the Western strikes have to be seen more as an operation of international police than as a war, which was reflected in the tactics used, which were more those appropriate for re-establishing law and order than for destroying an enemy.

Humanitarianism can lead to pacifism or to intervention. In the latter case, both the problem of ends or of *jus ad bellum* and that of means or of *jus in bello* reappear, but under a new form. Especially for intervention in a civil war or against an evil regime, when the intervener can hardly claim the motive of direct self-defence, the question of intervention in the name of whom and to achieve what goes beyond legitimation through national interests. And if the ends are explicitly ethical, the question of the means is all the more delicate. The answer, according to which intervention in the name of the common good is entitled to use whatever means are necessary, leads to the moral impasse of the USA taking as many lives as it saved in Somalia (ultimately to withdraw in order not to risk those of its own soldiers) or causing the death of hundreds of thousands of children through the embargo against Iraq in the name of avoiding the possible use of weapons of mass destruction by Saddam Hussein. Conversely, if the ethics of international intervention require multilateralism and impartiality, if they prohibit the use of force (except in self-defence), including its use for the defence of populations (as against the passive deterrence of attacks against them), the risk is that of paralysis, evidenced by the fate of UNPROFOR in Bosnia, with the tragic ethical as much as pragmatic problems evidenced by the case of Srebrenica.

Some of these problems are closer, as emphasized by Garapon,[33] to those faced by a police force, torn between protection and repression, than to those of a classical army engaged in interstate warfare. The search for weapons of deterrence and control that should not escalate violence, make martyrs of the law-breakers, and kill innocent bystanders or mobilize them against the authorities is familiar to the police forces of liberal states. It is now extended to their armed forces, or at least to those of the USA, with the help of technological progress: this is the so-called "revolution in military affairs" – which can be seen as a search for non-lethal weapons and the progress in sophisticated computers, lasers, and sensors promising to yield the international equivalent of tear gas. The idea is to paralyse or blind the opponent rather than destroy him.

Many of its American proponents have extolled the "revolution's" ethical dimension. Already, during a previous technological phase, strategists like Albert Wohlstetter[34] had hailed the progress of precision as resurrecting proportionality and discrimination and permitting the sparing of civilian populations even in nuclear warfare. Others have denounced this progress in counterforce capabilities as making war more acceptable, jeopardizing its moral delegitimization and creating the illusion of control, whereas in real life the reality of escalation would soon gain the upper hand.[35] This almost happened in Kosovo, when the escalation in the bombing of Serbian cities during the last phase of the war was, while still very limited, clearly no longer limited to military objectives and recalled the terror bombing of the Second World War and Viet Nam. Another aspect that was hard to reconcile with the spirit of the "revolution in military affairs" (RMA) was the use of cluster bombs.[36]

The danger is not the same with the new non-lethal technologies associated with the RMA, nor with its priority of information (and its denial) over destruction. Yet they have one flaw in common, as Lawrence Freedman[37] keeps tirelessly pointing out: the tacit assumption of symmetry. The RMA is particularly effective against an opponent of the same kind as the USA, which applies the same strategy using the same weapons. It can certainly have its uses in peace-keeping, but, conversely, weak adversaries may fairly easily develop a capacity for at least partially and temporarily disrupting the sophisticated systems of the technologically advanced: this is the ever-recurring theme of cyberwarfare. But predominantly, the smaller and weaker states, and even more the protagonists in civil wars subject to the intervention of the "international community" and of great powers acting or not acting on its behalf, have an interest in changing the rules of the game, in using their own less sophisticated and less costly weapons, and, above all, in escalating the costs for the "new interventionists"[38] by threatening or hurting what they value most: the life of their citizens, whether military or civilian.

This is all the more tempting when the weaker power or group is, anyway, targeting primarily civilian populations, when it is playing for the most absolute ends, those of religious fanaticism, or for the highest stakes, those of the creation or the collapse of nation-states, whereas for the interventionists or the peace-keepers, ends and stakes are relative and certainly subordinate to the peace, security, and prosperity of their own societies. The asymmetry in the physical power, on the one hand, and in the willingness to take and inflict pain and death, on the other, combines the dimension of ends and means. But it is clear that it involves even more than that. The key asymmetry which is emerging more and more clearly is that which concerns the nature or identity of the *actors* and the *structure* of the global arena.

The level-of-analysis problem is central to international relations theory. It acquires an ethical importance with the emergence of "situational ethics", and within a tradition that from Aristotle to Hegel refuses to separate the question of ethics from that of the political community. The moral subject, for this tradition, is neither the Kantian rational person defined by its relation to the pure form of the law, nor the unique individual defined by his existential solitude and his anxiety in front of his absolute freedom. He cannot be separated from a tradition, a heritage, a context, which inserts his rights, his duties, his moral education within a structure that he has not created. In a sense, this is the case even for the Kantian subject who is a member of a kingdom of ends or a republic of rational beings, or for the existential subject whose basic moral experience, for Levinas, is the encounter with the other.

Crucial to all these versions is the notion of reciprocity, or of a shared intersubjectivity that is reflected and channelled by institutions. But today, it is this sense of reciprocity that can less and less be taken for granted, it is these institutions which seem to have lost their reassuring stability. In this situation, which Hannah Arendt[39] calls "worldlessness", the individual and the universal seem to meet face to face in their immediate nakedness. Yet neither can be an agent in international relations without some mediating collective structures. The central point is that these structures, having lost their obvious and exclusive character, are felt as overlapping and conflicting, fragile and transient.

In a world of divided loyalties and cross-cutting alignments, the moral dilemmas of the individual between his social, national, ethnic, and religious identities are a source of deep anxiety, often resolved through violence. Precisely because one does not know what one is, one tries to find an identity by the exclusion of the other. As Ignatieff[40] remarks, very often being a Serb means above all not being a Croat, and vice versa.

At a second level, the moral subject is no longer the individual but the collective body, the Leviathan created by individuals but endowed with a moral authority and moral obligations of its own. The notion of a "moral person" is a legal one, but the notion of sovereignty can endow it in the case of a state with a moral and quasi-religious authority which defines not only the duties of the subjects towards the state, but those of the state towards them and its rights and duties towards other sovereign states.

One may argue indefinitely whether the ultimate kernel of the notion of sovereignty (the "*Kompetenz-Kompetenz*"; today, the Schmittian[41] freedom to decide on the exceptional situation) is still valid in the abstract, but there is no way of denying that its actual exercise is considerably weakened by the even stronger affirmation of substate, transstate and suprastate actors and forces, and, above all, by the necessity of a permanent compromise between sovereignty and responsibility.[42] This responsibility may be particular or universal, it may be based on the evils of the past or on the dangers of the future, but it is oriented both towards individuals and towards the planet, it is defined both by universal principles and by exceptional situations. As far as violence is concerned, it is again the shadow of the Holocaust and that of nuclear destruction which, ultimately, legitimize international intervention in violation of the sovereignty of states.

But whose intervention, and in whose name? What is important, here, is to resist the temptation of replacing the imagined abstractions of state sovereignty by other abstract entities such as "the international community" and "the rule of law". As Badie[43] shows, power and responsibility are in constant interplay; states, along with other actors, may use the claim of responsibility for their own aims of territorial sovereignty, or the intangibility of borders may be more and more honoured in the breach or conflict with other principles such as the self-determination of peoples, but they still correspond to a reality which, however much we may need to "re-imagine political community"[44] in the direction of cosmopolitan democracy, has not been replaced by a coherent and effective alternative.

The world is still, at the same time, Westphalian, pre-Westphalian and post-Westphalian. It is neither a hierarchical empire, nor a multipolar balance between sovereign states, nor a complete anarchy, but a combination of all three. Yet, in the interstices of the politics of power and inequality – whether interstate or transnational – some new elements are beginning to interject an ethical perspective. They range from voluntary movements such as "borderless" humanitarian organizations to institutions like the International Court of Justice and, even more, the International Criminal Tribunals on Former Yugoslavia and Rwanda, the International Criminal Court, the European Court of Human Rights, and the various "truth and reconciliation" commissions. They are alerting the public and challenging governments. The public doesn't listen for very long and the governments don't change their behaviour very deeply, but they have to react: they can less and less turn a blind eye or a deaf ear.

It is in this sense that we do witness the beginnings of an international civil society, even though it has to go against the two dominant trends of McWorld and Djihad (to use Benjamin Barber's[45] formulation), of a soulless globalization oblivious to and destructive of differences, and of an intolerant, fanatical, or nihilistic reassertion of national, ethnic, cultural, and religious identities.

As far as violence is concerned, the task consists of trying to break the cycle or the dialectic of the bourgeois and the barbarian, of an indirect, sanitized violence based on economics and technology, and of a brutal, murderous, or suicidal one based on the dehumanization of enemies. This means preventing the barbarization of the bourgeois and going beyond the embourgeoisement of the barbarian, in order to rediscover the virtues of dialogue and to reinvent the figure of the citizen. In this sense, the search for ethics in international relations should lead us beyond ethics and beyond international relations towards a rebirth of philosophy and a new birth of politics.

Notes

1. Toscano, R., 2001, "The Ethics of Modern Diplomacy", in this volume.
2. Goodin, R., 1988, "What's So Special about Our Fellow Countrymen?", *Ethics*, 98, July; Miller, D., 1988 "The Ethical Significance of Nationality", *Ethics*, 98, July.
3. Hassner, P., 1997, *Violence and Peace*. Budapest: Central European University Press.
4. Fishkin, J., 1986, "Theories of Justice and International Relations: The Limits of Liberal Theory", in Ellis, A., ed., *Ethics and International Relations*. Manchester: Manchester University Press, pp. 10–11.
5. Hassner, P., 1973, "On ne badine pas avec la paix", *Revue française de science politique*, March.
6. Walzer, M., 1977, *Just and Unjust War*. New York: Basic Books.
7. Arendt, H., 1969, "On Violence", in Arendt, H., ed., *Crises of the Republic*. New York: Harcourt.
8. Hosbawm, E., 1999, *Prospect*, p. 34.
9. Kant, I., 1960, *Religion Within the Limits of Reason Alone*. New York: Harper and Row.
10. Strauss, L., 1959, *What is Political Philosophy?* Glencoe: Free Press, p. 35.
11. Wight, M., 1991, *International Theory. Three Traditions*. Leicester: Leicester University Press.
12. Bull, H., 1977, *The Anarchical Society*. New York: Columbia University Press.
13. Beitz, C., 1979, *Political Theory and International Relations*. Princeton: Princeton University Press.
14. Ignatieff, M., 1998, *The Warrior's Horror. Ethnic War and Modern Conscience*. New York: Holt, pp. 18–21.
15. Garapon, A., 1999, "De Nürenberg au TPI: Naissance d'une justice universelle?", *Critique Internationale*, No. 5, pp. 167–180.
16. Hassner, P., 1998, "From War and Peace to Violence and Intervention", in Moore, J., ed., *Hard Choices*, Lanham: Rowman and Littlefield.
17. Ignatieff, note 14 above, p. 20.
18. Hassner, P., 1999, "Guerre sans morts ou morts sans guerre? Les paradoxes de l'intervention au Kosovo", *Critique Internationale*, No. 4.
19. Wolfers, A., 1962, *Discord and Collaboration*. Baltimore: Johns Hopkins University Press.

20. Hosbawm, E., 1994, The Age of Extremes: A History of the World, 1914–1994. New York: Random House.
21. Strauss, L., 1950, *Natural Right and History*. Chicago: University of Chicago Press, pp. 160–161.
22. *Ibid.*, p. 162.
23. Henrich, D., 1990, *Ethik zum nuklearen Frieden*. Frankfurt: Suhrkamp.
24. Jaspers, K., 1961, *The Future of Mankind*. Chicago: University of Chicago Press.
25. Diner, D., 1999, ed., *Zivilisations buch. Denken nach Auschwitz*. Frankfurt: Fischer.
26. Laignel-Lavastine, A., 1998, *Patocka*. Paris: Ed. Michalon.
27. Ricoueur, P., 2000, *La Mémoire, l'Histoire, l'Oubli*. Paris: Seuil.
28. Strauss, note 21 above.
29. Revault d'Allonnes, M., 1995, *Ce que l'homme fait à l'homme*. Paris: Seuil; Revault d'Allonnes, M., 1998, "A l'épreuve des camps: L'imagination du semblable", *Philosophie*, No. 6.
30. Gellner, E., 1995, *Anthropology and Politics*. Oxford: Blackwell.
31. Pangle, T. and Ahrensdorf, P., 1999, *Justice Among Nations. On the Moral Basis of Power and Peace*. Kansas: University Press of Kansas.
32. Garapon, note 15 above.
33. *Ibid.*
34. Wohlstetter, A., 1983, "Bishops, Statesmen and Other Strategists on the Bombing of Innocents", *Commentary*, June.
35. Hassner, note 3 above.
36. Dickey, C., 1999, "The Seeds of Carnage", *Newsweek*, 2 August, pp. 28–30.
37. Freedman, L., 1995, *The Revolution in Strategic Affairs*. London: IISS, Adelphi Papers, No. 318.
38. Mayall, J., 1996, *The New Interventionists*. Cambridge: Cambridge University Press.
39. Arendt, note 7 above.
40. Ignatieff, note 14 above.
41. Schmitt, C., 1927, *Das Begriff des Politischen*. Berlin: Dunkler-Humbolt.
42. Badie, B., 1998, *Un monde sans souveraineté. Les etats entre ruse et raison*. Paris: Fayard.
43. *Ibid.*
44. Archibugi, D., Held, D., and Kohler, M., 1998, *Re-imaging Political Community*. Cambridge: Polity Press.
45. Barber, B., 1995, *Djihad Against the World*. New York: Timsbooks.

5

Justice and international order: The case of Bosnia and Kosovo

David Campbell

Introduction

The war in Bosnia and the conflict in Kosovo were fought and responded to in terms of dominant international relations' framings of political possibilities (nationalist principles versus cosmopolitan relations, order versus justice, sovereignty versus responsibility, national interest versus humanitarianism, barbarism versus civilization, etc.). However, the widely registered abhorrence of certain actions and policies, and the much-maligned character of the international community's response (despite it appearing to be different in each case), call into question these framings – or at least expose their political costs. The purpose of this chapter is to discuss, from a perspective informed by continental philosophy (especially post-structuralism) the limitations of traditional renderings of justice and international ethics as exemplified in Bosnia and Kosovo. Important to this discussion is a reflection on the limited purchase of a continuing faith in the structuring of possibilities in terms of universalism/particularism, and how, in this context, politics can be rethought and a new political bond posited. The chapter does not claim, however, that a philosophical reworking of the problems will guide a political solution. Rather, the purpose is to expose the power of certain assumptions, consider their effects, and reflect on how they constrain debate.

Competing conceptions of justice

Despite the sense of justice being a universal if not natural category, it is, like all other political terms, open to different interpretations. Some interpretations have, however, come to be better established than others. Among the most dominant is a notion of justice with a formal and procedural cast. According to Brown,[1] justice involves the application of rules governed by impartiality, especially "the idea that some entity (an individual, a people, a community, a state, an ecosphere) is entitled, as a matter of right rather than charity, to receive the treatment proper to it".

Within international relations, of course, justice has been understood in these terms through its juxtaposition to order. Best explicated by Hedley Bull,[2] the contrast between justice and international order relies on a conventional rendering of the idea of justice. In particular, Bull invokes Aristotle's formulation that justice involves "a particular kind of right conduct, viz. conduct in which persons are treated fairly, or given the rights and benefits that are due to them". In this sense, right conduct can be achieved arithmetically (equality of principle) or proportionately (equality of outcome through distributive means).

Thus conceived, justice is a concern ancillary to the assumptions underpinning notions of order. Justice, though important and always desired, comes second to the prior emphasis accorded that most basic norm of international society, sovereignty. While conduct that supports the rights due to persons or like entities is to be pursued, it is always pursued within the already established strictures of international order. It is for this reason that arguments about the pursuit of justice in international practice – such as Walzer's[3] seminal argument about just and unjust wars – are more often than not focused upon exceptions or exceptional circumstances. Rarely if ever do they suggest a more thoroughgoing questioning of the way justice, order, and their coeval relationship have been problematized.

Alternative problematizations of justice nonetheless exist. From the perspective of post-structuralist thought, justice takes on a different hue, as another justice.[4] Rather than presuppose an already existing state of international order, a post-structuralist perspective takes a step or two back to rework some key ontological assumptions. Above all else, and before all else, post-structuralist conceptions of justice (and ethics generally) are concerned with the politics and production of subjectivity within the context of the unavoidable and inescapable relationship to the other. Rather than justice being ancillary to this relationship, justice is the relationship to the other. Accordingly, it is justice when we are open to the surprise of the other, acknowledge the other's summons, or are willing to be unsettled by our encounters with others. The relationship to the other is the context of the political; it is the site of an irreducible responsibility, and yet it is in the relationship to the other that responsibility is often suppressed or effaced by violence.[5]

Derrida,[6] for whom justice is outside and beyond the law, informs this understanding. For Derrida, "justice is the experience of the impossible". Justice is not a principle, or a foundation, or a guiding tradition. Justice is infinite, and – in a favourable comparison to Levinas's notion of justice – "the heteronomic relation to others, to the faces of otherness that govern me, whose infinity I cannot thematize and whose hostage I remain". In these terms, justice is the pre-original, anarchic relation to the other, and integral to the undecidable. It represents the domain of the impossible and unrepresentable that lies outside and beyond the limit of the possible and representable. But it cannot be understood as "utopian", at least in so far as that means the opposite of "realistic". It is not indeterminate. It is undecidable. It is that which marks the limit of the possible; indeed, it is that which brings the domain of the possible into being and gives it the ongoing chance for transformation and refiguration, that which is one of the conditions of possibility for ethics and politics.[7]

Conventional approaches to ethics: A critique

Because of their differing ontological positionings, post-structuralist themes have found little place in the growing literature on ethics and international relations. As Brown[8] concluded, "the postmodern turn seems unlikely to provide new thinking on international justice as conventionally understood". This might, however, say more about the conventional international relations literature – and the sense of justice conventionally understood – than post-structuralism. That is because, from a broader perspective, ethics sometimes finds little place in the international relations literature. Famous as a way of understanding how this has come to be the case is George Kennan's[9] oft-cited belief that "the interests of the national society for which government has to concern itself are basically those of its military security, the integrity of its political life, and the well-being of its people. These needs have no moral quality." Although perhaps a sharper and more unequivocal formulation than most would make, Kennan's declaration nonetheless encapsulates concisely the realist tradition's view that moral concerns are largely inappropriate to international affairs.[10]

Most importantly, what enabled Kennan and others to claim the divorce of national interests and state security from morality is a spatial imaginary in which the virtues of sovereignty are unproblematically affirmed.

However, this affirmation of sovereignty is itself insinuated with moral considerations, for it is a stance which is enabled by faith in the notion of *raison d'état*, an acceptance of the priority accorded the security of the state. Far from being a principle which keeps morality at bay, reason of state constitutes the realist problematic as a moral argument in which the claim is that "the reasons for overriding the constraints of ordinary morality in emergency situations are themselves moral".[11]

Kennan's problematization of the issue thus requires one to overlook the way in which the "the national" is itself a "moral" construction. Eliding the ethical investments of "amoral" formulations is something that, because of the recent march of "normative theory" in international relations, is superficially at least increasingly difficult to sustain. Indeed, the intellectual contestations of a discipline caught cold by the global transformations of the last decade have been marked by the resurgence of moral questions and dilemmas, with "ethics and international affairs" becoming something of a growth literature.[12]

This moral cartography of realism, manifest in Kennan's paradigmatic claim about the amorality of sovereignty, has, however, done more than legitimize the evacuation of ethical concerns from international relations. It has also circumscribed the "ethics and international affairs" literature that seeks to redress the moral lacunae of the field. In this literature, the dilemmas of ethical theorizing are generally posed in terms of ameliorating or overcoming – rather than contesting and problematizing – the parameters of anarchy and sovereignty.

As a result, the "ethics and international affairs" literature is based on some questionable fundamentals. In the first instance, there is the unsustainable assumption that "normative" concerns manifest issues and practices hitherto unknown or unrecognized, and that they can be distinguished from a realm called "empirical theory". Secondly, having allegedly disentangled the normative from the empirical, the claim that problems can be dealt with by the joining in intellectual marriage of an already established political theory literature of ethics and the untheorized domain of international relations is open to serious question. All of which suggests that this literature is compromised by the orthodox frames of reference within which enquiry is largely contained.

These orthodox frames of reference – and the accounts of the (im)-probability of ethical action in international relations they license – follow a familiar trajectory. They depend upon the notion of a prior and autonomous sovereign subjectivity (whether it be the individual, the state, or some other corporate actor) deploying either a supposedly universal moral code (the deontological view), or muddling through their situation in order to achieve what might be thought of as the best possible outcome (the consequentialist account). In more specific terms, these concerns are mostly articulated in the context of a debate between communitarians and cosmopolitans, with both camps searching for a singular ethical theory that could be devised in the abstract and applied in the concrete.[13] Judged from within these confines, where justice is said to be about impartial rules, the impact of more critical approaches is deemed to be insufficient.[14]

Any new approach to ethics and world politics must involve a shift of focus from that which constitutes the familiar field of "ethics and international affairs". Rather than engaging in the traditional search for a grounding for supranational principles, we have to investigate the contingencies involved in specific, historically situated encounters. This is because responding effectively to the dilemmas that emerge from the spatial assumptions of the realist *problematique*, as well as the communitarian/cosmopolitan debate, requires a sustained consideration of the relationship between space, subjectivity, and ethics. This can be revealed in the link between community and responsibility, which leads to the thought that the search for communities in which responsibility can be grounded should itself be reconsidered.

The most general insight, which integrates post-structuralist perspectives, is recognition of the radical entanglement between moral discourses and spatial imaginaries. Accordingly, a primary emphasis is placed on "moral spaces",[15] the bounded locations whose inhabitants acquire the privileges deriving from practices of ethical inclusion, and on the need to intervene in the dominant practices of intelligibility which allow geopolitical imaginaries at the expense of an ethics of encounter.

From ethical theory to the ethical relation

In constituting an alternative to the increasingly familiar field of "ethics and international affairs" that has dominated recent thinking about ethics and world politics, a post-structuralist perspective rethinks both the nature of "international" and "ethics" as well as the relationship between those terms. While this alternative – if we can speak of a singular position emerging from shared sensibilities – does not stand in opposition to all that has gone before, it does distinguish itself from some common and central formulations that predominate in international relations literature.[16]

Most obviously this alternative is "against theory" in so far as it resists the desire for *a* theory of ethics that articulates abstracted principles in a systematized manner. In consequence, rather than being concerned with a *theory of ethics*, the ethical relation in which our responsibility to the other is the basis for reflection motivates this perspective. Eschewing hierarchical constructions of moral value, it focuses instead on the ethical situation integral to experience. Such an argument might also be thought of as being "against ethics". This position does not mean people wish to promote or be associated with the non-ethical or the amoral. Instead, it contests the idea that the development of a theory of ethics produces a body of thought called "ethics" removed from the contexts of concern.

In this context, and given the centrality of universality/particularism to most discussions of this topic, some reflections on what rethinking ethics means for the status of the "universal" are warranted. A post-structuralist perspective refigures our understanding of the relationship between the universal and the particular, and, indeed, the manner in which that relationship is in the first place conceivable. Thought tagged in this manner has long been (mis)interpreted as inhabiting only one side of the dualism. It has been argued, in asides too numerous to mention, that post-structuralist critiques favour the particular and thereby denigrate the universal, inviting in consequence a host of illiberal outcomes; that, by questioning in a critical spirit all that is involved in the positing of the universal, relativism is celebrated. Yet such observations fail to heed the other side of the coin. In this context, the notion of the universal and the particular remains, but these terms come to represent something other than antinomies existing autonomously in a relationship of contradiction. Instead, they exist in a relationship of radical interdependence and are each contaminated by the trace of the other.

This can be best examined by reflecting on the emergent forms of conflict that are said to mark the post-Cold War world. What we have seen in so-called "ethnic" and "nationalist" struggles appears to be the political demise of universalism and its practical substitution by particularism. That is because each of these struggles operates not in terms of the aspirations of a "universal subject" (such as a class) or a "universal history" (such as class struggle), but in terms of a particular subject (a specific ethnic or national group) and a particular history (the aspirations of that group).

However, even in these terms, the apparent political demise of universalism cannot be said to have produced the theoretical dissolution of universalism. It has, instead, led to its reconfiguration. The universalism of today is one enabled by the assertion of particularism, it is a "universality that is the very result of particularism".[17] That is because the right of national self-determination involves the declaration of a universal principle, albeit a universal principle that derives its force from the plurality of particular groups seeking self-determination because of their heterogeneous singularity, rather than a universal subject confident of its homogeneity and global applicability. As Rodolphe Gasché, writing in terms of how best to comprehend a thought as philosophically radical as Derrida's, states: "Paradoxically, even the most radical singularity must, in order for it to be recognized for what it is, have an addressable identity, guaranteed by a set of universal rules that, by the same token, inscribe its singularity within a communal history, tradition, and problematics."[18]

However, the particular or singular does not exist and cannot be known as such. As with the radical interdependence of the decision and the undecidable, the possible and the impossible, the particular and the universal might only be conceivable in relation to one another. It might be said that the universal can only be witnessed in moments of particularity, and the particular can only be rendered through a universal concept. The claims of "ethnic" or "national" particularism would themselves then be regarded as a form of limited universalism.

Being "against" theory, ethics and justice are thus a matter of being against the orthodox renderings of those domains and the ethico-political effects of those renderings. Being "against" theory, ethics and justice stem in large part from a suspicion that those preoccupied with theories of ethics end up eliding the ethical relation; that the concern with "ethics" obscures the contingencies and complexities of the ethical; and that a striving for the rules and principles of justice, especially those that demand impartiality, effects injustice. In this context, being "against" theory, ethics and justice are an affirmative position designed to foster the ethical relation.

Integral to an affirmative position that fosters the ethical relation is a reworked basis for political action. It is possible to take the insights of the above argument about rethinking ethics – especially the need to intervene in dominant practices of intelligibility and to investigate contingencies and specific, historically situated encounters – and articulate a political sense animated by and consistent with these injunctions. However, as with the notion that a post-structuralist understanding of ethics and justice is "against" the conventional positions of ethical theory, this political rethinking involves being against some assumptions that many consider essential for politics *per se*.

Most importantly, the affirmative politics consistent with this argument resists the idea that a prior normative framework, generating established principles for action, is the requirement of a just politics. Instead, the argument here is that the centrality of the ethical relation, our responsibility to the other, provides a sufficient principle to serve justice. Specifically, this is the idea that we should engage in a struggle for – or on behalf of – alterity rather than a struggle to efface, erase, or eradicate alterity.[19] Importantly, this political figuration encourages distinctions between antagonisms, conflicts, pluralities, and multiplicities. All are permitted, but not all forms of difference permit all to be. In this sense, a principle concerned with struggle for and on behalf of alterity cannot be read as an ethic of tolerance for the intolerable. The principle being articulated here goes beyond the static confines of tolerance and maintains that the active affirmation of alterity *must* involve the desire actively to oppose and resist – perhaps, depending upon the circumstances, even violently – those forces that efface, erase, or suppress alterity and its centrality to the economy of humanity. That which is to be opposed is not simply that which causes disturbance or irritation. There will always be an agonistic and sometimes antagonistic relationship between the numerous identities and settlements which variously contain difference. Instead, what must be opposed are the relations of power which, in dealing with difference, move from disturbance to oppression, from irritation to repression, and, most obviously, from contestation to eradication. In other words, racism, xenophobia, neo-liberal globalization strategies, ethnic-nationalist violence, fascism, and the like; "moral visions which suppress the constructed, contingent, relational character of identity".[20]

Importantly, this principle establishes the basis for a new political bond that can foster solidarity and collective action. It speaks to the idea of a political bond enabled by government's continuing power and our implication in those practices of governmentality that traverse our lives. It figures a new form of universality that does not rely on any a priori sense of essential sameness. It is thus a political bond with some similarities to that identified by Derrida as marking "a new International":

> There is today an aspiration towards a bond between singularities [not "political subjects" nor even "human beings"] all over the world. This bond not only extends beyond nations and states, such as they are composed today or such as they are in the process of decomposition, but extends beyond the very concepts of nation or state. For example, if I feel in solidarity with this particular Algerian who is caught between F.I.S. and the Algerian state, or this particular Croat, Serbian or Bosnian, or this particular South African, this particular Russian or Ukrainian, or whoever – it's not a feeling of one citizen towards another, it's not a feeling peculiar to a citizen of the world, as if we were all potentially or imaginary citizens of a great state. No, what binds me to these people is something different than membership of a world nation-state or of an international community extending indefinitely what one still calls today "the nation-state". What binds me to them – and this is the point; there is a bond, but this bond cannot be contained within traditional concepts of community, obligation or responsibility – is a protest against citizenship, a protest against membership of a political configuration as such. This bond is, for example, *a form of political solidarity opposed to the political* qua *a politics tied to the nation-state*.[21]

The case of Bosnia

Bosnia was the second crisis of the post-Cold War world, following shortly after the allied success (at least from the official perspective) of

the Gulf War. But in contrast to the decisive action and clearly articulated objectives of that conflict, the war in Bosnia saw only military
inaction and political confusion on the part of Europe and the USA.[22]
While images of concentration camps and details of ethnic cleansing were
widely evident, and despite the post-Second World War conviction that
such things should "never again" happen, few governments regarded the
conflict a sufficient threat to their vital interests to warrant the commitment of men, women, or *matériel*. When a NATO plan (OpPlan 40-104)
for military deployment was drawn up, its aim was to provide cover for a
possible UN withdrawal from Bosnia. This indicated that the alliance was
willing to commit forces to implement a failure – to provide cover for a
retreat from even the hitherto limited "humanitarian" involvement – but
not to address the politics of the problem.[23]

Inaction with regard to Bosnia was a product of neither inattentivness
nor lack of discussion on the part of officials in the USA. The Bush
administration was aware of the forthcoming break-up of Yugoslavia and
its likely consequences, but concluded it knew of no way to prevent
it without reinforcing the idea that the USA should be the world's
policeman.[24] In the Clinton administration, Bosnia was much discussed,
but "most high-level meetings on Bosnia had a dispirited, inconclusive
quality ... Although no one could ignore the crisis, there was little en-
thusiasm for any proposal of action, no matter what it was. The result was
often inaction or half-measures instead of a clear strategy."[25]

Part of the reason for this "collective spinelessness" was that the policies that were implemented for Bosnia were not directed at Bosnia *per
se*.[26] Instead, as the second crisis of the post-Cold War period, Bosnia
became a symbol of US foreign policy, and, most significantly, a site upon
which the USA could trial aspects of its strategies for this new era in
which the Cold War guidelines for intervention were no longer operative.
Indeed, at various times during the four years of the Bosnian war, the
USA and its European allies declared that what was important was not so
much a specific event or issue in Bosnia, but what that event or issue
meant for the alliance between Europe and the USA, and especially the
"credibility" of one or other of the partners. If the inaction of allied
forces meant that the USA looked weak and unable to lead, then this was
a problem – not because it meant little was being done for Bosnia, but
because the image of the USA suffered. The pivot for US policy towards
Bosnia was therefore more often than not US concern about itself and its
allies, rather than a concern for Bosnia.

By the summer of 1995 the feeling that the ongoing war in Bosnia was,
regardless of US reluctance, an affront to the USA was particularly acute
in the highest reaches of the US administration. This egotism of policy
combined with developments in the war to produce a more robust
American commitment of diplomacy in sync with force designed to end

the war. As the chief negotiator of the Dayton accords, Richard Holbrooke, argued:

Strategic considerations were vital to our involvement, but the motives that finally pushed the United States into action were also moral and humanitarian. After Srebrenica and Mount Igman the United States could no longer escape the terrible truth of what was happening in Bosnia ... Within the Administration, the loss of three friends on Mount Igman carried a special weight; the war had, in effect, come home.[27]

For Holbrooke, the massacre of thousands of Bosnian Muslims at Srebrenica in July 1995, and the death in a road accident on Mount Igman above Sarajevo of three of his negotiating team, finally meant the war had "come home". Of course, for millions of Bosnians the war had been at home, and about their homes, for more than three years, with disastrous effects. But although the carnage of this period had been much evident to the world during that time, it took something more immediate to the self to force action.

When action was forthcoming it was in the form of a strategy combining NATO air-strikes and the ground forces of the Bosnian and Croation armies working in tandem with Contact Group, resulting in the Dayton agreement of November 1995. The result brooked few surprises, as it installed the same political anthropology of international diplomacy – that is, the same assumptions about identity, territory, and sovereignty – which had marked the international community's response from the outset of the Bosnian conflict in 1992. The result was an effectively partitioned polity organized along ethnic lines, resembling more than anything the logic of apartheid that had recently been defeated in southern Africa.[28] Much of the politics and prospects of post-Dayton Bosnia – especially the tension between integration and partition that constitutes the Dayton agreement, and the contrast between national interest and humanitarian interests which shapes the prospects for a continuing response by the international community – are governed by this framing of the issue. The ethical relation is thereby officially elided.

The case of Kosovo

In the aftermath of Operation Allied Force – NATO's extensive bombing campaign against the Federal Republic of Yugoslavia, in response to Serbian aggression against the Kosovan Albanian population – the contrast with the international community's response to the war in Bosnia seems clear and stark. On closer reflection, however, there are, regrettably, more similarities than are first apparent, as will be demonstrated via a brief overview of the situation in Kosovo up to and including the violent events of 1999. Moreover, the debate engendered by Operation Allied Force – especially the criticisms of those from the left opposed to NATO's actions – shows how conventional renderings of the situation, manifesting assumptions similar to the ethics and international affairs literature, appear empty in the face of violence, especially when it constitutes genocide. In this sense, addressing situations such as Kosovo requires a move away from traditional ethical theories towards an appreciation and cultivation of the ethical relation.

Post mortems of Operation Allied Force, in a manner similar to criticisms expressed throughout the campaign, have tended to focus on the immediate tactical issues of air power as an instrument used to address ethnic cleansing and genocide.[29] While not unimportant – especially in so far as a strategy designed to avoid allied casualties at all costs represents a questionable ethical calculus given the horrors it was supposed to address – this preoccupation is rather limited, narrow, and ultimately depoliticizing. It reduces everything to the issue of military tactics in the present, rather than political and military strategy in historical perspective. This depoliticization of the issues is something to be addressed by a renewed focus on the larger political strategies at stake in the conflict. Without such a perspective, which must include a reconsideration of the politics of identity pertaining to the protagonists in this context (something which, however, cannot be considered in detail here), the ethical relation cannot be fostered.[30]

Above all else, we have to recognize that Kosovo is not an isolated incident in a series of discrete Balkan problems; it is part of the end game in Milosevic's campaign for a greater, and largely "ethnically pure", Serbia. Nor does the "victory" of Operation Allied Force and the return of the refugees to their homes mark an end to such conflict. The vengeful instances of ethnic cleansing in reverse – the violence against remaining Serbs in Kosovo perpetrated by their prior victims – as well as concern for the future of Montenegro and the Sandzak region of Serbia illustrate that these issues live on.

As has frequently been noted, Kosovo was instrumental in the start of the wars of dissolution and secession that comprised the demise of Tito's Yugoslavia. Kosovo was the context from which, and the issue upon which, Milosevic mobilized nationalist politics and authorized nationalist violence in the late 1980s. Having been only partially successful in his ethno-political goals – the "success" being the establishment of an autonomous Serbian entity within the borders of Bosnia – the same logic of political identity and associated violence was operationalized in the same manner in Kosovo by the Serbian authorities.

As such, the "current" conflict in Kosovo dates most recently from the 1989 removal by Milosevic of the substantial autonomy Tito granted the province in the 1974 constitution. The implementation of direct, authoritarian, and colonial rule from Belgrade created an apartheid-like climate for the non-Serbian majority resident in Kosovo, with official strategies from Belgrade designed to marginalize the majority under the discriminatory rule of the minority. For example, school buildings were literally divided down the middle, with separate entrances for separate groups; laws on language that banned Kosovo Albanian and renamed all streets and public spaces in Cyrillic script were implemented; Kosovars were dismissed from their jobs in the public sector and systematically replaced with Serbs; and property laws – detailed in a not-so-subtly titled "Decree of Colonization" issued by the government of the Federal Republic of Yugoslavia (FRY) in 1995 – made Serb settlement easy and cheap, while banning sale or rental of property by Serbs to Albanians.[31] The overall climate has been termed by Human Rights Watch as constituting "the status quo of repression".[32] Throughout this time, of course, Milosevic's Belgrade regime was being actively engaged as a force for peace in the negotiations concerning the future of Bosnia. Despite ritual denunciations, Serbia's apartheid-like policies in Kosovo were not taken to be a problem of significance in their own right by the international community.

In the aftermath of the 1989 revocation of autonomy, Kosovars responded by developing their own parallel society, especially in the realms of education and health, as part of their self-proclaimed "Republic of Kosovo" (which was declared in 1991). Notwithstanding this organized, peaceful resistance, the discriminatory climate in Kosovo throughout the 1990s saw large-scale Kosovan emigration from the province, with 350,000 residents departing. Nearly 230,000 were relocated in Germany, but in October 1996 – at the same time as Germany was forcibly repatriating Bosnians to places other than their former homes – Germany and the FRY agreed to repatriate more than half the Kosovars. Only about 3,000 had returned by the end of 1997, with more than 70 per cent reapplying for asylum.[33]

Interestingly, the extensive emigration of Kosovars was not matched by widespread immigration of Serbs. Despite the much-promulgated mythology of the nationalist significance and religious symbolism of Kosovo as Serbia's "heartland", the region was not an attractive destination for Serbs from the Krajina in Croatia. Although the regime in Belgrade actively encouraged settlement by displaced Serbs – resulting in some 20,000 of the 150,000 Krajina Serbs moving to the province – they have been reluctant immigrants, often publicly protesting about their politically motivated relocation. Together, these confluences of population movement suggest some interesting conclusions: firstly, that implementing the idea of an Albanian-free Kosovo is a relatively new strategy for the Serbian regime, despite having been a long-standing ideological aim; secondly, that the power of nationalist myths concerning Kosovo is not as central as sometimes maintained, notwithstanding the obvious historical importance of certain cultural sites; and, thirdly, that Western European altruism *vis-à-vis* refugees is often less impressive and more infrequent than it first appears.

The most recent escalation of violence in Kosovo occurred in early 1998; it presaged a change, albeit a slow one, in the international community's policy concerning Kosovo. In February 1998, Serbian special police (the anti-terrorist units of the Ministry of Interior) and paramilitaries began an offensive loosely – very loosely – targeted against Kosovar separatists in the Drenica region. To some extent, the USA and its allies seemed to rationalize this campaign by declaring that the Kosovo Liberation Army (KLA) were – as in Serbian parlance – "terrorists" whose activities had to be condemned.

The novelty of armed repression in Kosovo – as opposed to the many and varied instruments of "civilian" repression pursued by the Serbian regime throughout the 1990s – stems in large part from the fact that the KLA is a very recent entrant to Kosovan politics. Beginning with isolated strikes against Serbian police in late 1996, the KLA expanded its activities in 1997 after social chaos in Albania saw that country's military stockpile looted. Better armed as a result, the KLA in September 1997 began a series of more coordinated raids against the Serbian regime's forces in Kosovo.[34]

The Serbian paramilitary response in the spring of 1998 used a "scorched-earth" policy to terrorize and uproot Kosovar populations from their homes. Unlike the mass killings associated with this strategy in Bosnia, this practice involved fewer deaths; in the Drenica valley, for example, some 80 people were murdered and some 15,000 properties were torched. Although the action was ostensibly targeted only against the "terrorist" KLA, civilians were its victims. The aim – and the effect – was to create a large refugee population, which the UNHCR calculated numbered more than 240,000 displaced Kosovars by August 1998.[35] When the operation was expanded and hastened in early 1999, it crucially included the confiscation or destruction of any documentary evidence (identity cards, birth certificates, property titles, and the like) which connected people to the places where they lived.[36]

Importantly, recalling these developments puts into question the commonly expressed view that the even larger forced displacement of the Kosovar population in the days and weeks after Operation Allied Force began on 24 March 1999 was a result of the bombing rather than Serbian policy. Recalling the conflict in 1998 and the refugee population that was deliberately created in the year prior to NATO's bombing demonstrates that forced population transfer was an established part of Serbian policy prior to NATO's air-strikes. While the Serbian regime probably accelerated its plans once the bombing began, those plans were in place well before 24 March. As Fred Abrahams[37] of Human Rights Watch observed:

Violations of the rules of war increased in both intensity and frequency in the wake of the NATO bombing, but indiscriminate attacks, summary executions, and the systematic destruction of civilian objects have been standard features of the Serbian government's anti-insurgency campaign since the outbreak of fighting in 1998.

Yet, despite international attention on what was clearly a humanitarian catastrophe, even in early to mid-1998, NATO officials privately observed that "current numbers of refugees are simply not sufficient to trigger any intervention".[38] Having ruled out a military response at this early stage, the USA and the EU embarked on a policy of encouraging dialogue between Kosovars and the Serbian regime. Despite the continuation of Serbian military activities in the province, by the summer of 1998 Western policy, embodied in the familiar shuttle diplomacy of Richard Holbrooke, was to broker an agreement between leaders in Belgrade and Pristina.

These talks resulted in little substantively, especially as the autumn of 1998 saw the Serbian regime inaugurate a new offensive against "terrorists" in Kosovo. As war crimes continued to be committed apace (by the end of 1998 more than 2,000 Kosovars had been killed and more than 300,000 were refugees), NATO was finally goaded into threatening air-strikes. On 13 October 1998 its first ever activation order was declared, readying plans for the first of three phases in an extended air campaign against Serbia. Despite talk of NATO's action signifying the possibility of a massive military response, the original activation order concerned targeting plans for no more than 50 air-defence targets. The notion of limited first use and later escalation of force was enshrined in NATO strategy from the beginning, something that in the wake of Operation Allied Force has been subject to sustained criticism. On 30 January 1999 a new activation order, with no pause between each of the three phases, was approved.[39]

NATO was not obliged to pursue its military threats in October 1998, as Holbrooke finally succeeded in getting a cease-fire agreement to cover Kosovo. The agreement had three principal obligations for the Serbian regime: Serbian forces were to be reduced to February 1998 levels (even though this number had then been sufficient to have commenced the "cleansing" policy); an amnesty for Kosovar prisoners detained since the operation began was to be implemented; and Serbia was to give assurances of cooperation with the International Criminal Tribunal for the Former Yugoslavia (ICTY) to ensure the effective pursuit of war criminals responsible for the indiscriminate killing. In the end, and not long after the agreement's coming into force, it was evident that none of these promises was being kept by the Serbian regime. Continued repression and fighting made a mockery of NATO's repeated military threats to act if the agreement was not honoured.

The Serbian regime's flouting of the October 1998 cease-fire occurred despite the fact that the accord was to be monitored and supposedly secured by the Organization for Security and Cooperation in Europe (OSCE), which was authorized to deploy 1,000 unarmed "verifiers" as the OSCE Kosovo Verification Mission (KVM). The fact that persistent diplomacy and non-military options were patently unsuccessful in their expressed aim left NATO with few options given its military threats and desire to be seen as credible.

Nearly a year on from the beginning of the offensive in the Drenica valley, the massacre on 15 January 1999 of 45 civilians in Racak – quickly verified by the OSCE KVM as a war crime – increased pressure on NATO to act. However, the alliance's reluctance actually to implement its oft-made threats was evident in the constant deferrals of the activation orders, and their insistence that diplomacy be pursued still further. This position became harder to maintain once the details of the chain of command behind the Racak massacre – involving authorization by the Yugoslav deputy prime minister and the Serbian interior minister – were obtained from intelligence sources.[40]

Further evidence that the events on the ground in Kosovo were manifestations of a coordinated and systematic policy was available to the alliance. After the October 1998 cease-fire, Milosevic purged the Yugoslav army (VJ) leadership and installed generals more willing to do his bidding. This involved putting in place commanders who worked up a scheme (now widely known as "Operation Horseshoe") for the removal if not eradication of the KLA, and with them large sections of the Kosovar population. As the *Washington Post* revealed, "the offensive [of 1999] – including random executions and the forced exodus from towns and cities – flowed from a coherent plan designed by Milosevic and his generals and prepared over many weeks by Yugoslav officials ... it was a 'pre-planned, premeditated and meticulously executed military campaign'".[41]

What was most significant about this plan, and what flowed directly from Milosevic's October 1998 purge of the VJ leadership, was the army's direct involvement in the ethnic cleansing of Kosovo. Up until the end of 1998 it had been the paramilitaries and the Interior Ministry police who had carried out the violence. The offensive against the northern Kosovo town of Podujevo, which started on Christmas Eve 1998 – three months before NATO's military action – demonstrated the new strategy, with all the arms of Serbia's (and the FRY's) militias operating in unison. At the same time, in an echo of moves taken in Sarajevo prior to the outbreak of hostilities there in early 1992, government records, historical manuscripts, and religious icons were removed from various sites in Kosovo and shipped to Serbia proper.[42] All this was taking place while the OSCE's KVM continued to monitor the supposed cease-fire.

While the cease-fire was supposed to see a reduction in Serbian military numbers to the levels present in February 1998, those numbers grew beyond October 1998 levels as more than 14,000 additional troops were sent to the province. This build-up continued and accelerated as the West reiterated military threats and pursued its next diplomatic strategy – peace talks at Rambouillet, France, in the first two weeks of February 1999. The attendance of delegations representing the FRY and the Kosovars was achieved by further military threats. However, unlike the Dayton negotiations concerning Bosnia in 1995, Milosevic refused to attend, and made it difficult for Kosovars to travel from the province. Moreover, the Serbian delegation contained no representatives of the Kosovo Serbs, nor consulted with them, suggesting that local Serbian interests were insignificant to the Serbian regime's overall strategy.[43]

After numerous delays and much cajoling, the negotiations at Rambouillet – initially unsigned by all parties, and steadfastly denounced by the Serbian regime – resulted in a plan for a NATO-led force of 28,000 peace-keepers to oversee the return of refugees and ensure three years of stable autonomy in Kosovo before a final determination.[44] Once internal divisions between various Kosovar factions had been overcome, representatives of the Kosovars signed the Rambouillet text on 18 March 1999. However, continuing opposition from Milosevic and others meant the agreement was doomed, and their reluctance to countenance acceptance became the precondition for military action by NATO. The final step in that direction was achieved when the OSCE's KVM withdrew on 20 March, a move that coincided with the beginning of another integrated offensive in the central Drenica valley.[45]

All in all, rather than rushing in to put in place (as many Western and Serbian critics claimed) its supposed desire for imperial hegemony, the above analysis suggests that the international community has at all times taken its time, looked the other way, pursued all and every non-military option despite their projected failure, and then finally, reluctantly acted when the evidence of atrocities could no longer be resisted.[46] In that sense, much of its performance in relation to Kosovo throughout 1998–99 is a continuation of its Balkan record since the early 1990s. Moreover, as in the case of Bosnia and elsewhere, this seemingly institutionalized reluctance to respond takes place in the face of what amounts to genocide.

There is, of course, and rightly so, much debate about the use of the term "genocide". But despite those who (erroneously) think that unless the Holocaust is replicated in all its unimaginable detail nothing worthy of the name genocide has taken place, the Serbian regime's policies in Kosovo fulfil at least the international legal standard of genocide, as expressed in Article 2 of the Genocide Convention of 1948: "the intention to destroy, in whole or in part, a national, ethnical, racial or religious group, as such". Detention centres, random killings, organised rape, and the forced expulsion of hundreds of thousands of people on previously organized bus and train convoys certainly fits the definition of an intention to destroy in whole or in part. The violence against the body – such as rape, and the carving of nationalist symbols into the flesh of victims[47] – and the violence against the body politic – the destruction of villages and their cultural symbols – intersect at the final point with the stripping from the refugees of all their identity documents to demonstrate the destruction of a group as such. As a result of the Serbian regime's systematically organized plan to displace the population from Kosovo – a plan which in its formation and execution demonstrates the chain of command and responsibility for the crimes against humanity – more than 90 per cent of the pre-war population fled from their homes to internal or external refuge.[48]

That genocide was taking place in Kosovo should hardly surprise those who have understood the course of the Balkan wars in the last few years. After all, the International Court of Justice in 1993 issued a preliminary finding against the FRY for genocide in Bosnia, and the ICTY has indicted key Bosnian Serbs such as Radovan Karadzic and Ratko Mladic for genocide. Many of the same paramilitaries implicated in the violence in Bosnia have been operating in Kosovo. Most telling in this regard is the fact that the Dutch armoured vehicles taken by Mladic's Bosnian Serb forces during the massacre of thousands at Srebrenica in 1995 have been spotted in the Serbian armoury during fighting in Kosovo.[49] Although genocide is not one of the counts against Milosevic and three other senior officials of the FRY (including the two ministers implicated in the Racak massacre), the ICTY's indictment of them for crimes against humanity for activities in the period 1 January to late May 1999 covers violent acts that could in time be legally considered consistent with genocide.[50]

The above overview of the key events and issues in the Kosovo conflict, emphasizing the planned nature of the Serbian atrocities and the untimely nature of the international community's response, does not mean that unquestioning support for NATO's Operation Allied Force is the logical conclusion of the argument. To the contrary, there are many justifiable and important criticisms of the bombing campaign, not the least of which is that the emphasis on degrading Serbian infrastructure rather than attacking the Serbian militias involved in the Kosovo "cleansing" resulted in too many innocent Serbian citizens dying. This deplorable state of affairs stemmed from the substantial political limits on the use of allied forces (such as the overweening desire to avoid casualties by, among other things, restricting flights to altitudes of 5,000 metres or above) that have come to characterize post-Cold War interventions, especially where the USA is centrally involved.[51] The effect of such constraints was to ensure that the losses incurred by Serbian militias were substantially less than intended. Serbia claimed that only 13 tanks were destroyed during the campaign,[52] a figure borne out by a US Munitions Effects assessment team report, leaked after the US Joint Chiefs of Staff suppressed its findings, which concluded that only 14 tanks, 18 armoured personnel carriers, and 20 artillery pieces had been destroyed by air-strikes.[53] Most importantly, and contrary to the oft-expressed war aim, the humanitarian catastrophe of forced population transfer was not prevented.

Nonetheless, just as making an understanding of the war crimes committed in Kosovo the centrepiece of an argument does not lead to a blanket endorsement of NATO's actions, neither do criticisms of NATO's tactics and strategy validate all opposition to military action against the violators of international humanitarian law. In the name of a different justice, a more discerning and discriminating judgement is required. What this involves can be best demonstrated by considering – from the perspective of the public debate in Britain – the flaws in the argument of those on the left who opposed NATO. Their reliance on assumptions and logics common to conservative positions demonstrates the limits of traditional ethical discourse in international affairs, and underscores the need to rethink the political effects of certain assumptions in the face of atrocities like those in Kosovo.

From the left

In the UK, NATO's military campaign against Serbia drew together former political adversaries in a new policy alliance opposed to the action. Prominent Conservatives (such as the Tory Party's former minister, Alan Clark MP), invoking the spatial imagery of sovereignty, failed to see why a country like Britain should be involved when no national interests were at stake. In the words of one of their American neo-conservative counterparts, the Kosovo crisis was "one of those small but nasty local disputes that happen regularly all over the world". As such, there was no point expending men and *matériel* "against a minor state on a peripheral issue".[54] They argued, in addition, that although Milosevic was surely unsavoury, what he was doing added up to little more than what the West had previously been happy to ignore in places such as Turkey, Rwanda, and Croatia.

Commentators on the left in Britain – such as the playwright Harold Pinter and the journalist John Pilger – concurred with the latter point. Both Pinter and Pilger had been prominent voices expressing a political bond with, in particular, the oppression of Kurds and East Timorese. Writing a month before Operation Allied Force, in the wake of the arrest of the Kurdish leader Abdullah Ocalan, Pinter recounted some of the human rights abuses (especially denial of language rights and access to publishing) the Kurds had suffered.[55] In a similar vein, Pilger has campaigned long and hard to make Indonesian violence against the East Timorese an international issue by drawing attention to the British and American arms trade with Indonesia.[56]

Given these expressions of a political bond by Pinter and Pilger, it might have been expected that they would include Kosovars within the sphere of concern the Kurds and East Timorese occupied for them. However logical this would have been – given that the human rights abuses which have so exercised Pinter and Pilger with regard to Turkey and Indonesia were replicated by Serbia in Kosovo, and them some – their response to the conflict was of a different order. Although careful to note in passing that Milosevic was no saint, Pinter and Pilger focused their critical energies on the USA and NATO as the problem. Pilger[57] acknowledged that "the parallels with Kosovo and East Timor are striking", but because the West was unlikely to take action against Indonesia he opposed action against Serbia. Pilger's writings gave greater weight to the civilian deaths in Serbia than the refugee massacres in Kosovo. He charged the media with suppressing the supposedly rising NATO casualty figures, and claimed that the alliance had ignored Serbia's offers for a diplomatic solution so that it could exercise its power.[58]

The positions of Pinter and Pilger demonstrated the way that new forms of violence as witnessed in Bosnia and Kosovo have unsettled traditional political positions. Whereas once it would have been standard for those on the left to have opposed the ethnic nationalism of Milosevic and others like him, the inversion of political certainties that marks much of the post-Cold War world has made many progressives uneasy. The idea that the military might of NATO could be deployed for humanitarian reasons devoid of national interest is regarded as impossible, while any action taken without the sanction of the UN Security Council is regarded as criminal.[59]

Indeed, it is a common and long-held suspicion of the motives of the USA and its allies – as well as a new-found faith in the justice of international law as exercised by the United Nations – that has underpinned many on the left, like Pinter and Pilger, in their stance against Operation Allied Force (see also Said[60]). Without diminishing the veracity of their well-made criticisms against the tactics of the campaign (such the reliance on bombing from a safe altitude and its attendant problems), or doubting the view that in many instances the USA acts with an unwarranted moral absolutism,[61] the inability of these critics to move beyond their general, blanket denunciations to an appreciation of the specific and situated context of Milosevic's campaign in Kosovo demonstrates an intellectual inflexibility that is at best unhelpful. For example, the criticism that NATO, in formally acting outside the United Nations, undertook a criminal act equates the power politics of the Security Council with justice, and assumes that international law, even when it is customary, is the best arbiter of right.[62]

In an attempt to overcome some of the obvious dilemmas with this form of generic criticism, some on the left argued that there are new codes or principles that could secure opposition to NATO. Prominent in this regard was an essay from Noam Chomsky,[63] which originally appeared in *Le Monde*. Chomsky invoked what is becoming a disturbingly common formulation amongst those who claim to be from the progressive stream of thought, yet want to oppose action in areas subject to prejudicial violence. It is the idea that, as in the Hippocratic oath (an analogy which medicalizes the issue), one should do nothing if what one proposes might in some way cause harm to someone. This argument is best known in development studies through Mary Anderson's essay "Do No Harm".[64] It is a position that promotes paralysis in the face of genocide, for there is never a stance which we can be sure will be free of all "harm", whether it be the unintentional side-effects borne by onlookers, or violence directed solely towards the perpetrators. Nonetheless, Chomsky argues as follows:

A standard argument [re Kosovo] is "We had to do something: we could not simply stand by as atrocities continued." That is never true. One choice, always, is to follow the Hippocratic principle: "First, do no harm." If you can think of no way to adhere to that elementary principle, then do nothing. There are always ways that can be considered. Diplomacy and negotiations are never at an end.[65]

Chomsky's politics have always been somewhat puzzling; critical of Foucault because he (allegedly and mistakenly) cannot advocate just positions, Chomsky has in the past been associated with individuals advocating Holocaust revisionism – as in his support for Robert Faurrison, documented by Pierre Vidal-Naquet[66] – and now seems content to advocate inaction whenever we are faced with violence. Is it uncharitable to ask what would he have argued in 1941 and 1942? No one wants violence for the sake of violence, but the naïve belief that when faced with the abhorrent we can avoid harm *per se* is quite breathtaking. And completely debilitating, for doing nothing is not an option, as it always implicitly involves doing something, such as standing by and doing nothing while others carry out the violence, thereby in effect aiding the aggressor who fails to heed the directive to do nothing.

What stands out from this debate from the left opposing Operation Allied Force is the importance of the *horizon of temporality* in the decision to support or oppose (which illustrates well Derrida's arguments on the politics of decisioning[67]). Pinter, Pilger, and others maintain that *in the past* the USA and its allies failed to oppose the oppression of peoples. Likewise, as argued above, the USA and its allies – in *the more recent past* of the Kosovo issue – have previously failed to act to oppose the violence of the Serbian regime. Yet we draw different conclusions. Pinter and others take the past failures to be a sufficient reason not to act now. In contrast, the present author takes the past failures to act – given the responsibility to the other, the necessity to affirm alterity and oppose its erasure, which comprises the ethical relation – as all the more reason to have acted *now*. Yes, many of the details of the action NATO undertook warrant criticism. But in the absence of a decision to act firmly in the face of genocide, what satisfaction would have been taken from the surety that, while *we* did no harm by refusing to act, *they* – the Serbian regime – engaged in war crimes to match the worst of the past 50 years? Would not that have placed a responsibility to ourselves over and above a responsibility to others?

This is the view in effect taken by Jose Ramos-Horta, the East Timorese independence leader who was jointly awarded the Nobel Peace Prize in 1996, in a letter to *The Guardian*. As a statement curiously overlooked by Pilger in his arguments, it bears (despite its questionable identity politics) quoting in full here:

At times the use of force is necessary. When all diplomatic efforts, dialogue and other means of pressure such as economic sanctions [have] failed to induce a tyrant to change his behaviour, the use of force is inevitable. Not doing so can have more tragic consequences with more loss of lives and dangers of wider aggression.

Nato intervention in Kosovo could have been avoided if only the Serbian dictator Slobodan Milosevic had shown flexibility, moderation and toleration towards the Kosovars. Those in the world who are critical of the Nato intervention should take some comfort that this time at least the predominantly Christian alliance of Nato is trying to protect a Muslim community threatened with genocide. It is one of the few moments since the second world war when a Western military alliance [has] taken up the fight of a small nation for purely humanitarian reasons.[68]

Conclusion

The purpose of this chapter has been to focus on the way in which the issues of justice and international order are framed as iterations of a conventional rendering of the universal/particular in which the spatial imaginary of sovereignty is accorded priority. The argument is that this framing itself constitutes many of the problems that subsequent debates about ethics and international affairs seek to overcome. Yet their attempt to overcome these problems is made impossible by the privilege they grant the dominant assumptions which render the issue in terms of sovereignty.

While rethinking matters does not make problems go away, there can be little doubt that an appreciation of the political effects of these representations is integral to an evaluation of future prospects. This was especially evident above in the consideration of how those (embodied here in the arguments of Pinter, Pilger, and others) traditionally critical of the state deployment of violence, such as Serbia deployed against the Kosovars, employed conservative notions of international order and thereby found themselves in an uneasy alliance against the claims to justice of a people subject to genocide.

A post-structuralist-inspired rethinking of the question of justice does not provide a clear-cut answer to the many dilemmas of situations such as Bosnia and Kosovo. But, with its emphasis upon our heteronomous responsibility to the other, it does undercut the idea that there are situations that can be of no concern whatsoever or situations where our concern has to be circumscribed by "higher" values such as sovereignty. While this by itself will not move state representatives whose position depends upon the constant reinvigoration of sovereignty, the new political bonds and transversal alliances animated by the ethical relation flowing from this reconfiguration of justice will contest, disturb, and unsettle potentially complacent reactions to violence. Far from the depoliticizing comforts of ethical theory, enacting the ethical relation will involve resistance and struggle. It is a messy business. But then, that is politics.

Notes

1. Brown, C., 1997, "Review Article: Theories of International Justice", *British Journal of Political Science*, Vol. 27, April, pp. 273–297.
2. Bull, H., 1984, *Justice in International Relations: The 1983–4 Hagey Lectures*. Ontario: University of Waterloo, p. 2.
3. Walzer, M., 1992, *Just and Unjust Wars*, revised edn. New York: Basic Books.
4. Dillon, M., 1999, "Another Justice", *Political Theory*, Vol. 27, No. 2, pp. 155–175.
5. Campbell, D., 1998, *National Deconstruction: Violence, Identity and Justice in Bosnia*. Minneapolis: University of Minnesota Press, ix.
6. Derrida, J., 1992, "Force of Law: The 'Mystical Foundation of Authority'", in *Deconstruction and the Possibility of Justice*, Cornell, D., Rosenfeld, M., and Gray Carlson, D., eds. New York: Routledge, pp. 14–15, 22.

7. Kellogg, C., 1998, "The Messianic Without Marxism: Derrida's Marx and the Question of Justice", *Cultural Values*, No. 2, pp. 51–69.
8. Brown, note 1 above, p. 295.
9. Kennan, G. F., 1991, "Appendix: 'Morality and Foreign Policy'", in *Morality and Foreign Policy: Realpolitik Revisited*, Jensen, K. M. and Faulkner, E. P., eds. Washington: United States Institute of Peace, p. 60.
10. Donnelly, J., 1992, "Twentieth-Century Realism", in *Traditions of International Ethics*, Nardin, T. and Mapel, D. R., eds. Cambridge: Cambridge University Press.
11. Nardin, T., 1992, "Ethical Traditions in International Affairs", in *ibid.*, p. 15.
12. The majority of contributions to the journal *Ethics and International Affairs*, published by the Carnegie Council on Ethics and International Affairs, are representative of this outlook. For overviews, see Brown, C., 1992, *International Relations Theory: New Normative Approaches*. New York: Columbia University Press; Smith, S., 1992, "The Forty Years Detour: The Resurgence of Normative Theory in International Relations", *Millennium*, Vol. 21, Winter, pp. 489–506. This literature, specifically Brown's book, is critically reviewed in Walker, R. B. J., 1994, "Norms in a Teacup: Surveying the 'New Normative Approaches'", *Mershon International Studies Review*, No. 38, October, pp. 265–270. This focus on normative concerns is more self-consciously evident in the UK and Europe, with those writing in North America addressing "normative" issues through other frames of reference, especially the renewed focus on culture and identity. See, for example, Lapid, Y. and Kratochwil, F., eds, 1995, *The Return of Culture and Identity in IR Theory*. Boulder: Lynne Rienner. Some of the problems associated with this focus on culture and identity are reviewed in the epilogue to Campbell, D., 1998, *Writing Security: US Foreign Policy and the Politics of Identity*, revised edn. Minneapolis: University of Minnesota Press.
13. Nardin and Mapel, note 10 above.
14. Brown, note 12 above; Cochran, M., 1995, "Postmodernism, Ethics and International Political Theory", *Review of International Studies*, No. 21, pp. 237–250.
15. Campbell, D. and Shapiro, M. J., eds, 1999, *Moral Spaces: Rethinking Ethics and World Politics*. Minneapolis: University of Minnesota Press.
16. Campbell, D. and Shapiro, M. J., 1999, "Introduction: From Ethical Theory to the Ethical Relation", in *ibid.*
17. Laclau, E., 1994, "Introduction", in *The Making of Political Identities*, ed. Laclau, E. London and New York: Verso, p. 5.
18. Gasché, R., 1994, *Inventions of Difference*. Cambridge, MA: Harvard University Press, p. 2.
19. Campbell, D., 1998, "Why Fight: Humanitarianism, Principles and Poststructuralism", *Millennium: Journal of International Studies*, Vol. 27, No. 3, pp. 497–521.
20. Connolly, W. E., 1997, "The Ethical Sensibility of Michel Foucault", in *The Later Foucault*, ed. Moss, J. London: Sage, p. 114.
21. Derrida, J., 1994, "Nietzsche and the Machine: Interview with Jacques Derrida by Richard Beardsworth", *Journal of Nietzsche Studies*, No. 7, pp. 47–48, emphasis added.
22. Bert, W., 1997, *The Reluctant Superpower: United States Policy in Bosnia, 1991–95*. New York: St. Martin's Press; Gow, J., 1997, *The Triumph of the Lack of Will: International Diplomacy and the Yugoslav War*. London: Hurst.
23. Holbrooke, R., 1998, *To End a War*. New York: Random House, pp. 65–67.
24. Gompert, D., 1996, "The United States and Yugoslavia's Wars", in *The World and Yugoslavia's Wars*, ed. Ullman, R. H. New York: Council on Foreign Relations, pp. 122–144.
25. Holbrooke, note 23 above, p. 81.

26. Weiss, T. G., 1996, "Collective Spinelessness: UN Actions in the Former Yugoslavia", in Ullman, note 24 above, pp. 59–96.

27. Holbrooke, note 23 above, pp. 359–360.

28. Campbell, D., 1999, "Apartheid Cartography: The Political Anthropology and Spatial Effects of International Diplomacy in Bosnia", *Political Geography*, Vol. 18, No. 4, pp. 395–435.

29. For example, *The Guardian*, 1999, "Call it a Victory", 30 June, p. 15.

30. The importance of identity categorizations, especially those named via "ethnicity", is central to a reconsideration of Bosnia; see Campbell, note 5 above. Isa Blumi begins to show how the same concerns are operative in the context of Kosovo and its Albanian inhabitants: Blumi, I., 1998, "The Commodification of Otherness and the Ethnic Unit in the Balkans: How to Think about Albanians", *East European Politics and Societies*, Vol. 12, No. 3, pp. 527–569.

31. The Federal Republic of Yugoslavia consists formally of the republics of Serbia and Montenegro. Because the latter was opposed to the former's policy with repect to the conflict in Kosovo, except with reference to specific legal agreements, this paper talks of Serbia as the entity which enacted policy with regard to Kosovo.

32. ICG, 1998, *Kosovo Spring*. International Crisis Group, 20 March. (http://www.crisisweb.org)

33. *Ibid.*

34. ICG, 1998, *Kosovo's Long Hot Summer: Briefing on Military, Humanitarian and Political Developments in Kosovo*. International Crisis Group, 2 September. (http://www.crisisweb.org)

35. *Ibid.*; Steele, J., 1998, "Learning to Live with Milosevic", *Transitions*, Vol. 5, No. 9, pp. 18–21.

36. *Washington Post*, 1999, "Serbs' Offensive was Meticulously Planned", 11 April. (http://washingtonpost.com/, 5 May 1999, 10:08)

37. Abrahams, F., 1999, "Comment: Investigating War Crimes", *IWPR Balkan Crisis Reports*, 18 June. (http://www.iwpr.net/balkans/news/bcr180699_4_eng.htm, 30 June 1999, 14:58)

38. ICG, note 34 above.

39. *Washington Post*, 1999, "The Path to Crisis: How the United States and its Allies Went to War", 18 April. (http://washingtonpost.com/, 21 April 1999, 14:42)

40. *Washington Post*, 1999, "Serbs Tried to Cover Up Massacre: Kosovo Reprisal Plot Bared by Phoned Taps", 28 January. (http://washingtonpost.com/, 5 May 1999, 10:12)

41. *Washington Post*, note 36 above.

42. *Ibid.*

43. ICG, 1999, *Kosovo: The Road to Peace*. International Crisis Group, 12 March. (http://www.crisisweb.org)

44. *Ibid.*

45. *Washington Post*, note 36 above.

46. Abrahams, F., 1998, "The West Winks at Serbian Atrocities in Kosovo", *Human Rights Watch*, 5 August. (http://www.hrw.org/hrw/campaigns/kosovo98/ihtoped.htm, 20 April 1999, 14:59)

47. *New York Times*, 1999, "European Group Cites Evidence of War Crimes", 24 April. (http://www.nytimes.com/library/world/europe/042499kosovo-atrocities.html, 30 April 1999, 10:49)

48. The equally abhorrent violence against Serbs by Kosovars since the end of NATO's campaign in June 1999 cannot be justified by the desire for revenge. It constitutes continuing crimes against humanity, even if, in the absence of a larger, systematic strategy, it does not constitute genocide.

49. Details of this sighting are contained in a Dutch TV documentary, aired on 5 June 1998, available at ⟨http:www.domovina.net/NOS/video/980606.ram⟩.
50. For details of the indictment, see the documents available at ⟨http:///www.un/org/icty⟩.
51. Campbell, D., 1999, "Contradictions of a Lone Superpower", in *The American Century: Consensus and Coercion in the Projection of American Power*, eds. Slater, D. and Taylor, P. Oxford: Blackwell.
52. *The Guardian*, note 29 above.
53. *The Guardian*, 2000, "MoD Leak Reveals Kosovo Failure," 15 August. (http:www.guardian.co.uk/Kosovo/Story/0,2763,354541,00.html, 17 August 2000, 14:45). The British Ministry of Defence similarly sought unsuccessfully to keep secret a report which revealed that fewer than half the bombs dropped by the Royal Air Force – and only 2 per cent of the unguided munitions – hit their designated targets. See *The Guardian*, note 29 above.
54. Harries, O., 1999, "First It Was Kosovo, Then Russia and Now China", *International Herald Tribune*, 18 May.
55. Pinter, H., 1999, "The Kurds Have Lifted the Veil", *The Guardian*, 20 February. (http://www.guardianunlimited.co.uk/Archive/Article/0,4273,3825124,00.html, 2 July 1999, 14:52)
56. Pilger, J., 1999, "Blood on Our Hands", *The Guardian*, 25 January. (http://www.guardianunlimited.co.uk/Archive/Article/0,4273,3812281,00.html, 2 July 1999, 14:32); Pilger, J., 1999, "Immoral Earnings", *The Guardian*, 29 June. (http://www.guardianunlimited.co.uk/Archive/Article/0,4273,3878924,00.html, 2 July 1999, 14:01)
57. Pilger, J., 1999, "Morality? Don't Make Me Laugh", *The Guardian*, 20 April. (http://www.guardianunlimited.co.uk/Archive/Article/0,4273,3856188,00.html, 2 July 1999, 14:24)
58. Pilger, J., 1999, "Acts of Murder", *The Guardian*, 18 May. (http://www.guardianunlimited.co.uk/Archive/Article/0,4273,3866125,00.html, 2 July 1999, 14:18)
59. Pinter, H., 1999, "Artists Against the War", *The Guardian*, 8 April. (http://www.guardianunlimited.co.uk/Archive/Article/0,4273,3851195,00.html, 2 July 1999, 14:49)
60. Said, E., 1999, "It's Time the World Stood Up to the American Bully", *The Observer*, 11 April. (http://www.guardianunlimited.co.uk/Archive/Article/0,4273, 3852806,00.html, 2 July 1999, 14:57)
61. Cf. Campbell, D., 1993, *Politics Without Principle: Sovereignty, Ethics and the Narratives of the Gulf War*. Boulder: Lynne Rienner.
62. Ironically, this argument, with its faith in the justice of the Security Council's deliberations (something those on the left did not share during the Gulf War, for example), ignores the many other expressions in the lesser organs of the United Nations which strenuously criticized the Serbian regime. Williams, I., 1999, "The UN's Surprising Support", *IWPR Balkan Crisis Reports*, 19 April. (http://www.iwpr.net/balkans/news/bcr190499_2_eng.htm, 30 April 1999, 11:06)
63. Chomsky, N., 1999, "Now It's a Free for All", *The Guardian*, 17 May, p. 18.
64. See the discussion in Campbell, note 19 above.
65. Chomsky, note 63 above.
66. Vidal-Naquet, P., 1993, *Assassins of Memory*. New York: Columbia University Press.
67. See Campbell, note 5 above, ch. 6.
68. Ramos-Horta, J., 1999, "When the Use of Force is Justified", *The Guardian*, 1 April. (http://www.guardianunlimited.co.uk/Archive/Article/0,4273,3847146,00.html, 2 July 1999, 15:06)

6

Ethics and international human rights

Jack Donnelly

Human rights have become, along with peace, development, and democracy, a defining normative theme of post-Cold War international society – making a "natural" subject for a volume on international ethics. This chapter explores the ethical contours of the concept as expressed in the 1948 Universal Declaration of Human Rights and the 1966 International Human Rights Covenants. These documents have not only been almost universally endorsed by states but are also widely appealed to by national, subnational, and transnational movements of political opposition in all regions of the globe. In addition, they reflect a coherent, and attractive, vision of national political societies composed of equal and autonomous persons with extensive civil, political, economic, and social guarantees.

International ethics under the shadow of realism

The chapter will start by focusing on the ways in which "ethics and international affairs", as the field is usually called in the USA, have – like so much else in the discipline of international studies – been shaped by political realism (*realpolitik*).

"Right is in question only between equals in power, while the strong do what they can and the weak suffer what they must."[1] Ethics and international affairs oppose this standard realist claim, advanced by the Athenian envoys to Melos. They also reject what Morgenthau called "the autonomy of politics",[2] the view that "what the Melians have tried to do is impossible in Thucydides' world. They have injected values and ideals into a sphere of interaction where they do not belong."[3] Ethics and international affairs insist that the impact of the Melian dialogue depends on accepting the appropriateness of the Melian appeal to justice and appreciating the barbarity of the arguments and behaviour of the Athenians.

The realist distinction between morality and "the national interest" cannot be allowed. Politics has inescapable ethical dimensions.[4] The distributions of goods, services, and opportunities that arise from political actions are appropriately subject to ethical evaluation. Survival, security, power, wealth, and related material interests are values, not facts or ethically neutral concerns.[5] We are "interested in", for example, security only because we value it. Security is no less a value than justice or alleviating suffering. To call security a vital national interest is to say that we value it so highly that we are willing to fight for it. Whether or not it is prudent to pursue security, justice, wealth, power, or any other interest/value is an empirical, not at logical, question. And the answer varies with time, place, and actor.

Even bracketing the ethical dimension often distorts the issues at hand. An example is treating the humanitarian impacts of (US-led) sanctions on Iraq as a second order, and thus appropriately subordinated; ethical concern is not a neutral description of American policy or behaviour. Rather, this example implicitly advances the *ethical* argument that the humanitarian suffering should be valued less than increasing our confidence that Iraq's capacity to produce weapons of mass destruction has been degraded. Segregating and subordinating the ethical dimension largely eliminates the need to *make* such an argument, and thus respond to criticisms.[6] As a result, many Americans view the suffering of Iraqi civilians as an unfortunate but "unintended" consequence for which they are somehow not really responsible – even though such consequences are well known and entirely predictable.

A more subtle manifestation of lingering realist conceptualizations persists in the common idea that ethics and international affairs are concerned principally with "soft" issues such as human rights, famine relief, refugees, and food aid rather than the hard core of international relations represented by the pursuit of security and prosperity. The principal exception is the well-established literature on the ethics of force.[7] But even here, segregation reigns. A book like Michael Walzer's *Just and Unjust Wars*,[8] although a staple of courses on ethics and international affairs, is rarely taught in standard security studies courses. Ethical issues are treated as separate concerns that for most ordinary purposes can, even should, be considered, at best, only after real(ist) political analysis has been completed.

One might suggest that ethics is a distinctive approach or methodology, and thus deserves to be treated separately. But ethics is *not* just a methodology, like game theory or structural equation modelling. To treat it as such is falsely to suggest that the substance of international politics can be studied without engaging ethical issues. Questions of justice, fairness, rights, and responsibilities are an inescapable part of the *substance* of international politics.

The existence of this volume is evidence of modest progress in reintroducing ethics into the discipline. International ethics is beginning to find a place at the table of international studies again – although far removed from the head of the table, "down" with the women, children, and awkward, unwanted, and unappreciated relatives. The development of the field of human rights, however, does provide hints of what a discipline of international studies which assumes that politics cannot be analysed separately from ethics might look like.

Thirty years ago, human rights were regularly studied only within the fields of international organization and international law – and even there only as peripheral issues. During the mid-1970s, the core of controversy, among both analysts and actors, was whether human rights were a fit subject for inclusion within a country's foreign policy.[9] Because of their ethical dimension, many argued that human rights were an inappropriate part of international politics.

Over the past decade, however, human rights have become accepted as a standard part of both the study and the practice of international politics. They still remain (at best) a secondary interest in the foreign policy of states and most regional and international organizations. But in policy circles, the ethical dimension is increasingly treated as a fact about the character of this particular national (or international) interest. Debate is over the proper substance of international human rights policies, not whether states ought to have such policies. And human rights have become a relatively well settled, if still peripheral, part of the discipline of international studies.

Ethical foundations

The following four sections seek to chart the ethical contours of internationally recognized human rights by unpacking the ethical perspective implicit in the leading international legal instruments. Although the author largely endorses this vision, arguing on behalf of it is not the central concern. The approach is more descriptive or analytical than prescriptive, with the aim of analysing, and developing a particular interpretation of, the underlying logic and presuppositions of contemporary international human rights norms and political practice.

International human rights

In the 50 years since it was adopted by the UN General Assembly, the Universal Declaration of Human Rights has been endorsed by virtually all states, arguably acquiring the status of customary international law.[10] The International Covenant on Civil and Political Rights currently (1 July 1999) has 144 parties. The International Covenant on Economic, Social, and Cultural Rights has 141 parties.[11] The Vienna Declaration and Programme of Action was adopted by consensus by the 171 states that participated in the 1993 World Conference on Human Rights. For better or worse – and in most regards, the author considers it for the better – these documents set the meaning of "human rights" in contemporary international society.

No less important than this endorsement by states is the fact that human rights have repeatedly been at the centre of struggles for social justice and against political oppression across the globe. Opposition to totalitarian party-state rule in the Soviet bloc was increasingly waged through the language of human rights in the late 1970s and 1980s, spurred in significant measure by the human rights provisions of the Helsinki Final Act.[12] The struggle against military dictatorship in Latin America also became largely a struggle for human rights.[13] And today in much of Africa and Asia, human rights activists are central to struggles against poverty and misrule. The language of international human rights has become almost as deeply embedded in contemporary struggles of political opposition as it is in the rhetoric of multilateral and bilateral diplomacy and the legitimating appeals of states.

Human rights are typically understood, following the manifest, literal sense of the term, as the rights that one has simply because one is human. They are universal rights: every human being has them. They are equal rights: one either is a human being (and thus has these rights equally) or not. And they are inalienable rights: one cannot stop being a human being, and thus cannot stop having these rights. Furthermore, in the Universal Declaration, the covenants, and the Vienna Declaration we can discern clear if thin answers to three basic conceptual and theoretical questions about human rights thus understood: what is the character of these rights (function), where do they come from (source), and what is their substance (list)?

The source of internationally recognized human rights is identified as the inherent (moral) nature of the human person. Article 1 of the Universal Declaration begins "All human beings are born free and equal in dignity and rights". Both covenants assert that "these rights derive from the inherent dignity of the human person". The Vienna Declaration uses almost the same language: "all human rights derive from the dignity and worth inherent in the human person".[14]

Every person, simply as a human being, is entitled to enjoy human rights. "Everyone has the right ..." "No one shall be ..." "Every human being has ..." Individuals are properly subject to a great array of social and political obligations. Human rights, however, specify an inalienable set of goods, services, and opportunities that the state and society are, in ordinary circumstances, required to respect or provide to those under their jurisdiction.

By thus restricting the legitimate range of state action, internationally recognized human rights function as a standard of political legitimacy, and thus as a ground for struggles against misrule and injustice. The Universal Declaration proclaims itself "a common standard of achievement for all peoples and all nations". The Vienna Declaration is unusually forthright, claiming in its first operative paragraph that protecting and promoting human rights "is the first responsibility of Governments".[15]

Other systems for regulating relations between individuals, states, and society have been the norm throughout most of history in all regions of the world. Tradition, gender, age, birth, divine right, charisma, ethnicity, superior culture, and religion have been some of the more prominent grounds for establishing a just title to rule. Contemporary international society, however, has endorsed human rights in the strongest possible terms.

The Universal Declaration and the covenants are primarily lists of internationally recognized human rights, summarized below. The International Bill of Human Rights recognizes the rights to:

- equality of rights without discrimination (D1, D2, E2, E3, C2, C3)
- life (D3, C6)
- liberty and security of person (D3, C9)
- protection against slavery (D4, C8)
- protection against torture and cruel and inhuman punishment (D5, C7)
- recognition as a person before the law (D6, C16)
- equal protection of the law (D7, C14, C26)
- access to legal remedies for rights violations (D8, C2)
- protection against arbitrary arrest or detention (D9, C9)
- hearing before an independent and impartial judiciary (D10, C14)
- presumption of innocence (D11, C14)
- protection against *ex post facto* laws (D11, C15)
- protection of privacy, family, and home (D12, C17)

- freedom of movement and residence (D13, C12)
- seek asylum from persecution (D14)
- nationality (D15)
- marry and found a family (D16, E10, C23)
- own property (D17)
- freedom of thought, conscience, and religion (D18, C18)
- freedom of opinion, expression, and the press (D19, C19)
- freedom of assembly and association (D20, C21, C22)
- political participation (D21, C25)
- social security (D22, E9)
- work, under favourable conditions (D23, E6, E7)
- free trade unions (D23, E8, C22)
- rest and leisure (D24, E7)
- food, clothing, and housing (D25, E11)
- health care and social services (D25, E12)
- special protections for children (D25, E10, C24)
- education (D26, E13, E14)
- participation in cultural life (D27, E15)
- a social and international order needed to realize rights (D28)
- self-determination (E1, C1)
- humane treatment when detained or imprisoned (C10)
- protection against debtors' prison (C11)
- protection against arbitrary expulsion of aliens (C13)
- protection against advocacy of racial or religious hatred (C20)
- protection of minority culture (C27).

This list includes all rights that are enumerated in two of the three documents of the International Bill of Human Rights or have a full article in one document. The source of each right is indicated in parentheses, by document and article number: D = Universal Declaration of Human Rights; E = International Covenant on Economic, Social, and Cultural Rights; C = International Covenant on Civil and Political Rights.

Underlying this list is an implicit account of the minimum political conditions for a life of human dignity in the conditions of the contemporary world. And these rights are seen, in the language of the Vienna Declaration, as "universal, indivisible and interdependent and interrelated ... it is the duty of States, regardless of their political, economic and cultural systems, to promote and protect all human rights and fundamental freedoms".[16] Thus the motto of the office of the High Commissioner for Human Rights for 1998, the fiftieth anniversary of the Universal Declaration, was "All human rights for all".

The duties correlative to internationally recognized human rights, however, fall largely on states. Although every person holds human rights, they target the state of which one is a national. International human rights treaties create obligations for states to respect, protect, and implement the rights of *their own* citizens (and foreigners under their jurisdiction). They do not provide international legal justification for coercive action to implement or protect the rights of foreigners abroad, and thus leave largely untouched the central international legal principle of non-intervention. Although human rights norms have been internationalized, their implementation remains largely national. Coercive uses of force, and thus international enforcement in a strong sense of that term, remain largely prohibited.[17]

Moral theory, political theory, and human rights

It is conventional to distinguish deontological (duty-based) theories, such as Kant's categorical imperative, from teleological (ends-, goals-, or consequence-based) theories, such as Bentham's utilitarianism.[18] Such theories posit radically different relationships between the right and the good.[19] Right is the moral primitive for deontological theories. We are required to do what is right (follow our duty), period, independent of the effects, for good or bad, produced by our actions. "Thou shalt not ..." The moral primitive in teleological theories, by contrast, is the good. Duty depends on the consequences of our actions. We are morally required, within the limits of our skill and resources, to increase human happiness or reduce human suffering.[20]

This common classification of moral theories, however, tells us little about human rights, which have played a vanishingly small part in the history of (Western) moral theory, even during the modern era. For example, rights are hardly mentioned in Kant's *Grounding for the Metaphysics of Morals*.[21] For utilitarians, rights are only second-order rules that save us the (often considerable) task of calculating utilities in particular cases. Although Ronald Dworkin has talked about rights-based moral theories,[22] such a category has historically been largely an empty one.[23] Human rights logically may be, but in fact rarely have been, taken to be a moral primitive.

They can, however, be relatively easily derived from many moral theories. Human rights might, for example, be seen as encoded in natural law.[24] Teleological theories might ground a system of rights in their tendency to further human good or flourishing. Nonetheless, one of the most striking theoretical features of human rights is their loose connection to modern moral theories.

When we turn to *political* theory, however, (human) rights often become central. This is perhaps most striking in Kant's "Theory and Practice".[25] Part I, which deals with individual morality, sketches a radically egalitarian deontological ethic that makes no significant reference to rights. But in Part II, which treats with what Kant calls "political right", rights (entitlements) become central. In fact, Kant's contractarian political theory is centred on the rights we have as human beings, as subjects, and as citizens. And as this example suggests, human rights are at the heart – in fact a defining feature – of contractarian political theories.

Other political theories may endorse a human rights standard of political legitimacy by other routes. One might even argue that the loose and weak link between human rights and leading moral theories is an attraction rather than a drawback, allowing for a considerable degree of *political* consensus despite otherwise important moral divergence. Although incompatible with virtually all inegalitarian theories, human rights, by remaining open to many egalitarian moral and political theories, may allow us to handle certain questions of political justice and right while circumventing difficult and often acrimonious disputes over moral foundations.

This is particularly attractive in a "post-modern" world sceptical of the possibility of finding logically unassailable foundations. Political theorists have increasingly turned their attention to notions such as deliberative consensus – for example, in the recent work of both John Rawls[26] and Jurgen Habermas[27] – and recognition (for example, Gutmann[28]). Human rights may provide a focal point for forging such a consensus or for negotiating mutual recognition. Certainly there is no other substantive ideal that has even come close to such widespread international endorsement by both governments and movements of political opposition across the globe.[29]

Therefore, the remainder of this chapter will be concerned with the political, rather than moral, theory of human rights. It will be concerned with questions of *political* rights and obligations. More particularly, it will explore the ways in which human rights, as expressed in the Universal Declaration and as explicated in the preceding section, establish particular relationships between individuals, political communities, and the state.

Human rights and political dignity[30]

The "universality" of human rights is a normative claim about the proper way to organize social and political relations in the contemporary world, not a historical or anthropological fact. All societies have conceptions of personal dignity, ideal visions of the life – or more often, lives – fit for (different groups of) human beings. All cultures and societies appeal to social values such as equity, fairness, compassion, and respect for one's fellows. Very few, however, have defined one's fellows as all members of the species *homo sapiens* or have sought to realize these values through equal and inalienable universal rights held by every citizen against society.

That is the perspective, however, that has been adopted by contemporary international society.

We are most immediately familiar with the regulative aspects of human rights norms: "No one shall be subjected to torture or to cruel, inhuman, or degrading treatment or punishment"; "All are equal before the law and are entitled without any discrimination to equal protection of the law"; "Everyone has the right to work, to free choice of employment, to just and favourable conditions of work, and to protection against unemployment." No less importantly, however, human rights norms *constitute* individuals as a particular kind of political subject – free and equal rights-bearing citizens – and define the requirements and limits of legitimate government.

Human beings are, of course, members of social groups and occupants of social roles. "Individuals" are also members of families and communities, workers, churchgoers, citizens, and occupants of numerous other social roles. Nonetheless, a human rights conception of politics insists that essential to their dignity, and to a life worthy of a human being, is the simple fact that they are distinct and separate individual human beings.

These individuals are in the first instance equal. But this core commitment to equality leads "naturally" to an emphasis on autonomy. Equal individuals have no right to force on one another ideas of what is right and proper. More precisely, they have no right to force on others obligations that treat them as less than equal moral agents. Human rights link equality and autonomy through the notion of (individual and collective) self-determination, an ideal with extremely wide and deep political resonance.

Without implying complete licence, human rights limit what society may legitimately prohibit or require of its members. Equal and autonomous rights-bearing individuals are entitled to make fundamental choices about what constitutes the good life (for them) and with whom they associate and how. Each individual must thus be treated by the state with equal concern and respect. A list of (human and legal) rights reflects a particular understanding of the meaning of equal concern and respect, based on a substantive conception of human dignity or the conditions required to permit human flourishing.

But human rights also promise to (re)shape political and social relations so that this moral vision will be realized. Equal, inalienable rights held by all against state and society provide a mechanism for realizing such a world of equal and autonomous human beings. The effective implementation of the specified rights will *produce* the envisioned person/ life (assuming a certain coherence and practicality in that vision). Human rights are thus simultaneously a "utopian" vision and a set of institutions

– equal and inalienable rights – for realizing at least an approximation of that vision.

Human rights and political legitimacy

As a political theory, human rights focus on relations between subjects and rulers – or, in the language of egalitarian politics, citizens and their governments. We can trace a progression over the past century and a quarter through four (overlapping) conceptions of international political legitimacy.

- "Classical" political realists and legal positivists granted full membership in international society to organized political groups (states) with the capacity to maintain their political autonomy and control their own territory, and a willingness to enter into international obligations and participate in established practices of diplomacy.[31] This "Hobbesian" vision presents international relations as a state of war, and international recognition as properly determined by the facts of control over people and territory. National legitimacy is left as a matter of sovereign prerogative.
- The late nineteenth and early twentieth-century "standard of civilization" added the requirements of respect for the laws of war and certain rights of (Western) aliens, as well as the prohibition of shockingly "uncivilized" practices such as slavery, polygamy, and "barbaric" penal practices.[32] These minimal international standards of national political legitimacy reflect a more "Burkean" conception of politics that sees some peoples as having greater virtue than others, and thus being entitled to more rights and a greater say in politics. It rejects Hobbes's egalitarian universalism, minimalist as it might be, in favour of an inegalitarian, "communitarian" conception of social and political development.
- The anti-colonial idea of "self-determination" – understood in Cold-War-era practice as decolonization of Western overseas holdings and punctilious respect for the legal principles of sovereign equality and non-intervention – in effect extended to all states the formal rights enjoyed by the nineteenth-century "powers". The conception of international legitimacy, however, remained largely Hobbesian: the right to life (sovereignty and territorial integrity) was recognized, but not much else. Furthermore, the international community largely refused to enquire into questions of national legitimacy, which were seen as a matter of self-determination.
- Human rights have become the dominant conception of political legitimacy over the past two decades. Like the classical standard of civili-

zation, it is a standard of national as well as international legitimacy. But it is an egalitarian standard. And its substantive requirements are quite extensive. Legitimacy is thus measured in terms of the interests of people as well as those of states. In fact, the interests of the people, and any plausible conception of human dignity, are seen to require the harnessing of the immense power and reach of the modern state.

The human rights strategy of state control has had two principal dimensions. Negatively, human rights prohibit a wide range of state interferences in the personal, social, and political lives of citizens, acting both individually and collectively. No less important, however, is the positive empowerment of the people, who are seen as above and in control of their government. Political authority is vested in a free citizenry endowed with extensive rights of political participation (universal suffrage, freedom of association, free speech, etc.). And by requiring the people, through the state, to provide certain goods, services, and opportunities (as specified in the reigning list of human rights), the regulation of economic markets is brought centrally within the purview of the state.

The state thus is seen not simply as a potential threat to human dignity, but no less importantly as the central institution with the capacity to implement internationally recognized civil, political, economic, and social human rights. "Failed states" such as Somalia suggest that one of the few things as frightening as an efficiently repressive state is no state at all. Human rights, in addition to seeking to prevent certain state-based wrongs, require the state to provide certain goods, services, and opportunities and to protect individuals and families from market-based suffering.

This positive role of the state is as central for civil and political rights as for economic and social rights. Effective implementation of the right to non-discrimination, for example, often requires extensive positive actions. Even procedural rights such as due process entail considerable positive endeavours by police, courts, and administrative agencies. The state must not merely refrain from certain harmful actions but must create a social and political environment that fosters the development of active, engaged, autonomous citizens.

Rights-bearing individuals alone cannot effectively implement their rights or make for themselves a life worthy of human beings. Hobbes put the point most forcefully in arguing that in a pre-social state of nature, life would be "solitary, poor, nasty, brutish, and short".[33] Human rights require social provision. And the substance of contemporary international human rights norms emphasizes collective, public activity as essential to a life of human dignity.[34]

The Universal Declaration of Human Rights and the International Human Rights Covenants codify an evolved shared understanding of the principal systematic public threats to human dignity in the contemporary world and the social and political practices necessary to counter them. To oversimplify only slightly, they set out a hegemonic political model very much like the liberal democratic (or social democratic) welfare state, in which all adult nationals are incorporated as full legal and political equals entitled to an extensive array of social welfare services, social and economic opportunities, and civil and political liberties.

This point is pursued in much greater detail below; here one need simply note that there is nothing fixed or inevitable about this political model or the list of rights with which it is associated. Quite the contrary, they are the result of particular historical political struggles and contingent processes of national, transnational, and international social learning. Nonetheless, the human rights ideal of political legitimacy is hegemonic in contemporary international society.

Contemporary issues

So far the discussion has been at a fairly high level of theoretical abstraction. The remainder of this chapter looks at four issues: the role of the state, international responsibility for human rights violations, cultural relativism, and the rise to normative prominence of democracy and markets. Although other issues might have been chosen, these have been extensively discussed in both the Cold War and post-Cold War eras. In addition, all four involve the central issue of the relationship between individuals, communities, and states.

In the first two sections, the approach will remain largely analytical, with a particular emphasis on evolving international practice with respect to human rights. In the following sections, however, the analysis becomes more normative and argumentative.

The state and human rights

However attractive one find the human rights vision of political dignity and legitimacy, the close tie to the state is problematic. The dominant contemporary conception of human rights mixes a cosmopolitan, universalistic vision of the source and subjects of human rights with a particularistic, nationalist vision of their implementation. This rather awkward compromise is most often assumed rather than justified.

Practically, it reflects the continuing dominance of the sovereign state, which remains the only agent widely capable of delivering the goods, services, and opportunities specified by international human rights norms. But can this political fact be morally justified? Consider (the little-discussed) Article 28 of the Universal Declaration: "Everyone is entitled to a social and international order in which the rights and freedoms set forth in this Declaration can be fully realized." Is a system of sovereign territorial states such an order? If so, is it the best such order? If not, is there a better practical alternative?

If, in contractarian terms, we can see the state as the free choice of self-determining individuals and communities, then a world of sovereign territorial states may satisfy the demands of Article 28. But even setting aside severely repressive regimes that cannot plausibly be imagined to reflect either the autonomous will of the people or the requirements of internationally recognized human rights, this privileging of the state is problematic. We should remain open to the possibility of right-holders choosing to exercise their rights collectively in communities smaller or larger than states.

Consider, for example, contemporary Europe, in which we see strong pressures towards both regional integration and subnational devolution of power. Individuals increasingly act within multiple political communities that reflect cross-cutting loyalties and identities, in contrast to the totalizing centralization of political power and identity in the nationalist state. In Belgium, Spain, and to a somewhat lesser extent Britain, we see fragmenting national identities and the emergence of non-state political communities that might suggest a more diverse and pluralistic conception of social actors with human rights obligations.

If recent talk about transnational or global civil society[35] is more than metaphorical or prescriptive, this is another possibility worth taking seriously. In any case, it would be dangerous to treat the currently dominant statist conception of political community uncritically as a fixed feature. Individual right-holders in principle have many more options within which they may choose to interact and seek to realize their rights.

International responsibility for gross violations

Recent efforts to establish international responsibility for genocide and related gross and systematic violations of internationally recognized human rights present a direct if implicit challenge to the statism of the Universal Declaration and the covenants. Under realist/positivist, standard-of-civilization, and self-determination conceptions of international legitimacy, how a state treats its own citizens within its own territory was largely unregulated by international standards.[36] International responsibility for national human rights practices was therefore virtually non-existent. Human rights violators were not legally accountable and international actors had no right to intervene even in response to the most gruesome violations. During the Cold War, most former dictators could expect, at worst, a comfortable retirement abroad in pleasant if somewhat isolated circumstances. Even genocide was met by expressions of shock and outrage coupled with inaction against the perpetrators.[37]

This is no longer the case. *Ad hoc* tribunals for the former Yugoslavia and Rwanda and the new International Criminal Court have established individual responsibility for genocide and crimes against humanity. Violators are seen as having international human rights obligations to international society, in addition to their direct and primary obligation to the right-holders under their jurisdiction.

In addition, multilateral field operations in places such as Somalia, Cambodia, Bosnia, Rwanda, and Kosovo suggest a different, but no less important, sort of international responsibility. These operations involve international society asserting a right to provide limited redress to victims, who are no longer left to the (often not-so-tender) mercies of a purely national system of implementing internationally recognized human rights. In certain cases, the international community will act on their behalf.

Such a limited doctrine of humanitarian intervention can be seen as an unfolding of the self-determination justification for sovereignty noted above. No free people could be imagined to choose for themselves treatment such as that suffered by, for example, Muslims and Croats in Bosnia or Serbs in Croatia following the break-up of Yugoslavia. International intervention is justified to restore the conditions under which self-determination is possible. But once a plausible argument of self-determination can be advanced, the obligation of non-intervention again takes priority.

Rights are enjoyed within nested political communities. And this nesting challenges the previously accepted exclusive claims of sovereign territorial states. Sovereign states and ruling governments are coming to be seen to have (limited) international human rights obligations not just to their own nationals but also to the international community. And these international responses have often been in situations where the victims were singled out in significant measure on the basis of their membership in an ethnic or other subnational community. In thus asserting both obligations to the international community and rights of subnational communities to a protected sphere of difference, the awkward compromise between statist and cosmopolitan conceptions of community would seem to be shifting, subtly yet significantly, against the state.

We should not overestimate the scope of these (undoubtedly important) changes. Humanitarian intervention remains a right rather than an obligation. Should international society fail to act forcefully, victims have no established recourse. And as Kosovo indicates, the nature and authority of the relevant "higher" community many not be clear or endorsed by anything close to the full range of interested and involved international actors.

Furthermore, we should not assume an inevitable, or even likely, spill-over from cases of genocide and crimes against humanity to more "ordinary" human rights violations. Coercive international enforcement of internationally recognized human rights remains rare and largely restricted to broader peace and security operations. Even severe violations in "ordinary" situations are usually not seen to authorize coercive international enforcement.[38]

Nonetheless, we do seem to be witnessing modest but important changes in dominant views of the obligations correlative to internationally recognized human rights. The international community, in at least some limited circumstances, may assert priority over states to assure the protection of internationally recognized human rights. And many of the leading cases involve the international community acting to protect subnational communities from a government that punishes them for their difference.

The simple state-citizen model of politics implicit in the Universal Declaration is at least fraying on the edges. States are coming to be seen as having (limited) human rights obligations to other states or the international community, as well as to their own citizens. In at least these limited cases, the political universality of human rights is significantly extended. Furthermore, human rights link individuals to both national and international communities, at least partially re-opening questions of national and international political legitimacy and the proper relation between individuals, seen as bearers of internationally recognized human rights, and the various communities in which they live their lives.

Cultural relativism

The idea that certain practices simply cannot be justified raises the issue of cultural relativism. An extensive literature in the 1970s and 1980s addressed the claim that there are radically different but entirely defensible regional, cultural, political, or religious conceptions of human rights – for example, African, Islamic, Western, socialist, and third world conceptions.[39] In the 1990s, a parallel argument about "Asian values" received considerable attention (at least prior to the Asian financial crisis).[40] The writer has been an active participant in many of these debates.[41] This section briefly summarizes the position developed by the author in earlier writings, considers some of its philosophical underpinnings, and extends it to the issues of community raised in the preceding two sections. Unlike the earlier sections where the argument was largely descriptive, here it will explicitly respond to the challenge posed by cultural relativism to the largely universalistic account of human rights developed earlier.

The theoretical challenge of relativism

The idea of *human* rights appeals to values and social practices that transcend cultural and political differences – however important those differences might be in other contexts. Any interesting sense of the adjective "human" requires that these rights be in some sense universal. And the standard language of universal human rights clearly reflects such an understanding.

The challenge of cultural relativism thus addresses the substantive extent of these (universal) rights, and their force relative to competing cultural and political claims. If there are few universal rights, and if the competing claims of society regularly take priority over even those rights, then the resulting vision of human rights is extremely relativist. Conversely, an extensive list of rights that usually take priority over competing social claims yields a relatively universalist vision of human rights.

Real disputes about the substance of internationally recognized human rights certainly do exist. For example, the right to property appears in the Universal Declaration, was not included in the covenants, but has made a considerable comeback in the 1990s. The international legal prohibition of "hate speech" is inconsistent with American constitutional law. Many Muslims reject the right to change one's religion (if it is Islam) or to have no religion at all.

Nonetheless, when we consider the extent of the list of rights in the Universal Declaration and the covenants, and the degree of cultural and political diversity in the world, there is a remarkable degree of consensus about the list of internationally recognized human rights. Few major states or social groups categorically reject more than a few of the rights in the Universal Declaration. Debate instead usually focuses on the implications of particular rights, priorities among them, and conflicts between human rights and other social and political values and concerns.

At its deepest level, the debate between relativism and universalism concerns our conception of human beings. Do we see them principally through the lens of what they share or how they differ? We might want to say that the issue is whether we think of people primarily as human beings or as social beings. But given the obvious fact that human beings live human lives only within rich and complex social settings, a better way to pose the question is "Do we see our social life more as an expression of a common humanity or as a series of often very different yet internally authoritative answers to the question of what it means to be human?"

The position to be defended here, already outlined earlier, is philosophically and historically relativist but politically much more universalist.

If the universality of human rights is a prescriptive claim about the proper way to organize society, and if human rights are constitutive norms, then the resulting account of human rights must be in some important sense relativist. Most societies have rejected these norms and have constituted social, political, and moral actors with identities very different from those of equal citizens with extensive rights against society. These visions cannot be dismissed as "wrong" or "immoral" without some neutral standard of evaluation – which the writer does not think exists.

Rather than transcendent values, the "grounds" or "foundations" of human rights are social acceptance in "our" world today. Their justification is ultimately functional: we accept human rights because of the social, political, and moral consequences of acting as required to realize these rights. The inherent human dignity on which human rights rest is a social project, not a fact of nature or reason.

Within this general theoretical relativism, however, a strong case can be made for the relative universality of internationally recognized human rights. Human rights represent our best effort to respond to the standard threats to human dignity posed by modern markets and modern states – which, in the contemporary world, have penetrated almost the entire globe.

In addition, the list of internationally recognized human rights reflects a relatively highly evolved, and still changing, conception of the minimum conditions for a life of dignity. Consider the case of economic and social rights. The "classic" Lockean list includes only the right to property. But we came to learn that this provided minimum economic dignity only for a small segment of society. And after many struggles by the excluded masses, dominant conceptions of economic and social rights changed dramatically. To take a very different example, in the contemporary world, where health is seen less as a matter of fortune and more as a matter for social provision, a right to health care has become central to our conception of a life of dignity – at least in countries other than the USA.

Given that it is relatively uncontroversial to say that the threats of states and markets are indeed (relatively) universal, the heart of the challenge of cultural relativism becomes a claim that in the contemporary world there is not considerable cross-cultural convergence on the underlying conception of human dignity expressed in the Universal Declaration. The author would argue, however, that most major cultural differences in the contemporary world could be relatively easily accommodated within the Universal Declaration.

The universality of the Universal Declaration

It is often argued that non-Western societies give more emphasis to the group, whereas Western societies give more emphasis to the individual. There is a lot of (politically dangerous) caricature here. For the sake of argument, however, let us accept this claim. What does it imply as a challenge to the universality of the Universal Declaration? Not much.

Articles 2 and 7, which require non-discrimination and equality before the law, are usually stressed at least as much by third world as Western governments and activists. The rights to life, liberty, security of the person, legal recognition, and protection against slavery and torture (Articles 3–6) have as wide an applicability in non-Western as in Western societies in the contemporary world. Much the same is true of legal rights to remedy, the presumption of innocence, and protection against arbitrary arrest or detention (Articles 8–11). Article 12's insistence that "No one shall be subjected to arbitrary interference with his privacy, family, home, or correspondence, nor to attacks upon his honour and reputation" has unusually wide cross-cultural resonance.

Even some "individualistic" civil and political rights have surprisingly wide appeal. Consider Articles 18–21. "Everyone has the right to freedom of thought, conscience, and religion." "Everyone has the right to freedom of opinion and expression." "Everyone has the right to freedom of peaceful assembly and association." "Everyone has the right to take part in the government of his country, directly or through freely chosen representatives." Even most governments that in practice systematically deny these rights rarely admit that this is what they are doing.

Certain rights are more genuinely problematic. Consider, for example, Article 16.

1. Men and women of full age, without any limitation due to race, nationality or religion, have the right to marry and to found a family. They are entitled to equal rights as to marriage, during marriage and at its dissolution.
2. Marriage shall be entered into only with the free and full consent of the intending spouses.

This does indeed seem to express a particular "modern", "Western" conception of marriage. But if we exercise a modest degree of interpretative liberty with the phrase "free and full consent of the intending spouses", considerable accommodation to "traditional" conceptions of the family and marriage are possible. In particular, so long as intending spouses are *legally* free to enter into a marriage or not, and are able to receive legal protection if they decide not to accept arranged marriages, the social pressures to accommodate broader family interests – which, of course, also exist in parts of many Western societies as well – will usually be acceptable.[42]

Furthermore, many of the group-oriented cultural differences to which relativists appeal can be accommodated by the way in which right-holders exercise their rights. For example, if Asians are more deferential, they will choose to exercise their civil liberties in more deferential ways than, say, Americans do. Those who are excessively aggressive or individualistic in the expression of their views are likely to have less attractive employment prospects and are unlikely to be elected to political office. They may even be shunned by wide segments of society. Human rights do not prohibit such social sanctions for behaviour that fails to conform to social norms. They only require that the state should not punish or discriminate against those with unpopular views or abrasive ways of expressing them.

But although societies do have considerable latitude in shaping their implementation of such rights, there are limits. The state may *not* incarcerate, harass, or deny otherwise available benefits or services to individuals simply because they hold or publicly express unpopular, or even offensive, religious or political beliefs. Female children may *not* be treated as chattels, to be disposed of in marriage at the discretion of their family. The claim of the Universal Declaration is that even where such practices have deep cultural roots – as they did in the West just a hundred years ago – they can no longer be justified.

For slavery, torture, the denial of legal personality, or the denial of food, such a claim is *relatively* unproblematic. Many societies have practised slavery. That simply does not justify it today – so long as we accept the basic notion that all human beings are entitled to certain basic goods, services, and opportunities. Torture has been a common practice in many societies. It is simply no longer acceptable, given the reigning conception of the right to personal security and bodily integrity. Many societies have allowed large numbers of people to starve in the face of natural or social disasters; almost nowhere is this accepted today.

Much the same is true, the author would argue, of just about all the rights in the Universal Declaration. They are in fact widely endorsed, by both governments and citizens. And where they are not, a very heavy burden of proof lies on those who would claim that the right ought not to apply in their society.

Occasionally, this may lead to a moral impasse. Perhaps the clearest examples involve religious fundamentalist regimes such as the Taliban in Afghanistan and the clerical governments that have ruled Iran for the past two decades.[43] These governments do explicitly claim that they recognize human rights only to the extent that they are already incorporated within divine revelation or established religious law and tradition. The fact that they are internationally recognized human rights is essentially irrelevant in the eyes of these regimes. Where there is conformity with international human rights norms, that is purely a matter of coincidence.

How should defenders of (universal) human rights respond in such cases? (In the remainder of this chapter the author speaks as a defender of a relatively universalistic vision of internationally recognized human rights.) We are significantly constrained by the overarching commitment to individual autonomy and collective self-determination. If people choose to make for themselves a life that rejects our vision of the good life, that is, within certain limits, their choice. The question then becomes determining whether indeed they have made that choice or have had it imposed upon them.

The politics of relativism

Often the "cultural" differences in question are relatively recent creations, or the creations of "outside" forces – such as the creation of Hutu and Tutsi ethnicities by Belgian colonial officials.[44] More often than not, they are political rather than cultural differences, involving at best a highly selective appropriation of local traditions. For example, revolutionary governments that engage in the massive repression of dissent usually have a hard time justifying their behaviour by truly cultural arguments (as is suggested by the growing dissent among even some clerical supporters of the Iranian revolution). China presents a particularly striking example of misplaced "cultural relativist" arguments: a Communist Party state dictatorship fully in control of the coercive apparatus of a modern state and army and actively hostile to most elements of traditional Chinese culture simply cannot plausibly be seen as an expression of "Chinese culture", however we might want to understand that term.

Even when political differences do have a deep "cultural" basis, political interests often hijack it. This is how the author reads much of the ethnic violence in the former Yugoslavia. Similar stories can be told about the political manipulation of ethnic differences in, for example, Nigeria, Kenya, and South Africa. And the "Asian values" touted by repressive ruling élites seem not to be shared even by other Asian governments, most notably in north-east Asia, or by many ordinary Asian people, as the examples of Indonesia and Myanmar suggest.

If we are to take cultural relativism seriously as an ethical position, we must abandon the unthinking statism that accepts whatever a government does as the expression of the will of its people. We must enquire, as a matter of fact, whether the practices in question have been chosen by or imposed upon a people. If the latter, there may be legal, political, or practical reasons not to intervene. But there is no moral reason to stand by idly.

Even the free choices of a people are subject to limits. If a majority chooses to massacre, enslave, or systematically subordinate a minority through force, outsiders face a choice of which side to support. (Silence and inaction effectively support the majority.) Only if we believe that all values are simply a matter of majority choice are we bound to choose a repressive majority – and even that is not clear if an international majority has condemned such practices. Conversely, there are a variety of good reasons, including universal human rights, for outsiders to choose to aid the minority.

What forms that aid should take is often a difficult question, as NATO's efforts in Kosovo vividly illustrate. When the violations of international human rights norms are less systematic or substantially less brutal, determining an appropriate international response is even more difficult. Nonetheless, outsiders are not ethically obliged to abandon foreigners to the mercies of their governments or societies.

States or societies that wish to make a plausible ethical appeal to an international obligation of non-intervention must be able to point to something more than their control over their territory by force. An argument that we have done it this way for a long time, or that some (larger or smaller) segment of the population wishes to do it this way now, is simply not persuasive. Those who wish to have their rights to sovereignty and self-determination respected can, in at least some cases, be plausibly required to respect the self-determination and basic human rights of those over whom they rule. And even if considerations of law or politics lead outsiders not to intervene with force, they have every right to condemn systematic violations of internationally recognized human rights and to use other means of foreign policy to encourage guilty governments to change their practices.

In practice, relativist arguments have had significant ethical force in few cases where there has been a strong ethical inclination to intervene on behalf of victims of gross human rights violations. Even if it is the way of Serbs to massacre Muslims in Bosnia and Kosovo, that is no reason for non-Serbs to accept that way. Much the same is true of Sudanese Muslims massacring non-Muslims in the south of their country, or governments in Guatemala and Paraguay massacring their native peoples, or Myanmar's government expelling a quarter of a million Myanmar Muslims (Rohingyas), or Somali clan leaders fighting one another and leaving hundreds of thousands to die of starvation.

When it comes to cases such as the Khmer Rouge in Cambodia, where traditional culture was an explicit target of repression, arguments of cultural relativism become a cruel joke. Much the same is true today of the Democratic People's Republic of Korea and Sierra Leone, where barbarism seems to have replaced any plausible conception of culture. And in countless other cases – such as China, Cuba, Iraq, Myaumar, and

Afghanistan to take some of the more extreme cases; or, less extremely, Indonesia, Cambodia, and Pakistan – where people are daily being forced to be what their government insists their cultural or political destiny commands them to be, the joke is only somewhat less cruel.

Perhaps the strongest evidence in support of the relative universality of internationally recognized human rights is the fact that the protections provided by these human rights seem to be widely desired by most people in most parts of the world. This is how the author reads the collapse of the Soviet empire and the near-universal delegitimation of military rule in Latin America and Africa, and even most of Asia, over the past dozen years. When allowed a choice, most people in all regions of the world have chosen human rights. And most regimes that systematically reject extensive portions of the Universal Declaration retain power only through systematic repression – which clearly evidences the regime's lack of legitimacy in the eyes of its own people.

If we are not to treat human beings as objects at the mercy of their government or society, some substantial appeal to "higher" values is required. Such appeals are undoubtedly morally problematic. But strong cultural relativism faces even more severe moral problems. And when the universalistic appeal is to international human rights norms, which have been remarkably widely endorsed by both states and citizens more or less across the globe, a position of relative universalism seems by far the least problematic course.

Democracy, markets, and human rights[44]

The post-Cold War world has also seen growing international endorsement of democracy as a form of political rule and markets as the basis of economic organization. The mutually reinforcing linkages between human rights, democracy, and markets are well known and regularly noted. In the USA, and in certain political circles in Britain and other countries, it has even become common to speak of the ideal regime type as "market democracies". The purpose here, however, is to draw attention to fundamental divergences between the political logic of human rights on the one hand and democracy and markets on the other.

Human rights and democracy

"Democracy is based on the freely expressed will of the people to determine their own political, economic, social and cultural systems and their full participation in all aspects of their lives." This statement from the Vienna Declaration, like all plausible definitions, is rooted in the etymology of the term "democracy", the Greek *demokratia*, literally, rule or power (*kratos*) of the people (*demos*). Thus David Held begins *Models of*

Democracy, an often-cited recent scholarly work, by defining democracy as "a form of government in which, in contradistinction to monarchies and aristocracies, the people rule".[45]

Exactly what it means for the people to rule has been, and remains, a matter of the most intense controversy. Of particular salience are the continuing debates over balancing democratic procedures (government by the people, in Jefferson's famous formula) with "substantive" democracy (government for the people). As a result, discussions of democracy as a political ideal usually shift their attention fairly rapidly to the adjectives – substantive, procedural, electoral, direct, representative, liberal, guided, people's – rather than the noun democracy.

Here, however, the author wants to keep the focus on the core sense of the term captured in the noun. Doing so, it quickly becomes evident that rule of the people and respect for human rights often point in very different directions, as a result of their very different visions of the relationship between society and its individual members.

Democracy in this root sense aims to empower the people, to assure that they, rather than some other group in society, rule. But it requires little of the sovereign people, who, as the Vienna Declaration put it, are free "to determine their own political, economic, social and cultural systems". Only if a sovereign people show respect for human rights, and thus constrain their own interests and actions, will democracy contribute to realizing human rights. In practice, however, the will of the people, no matter how it is ascertained, often diverges from the rights of individual citizens.[46]

Human rights, by contrast, aim to empower individuals, thus *limiting* rather than empowering the sovereign people and their government. By requiring that every person receives certain goods, services, and opportunities, the acceptable range of political, economic, social, and cultural systems and practices is severely restricted. Beyond *who* ought to rule – which is indeed given a democratic answer – human rights are concerned with *what* rulers do, with *how* the people (or any other group) rule.

Human rights are thus in an important sense profoundly anti-democratic. Their aim is to frustrate the will of the people when it diverges from the requirements of human rights. The American system of constitutional review by an "undemocratic", even "anti-democratic", Supreme Court provides a good example. One of its central purposes is to ensure that the people, through their elected representatives, do not exercise their sovereignty in ways that violate basic rights.

Governments in Britain, France, India, Japan, Costa Rica, South Africa, and the USA are indeed democratic. But what makes them truly attractive is the fact that they are what students of comparative politics typically call *liberal* democracies, a very specific kind of (democratic) government in which the morally and politically prior rights of citizens (and the requirement of the rule of law) limit the range of democratic decision-making. Democracy and human rights are mutually reinforcing in contemporary liberal democracies only because of a particular resolution of the *competing* claims of democracy and human rights that gives priority to human rights.

The democratic logic of popular rule operates only within the constraints set by individual human rights. The adjective "liberal"[47] rather than the noun "democracy" does most of the human rights work. The struggle for liberal democracy is a struggle for human rights – but only because human rights have been built into the definition through the adjective.

These vital distinctions have been obscured in many discussions of the late Cold War and early post-Cold War spread of (largely electoral) democracy, especially in Latin America and Eastern Europe. These "democratic revolutions" have undoubtedly benefited human rights. But even where anti-democratic forces have not reasserted themselves, many of these countries continue systematically to violate numerous internationally recognized human rights. Those not part of the majority – or whatever group exercises the power of the people – need the protection of human rights against the interests and will of "the people".

This is *not* a matter of "immature" (merely electoral) versus "mature" (liberal) democracies.[48] Liberal democracy is tempered or constrained, rather than matured (fully developed), electoral democracy. Similar difficulties beset efforts to talk about liberal democracy as thick, full, or robust, in contrast to a thin electoral democracy. The differences are qualitative, not quantitative. Rather than completing or realizing the full logic of popular rule, liberal democracy puts popular rule in its "proper" place, subordinate to human rights in most cases of conflict.

Human rights draw our attention to the fact that all individuals, simply as human beings, have powerful claims against society that typically override the preferences of even the vast majority. Democracy, by contrast, is a fundamentally collectivist or "communitarian" political logic. Its concern is not to protect individual rights, but to assure popular control of government. These very different political logics can be combined in a variety of ways. Only when human rights set the limits of democratic governance are democratic governments likely to be rights-protective regimes.

Development and human rights

Definitions of development are almost as diverse as, and perhaps even more contentious than, definitions of democracy. As in the case of democracy, human rights and development can be made compatible. But "development", in a standard, plausible, and even attractive sense of that term, can be pursued in ways that undermine internationally recognized human rights. Not all good things necessarily go together.

Consider the currently popular notion of "sustainable human development". As defined by the United Nations Development Programme (UNDP),[49] it includes empowerment, cooperation, equity, sustainability, and security.[50] It may be true that "human rights and sustainable human development are inextricably linked"[51] – but only because human rights, along with democracy, peace, and justice, have been thus defined as subsets of development. Even if we agree that "true" development is "sustainable human development", we still face the problem that *economic* development can be, and regularly is, pursued in ways that do not aim to realize internationally recognized human rights.

This is particularly true when economic development is understood – as it typically is today – as having at its core a matter of fostering market-based systems of production and exchange. Markets are social institutions designed to produce economic efficiency. Smoothly functioning market systems of production and distribution characteristically produce a greater output of goods and services with a given quantity of resources than alternative schemes. There is thus an almost tautological relationship between markets and rapid growth – which does seem to be substantively linked to realizing economic and social rights. Countries such as Cuba and Sri Lanka, which achieved short- and medium-run success but long-run failure under development plans that emphasized state-based (re)distribution over market-based growth, suggest that a considerable degree of economic efficiency (and thus market mechanisms) is necessary for *sustainable* progress in implementing economic and social rights.

Nonetheless, like (pure) democracy, (free) markets are justified by arguments of collective good and aggregate benefit, not individual rights (other than, perhaps, the right to economic accumulation). Markets foster efficiency, not social equity or the enjoyment of individual rights *for all*. Rather than ensure that every person is treated with concern and respect, markets systematically deprive some individuals to achieve the collective benefits of efficiency.

Markets distribute growth without regard for individual needs and rights (other than property rights), *necessarily and by design*. Market distributions are based on contribution to economic value added, which varies sharply and systematically across social groups (as well as between individuals). The poor tend to be "less efficient"; as a class, they have fewer of the skills valued highly by markets. Therefore, they are systematically disadvantaged. And their plight is exacerbated when economic and political disadvantage interact in a vicious rights-abusive cycle.

Market advocates typically argue that in return for such short-run dis-advantages for the few, everyone benefits from the greater supply of goods and services made available through growth. "Everyone", how-ever, does not mean each (every) person. The referent instead is the *average* "individual", an abstract collective entity. And even "he" is as-sured significant gain only in the future. In the here and now, and well into the future, many real, flesh-and-blood human beings and families suffer.

Efficient markets improve the lot of some – ideally the many – only at the (relative and perhaps even absolute) cost of suffering by others. That suffering is concentrated among society's most vulnerable elements. Even worse, because markets distribute the benefits of growth without regard to short-term deprivations, those who suffer "adjustment costs" – lost jobs, higher food prices, inferior health care or education – acquire no special claim to a share of the collective benefits that efficient markets produce. One's "fair share" is a function solely of efficiency, of monetary value added. The human value of suffering, the human costs of depriva-tion, and the claims they justify, are excluded from the accounting of markets.

The trick, as in the case of democracy, is to tame markets by allowing them to operate only within the constraints of the "higher" demands of internationally recognized human rights. In the liberal democracies of the Western world, the mechanism for achieving this has been the welfare state.

All existing liberal democracies compensate (some of) those who fare less well in the market through the welfare state (which, despite cutbacks, remains a powerful force in all existing liberal democratic regimes, and a central source of their legitimacy). Individuals who are harmed by the operation of social institutions that benefit the whole – markets and pri-vate property rights – are recognized to have a right to a fair share of the social product their participation has helped to produce. The collectivity that benefits in the aggregate has an obligation to look after individual members who are disadvantaged in or harmed by markets. The welfare state guarantees *all* individuals certain economic and social goods, ser-vices, and opportunities irrespective of the market value of their labour.

Assuaging short-term suffering and assuring long-term recompense are the work of the (welfare) state, not the market. These are matters of justice, rights, and obligations, not efficiency. They raise issues of indi-vidual rights. Markets simply cannot address them – because they are not designed to.

Free markets are an economic analogue to a political system of major-ity rule without minority rights. The welfare state, from this perspective, is a device to ensure that a minority who are disadvantaged in or deprived by markets are treated with minimum economic concern and respect. And because this minority is shifting and indeterminate – much like the minority who would engage in unpopular political speech or be subject to arbitrary arrest – these "minority rights" are actually individual rights for all.

Rights-protective regimes will pursue economic development. But development is desirable as much for the resources it makes available to provide economic and social rights for members of disadvantaged groups as for the intrinsic values of the goods produced. Rights-protective regimes will also be democratic. They are desirable, however, not primarily because they empower the people, but because we think that we have good reason to believe that empowering the people is the best political mechanism we have yet devised to secure all human rights for all.

Conclusion: Human rights and the contemporary state

Human rights are required to civilize both democracy and markets by restricting their operation to a limited domain. Free markets, like pure democracy, sacrifice individuals and their rights to a "higher" collective good. The liberal democratic welfare states of Western Europe, Japan, and North America are attractive models for much of the rest of the world because of the particular balance they have struck between the competing demands of democratic participation, market efficiency, and internationally recognized human rights.

All three adjectives – liberal, democratic, and welfare – are important. The state envisioned by international human rights norms is liberal in the fundamental sense that it is based on and committed to realizing the rights of its citizens. It is democratic. And it is a welfare state, committed to an extensive array of economic and social rights.

Democracy and development – and human rights as well – are not ends, but means to a life of dignity. Contemporary international society has in substantial measure defined such a life of dignity in terms of respect for internationally recognized human rights. And that vision, for all its problems, is an attractive one. In fact, the author would argue that the current hegemony of human rights and the liberal democratic welfare state owes more to the normative power of this vision than to the economic and military power of the states that support it.

Legitimate government in the contemporary world is government fit for the human beings envisioned in the Universal Declaration of Human Rights: equal and autonomous individuals, collectively in control of their destiny, and committed to all rights for all of their fellow citizens. Human rights are not a complete answer to the ongoing problems of creating such individuals and states. Even in the liberal democracies of northern Europe, where progress toward this ideal has been greatest, there is a long way to go. The post-Cold War world has been marked by tragedies such as Rwanda, which match in their horror some of the worst episodes of preceding decades. Nonetheless, the writer would like to close by suggesting that we do have good reason to think that, in part through the international spread of human rights ideas, we are lucky to be living in a time where we are seeing real political progress toward realizing an attractive vision of human dignity for all.

Notes

1. Thucydides, 1982, *The Peloponnesian War.* New York: Modern Library.
2. Morgenthau, H. J., 1954, *Politics Among Nations: The Struggle for Power and Peace,* 2nd edn. New York: Alfred A. Knopf, pp. 10–12.
3. Saxonhouse, A. W., 1978, "Nature and Convention in Thucydides' *History",* *Polity,* No. 10, Summer, pp. 461–487, at pp. 479–480.
4. Thus even Morgenthau, perhaps the most forceful advocate of separating power and interest from morality, notes "the curious dialectic of ethics and politics, which prevents the latter, in spite of itself, from escaping the former's judgment and normative direction": Morgethau, H. J., 1946, *Scientific Man Versus Power Politics.* Chicago: University of Chicago Press, p. 177. Nonetheless, one of the explicit defining elements of Morgethau's realism is that "universal moral principles cannot be applied to the actions of states": Morgenthau, note 2 above, p. 9.
5. We see this same misunderstanding in mainstream (realist and liberal institutionalist) discussions of norms, which are usually presented as categorically distinct from (material) interests. For a striking example from someone who considers herself a constructivist, see Klotz, A., 1995, *Norms in International Relations: The Struggle Against Apartheid.* Ithaca: Cornell University Press, especially p. 20. In Klotz's model, norms interact with interests, but interests remain defined in largely realist terms. Klotz does recognize, and even periodically call attention to, the constitutive nature of norms. When she presents her basic theoretical logic, however, norms are treated largely as an intervening causal variable – a position that all but the crudest realists can probably accept.
6. There is a strand of realist argument that treats the national interest as an ethical principle, and thus makes an ethical argument for an "amoral" foreign policy. For example, Robert Tucker argues that "the statesman has as his highest moral imperative the preservation of the state entrusted to his care": Osgood, R. E. and Tucker, R. W., 1967, *Force, Order, and Justice.* Baltimore: John Hopkins University Press, p. 304, n. 71. Morgenthau even speaks of "the moral dignity of the national interest": Morgenthau, H. J., 1951, *In Defense of the National Interest: A Critical Examination of American Foreign Policy.* New York: Alfred A. Knopf, pp. 33–39. Such views, however, are at least as problematic as the more common position represented by the Athenians at Melos. Most obviously , it is unclear, to say the least, why the interests of one's own group ought to count as an overriding ethical principle in dealings with others, except in a radically communitarian (almost egotistic) and inegalitarian account of ethics.
7. A second, somewhat more partial, exception is the literature on international distributive justice, which is addressed in Chapter 10 in this volume by Ethan Kapstein.

8. Walzer, M., 1977, *Just and Unjust Wars: A Moral Argument with Historical Illustrations*. New York: Basic Books.

9. In the USA, see for example Frankel, C., 1978, "Human Rights and Foreign Policy", *Headline Series*, No. 241, October; Brown, P. G. and MacLean, D., eds, 1979, *Human Rights and US Foreign Policy: Principles and Applications*. Lexington: Lexington Books; Morgenthau, H. J., 1979, *Human Rights and Foreign Policy*. New York: Council on Religion and International Affairs; Schlesinger, A. Jr, 1979, "Human Rights and the American Tradition", *Foreign Affairs*, No. 57, pp. 503–526; Buckley, W. F. Jr, 1980, "Human Rights and Foreign Policy", *Foreign Affairs*, No. 58, Spring, pp. 775–796. These writers cover what passes for the political "spectrum" in the American mainstream. The "radical" critique of Chomsky takes human rights no more seriously than realists, reducing the American pursuit of human rights to a convenient cover for narrow material interests: Chomsky, N., 1978, *Human Rights and American Foreign Policy*. Nottingham: Spokesman Books. This is more or less what William Calder in the case of Thucydides called a "pleasing introduction to the concrete and effective factor" of power: Calder, W. M., 1955, "The Corcyraean-Corinthian Speeches in Thucydides I", *Classical Journal*, No. 50, pp. 179–180, at p. 179.

10. See Meron, T., 1989, *Human Rights and Humanitarian Norms as Customary Law*. Oxford: Clarendon Press, ch. 2; Simma, B. and Alston, P., 1992, "The Sources of Human Rights Law: Custom, *Jus Cogens*, and General Principles", *Australian Year Book of International Law*, No. 12, pp. 82–108. For a forceful presentation of the alternative view, see Watson, J. S., 1999, *Theory and Reality in the International Protection of Human Rights*. Ardsley: Transnational Publishers.

11. Up-to-date ratification figures can be found at http://www.un.org/Depts/Treaty/final/ts2/newfiles/part_boo/iv_boo/iv_4.html and .../iv_3.html.

12. See, for example, Gubin, S. L., 1995, "Between Regimes and Realism – Transnational Agenda Setting: Soviet Compliance with CSCE Human Rights Norms", *Human Rights Quarterly*, No. 17, May, pp. 278–302; Thomas, D. C., forthcoming, *The Helsinki Effect: International Human Rights Norms and the Demise of Communism*.

13. See, for example, Brysk, A., 1994, *The Politics of Human Rights in Argentina*. Stanford: Stanford University Press; Steinmetz, S., 1994, *Democratic Transition and Human Rights: Perspectives on US Foreign Policy*. Albany: State University of New York Press; Keck, M. E. and Sikkink, K., 1998, *Activists Beyond Borders: Advocacy Networks in International Politics*. Ithaca: Cornell University Press.

14. A similar source is specified in regional instruments. The American Convention on Human Rights declares that "the essential rights of man ... are based upon attributes of the human personality". The Protocol of San Salvador bases human rights "on the recognition of the dignity of the human person". The African Charter on Human and Peoples' Rights declares that "fundamental human rights stem from the attributes of human beings". The Helsinki Final Act repeats the language of the covenants: human rights "derive from the inherent dignity of the human person".

15. In much the same vein, the preamble emphasizes "the responsibilities of all States ... to develop and encourage respect for human rights and fundamental freedoms for all", and calls upon "the peoples of the world and all States Members of the United Nations to rededicate themselves to the global task of promoting and protecting all human rights and fundamental freedoms so as to secure full and universal enjoyment of these rights".

16. This understanding has been reaffirmed in a series of UN Commission on Human Rights resolutions asserting "the universality, indivisibility, interdependence and interrelationship of all human rights" and claiming that "promoting and protecting one category of rights should therefore never exempt or excuse States from the promotion and protection of other rights". See Resolutions 1999/33, paragraph 3[d]; 1998/33, paragraph 4(d);

1997/17, paragraph 3(c); 1996/11, third preliminary paragraph; and 1995/15, third preliminary paragraph.

17. The possibly emerging exception in cases of genocide is discussed below.

18. Aristotelian virtue-based theories are another increasingly popular example of ends-based (teleological) theories. See, for example, MacIntyre, A. C., 1984, *After Virtue: A Study in Moral Theory*, 2nd edn. Notre Dame: University of Notre Dame Press; MacIntyre, A. C., 1999, *Dependent Rational Animals: Why Human Beings Need the Virtues*. Chicago: Open Court; Galston, W. A., 1980, *Justice and the Human Good*. Chicago: University of Chicago Press; Galston, W. A., 1991, *Liberal Purposes: Goods, Virtues, and Diversity in the Liberal State*. Cambridge: Cambridge University Press; Chapman, J. W. and Galston, W. A., 1992, *Virtue*. New York: New York University Press.

19. Within Anglo-American philosophy, a classic discussion can be found in Ross, W. D., 1930, *The Right and the Good*. London: Oxford University Press.

20. Deontological and teleological theories thus posit radically different accounts of the relationship between means and ends. Teleologists are concerned primarily with consequences, and thus ends. Actions ("means") are evaluated by their contribution to realizing the defining moral end (for example, utility maximization). Deontological theories of course recognize acts that have instrumental value, but they see the morality of an act as determined by its inherent nature, not by its consequences. Moral acts are required because they are right, not because they produce some other effect in the world. They are not a means to anything at all.

21. Kant, I., 1981, *Grounding for the Metaphysics of Morals*. Indianapolis: Hackett, pp. 71–77.

22. Dworkin, R., 1977, *Taking Rights Seriously*. Cambridge, MA: Harvard University Press, pp. 171–172.

23. Even Dworkin is at best a limited exception, given that his work is primarily concerned with legal and political, not moral, theory (a distinction discussed below). Perhaps a clearer example of a real exception is the work of Alan Gewirth: Gewirth, A., 1982, *Human Rights: Essays on Justification and Applications*. Chicago: University of Chicago Press; Gewirth, A., 1996, *The Community of Rights*. Chicago: University of Chicago Press.

24. The best-known such argument is probably Finnis, J., 1980, *Natural Law and Natural Rights*. Oxford: Clarendon Press. See also Maritain, J., 1943, *The Rights of Man and Natural Law*. New York: C. Scribner's Sons.

25. Kant, I., 1983, *Perpetual Peace and Other Essays*. Indianapolis: Hackett.

26. Rawls, J., 1996, *Political Liberalism*. New York: Columbia University Press.

27. Habermas, J., 1993, *Justification and Application: Remarks on Discourse Ethics*. Cambridge, MA: MIT Press; Habermas, J., 1996, *Between Facts and Norms: Contributions to a Discourse Theory of Law and Democracy*, transl. Rehg, W. Cambridge, MA: MIT Press; Habermas, J., 1998, "Remarks on Legitimation through Human Rights", *Philosophy and Social Criticism*, No. 24, pp. 157–171.

28. Gutmann, A., 1994, *Multiculturalism: Examining the Politics of Recognition*. Princeton: Princeton University Press.

29. If this is an exaggeration, it is a modest one. "Peace" and "development" are probably more widely endorsed. But neither – at least in their common senses of absence of war and sustainable economic growth – provides anything like the attractive comprehensive standard of political legitimacy offered by human rights. "Justice" may also be more widely endorsed, but only in a very abstract form – in contrast to the considerable substantive detail of lists of internationally recognized human rights.

30. This and the following section draw on arguments developed at greater length in Donnelly, J., 1989, *Universal Human Rights in Theory and Practice*. Ithaca: Cornell

University Press, chs 3–5; Donnelly, J., 1999, "Human Rights, Democracy, and Development", *Human Rights Quarterly*, No. 21, August, pp. 608–632.

31. For a good recent survey of the theory and practice of recognition, the branch of positive international law most closely related to such judgements of legitimacy, see Peterson, M. J., 1997, *Recognition of Governments: Legal Doctrine and State Practice, 1815–1995*. New York: St Martin's Press.

32. See Gong, G. W., 1984, *The Standard of "Civilisation" in International Society*. Oxford: Clarendon Press; Schwarzenberger, G., 1955, "The Standard of Civilisation in International Law", *Current Legal Problems*, No. 17, pp. 212–234. See also, more briefly, Donnelly, J., 1998, "Human Rights: A New Standard of Civilization?", *International Affairs*, No. 74, pp. 1–24. The following paragraphs draw on these works.

33. Hobbes, T., 1986, *The Leviathan*. Harmondsworth: Penguin.

34. At the risk of belabouring the point, in order to counter the common tendency to downplay the social dimension of international human rights, consider the following passages from the Universal Declaration. Human beings "should act towards one another in a spirit of brotherhood" (Art. 1). "Everyone has the right to a nationality" (Art. 15). "Men and women of full age, without any limitation due to race, nationality or religion, have the right to marry and to found a family ... The family is the natural and fundamental group unit of society and is entitled to protection by society and the State" (Art. 16). "Everyone has the right to own property alone as well as in association with others" (Art. 17). "Everyone has the right to ... freedom, either alone or in community with others and in public or private, to manifest his religion or belief in teaching, practice, worship and observance" (Art. 18). "Everyone has the right to ... seek, receive and impart information and ideas through any media and regardless of frontiers" (Art. 19). "Everyone has the right to freedom of peaceful assembly and association" (Art. 20). "Everyone has the right to take part in the government of his country ... The will of the people shall be the basis of the authority of government" (Art. 21). "Everyone, as a member of society, has the right to social security and is entitled to realization, through national effort and international co-operation and in accordance with the organization and resources of each State, of the economic, social and cultural rights indispensable for his dignity and the free development of his personality" (Art. 22). "Everyone who works has the right to just and favourable remuneration ensuring for himself and his family an existence worthy of human dignity, and supplemented, if necessary, by other means of social protection. Everyone has the right to form and to join trade unions" (Art. 23). "Everyone has the right to a standard of living adequate for the health and well-being of himself and of his family" (Art. 25). "Everyone has the right freely to participate in the cultural life of the community" (Art. 27). For an account of human rights that emphasizes its compatibility with strong communities, see Howard, R. E., 1995, *Human Rights and the Search for Community*. Totowa: Rowman and Littlefield.

35. For example, Lipschutz, R. D., 1996, *Global Civil Society and Global Environmental Governance: The Politics of Nature from Place to Planet*. Albany: State University of New York Press.

36. Even the nineteenth-century standard of civilization restricted the sovereignty of countries such as China, primarily in their external relations and in their dealing with foreigners. A selected set of "barbaric" practices were condemned and there was an expectation that "civilized" states would have some sort of representative political institutions. But these requirements were secondary, and they were not seen to extend to Western colonial powers in their imperial domains.

37. The principal exception was intervention by neighbouring countries – India in East Pakistan (Bangladesh), Tanzania in Uganda, Viet Nam in Cambodia – for reasons that had at least as much to do with non-humanitarian interests.

38. Haiti is the exception that proves the rule.
39. For strong general statements of this argument see Espiell, H. G., 1979, "The Evolving Concept of Human Rights: Western, Socialist and Third World Approaches", in Ramcharan, B. G., ed., *Human Rights: Thirty Years After the Universal Declaration*. The Hague: Martinus Nijhoff; Pollis, A., 1982, "Liberal, Socialist, and Third World Perspectives on Human Rights", in Schwab, P. and Pollis, A., eds, *Toward a Human Rights Framework*. New York: Praeger. For representative regional arguments, see Said, A. A., 1979, "Precept and Practice of Human Rights in Islam", *Universal Human Rights*, No. 1, pp. 63–80; Buultjens, R., 1980, "Human Rights in Indian Political Culture", in Thompson, K. W., ed., *The Moral Imperatives of Human Rights: A World Survey*. Washington: University Press of America; Leng, S-c., 1980, "Human Rights in Chinese Political Culture", in *ibid.*; Mojekwu, C. E., 1980, "International Human Rights: The African Perspective", in Nelson, J. L. and Green, V. M., eds, *International Human Rights: Contemporary Issues*. Stanfordville: Human Rights Publishing Group; Khushalani, Y., 1983, "Human Rights in Asia and Africa", *Human Rights Law Journal*, No. 4, pp. 403–442; Hsiung, J. C., 1985, "Human Rights in an East Asian Perspective", in Hsiung, J. C., ed., *Human Rights in an East Asian Perspective*. New York: Paragon House; Cobbah, J. A. M., 1987, "African Values and the Human Rights Debate: An African Perspective", *Human Rights Quarterly*, No. 9, August, pp. 309–331. For a general defence of a strong relativist approach to human rights, see Renteln, A. D., 1985, "The Unanswered Challenge of Relativism and the Consequences for Human Rights", *Human Rights Quarterly*, No. 7, November, pp. 514–540.
40. For representative statements, see Kausikan, B., 1993, "Asia's Different Standard", *Foreign Policy*, No. 92, pp. 24–41; Zakaria, F., 1994, "Culture is Destiny: A Conversation with Lee Kuan Yew", *Foreign Affairs*, No. 73, March/April, pp. 109–126. Two edited collections provide recent, often critical, assessments of these arguments: Bauer, J. R. and Bell, D. A., eds, 1999, *The East Asian Challenge for Human Rights*. Cambridge: Cambridge University Press; Van Ness, P. and Aziz, N., eds, 1999, *Debating Human Rights: Critical Essays from the United States and Asia*. New York: Routledge.
41. See Donnelly, J., 1982, "Human Rights and Human Dignity: An Analytical Critique of Non-Western Human Rights Conceptions", *American Political Science Review*, No. 76, pp. 303–316; Donnelly, J., 1984, "Cultural Relativism and Universal Human Rights", *Human Rights Quarterly*, No. 6, November, pp. 400–419; Donnelly, J., 1990, "Traditional Values and Universal Human Rights: Caste in India", in Welch, C. E. Jr and Leary, V. A., eds, *Asian Perspectives on Human Rights*. Boulder: Westview Press; Donnelly, J., 1990, "Human Rights, Individual Rights and Collective Rights", in Berting, J. *et al.*, eds, *Human Rights in a Pluralist World: Individuals and Collectivities*. Westport: Meckler; Donnelly, J., 1999, "Human Rights and Asian Values: A Defense of 'Western' Universalism", in Bauer and Bell, note 40 above.
42. If women choose to defer to men in family settings (as, for example, many American religious conservatives, and other religious fundamentalists across the world, argue that they should) this too is entirely defensible – so long as they are not legally required to do so and are protected against violence and certain other forms of reprisal if they get "uppity".
43. These examples are *not* intended to suggest that there is anything in Islam in particular that is hostile to internationally recognized human rights. It merely reflects the fact that there are no examples of fundamentalist regimes based on another religion. Religious fundamentalist political movements in countries such as the USA, Israel, and Poland have not acquired political power.
44. This section draws heavily on Donnelly, 1999, note 30 above.

44. Newbury, C., 1988, *The Cohesion of Oppression: Clientship and Ethnicity in Rwanda, 1860–1960*. New York: Columbia University Press.
45. Held, D., 1987, *Models of Democracy*. Stanford: Stanford University Press, p. 2.
46. This is not exactly correct. One may stipulate that the people don't *really* will anything inconsistent with internationally recognized human rights. For example, Rousseau claims that the general will is always perfect and incorruptible (*Social Contract*, Book I, ch. 3). In such a case, however, either democracy or human rights becomes superfluous.
47. In contemporary discourse, especially in the USA, "liberal" is used in reference to the non-Marxist left (antonym: conservative); supporters of economic markets (usually "conservatives"); and supporters of rights-based political systems (across the political spectrum). Liberal is used here only in this last sense, although below the author implicitly argues (rather contentiously) that it is more properly associated with the first than the second sense. Compare Dworkin, R., 1985. "Liberalism", in *A Matter of Principle*. Cambridge, MA: Harvard University Press; Donnelly, 1989, note 30 above, chs 4 and 5.
48. See Linz, J. A. and Stepan, A., 1996, *Problems of Democratic Transition and Consolidation: Southern Europe, South America, and Post-Communist Europe*. Baltimore; John Hopkins University Press; O'Donnell, G., 1996, "Illusions About Consolidation", *Journal of Democracy*, No. 7, pp. 34–51.
49. UNDP, 1997, *Governance for Sustainable Development: A UNDP Policy Document*. UNDP.
50. Compare Anand, S. and Sen, A. K., 1996, *Sustainable Human Development: Concepts and Priorities*. New York: UNDP, Office of Development Studies; Nussbaum, M. and Sen, A. K., eds, 1996, *The Quality of Life*. New York: Oxford University Press.
51. UNDP, 1998, *Integrating Human Rights with Sustainable Human Development: A UNDP Policy Document*. UNDP.

7

Environmental ethics in international society

Oran R. Young

Are we witnessing the emergence of a meaningful system of environmental ethics at the international level? To ask this question is to launch an enquiry into the roles that principles of proper conduct play in the realm of international environmental affairs. The concern here is not whether ethical principles ought to guide behaviour in this realm or what the content of such principles ought to be. Rather, the question to be addressed concerns the roles that ethical standards or codes of conduct actually play in a social setting considered by many to be antithetical to the operation of normative principles.

What is a meaningful system of ethics? As the term is used in this enquiry, an ethical system is an interlocking set of principles of proper conduct that address in a comprehensive manner the behaviour of actors in a recognized field of human endeavour. Legal ethics and medical ethics, for instance, constitute ethical systems in this sense. Ethical systems become meaningful to the extent that they guide the behaviour of identifiable groups of actors in significant ways. There is no need for all the members of a group to behave in ways that conform to the highest standards at all times for an ethical system to make a difference. The relevant question is: how much importance do individual members of the group attach to ethical principles in weighing the pros and cons of the choices they are called upon to make under a variety of circumstances? Looked upon in this way, both the comprehensiveness and the meaningfulness of ethical systems are variables whose value may range from high to low.

The principles of international environmental ethics have not been spelled out clearly, refined through repeated applications to concrete situations, and codified in a single authoritative text. There is no universal declaration or charter of environmental ethics that all or virtually all the actors in international society acknowledge as authoritative. Nonetheless, it is reasonable to focus in this discussion on a small number of well-known texts that most observers treat as particularly salient and influential expressions of environmental principles intended to guide the behaviour of actors at the international level. The following discussion pays particular attention to the ethical principles set forth in three key documents: the Stockholm Declaration on the Human Environment (1972), the World Charter for Nature (1982), and the Rio Declaration on Environment and Development (1992).[1] A fourth document, the draft Earth Charter, is worthy of some consideration in this connection as well.

This response to the question posed at the outset begins by endeavouring to extract and frame the major environmental principles embedded in these key texts; then poses and seeks to answer a series of interrelated questions about these principles. What are the nature and status of the environmental principles set forth in these sources? In what ways and to what extent do they influence the behaviour of the actors in international society? Do these principles in their current form add up to a coherent system of environmental ethics applicable throughout international society or, for that matter, global civil society? Has the content of this ethical system evolved or changed significantly over time? If so, what forces account for such changes?

The emergence of international environmental principles

The Stockholm Declaration adopted at the close of the UN Conference on the Human Environment (UNCHE) in 1972 spells out 26 separate principles. The Rio Declaration emanating from the UN Conference on Environment and Development (UNCED) in 1992 contains 27. For its part, the World Charter for Nature, approved in the form of a UN General Assembly resolution in 1982, has 24 operative paragraphs. Under the circumstances, it is impossible to canvass or even to summarize the full range of the emerging collection of normative prescriptions intended to apply to human/environment relations throughout international society. Even so, a brief account of the contents of these key sources will serve to lend substance to the concept of ethical principles pertaining to international environmental matters, and to ground the discussion in subsequent sections of the analytic questions posed at the outset.

Some environmental principles have been stated and restated in a highly consistent manner throughout the last several decades. Both Principle 21 of the Stockholm Declaration and Principle 2 of the Rio Declaration, for instance, set forth – in nearly identical language – the proposition that "States have ... the sovereign right to exploit their own resources pursuant to their own environmental policies and the responsibility to ensure that activities within their jurisdiction or control do not cause damage to the environment of other States or of areas beyond the limits of national jurisdiction."[2] The World Charter for Nature articulates much the same normative standard in somewhat different language. Paragraph 22 of the charter, for instance, states that "[t]aking fully into account the sovereignty of States over their natural resources, each State shall give effect to the provisions of the present Charter through its competent organs and in co-operation with other States".

In other respects, however, the last three decades have witnessed some significant developments in the normative discourse pertaining to proper conduct in the realm of human/environment relations as reflected in the three texts. At Stockholm, for example, issues relating to decolonization and racial discrimination were still very much on the minds of participants. Thus, Principle 1 of the 1972 declaration asserts that "policies promoting or perpetuating *apartheid*, racial segregation, discrimination, colonial and other forms of oppression and foreign domination stand condemned and must be eliminated". For its part, the 1982 charter is largely a product of rising concern throughout the world about the impacts of human activities on the natural environment. To illustrate, Paragraph 2 of the charter asserts that "[t]he genetic viability of the earth shall not be compromised; the population levels of all life forms, wild and domesticated, must be at least sufficient for their survival, and to this end necessary habitats shall be safeguarded". By 1992, on the other hand, the pursuit of human welfare in a sustainable manner had become a theme of transcendent importance. Principle 1 of the Rio Declaration, for instance, states that "[h]uman beings are at the centre of concerns for sustainable development. They are entitled to a healthy and productive life in harmony with nature."

Are there some central trends reflected in these ethical expressions of the 1970s, 1980s, and 1990s? It is appropriate to flag here the distinction between the concepts of environmental protection and sustainable development as platforms for normative discourses that overlap but that nevertheless suggest distinct approaches to human/environment relations. Characteristic of the earlier documents is the concern for environmental protection, framed in provisions like Paragraph 1 of the 1982 charter, which states that "[n]ature shall be respected and its essential processes shall not be impaired". Contrast this with the perspective underlying Principle 3 of the Rio Declaration, which asserts that "[t]he right to development must be fulfilled so as to equitably meet developmental and environmental needs of present and future generations". In many concrete situations, the discourses of environmental protection and sustainable development yield normative prescriptions that are the same or at least broadly compatible. Both provide ample justification, for instance, for acting in ways that protect biological diversity and show respect for the welfare of future generations. In the final analysis, however, sustainable development is an anthropocentric discourse. It conceives of development in terms of human welfare, even though it clearly recognizes the importance of maintaining the integrity of biogeophysical systems as a basis for enhancing human welfare over time.

Is there a way to synthesize these divergent but not necessarily discordant discourses? Although the language it employs is somewhat flowery, the Earth Charter represents one interesting response to this challenge. The preamble of the charter begins with the proposition that "it is imperative that we, the People of Earth, declare our interdependence with and responsibilities to each other, the larger community of life, and the evolving universe. In the midst of a magnificent diversity of cultures and life forms, we are one humanity and one Earth community with a common future." This leads directly to the conclusion that "[t]he choice is ours: to care for Earth and one another or to participate in the destruction of ourselves and the diversity of life". On this account, the ethics of environmental protection and the ethics of sustainable development converge. The pursuit of human welfare presupposes an effective effort to protect major ecosystems and vice versa.

The ethical core

The discussion will return to this question of evolution in the normative premises underlying the major discourses pertaining to human/ environment relations in a later section. In the meantime, however, it is possible to identify with some precision a small core of ethical guidelines or standards that have achieved widespread acceptance at the international level or are well on their way to attaining this status. Despite the absence of a single authoritative statement of these ethical principles, most observers would concur in including the following principles in the core.

The polluter pays principle

Perhaps the oldest and most widely shared principle of international environmental ethics centres on an acknowledgement that those whose actions cause harm to the welfare of others are responsible for the consequences of their actions. As phrased in Principle 21 of the Stockholm Declaration, the emphasis is on damage to the environment of "other States or of areas beyond the limits of national jurisdiction". The basic idea of this principle is clear enough. It features an extension of what is commonly known as the nuisance doctrine in municipal settings to international society and introduces, at least implicitly, the concept of liability as a normative construct applicable to international affairs. That said, however, the polluter pays principle raises a host of subsidiary issues which require attention but have not been addressed fully at the international level. Although Principle 21 refers explicitly to states, it seems reasonable to conclude that the doctrine applies also to the actions of non-state actors, such as corporations, whose actions may affect the welfare of those residing in other jurisdictions. What is less clear, however, is whether states are ultimately responsible for the damages caused by the actions of their nationals, including non-governmental organizations and multinational corporations incorporated within their jurisdictions. Unclear as well are the standards of liability associated with the polluter pays principle. Does the principle presuppose a standard of strict liability, in the sense that actors are responsible for the consequences of their actions regardless of knowledge or intent? Is it sufficient to compensate victims after the fact, in contrast to making a concerted effort to avoid causing harm in the first place? Are there workable guidelines concerning the calculation of damages in transboundary settings? Who represents interests that lie "beyond the limits of national jurisdiction"? The polluter pays principle does not offer any simple or straightforward answers to these and variety of similar questions.

Nor does international practice carry us very far in understanding the operational content of this ethical principle. Many commentators have viewed the Trail Smelter case, involving damages caused by a smelter operating in British Columbia to various actors located in the state of Washington, as an important step in this connection.[3] But subsequent efforts to flesh out the polluter pays principle have proven somewhat disappointing. In fact, there are a number of instances in which pollutees have paid or at least shared the cost of repairing damages attributable to the actions of others. In the 1976 convention dealing with discharges of sodium chloride into the Rhine river, for instance, the Netherlands as the downstream victim shouldered a larger share of the cost of clean-up than France, the state in which the source of the pollution was located.[4] Similarly, Finland and Sweden have found it cost-effective to provide financial assistance to several Eastern European countries in an effort to reduce the volume of airborne pollutants originating in that area but affecting ecosystems located in the Nordic countries.[5] Much the same can be said of a variety of instances in which advanced industrial states have sought to assist developing countries in efforts to eliminate or mitigate transboundary movements of airborne or waterborne pollutants. None of this should be taken as evidence that the polluter pays principle is invalid as an ethical standard. There can be no doubt that it is now regarded as improper or antisocial to act in ways that damage the welfare of those located in other jurisdictions. But these comments do point up the difference between the idea of polluter pays treated as an ethical principle, and the development of a system of liability rules that are sufficiently operational to be used in handling claims for compensation arising in specific situations.

The precautionary principle and the corollary of reverse onus

The basic idea underlying the precautionary principle is straightforward. In dealing with large atmospheric, marine, and terrestrial ecosystems, it is often impossible to pin down causal connections in a clear and generally accepted fashion. There is substantial evidence to support the propositions that overharvesting is a major cause of stock depletions in a variety of fisheries, that the long-range transport of sulphur dioxide and other airborne particulates is damaging lakes and forests, and that the emission of greenhouse gases (GHGs) into the atmosphere is leading to changes in the earth's climate system. Yet definitive proof is often hard to come by, especially in time to support decisions about steps needed to avoid irreparable damages. In situations of this sort, the precautionary principle asserts that definitive proof regarding the relevant causal links is not required as a basis for taking steps needed to prevent serious disruption of important ecosystems. The signatories to the 1987 Montreal Protocol, for instance, committed themselves to phasing out CFCs and related chemicals before the emergence of a scientific consensus regarding the causal mechanisms involved.[6] More recent efforts to agree on targets and timetables regarding reductions in GHG emissions constitute an even more dramatic example, since the uncertainties surrounding climate change today are considerably greater than those relating to ozone layer depletion during the mid-1980s.[7] But in all these cases, the underlying message is the same. Ethical behaviour at the international level requires policymakers to act in a timely manner to deal with major environmental threats, even when significant uncertainties remain regarding the biogeophysical processes involved.

Stated in this form, the precautionary principle is now widely accepted; it shows up regularly in international agreements and even in legally binding conventions and treaties.[8] The corollary of reverse onus, on the other hand, is a much more contentious prescription. In essence, this corollary asserts that in cases involving significant uncertainties regarding the environmental effects of proposed actions, the burden of proof rests with proponents to show that their actions will not cause serious harm to important ecosystems rather than with the opponents to show that these actions will prove injurious. Proving beyond a reasonable doubt that a given action will be environmentally benign is typically difficult and often impossible. Consider the matter of harvesting whales as a case in point. Proponents of the revised management procedure (RMP) have gone to great lengths to demonstrate that a controlled harvest of minke whales would pose no threat to exploited stocks of these animals.[9] Most thoughtful and informed observers find this reasoning convincing. Yet it remains difficult to overcome definitively the objections raised by those who oppose the consumptive use of whales under any circumstances. In such cases, it becomes important to ask what constitutes a reasonable doubt, and who should be authorized to resolve disagreements about such matters? Given the nature of ethical systems in contrast to legal systems, this is ultimately a matter to be settled by individual actors who must live with the consequences of their actions. This may strike some as evidence of the weakness of ethical principles. Yet the intensity of the controversy surrounding the corollary of reverse onus is itself a clear indication of the perceived importance of ethical principles, even in a highly decentralized setting of the sort exemplified by international society.

The principle of environmental equity

Environmental equity is, first and foremost, a matter of taking steps to ensure that the rich and powerful do not insulate themselves from environmental harm largely by displacing problems on to the poor and weak. Of course, such concerns arise regularly within societies in such forms as debates over the siting of facilities for storing wastes and industrial facilities involving the use of hazardous chemicals or the production of toxic wastes.[10] Given the growing gap between the rich and the poor in many societies, concern about the environmental victimization of the poor has emerged as a focus of growing importance at the policy level.[11] In international society, the principle of environmental equity applies to relations between and among states or whole societies. But the fundamental issues are much the same.[12] Three distinct sets of concerns regarding international environmental equity have come into focus in recent years. One has to do with opposition to the exploitation of developing countries as sites for the disposal or reprocessing of hazardous wastes. Much of the opposition to the Basel Convention on transboundary movement of hazardous wastes, for instance, rests on ethical sentiments of this sort. A second set of concerns centre on questions about the appropriateness or propriety of investing scarce resources in combating problems like climate change when many of the world's poorest countries lack safe drinking water, adequate sanitation facilities, and even secure food supplies. Beyond this lies a set of questions encompassing issues having to do with the provision of assistance to poor countries to allow them to participate effectively in global environmental regimes.[13] Such considerations are clearly reflected, for example, in the creation in 1990 of the Multilateral Fund as a means of providing financial assistance to developing countries in return for their active participation in the regime created to protect the stratospheric ozone layer.[14]

A dramatic current issue involving environmental equity centres on the effort to find ways to reduce or curb GHG emissions. Most developing countries have taken the view that the problem of climate change is a consequence of the actions of advanced industrial countries, so that it is unfair to expect developing countries to join any effort to protect the earth's climate system unless and until the wealthy countries take effective steps to come to terms with this problem. For their part, the wealthy countries, noting that large developing countries like China and India are on course to become major sources of GHG emissions in the near future, are anxious to find ways to persuade the developing countries to join in efforts to control GHG emissions sooner rather than later. In part, of course, this is a simple matter of bargaining. Perceiving that they have real leverage with regard to the issue of climate change, countries like China and India are determined to drive a hard bargain in their dealings with the advanced industrial countries on this issue. If anything, their determination has been strengthened by the relative failure of their efforts to gain support for a "new international economic order" (NIEO) during the 1970s.[15] But it would be a serious mistake to overlook the ethical dimension of this issue. There is clearly a sense in which the views of those representing developing countries are shaped by a feeling that it is improper for them to be asked to pitch in to solve a problem arising from the behaviour of others.[16] Unless countries like the USA, Japan, and Germany acknowledge the ethical basis of these views, progress toward forming a global coalition that is able to deal effectively with climate change is likely to be limited.

The principle of common but differentiated responsibility

In some ways, the principle of common but differentiated responsibility is an outgrowth of the principle of environmental equity. The essential idea underlying this principle involves joining a general acceptance of the proposition that we are all in the same boat with respect to many large-scale environmental problems, on the one hand, with an acknowledge-ment that the circumstances of individual countries differ markedly, on the other. There are at least two types of circumstantial differences that are worthy of consideration in this discussion. One type involves variations among states regarding actions that are causes of major envi-ronmental problems. The problem of climate change discussed in the preceding paragraph is a case in point. It would be absurd not to recog-nize the difference between the USA and a country like India with regard to responsibility for increases in levels of GHGs resident in the earth's atmosphere. The other type of difference centres on various measures of ability to pay or capacity to contribute to solving major environmental problems. It is obvious that poor countries, which are preoccupied with domestic problems like providing for the basic needs of their own citi-zens, are not in a position to make large contributions to efforts to solve transboundary or global environmental problems. The central thrust of the principle of common but differentiated responsibility in situations of this kind is to couple an acknowledgement that everyone bears some re-sponsibility for coping with large-scale environmental problems with a recognition of the fact that some members of international society are much better situated than others to provide the resources needed to ad-dress these problems. In effect, the principle combines a universal ethical standard with a pragmatic acceptance of marked differences in the mate-rial circumstances of individual members of international society.

In practice, of course, many difficulties arise in efforts to apply this principle to specific situations. One way to operationalize the idea of dif-ferentiated responsibility is to develop a sliding scale of contributions along the lines of the scale used to calculate contributions to the general fund of the United Nations. Yet experience with devising and periodically reforming such scales is far from reassuring from an ethical point of view. What is more, there are many cases in which the essential issue involves finding ways to help others to meet their obligations rather than agreeing on a specific scale of contributions. In some instances, efforts to come to terms with such matters have worked reasonably well. The role of the Multilateral Fund in the case of ozone has already been mentioned as a positive example. Some of the activities of the Global Environment Facility (GEF) with regard to the protection of biological diversity and the control of GHG emissions are worthy of note in this connection as well.[17] In more general terms, however, there are major problems in living up to this element of the principle of common but differentiated responsibility.[18] At the UNCED conference in 1992, for instance, there was a recognition of the need for the advanced industrial countries to provide new and additional assistance to developing countries ready and willing to make a serious commitment to coming to terms with issues such as the protection of biological diversity. But the actual performance of leading countries like the USA in these areas during the years that have elapsed since the close of UNCED can only be described as disappointing.[19] This does not call into question the validity of the principle of common but differentiated responsibility. But it does underline the magnitude of the gap between the ideal and the actual in this realm.

The principle of obligation to future generations

There is nothing new about the general idea that those alive today have an ethical or moral obligation to pass on biogeophysical systems to the members of future generations that are as productive and resilient as those they inherited from their predecessors.[20] The essential idea here is that, contrary to what some legal systems suggest about the ownership of land and natural resources, the members of each generation are merely temporary residents of the earth who are entitled to use major ecosystems to enhance their own welfare but only on the condition that their activities do not impair the ability of members of future generations to use the same resources to pursue their welfare.[21] Many cultures have developed their own versions of this principle. The indigenous peoples of North America, for instance, often emphasized the need to think about the welfare of the seventh generation beyond the present. Others have suggested an approach in which each generation is seen as owing a debt to the preceding generation that it can only discharge by making a concerted effort to leave ecosystems in good condition for the members of the next generation.[22] But however we choose to conceptualize this principle, its ethical character is crystal clear. The fact that current users of natural resources and environmental services will disappear from the scene in the future makes it exceedingly difficult to devise any ordinary system of sanctions designed to constrain the behaviour of these users in the interests of securing or even enhancing the welfare of future users. Yet the limitations of utilitarian considerations of this sort do not weaken the influence of the obligation to members of future generations treated as an ethical precept.

What does require comment in this account is the proposition that the principle of obligation to future generations has become an ethical standard operative in international society. In essence, this development is a simple corollary of the growing capacity of humans to cause lasting damage to ecosystems on a very large scale. Consider the ethical issues surrounding the use of nuclear energy in this connection. As the Chernobyl catastrophe has made abundantly clear, nuclear accidents can produce dramatic transboundary impacts whose consequences will affect the welfare of large numbers of people over a period of hundreds or even thousands of years. In the face of dangers of this magnitude, it may not seem surprising that even those policy-makers who regard themselves as realists and whose decisions are grounded in the realities of power politics find themselves thinking hard about the ethical dimensions of their choices and backing away from actions that may seem attractive in terms of their short-run political consequences. Similar remarks are in order about human actions that are likely to drive numerous distinct species to extinction and, in the process, alter forever the composition of some of the earth's major ecosystems. In an important sense, therefore, the emergence of an obligation to future generations as an international environmental principle is simply a reflection of the scale of many human actions undertaken in today's world, or the advent of what some observers describe as human-dominated systems.[23] Where it once was sufficient to apply this principle to the actions of individuals or local communities, it now seems appropriate to bring the same principle to bear in assessing the actions of states and other large and powerful actors such as multinational corporations.

The principle of stewardship

The idea of stewardship points to the unique role that humans play as actors in major earth systems. It is pointless to ask members of other species to behave in ways that demonstrate a concern for the maintenance of large ecosystems; they are not moral agents in the ordinary sense of the term. In many cases, it is possible to justify a concern for the maintenance of ecosystems in purely utilitarian terms. Those who deplete stocks of living resources today, for example, will be faced with more or less severe shortages of these resources tomorrow. Similarly, those who pollute ecosystems in the short run may well suffer from the health effects arising from pollution in the future. Important as these utilitarian considerations undoubtedly are in some cases, it seems clear that the idea of stewardship is now emerging as a more general ethical principle. The premise here is that the uniqueness of the role that humans play as moral agents carries with it an ethical responsibility to look after the welfare of physical, and especially biological, systems that goes well beyond simple utilitarian calculations concerning the specific benefits accruing to humans from the maintenance of healthy ecosystems.[24] Embedded in this perspective is a clear sense that those whose superiority allows them to dominate the earth must also accept a special obligation to sustain those ecosystems that are critical to the maintenance of life on the planet.

The principle of stewardship should be distinguished from two other ethical perspectives that have received a good deal of attention in general discussions of environmental ethics. One is the idea that at least the higher orders of animals (such as whales and wolves) have a right to life, a proposition that would make it unethical for humans to kill these animals intentionally or to engage in actions whose side-effects are likely to deprive them of life.[25] This ethical position surfaces at the international level with some regularity, just as it does in various domestic settings. Yet there is little evidence to suggest that respect for the life of non-human organisms is emerging as a universally accepted principle of international environmental ethics at this stage. Nor is any such perspective implicit in the principle of stewardship, which is perfectly compatible with efforts to harvest fish and wildlife so long as these activities are carried out in a manner that is sustainable and humane. Another idea centres on Aldo Leopold's concept of biotic citizenship,[26] which treats humans as members of large ecosystems or "biotic citizens" and seeks to shift attention from the pursuit of human welfare to the pursuit of biotic welfare. Such a view leads, in Leopold's well-known formulation, to the dictum that "[a] thing is right when it tends to preserve the integrity, stability, and beauty of the biotic community". Whatever the general attractions of this way of approaching environmental ethics, there is little reason to believe that such a shift from anthropocentric to biocentric perspectives is under way at the international level at this time. The rapid growth of the world's human population is sufficient by itself to ensure that anthropocentric perspectives on sustainability are likely to dominate the international discourse on environmental ethics for the foreseeable future. Yet none of this undermines the validity of the principle of stewardship, which enjoins humans to act as moral agents and behave in ways that do not drastically upset the functioning of the earth's major ecosystems.

The principle of caring for the earth

Stewardship is an idea that applies to human/environment relationships regardless of the circumstances in which they occur. But today it has become apparent that human actions have reached a stage where they can affect the operation of major components of the earth's atmosphere, biosphere, and hydrosphere that are vital not only to human life but also to other life forms on the planet. Partly, this is a matter of the dramatic growth in the human population, which has now reached six billion and is expected to grow to 10–12 billion before reaching equilibrium.[27] In part, it is a result of technological developments that allow individuals to make much greater demands on the earth's resources than they did in the past. Not surprisingly, these developments have triggered the growth of new ways of thinking about human/environment relationships. Thus, we now find ourselves devoting more and more attention to the dynamics of human-dominated ecosystems and the role of anthropogenic drivers as major forces affecting the evolution of large atmospheric, marine, and terrestrial ecosystems.[28] Such developments have led as well to the emergence of more evocative ideas, like the vision of spaceship earth and the concept of the limits to growth.[29] Clearly, there is much that we do not understand about the role of humans as the dominant players in large biogeophysical systems. Much remains to be done, for instance, in identifying conditions that determine whether various practices involving consumptive uses of living resources are sustainable or unsustainable. Yet it is hard to avoid the conclusion that this dramatic rise in the role of humans as dominant players in large biogeophysical systems has raised pressing ethical issues that did not merit serious consideration in earlier eras.

The result in ethical terms has been a striking increase in the development of normative precepts centred on the idea of caring for the earth and its vital life-support systems. As the current draft of the Earth Charter puts it, "[w]e affirm that Earth's life support systems and resources are the common heritage of all and a sacred trust". The result is a growing insistence on the importance of "promoting the well-being of the planet" and conserving "the ecological processes that sustain and renew life, ensuring the long-term biotic regulation of these processes". For some, these ethical precepts are undergirded and strengthened by the idea that the earth itself is a living organism that must be accorded respect and cared for as an entity that deserves compassionate treatment in its own right.[30] But it is not necessary to rely on this perspective – sometimes described as the Gaia hypothesis – to frame a set of ethical injunctions centred on the principle of caring for the earth. As in a number of other cases, it is perfectly possible to formulate a utilitarian rationale for adopting the basic argument underlying the principle of caring for the earth. Some will see this utilitarian calculus as a sufficient basis for engaging in appropriate conduct in this realm. But others point to the role of ethical principles as behavioural guidelines whose influence extends well beyond the realm of utilitarian calculations, and which may prove more effective in shaping behaviour than injunctions requiring actors to weigh the costs and benefits associated with the options confronting them. In effect, the idea embedded in this principle is that caring for the earth is always the right and proper or appropriate thing to do, so there is no need to resort to elaborate computations of costs and benefits to convince oneself of the rectitude of this course of action.[31]

The character of international environmental principles

What is the essential character of these ethical principles, whose formulation and codification has become the focus of animated debates and vigorous negotiations over the past few decades on the part of sizeable groups of actors at the international level? Have some of these principles (such as Principle 21 of the Stockholm Declaration) passed into customary international law, thereby acquiring the force of law with regard to the behaviour of identifiable groups of subjects? Does the articulation of these principles in formal declarations or resolutions of the UN General Assembly signify a high level of political commitment on the part of sponsors and signatories to their implementation? If the answers to these questions are negative, what is it that accounts for the influence of international principles, and why should we pay attention to them?

To address these questions, this discussion will start with a definition and then proceed to unpack this general formulation. International principles are norms of social – in contrast to antisocial – conduct that are neither legally binding nor backed by firm political commitments but which nevertheless have demonstrable consequences for the ways in which key actors frame current issues and go about dealing with them. Principles, on this account, are not simply primitive, underdeveloped, or evolving rules that stand in need of further refinement and "upgrading" in order to move them over time towards the status of legally binding prescriptions. Rules are more or less well-defined behavioural prescriptions spelling out prohibitions, requirements, and permissions that members of specified groups of subjects are expected to comply with on a regular basis.[32] We know from domestic experience that rules – at least in their initial and more general formulations – are often articulated in ways that leave a lot to be desired in providing guidance that is sufficiently specific to prove helpful in directing the actions of individual subjects in concrete situations. The resultant need to make a transition from paper to practice is what gives rise to extended efforts to devise regulations to operationalize rules, and to the elaborate procedures often associated with the promulgation and interpretation of regulations. Yet none of this alters the fact that rules are normally intended to be treated as prescriptions requiring compliance on the part of identifiable subjects under more or less well-defined circumstances. Principles, by contrast, reflect more general normative aspirations that are meant to be viewed as guidelines for proper conduct that may or may not determine the choices actors ultimately make in specific situations.

Similarly, it would be a mistake to assume that the articulation of principles in the form of declarations or UN General Assembly resolutions implies that, in crafting and approving the language of these documents, their authors are committing themselves politically to a sustained effort to conform to the resultant norms. In saying this, the writer does not mean to imply that the framing of environmental principles is an exercise in political cynicism or a conspiracy on the part of diplomats to delude themselves and deceive others about the true nature of their endeavours. The fact that the authors of these documents know that they cannot count on their governments to make a sustained effort to conform to their requirements in specific situations does not constitute proof that the articulation of principles is ultimately an empty gesture. In effect, the framing and publicizing of principles is an exercise in spelling out normative aspirations. The assumption is that the establishment and periodic reaffirmation of these principles will exert a normative pull over time that affects the behaviour of a wide range of actors, even if they fail to conform to the standards in specific situations. Those who acknowledge the normative validity of ethical standards will experience – often internalized – pressure to justify their actions in terms that make them compatible with the standards. And those who feel the need to justify their actions in this manner will find that it makes life easier to conform to the standards whenever it is not unduly difficult or costly to do so. In short, the authors of international principles are in the game for the long haul. They will be more interested in the broad flow of behaviour over time than in statistics regarding levels of compliance at any given time.

With these distinctions in mind, we can begin to make sense out of several attributes of international principles that many observers have found puzzling or even downright confusing. For starters, it is perfectly normal to express ethical principles in generic or highly abstract terms.[33] Broadly speaking, this is true in all social settings. If anything, however, the abstractness of international principles is even more striking than that of their domestic and especially their local counterparts. Consider, in this connection, the principles that states have a "responsibility to ensure that activities within their jurisdiction or control do not cause damage to the environment of other States or of areas beyond the limits of national jurisdiction" and that human beings "are entitled to a healthy and productive life in harmony with nature". How much damage does it take to trigger the first of these principles? What about psychic damage, in contrast to material damage? How can we separate out the causal significance of the activities of specific actors in complex multivariate relationships? What is the test of the ability of states to control the impacts of activities outside their jurisdiction? What measures of health and productivity are appropriate in measuring human welfare? How should we interpret the phrase "in harmony with nature"? Do residents of advanced industrial societies live in harmony with nature? This is not just a simple matter of authoritative interpretation of the sort that is familiar in efforts to apply legal rules to specific situations. The fact is that the range of situations to which ethical principles apply is so great that there is little hope of operationalizing them through any straightforward process of interpretation. Is this a fatal flaw? Not necessarily. Unlike rules that require compliance, principles are better understood as broad normative guidelines. There is no expectation that actors will comply with them in any explicit or uniform sense. Their role is to provide direction for those seeking guideposts in terms of which to judge the appropriateness of alternative choices in a wide range of situations.[34]

Under the circumstances, it should come as no surprise that ethical principles framed in generic terms frequently run counter to – or even contradict – one another.[35] More or less pronounced tensions are even embedded within some individual principles. Consider Principle 21 of the Stockholm Declaration/Principle 2 of the Rio Declaration as a case in point. This principle asserts, at one and the same time, that states are entitled to exploit their resources without interference on the part of others and that they have an obligation to do so without harming either the environment of others or the global commons. Of course, there is nothing unusual about rights that are accompanied by restrictions serving to limit the freedom of action of the right-holders. But in this case, the assertion of the principle of sovereignty makes it hard to see how outsiders who suffer injuries can have any assurance of receiving just compensation, given that those responsible for the damages may refuse to allow outsiders access to their municipal legal systems and that international legal proceedings require a willingness on the part of both parties to accept the jurisdiction of relevant courts (such as the International Court of Justice). There are, in addition, obvious possibilities for conflict between distinct ethical principles. Consider the principles of environmental equity and responsibility to future generations in this connection. Given the rapid growth of the earth's human population, it may prove exceedingly difficult to provide a "healthy and productive life" to those alive today while at the same time taking steps to ensure that members of future generations can look forward to a similar quality of life. If we now add the precautionary principle to this mix, matters become even more complex. According to many who have paid attention to these issues, we should be cutting back on current rates of use of nature's capital in order to ensure that the earth remains hospitable to humans who will inhabit it in the future. Yet it would be difficult to persuade anyone that the principle of environmental equity can be fulfilled at the level of consumption characteristic of the developing world today, and the prospects for inducing residents of advanced industrial societies to cut back voluntarily on current consumption levels are dim.

There is nothing unusual about these difficulties in operationalizing abstract principles and sorting out the tensions arising between or among them. Doctors face problems of this kind on a regular basis in making decisions about the use of procedures designed to prolong the life of terminally ill patients. So do lawyers who find themselves in the position of defending clients, including corporations as well as individuals, whose behaviour they regard as ethically suspect and whose actions they have reason to believe violate existing laws. It may be that these problems are particularly severe with regard to international ethics in general and international environmental ethics more specifically. International environmental problems, such as what to do about climate change or the loss of biological diversity, tend to be extremely complex; they lend themselves to a variety of plausible interpretations from an ethical point of view. What is more, those who make decisions on behalf of states and other international entities often find themselves confronted with severe conflicts arising from the fact that they occupy a number of distinct roles at the same time. It is tempting, for example, to opt for courses of action that promise to enhance national security, at least in the short run, even when the results may be difficult to justify in terms of any reasonable standard of equity covering relations among the members of international society. But it would be a mistake to exaggerate such differences between the operation of ethical systems in international society and the operation of similar systems in a variety of other settings. Rather, it seems more productive at this juncture to turn to a discussion of ways to think about the effectiveness of international environmental principles.

The effectiveness of international environmental principles

If international environmental principles are construed as norms of proper conduct rather than as primitive or underdeveloped rules, how should we think about their effectiveness or, in other words, the role(s) they play in guiding or shaping the course of events in international society? We know – or think we know – what questions to ask in evaluating the effectiveness of rules.[36] Have the rules been operationalized through some process of promulgating detailed regulations? What is the level of compliance with the rules on the part of members of the relevant groups of subjects? Is there some procedure available to generate authoritative interpretations of individual rules in cases where affected parties disagree about their operational meaning? To the extent that this account of the character of ethical principles is correct, however, it will not do to approach the issue of their effectiveness in terms of questions of this sort. Instead, they require a different approach to the assessment of effectiveness. This section suggests four distinct – albeit related – ways to assess the effectiveness of ethical principles in international society. Although these perspectives do not lend themselves easily to the development of quantitative indicators, it will be argued that they nevertheless provide a basis for understanding the importance of ethical principles, even in a highly decentralized social setting of the sort prevailing at the international level.[37]

Ethical agendas

One way in which the emergence of ethical principles influences the course of world affairs is through the development of a clear vocabulary that actors can and do use in framing items for inclusion on the international agenda and defining appropriate ways to address the issues embedded in them. During much of the post-war era, the dominant discourse in world affairs has featured a (neo)realist emphasis on the role of states construed as unitary actors that pursue their interests through interactions guided for the most part by considerations of power in the material sense. This discourse lends itself to detailed assessments of initiatives designed to enhance the power of individual actors or to counter similar actions on the part of others.[38] But the realist lexicon does not offer much scope for sophisticated efforts to expand the international agenda to include issues framed as matters of environmental equity or obligations to care for the earth's life-support systems. In this context, the role of environmental principles is, first and foremost, to frame a new set of questions for consideration at the international level and, having done so, to provide a coherent array of terms and concepts that policy-makers can use in seeking to develop persuasive answers to such questions as they arise in specific situations.

No one expects the polluter pays principle to lead in the near future to an established practice in which states routinely comply with legally binding liability rules and regularly compensate victims located in other countries for damages arising from actions taken within their own jurisdictions. Yet the emergence of the polluter pays principle has provided a basis for talking about the environmental responsibilities of states, and more specifically the obligation to avoid causing injuries to others and compensate those who do suffer injuries, even in a world in which the influence of the doctrine of sovereignty remains strong. Similarly, the principle of caring for the earth provides a frame of reference for addressing issues that transcend mundane considerations of power politics. No one expects this principle to deter influential actors from engaging in various forms of power politics. But it does pose and offer a way to think about questions concerning the appropriateness or legitimacy of using environmentally destructive means (for example, detonating nuclear weapons, or setting fire to oil wells) in the pursuit of ends defined in terms of national interests. The issue here has more to do with providing the vocabulary needed to frame ethical questions than with determining how actors should respond to these questions in specific situations.[39] Powerful actors may seek to deny the relevance of ethical questions under particular circumstances. But once clear and compelling formulations of these questions make their way on to the international agenda, it becomes harder and harder for policy-makers to ignore them with impunity.

Discursive contexts

An important role that the resultant linguistic capital can and often does play is to provide a normative foundation on which to base efforts to devise the operative rules or behavioural prescriptions that comprise the operating provisions of environmental regimes (such as the regimes dealing with the control of climate change or the protection of biological diversity). For the most part, this normative foundation is reflected in the preambular language of the relevant conventions and treaties, where it is not intended to offer a substitute for legally binding rules. References to the polluter pays principle, the precautionary principle, and the principle of common but differentiated responsibility, for instance, are now common features of the preambles of international environmental agreements. Thus, the preamble of the climate change convention restates the gist of UNCED Principle 2 and then goes on to call for "the widest possible cooperation by all countries ... in accordance with their common but differentiated responsibilities and respective capabilities" in the effort to avoid anthropogenic disruptions of the earth's climate system. Similarly, the biodiversity convention's preamble asserts that "lack of full scientific certainty should not be used as a reason for postponing measures to avoid or minimize" the loss of biological diversity. The significance of the inclusion of this language does not arise from any expectation that the parties to the relevant agreements will treat these principles as behavioural prescriptions and judge each other's performance in terms of compliance with the requirements of the principles. Rather, these preambular assertions serve a discursive function that helps to establish the overall character or identity of collections of rules that are undoubtedly significant in their own right but which do not form cohesive wholes in the absence of the conceptual foundation provided by the normative precepts set forth in preambles, which set the stage for the operational provisions to follow.

Non-utilitarian reasons

One of the attractions of utilitarianism as an approach to decision-making is that it offers a mode of reasoning about specific choices that is straightforward, at least in conceptual terms. Once an issue is framed and the options identified, it is a relatively straightforward matter to enquire into the benefits and costs associated with individual options and to select the alternative yielding the greatest net benefit. Nonetheless, most policy-makers are well aware of the limitations of this mode of reasoning. This is partly a matter of appreciating the complications involved in making calculations of benefits and costs in situations involving multiple actors, complex interdependencies, and high levels of uncertainty. In part, however, it arises from the fact that utilitarian calculations do not offer a simple way to incorporate a variety of factors which loom large in the minds of many but which are difficult to represent in terms of conventional ways of thinking about benefits and costs.[40] Such factors range from the role of custom or tradition to considerations of legitimacy and propriety. Of course, reasons of this kind can influence behaviour without being introduced into policy-making processes on a conscious level. But in many cases, the problem of coming to terms with these non-utilitarian reasons to act in one way or another arises from the absence of suitable concepts in terms of which to articulate such considerations and juxtapose them to more conventional considerations expressed in terms of benefits and costs.

An important function of ethical principles, in this connection, is to provide structure and content to arguments about the merits of alternative courses of action that are not – and sometimes cannot be – expressed in the language of benefits and costs. The idea that the current generation should acknowledge obligations to the members of future generations has far-reaching implications for policy-making in a variety of situations, for instance, but it is not a simple matter of imputing costs to particular options that can be compared directly with other costs or benefits. Much the same can be said about the role of environmental equity as an ethical consideration that demands attention regardless of its impact on benefit/cost calculations. Needless to say, no one expects ethical reasons to trump utilitarian reasons on a regular basis and, in the process, alter dramatically the behaviour of important actors in world affairs.[41] Even so, providing a coherent language in terms of which to express non-utilitarian reasons constitutes an important step, in the sense that it makes it harder to ignore such considerations or to dismiss them on the grounds that they do not offer behavioural guidance that is sufficiently clear to compare and contrast with preferences derived from utilitarian calculations.

Normative benchmarks

Defining questions and providing a mode of reasoning in terms of which to address them are important contributions. But ethical principles also play a role in spelling out standards to be used in evaluating and judging behaviour after the fact. Many policy-makers are goal-oriented actors who exhibit a pronounced tendency to take the view that the ends justify the means under a wide range of circumstances. Yet it would be a mistake to assume that policy-makers are insensitive to the importance of justifying their actions in normative terms, whether this is a matter of assuaging their own guilty consciences or of avoiding shame in the eyes of others. In this connection, environmental principles enjoining actors to make contributions to solving common problems (such as controlling transboundary pollution), to pay attention to the needs of future generations, and to care for the earth's life-support systems emerge as normative benchmarks, in the sense that they offer standards against which to assess actual performance. This is not a matter of passing judgement about compliance in any strict sense of the term, or even about conformance in a more general sense. Most ethical principles are too abstract to be used for this sort of assessment. In any case, no one expects policy-makers to treat the environmental principles under consideration in this chapter as prescriptive requirements or prohibitions to be adhered to in any precise sense on a case-by-case basis. Nonetheless, such principles do stand as beacons that can be used to assess broad trends or the overall flow of events over time. Are we making progress in providing those residing in developing countries with safe drinking water and adequate sanitation facilities, as called for by the principle of environmental equity? Are there indications that humans are assuming increased responsibility for the maintenance of large atmospheric, marine, and terrestrial ecosystems, as mandated by the principle of stewardship? Dramatic progress regarding issues of this sort is not likely to occur over the short run. But to the extent that policy-makers anticipate that their overall records will be assessed after the fact in terms of broad normative criteria of this sort, we can expect a slow but ultimately significant shift in the flow of day-to-day behaviour over the long run.

Do these perspectives justify an affirmative response to the question posed at the beginning of this chapter about the development of a meaningful system of international environmental ethics? It is difficult to devise any precise way to measure the impact of environmental principles in setting agendas, lending character to regulatory arrangements, providing language for the expression of non-utilitarian reasons, and establishing normative benchmarks in terms of which to assess the course of events. Certainly, there are good reasons to avoid jumping to optimistic conclusions about such matters. It would be naive to expect the requirements of the principle of environmental equity to be satisfied under the conditions of inequality prevailing in today's world, for instance, and there are good reasons to be concerned about the efficacy of efforts to redirect behaviour in areas highlighted by the principle of caring for the earth. At the same time, it would be a mistake to dismiss these international environmental principles out of hand. The importance of paying attention to the side-effects of actions that harm the welfare of others can no longer be denied at the international level. The proposition that uncertainty is not an adequate justification for inaction in responding to major environmental problems is now widely regarded as legitimate. The importance of caring for the earth is undeniable in a world in which global environmental change caused, at least in part, by human actions has become a major issue on the international agenda. The author does not anticipate the occurrence of a sharp or unambiguous turning point in this realm after which the major actors in international society will adopt or explicitly embrace a coherent set of well-defined international environmental principles. Even so, there is much to be said for the proposition that the discourse associated with these principles is steadily infiltrating the realm of world affairs, and that this movement is likely to gather momentum in the early decades of the new millennium.

A system of international environmental ethics

Do the principles discussed in the preceding sections add up to a system of international environmental ethics? Note that this is not so much a question about the effectiveness of individual environmental principles as it is a query about the extent to which the collection of environmental principles taken together form a coherent ensemble. There is no implication here that a system of environmental ethics must reflect the concerns of all those currently active in international society. In most social settings, ethical systems are particularly responsive to the concerns and preferences of a subset of the most influential players, in contrast to the concerns and preferences of subordinate stakeholders. With regard to the case at hand, for example, it is notable that current discussions centre more on issues like climate change and biological diversity that seem important to the advanced industrial states than on issues like safe drinking water and adequate sanitation facilities that preoccupy many of the developing countries. An unbiased observer might react to these observations by questioning the ethics of ethical systems. This is surely a legitimate concern. But there is nothing peculiar about international society in these terms. Ethical systems are not correct or appropriate in some objective sense. They are products of social interactions, and they evolve in ways that reflect patterns of influence prevailing in the social settings in which they operate.

The international environmental principles under consideration here have several attributes that serve to define the character of this embryonic ethical system. First and foremost, this is fundamentally a system of international ethics in the strict sense of the term, or, in other words, a set of principles applying primarily to the actions of states. In a good many instances, this feature of the system is explicitly articulated. Stockholm Principle 21/Rio Principle 2, for example, assert that states have "the sovereign right to exploit their own resources ... and the responsibility" to ensure that activities within their jurisdiction do not harm outsiders. In other cases, this aspect of the principles is unambiguous, even though it is not stated in such explicit terms. Thus, the propositions that the polluter should pay and that actors should proceed with caution in dealing with large ecosystems are addressed in the first instance to national policy-makers. So also are concerns about environmental equity and caring for the earth. This means, to begin with, that states will have to address a range of questions about their responsibility for the activities of non-state actors operating "within their jurisdiction or control". How can national governments regulate the behaviour of large corporations whose actions give rise to long-range transboundary pollution, and to what extent are states ultimately responsible for damages resulting from the actions of their nationals? This feature of the system raises questions about the need to adjust international environmental principles to accommodate the growing role of non-state actors and the emergence of what some observers have begun to describe as global civil society.[42] It is fashionable in some quarters to see the state as the problem and various non-state actors, including both non-governmental organizations (NGOs) and multinational corporations (MNCs), as entities that can play significant roles in solving the problem.[43] But this seems overly optimistic. Much of the action regarding the development of international environmental ethics during the foreseeable future is likely to turn on debates about the proper roles of states and various non-state actors in this realm.

It is worth noting as well that the emerging international environmental principles typically deal with interactions between or among human actors regarding environmental matters, rather than – as Leopold would have it – with "man's relation to the land and to the animals and plants which grow upon it".[44] We are concerned, for example, with matters like the extent to which polluters are obligated to compensate those whose welfare their actions harm, the prospect that weak states will end up as victims of the environmentally significant actions of powerful states, and the obligations of those who make decisions today to pay attention to the consequences of their actions for the welfare of future generations. All these concerns raise issues pertaining to the impact of human actions on the earth's biogeophysical systems. In the final analysis, however, they are not rooted in Leopold's injunction to the effect that "[a] thing is right when it tends to preserve the integrity, stability, and beauty of the biotic community. It is wrong when it tends otherwise."[45] The emerging system of international environmental ethics consists in large measure of principles concerning the treatment of human stakeholders with regard to the environmental impacts of actions motivated by a desire to enhance human welfare. Of course, this does not rule out the emergence over time of injunctions arising from the idea of biotic citizenship as a force to be reckoned with at the international level. But it seems hard to avoid the conclusion that this perspective does not constitute a key feature of the system of international environmental ethics that is emerging at the present time.

Quite apart from these attributes of the system as a whole, it is relevant to ask whether the emerging system of international environmental ethics is inclusive or comprehensive in the sense that it covers the major sets of environmental issues arising at the international level. In this connection, it is helpful to divide environmental issues into four broad categories and to comment on the applicability of individual environmental principles to each category. This procedure yields the following taxonomy: standards pertaining to internal impacts of environmental activities, or household principles; guidelines relating to impacts of environmentally significant activities on adjacent states, or neighbourhood principles; codes of conduct relating to the use or management of shared natural resources, or principles of partnership; and standards relating to international or global commons, or community principles.

An assessment of the collection of international environmental principles under consideration in this chapter suggests uneven results in these terms. Progress is most apparent with regard to neighbourhood principles and community principles. The principle of the polluter pays, for example, is based in large measure on familiar doctrines about the importance of avoiding actions likely to damage the welfare of neighbours, or failing that to accept responsibility for compensating them for the damages they sustain. The injunction articulated explicitly in Stockholm Principle 21/ Rio Principle 2 to ensure that activities "do not cause damage to the environment of other States" is also predicated on the proposition that actors in international society are responsible for avoiding damage to their neighbours, even as they exercise their right to develop their own resources as they see fit. At the same time, the precautionary principle and the principles of stewardship and caring for the earth reflect a growing sense of the need for community principles in international society. The applicability of such principles seems relatively straightforward when it comes to the obligation to protect global systems, such as the stratospheric ozone layer and the earth's climate system. Considerably more complex are cases, such as the protection of biological diversity, in which the development of community principles leads to injunctions involving matters normally regarded as falling within the domestic jurisdiction of individual members of international society.

As this last observation suggests, meaningful household principles are particularly difficult to develop at the international level. The idea of non-intervention as an element of the doctrine of sovereignty remains highly influential at this stage. This is particularly true with regard to the sensitivities of small and relatively weak states that fear the effects of environmental imperialism perpetrated by powerful states whose priorities bear little resemblance to the priorities of most members of the developing world.[46] In the end, however, household principles are critical. It is difficult to see how a system of international environmental ethics can flourish in the absence of a well-developed code of appropriate conduct covering the internal environmental consequences of what the members of international society do within their own jurisdictions. For its part, the problem of devising ethical principles to address the use of shared natural resources, such as rivers that cross national boundaries and migratory animals that move from one jurisdiction to another on a seasonal basis, seems to lie in the fact that these resources often become focal points of more or less intense conflicts between or among the prospective partners.[47] Needless to say, this suggests that there is a compelling need for ethical principles to blunt the natural tendency toward polarization in dealing with shared natural resources. But from an ethical perspective, efforts to come to terms with this range of issues benefit neither from the obvious parallel with nuisance doctrines that undergird neighbourhood principles nor from the rapid growth of intellectual capital relating to global environmental change that underpins community principles.

If this assessment is correct, it suggests a mixed response to the question posed at the beginning of this section. The embryonic system of environmental ethics that has emerged in international society is state centric, and rooted more in a concern for human welfare than in a concern for the well-being of the earth's biogeophysical systems as such. There is as well more progress to report with regard to some issue areas than others. Not surprisingly, neighbourhood principles have become an important area of concern at the international level. Equally if not more striking is the emergence of global concerns that support ethical precepts in such forms as the precautionary principle and the principle of caring for the earth. In many ways, these developments constitute an early stage in the formulation of a meaningful system of international environmental ethics; it would be naive to suppose that a coherent – much less highly effective – system of environmental ethics is in place or on the verge of crystallizing in international society today. Yet it would be equally wrong to dismiss the developments under consideration here as mere window dressing designed to legitimize business as usual or the continued exercise of power politics. Policy-makers respond to a wide range of stimuli in framing issues, assessing their options, and evaluating outcomes at the international level. Surely, the emerging system of international environmental ethics has reached a stage in its development where it deserves to be treated as one of the forces to be reckoned with in these terms.

The future of international environmental ethics

All ethical systems are dynamic. Partly, this is a matter of the rise of new issues on public agendas that call either for the development of distinct codes of conduct or the adaptation of existing standards to come to grips with emergent concerns. In part, it is a consequence of shifts in the interests and influence of major actors in specific social settings. Although the rise and fall of major actors need not lead to drastic changes in ethical systems, it will come as no surprise that ethical systems do shift over time to reflect the viewpoints of the dominant members of specific societies. It would be a mistake to infer from this that ethical systems evolve on a continuous and gradual basis. There are good reasons to conclude, in fact, that such systems change by fits and starts, or in a fashion that may be described in terms of the idea of punctuated equilibrium. Existing principles can withstand a certain amount of stress without losing their normative force. But once these principles give way, a relatively rapid shift toward some alternative system of ethical standards is likely to ensue.

What can we say about the probable trajectory of international environmental ethics over the foreseeable future? No doubt, many specific changes in the principles discussed in this chapter are in store. But the fundamental debate, in the author's judgement, is likely to focus on differences between the ethical perspectives embedded in the discourses of environmental protection and sustainable development. To a point, these discourses support similar or at least compatible ethical precepts. They both encourage the development of the principle of caring for the earth and the precautionary principle as ethical standards governing human/ environment relations. But at bottom, the two discourses rest on different premises regarding the place of human beings in the overall scheme of things. In the final analysis, environmental protection is a biocentric perspective that mandates a concern for the well-being of biogeophysical systems as a first principle and emphasizes the idea of stewardship or even the concept of biotic citizenship as an overarching frame of reference in terms of which to approach specific issues involving human/environment relations. Paragraphs 1 and 2 of the World Charter for Nature, a product of the environmental debates of the 1970s and early 1980s, exemplify this perspective. Paragraph 1 lays down the foundational norm that "[n]ature

shall be respected and its essential processes shall not be impaired".
Paragraph 2 then seeks to flesh out this injunction by asserting that "[t]he
genetic viability of the earth shall not be compromised; the population
levels of all life forms, wild and domesticated, must be at least sufficient for their survival, and to this end necessary habitats shall be safeguarded".

Contrast this vision with the anthropocentric perspective of sustainable
development which, at its core, mandates a concern for the well-being of
biogeophysical systems not as an end in itself but rather as a means of
securing human welfare. As the 1992 Rio Declaration puts it, "[h]uman
beings are at the centre of concerns for sustainable development" (Principle 1) and "[i]n order to achieve sustainable development, environmental protection shall constitute an integral part of the development
process" (Principle 4). To be sure, principles like stewardship, caring for
the earth, and a concern for future generations are all important from the
perspective of sustainable development. But so, too, are explicitly anthropocentric concerns like the injunction to "cooperate in the essential
task of eradicating poverty" (Principle 5) and to accord "special priority"
to "the needs of developing countries, particularly the least developed
and those most environmentally vulnerable" (Principle 6). Many of those
committed to the goal of developing an effective system of international
environmental ethics have sought to minimize the differences between
the discourses of environmental protection and sustainable development
in the interests of maintaining solidarity among those actively concerned
about the course of human/environment relations. Tactically speaking,
this makes perfectly good sense. But given the observations set forth in
this and the preceding paragraph, it will come as no surprise that the occurrence of more or less severe tension between the biocentric ethics of
environmental protection and the anthropocentric ethics of sustainable
development is unavoidable.

Is one of these ethical visions likely to triumph over the other during
the foreseeable future? It would be a mistake to assume that one ethical
system must eventually drive out others. The coexistence of ethical systems that converge on some principles but diverge on others is by no
means uncommon. Even so, it is interesting to speculate here on the fate
of environmental protection and sustainable development as alternative
approaches to environmental ethics at the international level. Each
approach faces serious obstacles that will impede its progress toward becoming an effective ethical system. In the final analysis, environmental
protection requires a shift from an anthropocentric to a biocentric mode
of thinking. Although a shift of this sort appeals to some affluent citizens
of the advanced industrial societies, it is difficult to see how it can come to
dominate a world characterized by both a dramatic growth in the popu-

lation of humans and a strong desire on the part of those residing in developing countries to gain access to the material benefits associated with affluence. For its part, the idea of sustainable development has proven difficult to translate from the status of an appealing slogan to the formulation of a system of comprehensible principles dealing with more specific concerns. While it points the way towards principles highlighting concerns like environmental equity and the welfare of future generations, the influence of this perspective will remain limited unless and until its proponents succeed in constructing an interlocking set of clear and appealing principles on the foundation provided by the basic vision of sustainable development.

Those who approach such matters from a (neo)realist point of view will naturally ask who stands to benefit from the development of ethical systems rooted in the visions of environmental protection and sustainable development, and how influential are these stakeholders in international society? In effect, they assume that issues pertaining to ethical systems are much like other issues, in the sense that the rich and powerful are likely to dominate their treatment. But this simple approach has important limitations as a way of thinking about the dynamics of international environmental ethics. To begin with, it is not apparent that the leading actors in international society, such as the USA, the European Union, and Japan, have unambiguous preferences with respect to the content of environmental principles. Those committed to the ethics of environmental protection have achieved remarkable influence in recent years within the policy arenas of a number of OECD countries. Yet there is little evidence that the general public in these countries is ready to accept an ethical system rooted in biocentric principles. In any case, any serious effort to promote biocentric principles over anthropocentric principles as the basis for a system of international environmental ethics would almost certainly run into profound opposition on the part of influential groups located in the developing world. Such an effort would be interpreted – with some justification – as an example of the worst sort of environmental imperialism; any serious campaign to impose biocentric principles on the developing world would consequently require a massive exercise in what Thomas Schelling and others have described as compellence in contrast to deterrence.[48]

Beyond this, there is much to be said for the proposition that the spread of ideas in most social settings, including international society, involves processes that are difficult for powerful actors to control, even in situations featuring dramatic asymmetries in the distribution of material resources.[49] The USA is widely regarded as a dominant actor – the only remaining superpower – at the international level today. But American policy-makers have found it exceedingly difficult to control or even to guide the spread of ideas underlying efforts to come to grips with a range of large-scale environmental problems, such as climate change, the protection of biological diversity, and transboundary movements of hazardous wastes. This has resulted in the USA being cast repeatedly in the role of laggard, dragging its feet on initiatives designed to address major environmental problems and signing on grudgingly to agreements worked out largely by others.[50] Needless to say, it is difficult – even impossible – to solve many of today's environmental problems in the absence of at least *de facto* cooperation on the part of the USA. But the point here is that the formulation and diffusion of ideas, including ethical principles, exhibit a dynamic that does not lend itself readily to interpretation on the basis of conventional calculations regarding the role of power in international society. A particularly interesting aspect of this dynamic in the decentralized setting characteristic of international society concerns the roles that specific individuals (such as Gro Harlem Brundtland and Mostafa Tolba) have been able to play as leaders who nurture or even ignite processes leading to the diffusion of new normative standards, whether or not these standards appeal to policy-makers located in the most powerful states.[51] There is much to be learned about the specific conditions under which individual leadership can make a difference at the international level.[52] But it would be wrong to overlook the roles that individuals can and do play, especially with regard to ideational matters like the emergence of ethical principles.

Conclusion

It is tempting to regard international society as an arena in which power politics reign supreme and there is little scope for the operation of ethical principles of the sort familiar in a wide range of domestic settings. Even among those who accept the relevance of ethical principles at the international level, there is a pronounced tendency to treat such principles as primitive or underdeveloped rules that stand in need of refinement of a sort expected to lead eventually to their promotion to the status of legally binding prescriptions. In this chapter, the author has sought to challenge both these assumptions, arguing that each has severe drawbacks as an approach to understanding significant trends unfolding in international society today. No one would argue that a comprehensive and highly effective system of environmental ethics is currently in place at the international level, or even that such a system is now well along in the process of taking shape. Yet we have come some distance in this realm over the last few decades. Propositions like the polluter pays principle and the precautionary principle have entered the discourse of international affairs in a manner that is undeniably significant. This does not mean that environmental ethics offers simple prescriptions regarding proper conduct in complex situations of the sort policy-makers regularly confront, much less that it has become a dominant force in international affairs. As in other social settings, ethical principles achieve influence at the international level by contributing to the framing of issues for conscious consideration, defining the character of regulatory systems, providing reasons to act in one way or another, and establishing criteria or benchmarks against which to evaluate performance. They seldom prescribe clear and simple ways to handle specific problems.

Are we witnessing the development of a meaningful system of international environmental ethics? If so, what vision of human/environment relations lies at the core of this system? We are, at best, at an early stage in the development of international environmental ethics. Although the principles outlined in this chapter are far from trivial, they certainly do not constitute a coherent and effective ethical system covering the full range of environmental issues arising in international society. Of particular interest, in this connection, is the issue of whether this emerging system is likely to evolve during the foreseeable future as a biocentric ethics of environmental protection or as an anthropocentric ethics of sustainable development. Of course, the two visions may coexist and even reinforce one another for a period of time. In the author's judgement, however, the forces leading to an ethical system rooted in the idea of sustainable development are likely to prove stronger than the forces supporting a biocentric system, at least over the short to medium run. The need to come to terms with the tension between these approaches is a topic of obvious importance in any consideration of the development of environmental ethics over the longer run. But at this stage, the fact that this tension exists and is treated by many as a matter of some importance actually constitutes evidence that there are issues of substance to be discussed with regard to the development of environmental ethics in international society.

Notes

1. The Stockholm Declaration is included in UN Doc. A/CONF.48/14/Rev. 1 (1973). The Rio Declaration appears in UN Doc. A/CONF.151/5/Rev. 1 (1992). The World Charter for Nature is UN General Assembly Resolution 37/7 printed in *General Assembly Official Records: Thirty-Seventh Session*, Supplement No. 51 (A/37/51), 17–18. The latest draft of the Earth Charter, circulated as an unpublished document, is dated 14 October 1998.
2. Principle 2 of the Rio Declaration augments Principle 21 of the Stockholm Declaration with the phrase "environmental *and developmental* policies" (emphasis added).

3. Goldie, L. F. E., 1972, "The Management of Ocean Resources: Regimes for Structuring the Marine Environment", in Black, C. E. and Falk, R. A., eds, *The Structure of the International Environment*. Princeton: Princeton University Press, pp. 155–247.

4. Bernauer, T., 1996, "Protecting the Rhine River Against Chloride Pollution", in Keohane, R. O. and Levy, M. A., eds, *Institutions for Environmental Aid*. Cambridge, MA: MIT Press, pp. 201–232; Dupont, C., 1993, "Switzerland, France, Germany, the Netherlands: The Rhine", in Foure, G. O. and Rubin, J. Z., eds, *Culture and Negotiation: The Resolution of Water Disputes*. Newbery Park, CA: Sage Publications, pp. 97–115.

5. Hiltunen, H., 1994, *Finland and Environmental Problems in Russia and Estonia*. Helsinki: Finnish Institute of International Affairs. For a discussion of the broader context in which such calculations occur see Connolly, B., 1996, "Increments for the Earth: The Politics of Environmental Aid", in Keohane and Levy, note 4 above, pp. 327–365.

6. Litfin, K. T., 1994, *Ozone Discourses: Science and Politics in Global Environmental Cooperation*. New York: Columbia University Press.

7. Mintzer, I. M., ed., 1992, *Confronting Climate Change: Implications and Responses*. Cambridge: Cambridge University Press.

8. Freestone, D. and Hay, E., eds, 1996, *The Precautionary Principle and International Law: The Challenge of Implementation*. The Hague: Kluwer Law International.

9. Friedheim, R. L., ed., forthcoming, *Toward a Sustainable Whaling Regime*. Seattle: University of Washington Press.

10. Camacho, D. E., ed., 1998, *Environmental Injustices, Political Struggles: Race, Class, and the Environment*. Durham: Duke University Press.

11. Dowie, M., 1995, *Losing Ground: American Environmentalism at the Close of the Twentieth Century*. Cambridge, MA: MIT Press.

12. Weiss, E. B., 1995, "Environmental Equity: The Imperative for the Twenty-First Century", in Lang, W., ed., *Sustainable Development and International Law*. London: Graham and Trotman/Martinus Nijhoff, pp. 17–27.

13. Keohane and Levy, note 4 above.

14. Benedick, R. E., 1998, *Ozone Diplomacy: New Directions in Safeguarding the Planet*. Cambridge, MA: Harvard University Press.

15. On the experience with the NIEO, see Hart, J., 1983, *The New International Economic Order: Conflict and Cooperation in North-South Economic Relations*. New York: St Martin's Press.

16. Miller, M. A. L., 1995, *The Third World in Global Environmental Politics*. Boulder: Lynne Rienner.

17. Sand, P. H., 1995, "Trusts for the Earth: International Financial Mechanisms for Sustainable Development", in Lang, note 12 above, pp. 167–184.

18. Keohane and Levy, note 4 above.

19. Shabecoff, P., 1996, *A New Name for Peace: International Environmentalism, Sustainable Development, and Democracy*. Hanover: University Press of New England.

20. For a range of general perspectives on the issue of obligations to future generations, see Sikora, R. I. and Barry, B., eds, 1978, *Obligations to Future Generations*. Philadelphia: Temple University Press.

21. Readers will recognize the influence of this idea on the Brundtland Commission's definition of sustainable development: World Commission on Environment and Development, 1987, *Our Common Future*. New York: Oxford University Press.

22. Rothenberg, J., 1993, "Economic Perspective on Time Comparisons: Alternative Approaches to Time Comparisons", in Choucri, N., ed., *Global Accord: Environmental Challenges and International Responses*. Cambridge, MA: MIT Press, pp. 355–397.

23. Vitousek, P. M., Mooney, H. A., Lubchenko, J., and Melillo, J. M., 1997, "Human Domination of Earth's Ecosystems", *Science*, No. 277, 25 July, pp. 494–499.

24. On the philosophical underpinnings of the idea of stewardship, see Passmore, J. 1974, *Man's Responsibility for Nature: Ecological Problems and Western Traditions*. New York: Charles Scribner's Sons.

25. For a seminal statement of the principles underlying the animal rights movement, see Singer, P., 1977, *Animal Liberation: A New Ethic for our Treatment of Animals*. New York: Avon. A critical appraisal appears in Herscovici, A., 1985, *Second Nature: The Animal-Rights Controversy*. Montreal: CBC Enterprises.

26. Leopold, A., 1966, "The Land Ethic", in Leopold, A., *A Sand County Almanac: With Essays on Conservation from Round River*. New York: Ballantine Books, pp. 237–264, at p. 262.

27. Brown, L. R., Gardner, G., and Halweil, B., 1998, "Beyond Malthus: Sixteen Dimensions of the Population Problem", *Worldwatch Paper 143*. Washington, DC: Worldwatch Institute.

28. Stern, P., Young, O. R., and Drukman, D., eds, 1992, *Global Environmental Change: Understanding the Human Dimensions*. Washington, DC: National Academy Press.

29. Meadows, D., Meadows, D. L., Randers, J., and Behrens, W. W. III, 1972, *The Limits to Growth*. New York: Universe Books.

30. Lovelock, J. E., 1979, *Gaia: A New Look at Life on Earth*. New York: Oxford University Press.

31. March, J. G. and Olsen, J. P., 1998, "The Institutional Dynamics of International Political Orders", *International Organization*, No. 52, Autumn, pp. 943–969.

32. Ostrom, E., 1990, *Governing the Commons: The Evolution of Institutions for Collective Action*. Cambridge: Cambridge University Press.

33. Sands, P., 1995, "International Law in the Field of Sustainable Development: Emerging Legal Principles", in Lang, note 12 above, pp. 53–66.

34. For a helpful distinction between the logic of expected consequences and the logic of appropriateness, see March and Olsen, note 31 above.

35. Sands, note 33 above.

36. Mitchell, R. B., 1996, "Compliance Theory: An Overview", in Cameron, J., Worksman, J., and Roderick, P., eds, *Improving Compliance with International Environmental Law*. London: Earthscan Publications, pp. 3–28.

37. The distinction, set forth in March and Olsen, note 31 above, between the logic of expected consequences and the logic of appropriateness provides a helpful context for this discussion. For an account of the impact of international norms that appeals explicitly to the logic of appropriateness, see Finnemore, M. and Sikkink, K., 1998, "International Norm Dynamics and Political Change", *International Organization*, No. 52, Autumn, pp. 887–917.

38. Bull, H., 1977, *The Anarchical Society: A Study of Order in World Politics*. New York: Columbia University Press.

39. See Litfin, note 6 above, for an account of the role of discourses in framing issues for consideration in policy arenas.

40. For an account that accords particular weight to this proposition, see Ruggie, J. G., 1998, *Constructing the World Polity: Essays on International Institutionalization*. London: Routledge.

41. For an influential formulation of the idea that non-utilitarian reasons may trump utilitarian calculations under some conditions, see Dworkin, R., 1978, *Taking Rights Seriously*. Cambridge, MA: Harvard University Press.

42. The idea of a global civil society is discussed in a thoughtful manner in Wapner, P., 1997, "Governance in Global Civil Society", in Young, O. R., ed., *Global Governance: Drawing Insights from the Environmental Experience*. Cambridge, MA: MIT Press.

43. Wapner, P., 1996, *Environmental Activism and World Civic Politics*. Albany: State University of New York Press.
44. Leopold, note 26 above, p. 238.
45. *Ibid.*, p. 263.
46. Hurrell, A., 1992, "Brazil and the International Politics of Amazonian Deforestation", in Hurrell, A. and Kingsbury, B., eds, *The International Politics of the Environment*. Oxford: Clarendon Press, pp. 398–429.
47. Gleick, P. H., 1998, *The World's Water: The Biennial Report on Freshwater Resources*. Washington, DC: Island Press; Lyster, S., 1985, *International Wildlife Law*. Cambridge: Grotius Publishers.
48. Schelling, T. C., 1966, *Arms and Influence*. New Haven: Yale University Press.
49. Finnemore and Sikkink, note 37 above.
50. von Moltke, K., 1997, "Institutional Interactions: The Structure of Regimes for Trade and the Environment", in Young, note 42 above, pp. 247–272.
51. Tolba, M. K., 1998, *Global Environmental Diplomacy: Negotiating Environmental Agreements for the World, 1973–1992*. Cambridge, MA: MIT Press.
52. Young, O. R., 1991, "Political Leadership and Regime Formation: On the Development of Institutions in International society", *International Organization*, No. 45, Summer, pp. 281–309.

8

Ethics, feminism, and international affairs

Kimberly Hutchings

Why feminism now?

The bringing together of the three key terms in the title of this chapter (ethics, feminism, and international) has traditionally been seen as inappropriate. Ethics and international refer to ways of analysing, judging, and organizing the world which operate at a level of objectivity and generality to which categories such as "humanity", "citizen", or "state" are central but to which the category of women as women has been thought to be irrelevant. The term feminism placed between ethics and international therefore promises to disrupt the predominant ways in which the latter have been defined, and indeed this has been the effect of a variety of feminist interventions in the realm of ethics and the international in both theory and practice over the past 25 years. In this chapter, the aim is to assess the contribution which feminist thinking can make to ethics in the international context by examining two specific feminist responses to well-established areas of ethical debate in international politics: just war theory and international human rights. Although the arguments explored are distinctive, the chapter will conclude that they have in common a simultaneous commitment to both ethical universality and ethical particularity. It is in working through the meaning and practical implications of this stance, which appears oxymoronic in terms of conventional approaches to international ethics, that the distinctive contribution of feminism to thinking about ethical issues in the international context becomes apparent.

Before moving on, however, it is useful to reflect on why the feminist disruption of the traditional reference points of ethics and international has become so prominent in the last quarter of the twentieth century. The most obvious reason for the increasing importance of feminist perspectives in analysing and judging international politics is the worldwide phenomenon of the growth of feminist and women's political movements in both state and interstate politics. This is not a straightforward matter to describe, as feminist/women's movements have different contexts and histories and differ in their understandings of the key values and goals of feminism – to the extent that for some campaigners on behalf of women the very label "feminism" is suspect.[1] For the purposes of this chapter, however, the term "feminism" will be used in the broadest way possible, to refer to political movements or scholarly works which are in some sense premised on the need to address the ways in which women are, throughout the world, systematically disadvantaged by being assigned to the category "women".

The fact of women's systematic disadvantage has been well documented. Even in the richest, most developed, and liberal states, women are, overall, in a worse position in relation to political and economic power and rights than men. This is not to suggest that some women are not systematically advantaged in relation to some men or that some men are not systematically disadvantaged in the current world order, but the evidence clearly bears out the continuing relevance of gender as a principle of stratification in all parts of the world.[2]

Feminist movements and campaigns have focused on many different goals. In some cases priority has been given to ensuring equal civil and political rights for women and transforming political institutions to be more representative and inclusive of women's interests. In other cases women's material disadvantage has been the crucial issue in both developed and developing economies. In yet others, attention has focused on violence against women, on women's rights over their own bodies, or on social institutions and practices that discriminate against women. As Basu points out, it is difficult to measure how successful feminist politics has been in relation to different issues and in different parts of the world or at the international level.[3]

There have clearly been considerable successes in some contexts and, in general, women's issues and interests have gained a greater visibility across the board, including in state and international institutions. But in many instances there has been little progress and even, some feminists would argue, actual regression in women's position. One of the clearest things to emerge from feminist critiques of women's oppression is the importance of frameworks of thinking which exclude, marginalize, or devalue women in maintaining that oppression. Feminists routinely argue that improving women's position civilly, politically, and materially means changing minds as well as institutions. It is in challenging such frameworks that feminist practice and theory make their most significant contribution to thinking about ethical issues in the international context.

In common with other political and social movements whose constituency is in principle global, feminism has operated as a force at both local and international levels. In doing this it has constantly cut across traditional ways of conducting and thinking about international politics. Two of the ways in which it has done this have been particularly important for rethinking ethical questions and frameworks of judgement in the international context. Firstly, feminist politics has drawn attention to consistent blind spots in accounts of what is ethically relevant to the international realm. Feminists point out that both communitarian ethical perspectives and cosmopolitan (utilitarian and deontological) ethical perspectives actually fail to "see" women, whether in thinking about just war or social justice. The relevant ethical actor/victim in all of the above perspectives is either a state or the ethical community which legitimates the state, or it is the generic human individual, a category which has notoriously been defined in masculine terms.[4] This means that ways in which women act as well as the ways in which they are acted upon in the international context are rendered invisible or, alternatively, marginalized and devalued as significant for ethical judgement and prescription. Secondly, feminist politics has opened up the question of what more traditional ethical frameworks might learn from "seeing" women, and the nature of their position and role, as part of a quest to identify alternative resources for challenging the economic, social, and political *status quo*. This can be illustrated by looking briefly at two international issues about which feminist campaigning has been particularly prominent: peace and human rights.

The early 1980s was marked by the emergence of a distinctively feminist anti-nuclear peace politics in several Western European countries, as well as the USA and Australia. Although clearly sharing much ground with other anti-war and pacifist movements, this feminist peace politics was premised on the idea of a special link between women and peace.[5] One of the interesting things about it was its use of the technique of relying on certain traditional stereotypes of womanhood as the basis for an evaluation of strategic and just-war thinking. Essentially, these feminist peace activists reversed the dominant hierarchy of evaluation of masculine civic virtue and feminine private virtue, in which the former takes priority over the latter and the latter is essentially supposed to sustain the former. As Elshtain argues, in dominant thinking about war, women have been placed in the position of the naturally peaceful sex whose role is to provide comfort and care for the "just-war hero" and who are invoked (along with the children) as the party on behalf of whom resort to political violence has been necessary.[6]

In opposition to this, in the feminist peace activism of the 1980s, feminine private virtue was taken into the public realm and held up as the (subversive) yardstick of ethical conduct within that realm. The ways in which the 1980s' feminist peace movement campaigned against militarism, nuclear weapons, and Cold War politics clearly illustrate the two features of feminist cross-cutting of standard ethical frameworks in the international context mentioned above. Firstly, a key part of the tactics of these campaigners was, quite literally, to make themselves visible to a world which recognized states as friends or enemies and humans as elements to be aggregated in statistics of putative death tolls, but not women as women. These tactics ranged from mothers taking babies and children with them on demonstrations (thereby quite literally putting the realm of private virtue in the public domain) to counterposing traditional symbols of women's work and femininity to the machinery of militarism held within the bases where nuclear weapons were kept. Flowers, ribbons, and wool were woven into the fences surrounding military bases. Women broke into bases and danced on or decorated missile silos. Camps were set up at the gates of bases as a constant reminder of a world which included women and families, not simply states and individuals.

In engaging in the above kinds of activities the first feature of feminist cross-cutting – in which women are affirmed as part of and actors within the international realm – becomes tied up with the second. The campaigners at peace camps such as Greenham Common in England were not simply declaring their presence on the international stage, but were also arguing that the international stage should learn from them. Implicit within the tactics employed at Greenham Common was the ethical superiority of the notions of care, connection, and responsibility embedded in women's work within the family to the strategic and just-war thinking that could contemplate the destruction of large swathes of the human race in the pursuit of some greater goal.

The experience of feminist peace politics mentioned above has been accompanied by alternative experiences of women as protagonists and victims in modern warfare over the last quarter of a century. Research has shown that at the same time as women are gaining entry into the military and engaging in combat in increasing numbers, women also make up the vast majority of those dispossessed by war (whether as refugees or as the mediators between international sanctions and the needs of their families), as well as bearing the burden of responsibility for rebuilding lives in the aftermath of war.[7]

The variety and complexity of women's actual relation to political violence puts into question the straightforward equation between women and peace which characterized the thinking of the 1980s' women's peace camps. In contrast to the focus on specifically female practices as a source for ethical and political engagement which was found at Greenham, other feminist activists have been concentrating on utilizing existing discourses of negative and positive rights to address the numerous ways in which women are specifically vulnerable in the contemporary world. Struggles over rights for women have been carried out in a variety of ways within states and internationally, and in relation to the range of civil, political, social, and economic rights. Women's movements demanding equal rights to men have been most obviously successful within the context of the domestic state, particularly within more affluent liberal states in the postwar period. However, even where campaigns for equality of right have been most successful, feminist movements have found themselves often dissatisfied with their achievements because the legal equality they have gained does not seem to translate into full equality in practice. An obvious instance is the principle of a right to equal pay for equal work. Feminists have found that enshrining this principle in positive law gets rid of some overt pay discrimination on grounds of sex, but it does not tackle the fact of a sexually differentiated labour force, in which women do some kinds of work and men do others and the latter work is more highly paid than the former. In spite of legislation on equal pay, even women in developed liberal states continue to earn less than men.

Feminist struggles for equality of rights beyond the boundaries of specific states seek to utilize the existing principles and protocols enshrined in international law. Here, however, the bringing of change is even more difficult and complex than in the domestic context. This is partly because the recognition of rights in international law is notoriously poorly translated into the actual practices of many states, whilst at the same time states themselves are the only effective enforcers of international law. However, it is partly also because such rights are understood as human rights, and feminists have found themselves powerfully dissatisfied with the capacity of international human rights declarations and protocols to recognize and address harms done to women because they are women. Ashworth[8] notes how the Universal Declaration of Human Rights (UDHR) and the covenants on civil, political, social, and economic rights respectively have been ineffective even in recognizing the violation (or vulnerability to violation) of women's rights. In the case of civil and political rights, women's rights to bodily integrity are routinely violated in the context of widespread practices of domestic violence, female circumcision, and non-consensual marriage. In the case of socio-economic rights, women's rights are particularly badly affected by women's systematically disadvantaged position in relation to property ownership and waged and unwaged labour.[9] Yet until feminist groups began to campaign for more explicit recognition of the differential position of women as rights bearers, there was no accepted understanding that human rights might need to be specified as women's rights, or vice versa. Over the past 25 years international organizations have been increasingly subject to pressure from feminist campaigners to make sure that women are explicitly included in the category "human". The recent and shocking experience of the systematic rape of women which featured in the conflicts in Bosnia in the mid-1990s pushed feminist groups into campaigning for the international recognition of rape as a war crime, and provides another example of using rights as the appropriate feminist ethical discourse.

What is clear from the feminist politics of international rights, however, is that although the universality of rights discourse is recognized as a potentially powerful protector and promoter of the interests of women, the more generically specified such rights are, the less they are likely to be, even rhetorically, effective for women. Thus if we go back to the way in which feminist politics cuts across traditional ethical paradigms, in the case of the feminist rights discourse we again find the two previously outlined features of feminist work in relation to international ethics. Firstly, feminist work points out the blind spots in mainstream perspectives and asserts women's inclusion in the international, in this case the category of international rights bearers (humans).[10] Secondly, feminists assert the relevance of the particularity of women's position to a re-thinking of rights in terms of the specific ways in which women's rights are vulnerable to violation. This means paying attention to the fact that the ways in which people are human actually differ, and it also implies that the meaning of equality of right may be about the recognition of difference rather than the assumption of sameness.

Feminist ethical and political theorists have responded in different ways to the challenges made by feminist political activists to mainstream masculine world views in the contexts of both just war and human rights thinking. This discussion will now move on to look more closely at the difference feminism makes to ethical thinking in relation to these issues by focusing on Ruddick's work on just war and Mackinnon's feminist critique of the idea of human rights.[11] In each case the practical as well as the theoretical implications of the particular perspective will be drawn out. What emerges indicates links between feminist international ethics and some other recently articulated critical ethical paradigms (see Chapter 2, Kratochwil, and Chapter 5, Campbell, in this volume). Feminist ethics distinguishes itself from the foundationalism and universalism of standard deontological ethical paradigms, but is always also critical of taking the community as the source of ethical value, given the fact that all communities in the modern world rely on the disempowering of women in relation to men. Although feminists differ about the practical and institutional means of putting their ideals into practice, feminist thinking, which has its origins in addressing the systematic disadvantage of women, has built on the resources of the experience of that disadvantage to suggest the need for an ethics of universal relevance and particularist sensitivity which refuses the choice offered by mainstream ethics between communitarianism and cosmopolitanism as well as reflecting the actual complexity of feminist politics and values.

Feminism and just war

The most important strand in feminist moral theory since the early 1980s has been the idea of a feminist ethic of care, pioneered by the work of the social psychologist Carol Gilligan.[12] In the course of research into the patterns of moral reasoning of women, Gilligan came to challenge the accepted hierarchy of moral psychological development established by Kohlberg,[13] in which the most mature moral point of view is identified with the development of an impartial, universalist, and principled perspective on moral issues (the ethic of justice). Kohlberg had observed in his own research that, according to his criteria, adult women were less likely to manifest an ethic of justice and more likely to remain at (again according to his criteria) an earlier stage of moral development in which moral problems continued to be addressed in an *ad hoc*, highly personalized, and contextualized way. In a familiar feminist move, Gilligan did not so much overturn Kohlberg's findings as re-evaluate them, arguing that the characteristics of women's moral thinking were not inferior to an ethic of justice but demonstrated an equally advanced and sophisticated post-conventional moral point of view.

Women's moral judgement is more contextual, more immersed in the detail of relationships and narratives. It shows a greater propensity to take the standpoint of the "particular other", and women appear more adept at revealing feelings of empathy and sympathy required by this.[14]

In the wake of the argument between Kohlberg and Gilligan, a huge literature has arisen in social psychology and ethical and political theory which both criticizes and develops Gilligan's original insight.[15] In terms of feminist ethical and political theory, the concerns of the debate quickly shifted from arguments about whether men and women actually think differently in relation to moral problems to exploring the pros and cons of the features of women's moral reasoning identified by Gilligan, features which have come to be defined as those of an "ethic of care". The key feature of an ethic of care is that it is embedded in the practicalities of relationships of responsibility for others. Crucial to ethical judgement from the perspective of care is the importance of particularity (knowing who and what you are making a moral judgement about); connectedness (recognizing your actual relationship to others in the process of judgement); and context (paying attention to the broad and narrow context of ethical judgement).

In her book *Maternal Thinking: Towards a Politics of Peace*, Ruddick draws on the idea of an ethic of care as a central part of her argument for a feminist moral orientation in the context of international politics.[16] The book involves a rejection of realist arguments as to the tragic inevitability or structural necessity of war and communitarian claims as to the special ethical status of the collective group or nation. In addition it develops a critique of traditional just-war thinking – in both utilitarian and Kantian variants – as well as a positive characterization of how a different kind of moral judgement and political practice is possible in relation to war. There are essentially two stages to Ruddick's argument. In the first stage she offers a phenomenology of what she terms "maternal thinking"; in the second stage she reads off the implications of using maternal thinking as a critical "feminist standpoint" for making judgements about the ethics of war and the appropriate feminist response to war.

"Maternal thinking", according to Ruddick, "is a discipline in attentive love", a discipline which is rooted in the demands of a particular relation of care, that between mother and child, and which reflects a particular range of metaphysical attitudes, cognitive capacities, and virtues.[17] Ruddick is careful to insist that she is neither equating mothers with biological mothers, nor presuming that actual mothers are all good at maternal thinking. Ruddick draws a contrast between the ideals of response to threat, conflict, and harm which are inherent in any practice in which violence is understood as a permissible instrument for the attainment of goals, and modes of responding to threat, conflict, and harm which are premised on the unacceptability of violence. She finds paradigmatic examples of the former in militarism and of the latter in the labour of care.

Caregivers are not, predictably, better people than are militarists. Rather, they are engaged in a different project. Militarists aim to dominate by creating the structural vulnerabilities that caregivers take for granted. They arm and train so that they can, if other means of domination fail, terrify and injure their opponents. By contrast, in situations where domination through bodily pain, and the fear of pain, is a structural possibility, caregivers try to resist temptations to assault and neglect, even though they work among smaller, frailer, vulnerable people who may excite domination.[18]

Ruddick is aware of the problems of simply taking and applying the regulative ideals of care-giving practices to the realm of international politics, but nevertheless she extrapolates criteria of ethical judgement from care-giving practice which she argues do have implications for what should or should not be permissible within the international realm.

When maternal thinking takes upon itself the critical perspective of a feminist standpoint, it reveals a contradiction between mothering and war. Mothering begins in birth and promises life; military thinking justifies organized, deliberate deaths. A mother preserves the bodies, nurtures the psychic growth, and disciplines the conscience of children; although the military trains its soldiers to survive the situations it puts them in, it also deliberately endangers their bodies, minds and consciences in the name of victory and abstract causes.[19]

The idea of a feminist standpoint derives from Hartsock's appropriation of Marx's analysis of capitalism as being based on the standpoint (serving the objective interests) of the oppressed class. According to Hartsock,[20] the exploitative character of capitalist relations of production becomes clear when understood from the vantage point of the proletariat. Similarly, the patriarchal character of relations of reproduction as well as production under capitalism is revealed from the standpoint of the women who bear the brunt of those relations. Building on this notion, Ruddick argues that maternal thinking, located as it is in the marginalized and denigrated sphere of caring labour, provides a standpoint from which the absurdity of both strategic military and just-war thinking becomes evident. Although Ruddick does not claim that the feminist standpoint provides a universally valid ground for ethical judgement, she does make a strong claim for the potential of maternal thinking to illuminate the meaning of war from a critical perspective.[21] For Ruddick, both militarism and just-war theory share a commitment to the expendability of concrete lives in abstract causes to which maternal thinking is inherently opposed. Ruddick claims that this means that the implication of maternal thinking is not just the rejection of war but the active embracing of peace politics, a fight against war which draws on the acknowledgement of responsibility and relationship and the specificity of need and obligations which are inherent in a proper understanding of the labour of caring.[22]

The analytic fictions of just war theory require a closure of moral issues final enough to justify killing and "enemies" abstract enough to be killable. In learning to welcome their own and their children's changes, mothers become accustomed to open-ended, concrete reflection on intricate and unpredictable spirits. Maternal attentive love, restrained and clear sighted, is ill adapted to intrusive, let alone murderous judgements of others' lives.[23]

In Ruddick's theory the logic of domestic relations in the restricted sense of the domestic or private sphere is set against the logic of the public sphere of both state and interstate relations, although with the acknowledgement that in practice the former has tended to support and reinforce the latter. Ruddick places realism, morality of states, Kantianism, utilitarianism, and communitarianism all firmly in the realm of the logic of public "masculinist" theory and practice. Although it is clear that Ruddick does put an ethical value on humans, this is based not on a notion of inherent individual right, but on relation – value inheres in relations to others, in particular in the recognition of responsibility for others. For Ruddick, then, the realm of international politics is primarily a realm of human relations, not of human, nation, or state rights or an international state system. Ruddick assumes that ethical perspectives are the outcome of concrete practices and can never be neutral, but at the same time clearly suggests that some kinds of practice are inherently better than others. This distinction draws attention to the fact that although Ruddick presents an understanding of the international realm very different from mainstream ethical theories, nevertheless she argues for the notion of a standpoint from which critical judgements of international politics can be made. This standpoint is inherently prescriptive, and involves a commitment to the practical and political struggle against violence and for peace.

There are several different implications of Ruddick's argument in relation to ethical judgement on the one hand and ethical prescription on the other. As far as ethical judgement is concerned, the emphasis on particularity, connectedness, and context identified above as characteristic of the idea of an "ethic of care" suggests the following features. Firstly, from the standpoint of maternal thinking, the appropriate stance to take in ethical judgement is to attempt to build on particular experiences of the practice of care to help to identify with and take responsibility for the needs and suffering of others. Ruddick frequently cites the example of the Argentinian mothers of the disappeared, whose movement gradually grew to embrace concerns with children across the world who had suffered harm: "This is not transcendent impartiality but a sympathetic apprehension of another grounded in one's own particular suffering."[24] This is not just a matter of "feeling for" another's pain, but assuming an attitude of responsibility for it and therefore trying to do something about it. Secondly, however, maternal thinking is sensitive to the specific contexts in which ethical dilemmas are embedded, and the importance of appreciating the ethical weight of the perspectives of all parties to any dispute or conflict. For Ruddick, ethical judgement has to be on a case-by-case basis, but without ready-made principles of adjudication. Although the idea of maternal thinking is in principle non-violent and therefore rules out certain types of action, it also makes clear that there are no universally applicable algorithms that can be applied to any given situation to render definitive answers to ethical questions. The judgement of the maternal thinker is oriented by the ideals implicit in care, but these are regulative rather than determining in their effects. This brings us to the third feature of ethical judgement from the standpoint of maternal thinking. In contrast to the traditional picture of ethical judgement as a matter to be worked through at the level of the individual conscience in relation to specified criteria, maternal thinking implies that ethical judgement is a matter of dialogue and relies crucially on the capacity to hear what others are saying in arriving at the criteria for judgement. Judgement can only be made after what Benhabib refers to as engagement between "concrete others", in which it is recognized that no one party occupies a privileged position; judgement is therefore in principle an interactive and collective rather than an individual project.[25]

As well as suggesting new ways of conceptualizing ethical judgement, Ruddick's maternalist ethic of care has specific implications for practical ways of addressing classic problems of violence and oppression in the international context. At the broadest level, maternal thinking involves commitment to peace politics. In other words, violence is outlawed as a political tool, even for the righting of injustices. One of Ruddick's key preoccupations is that of working out non-violent strategies to combat violence and oppression. She is clear that such strategies are as risky as the use of violence in the contemporary world, and require levels of organization and commitment just as great as those used to support any military machine. But she also emphasizes the resources already present in women's lives which can be turned from sustaining political violence to resisting it; here the example of the mothers in Argentina mentioned above is taken as exemplary. Through non-violent protest, drawing on the generally recognized private feminine virtues of motherhood, these mothers operated effectively to help to bring about political change. This example confirms for Ruddick both the connection between maternal virtues and peace politics and the potential effectiveness of peace politics. More generally, it is clear that Ruddick's peace politics has elective affinities with a variety of examples of new ways of doing politics pioneered by peace movements, human rights movements, and green movements which emphasize the idea of local non-violent resistance to the powers of states, international organizations, and corporations. Such politics frequently makes use of the technique of subverting or overturning the dominant value hierarchy by asserting the value of that which has been marginalized or excluded, whether it is women's work, traditional economic practices, or particular cultural identities.[26] Ruddick argues that the idea of maternal thinking as a feminist standpoint for ethical judgement or prescription should be understood as a possible strategy for feminist work, one amongst a range of universalist and relativist ethical theories which may contribute towards peace.

Caregiving is only one of many ordinary practices that offers hints of peace and of the price of its violation. Given the pervasiveness of warism and the multiple costs of war, peacemakers can ill afford a competition among themselves to decide who is the best peacemaker. It is enough to identify a practice whose ubiquity and emotional potency make it one distinctly valuable resource for peace.[27]

Ruddick is clear that the idea of maternal thinking has its origin in maternal practice, features of which, she argues, are present in the work of mothering in radically different cultures. She therefore claims that her account of maternal thinking is likely to be generalizable across contexts, providing "at hand" an accessible basis for criticizing and resisting political violence of all kinds, as well as suggesting limitations to the kinds of strategies it is permissible to employ in critique and resistance.

Human rights

Ruddick's ethic of maternal thinking is essentially an example of virtue ethics. That is to say, that rather than presenting us with rules to govern conduct, it specifies forms of exemplary conduct and the values by which such conduct is oriented. In this respect there are clearly certain tensions between the maternal-thinking stance and rights-based ethics as traditionally understood. These tensions lie, firstly, between the ontological presumptions of an ethic of rights as opposed to an ethic of care, and secondly, between the universalist basis of rights-based thinking as opposed to the contextualist basis of maternal thinking. On the first point, the crucial ontological presumption of human rights thinking is that ethical value resides within the individual human being. In contrast to this, care thinking puts value not on any characteristic located within the human being but on a particular kind of relation between human beings, one in which care and dependence are a primary feature. An ethic of care does not simply require that rights are not violated but that positive responsibility (or at least the possibility of that responsibility) towards others is recognized.[28] Moreover, in foregrounding mutual dependence, maternal thinking does not draw clear lines between self and other; the ethical project is not solely that of defending or promoting the interests/needs/desires/freedom of each individual, it is that of nourishing a particular ideal of ethical life – the ways in which human beings are mutually sustaining. On the second point, a key feature of traditional rights-based thinking is the idea that what grounds human rights, that is to say what gives the human individual unique ethical value, is something which is universally common to all human individuals. There are different accounts of the source of this ethical value – alternatives include the capacity to feel pain, to reason, to act autonomously, or to know the moral law. Nevertheless, it is the fact that human beings are the same in some relevant respect, regardless of specific differences, that is the crucial reference point for how they should be treated. In contrast to this, an ethic of care grounds judgement and prescription in specific context and without the presumption of some fundamental sameness as the justification for the possession of rights. This is not to say that Ruddick would necessarily object to the idea of universal human rights, but such rights would have to be justified not in terms of a moral ontology of the human individual, but in terms of their (the rights') compatibility with the regulative ideal of maternal thinking.

In the discussion in the first section above it was clear that feminist activists have found rights-based thinking useful (even if also problematic) in the context of practical struggles to improve women's position. For feminists drawing upon rights discourses, the ethic of care is regarded ambivalently. On the one hand, they (feminist rights campaigners) are wary of Ruddick's reliance on the technique of re-evaluation of women's traditional work and her shift away from a legal/institutional dimension to ethical thinking. There is no question that, for Ruddick, maternal thinking constitutes an ethic of resistance and one that is fully compatible with the feminist aim of addressing and redressing the ways in which women are systematically disadvantaged within the current world order. However, feminist rights activists are suspicious of the apparent confirmation and affirmation of the traditional role of women in the idea of maternal thinking. Revaluing work within the family and the private sphere, in their view, threatens to perpetuate women's peculiar vulnerabilities as well as (arguably) their peculiar strengths within the current world order. For such theorists, an ethic of care does not do enough to protect and support women in the world as it is, even if it does set up a pleasing notion of the world as it might be.

On the other hand, as mentioned above, focus on women's rights in the international context has involved putting the generic universalism of rights thinking into question. In this sense there are points of overlap between the ethic of care and its careful contextuality and feminist rights arguments. This has given rise to a strand of feminist argument which objects to human rights thinking on the grounds that "human" is too general a category, and that both the theory and the practice of human rights have failed to provide the same ethical resources for women as they have done for men, but which does not issue in the rejection of rights thinking altogether. The discussion will now go on to explore this argument and its implications as carried through in the work of Mackinnon.[29] The upshot of Mackinnon's work is to shift the feminist perspective on international ethics and politics away from the ethical potential of care-giving practice towards a politics of sexually differentiated rights and a more pessimistic and conflictual vision of the future. The chapter will return in conclusion to compare and assess the rather different feminist ethical vocabularies with which Ruddick and Mackinnon present us.

Like Ruddick, Mackinnon bases her argument on the assumption that ethical perspectives and political and legal principles have their basis in social experience and practice. In Mackinnon's case, her focus is on the political and legal institutionalization of the concept of human rights within states and internationally. Mackinnon's argument about rights discourse and practice has two sides. On the one hand, she formulates a critique of the idea of human rights from a feminist perspective, and casts doubt on the capacity of the idea of international human rights to serve not only women's interests but also the interests of people in general. On the other hand, she argues in defence of the idea of rights understood not as generic human rights but as civil rights, which she argues are capable of being used to recognize and affirm relevant difference without this being translated into hierarchical terms. Mackinnon argues that contemporary human rights thinking has been characterized by the exclusion of women from the category of humanity:

If you are hurt as a member of a group, the odds that the group will be considered human are improved if it includes men. Under guarantees of international human rights, as well as in everyday life, a woman is "not yet a name for a way of being human".[30]

The root cause of this exclusion is, in Mackinnon's view, the lack of recognition in the discourse on human or individual rights of the fundamentally patriarchal structure of both states and interstate relations in the modern world. Where Ruddick looks to women's experience under patriarchy as care-givers as the source of a new ethics, Mackinnon's focus is on the systematic and institutionalized power differential between men and women in modernity, and the ways in which this results in women persistently failing to qualify as fully fledged human beings in terms of their effective protection under state and international law. This argument, that women have been incorporated into the ranks of rights bearers on different terms from men, is a familiar one in feminist political theory.[31] Mackinnon makes the argument in relation to women as bearers of international rights by focusing on the lack of fit between the ideology of human rights and the actuality of women's position. Mackinnon argues that there are two major influences on rights ideology in the international context: firstly, the original understanding of the "rights of man" as it emerged in Western legal and political theory, originating in Aristotle's principle of justice as meaning to treat the like alike; secondly, the experience of the Nazi Holocaust and genocide as the definitive example in the modern period of the violation of human rights on grounds of particular difference.

Mackinnon traces the principle of human rights back to Aristotle and his assertion that justice involved treating equals equally and unequals unequally. In Aristotle's terms the category of "equals" was heavily restricted to certain male citizens, with women and slaves definitively (and inherently) classed as unequals – in relation to male citizens and each other. According to Mackinnon, to treat equals equally in Aristotle's terms is to treat them as being the same. This notion of equal/sameness is then carried over, as the understanding of who counts in the class of equals is massively extended in the modern period, even to the point when women are included and slavery is abolished. Thus in the language of "natural" rights, the "rights of man", or in the post-1945 period, "human rights", what remains constant is the understanding that in being bearers of equal rights all human beings are essentially the same. In other words, any differences between them are morally irrelevant. This has specific consequences for women (amongst others) as rights bearers in two interrelated respects. Firstly, what it means to be the same, according to Mackinnon, is defined in terms which fit certain categories of men and which therefore necessarily exclude/marginalize women in practice. Secondly, it frequently turns out that women are not actually included in the category of the "same" after all, in theory or in practice. The former phenomenon is exemplified by instances standardly pointed out by feminist critics of the UDHR, such as the identification of human with head of household, property owner, wage earner, or independent discrete individual (in other words, not pregnant).[32] This means that for those humans who don't fit into this mould, the working assumption is always that these differences, being morally irrelevant, do not require recognition; hence the standard difficulties women face in the public and private sphere over equal treatment and opportunities across many different kinds of legal order. The latter phenomenon is clearly demonstrated by the lack of rights over their bodily integrity that is commonplace for women. The everyday abuse suffered by women in terms of sexual assault and domestic violence indicates how, in practice, women are routinely seen as "less than human". Both of these phenomena, argues Mackinnon, reflect the reality of women's subordinate civil and political status within modern states and the international community, a subordination which is masked by state endorsement of the idea of universal rights but which has its roots not in the state and international law as such but in patriarchy, a system of subordination in which men have power over women.[33] It is interesting that where the UDHR does recognize entities other than humans or men and women, it includes both nation and family, neither of them entities which have been unambiguously woman-friendly. In particular, the UDHR's endorsement of the "naturalness" of the family as the basic unit of society reinforces Mackinnon's point of the ambivalence of modern liberal discourse, which deconstructs the idea of natural hierarchy amongst humans but then condones it in the case of humans who are also women within the private sphere.

The second major influence on women's exclusion from the category of human in human rights discourse, according to Mackinnon, relates not to the generic nature of the category of humanity but to the one particular, collective identity which has been recognized as of supreme importance in the history of the violation of human rights: that of race or ethnicity. Mackinnon argues that the Nazi genocide, in powerfully influencing the ethical sensibilities of those who went on to formulate the human rights discourse in the post-1945 period, effectively reinforced the blind spot towards women already incorporated into generic human rights discourses. The latter set up the positive understanding that rights are given in virtue of humanity; the former set up the understanding that the paradigmatic violation of human rights is for people to be killed or hurt not because they are a male or female human individual but because they have a particular ethnic/racial identity. According to Mackinnon, what became clear in the light of the systematic rape of women in the wars in Bosnia in the mid-1990s was that the ambiguities of women's status were obvious not only in explicitly patriarchal cultures, not only within modern liberal states and nationalisms, but also within the international sphere amongst those observing, recording, and judging these events with the standards of the UDHR in mind. From the point of view of the international human rights discourse, women were rights bearers as humans and had their rights violated as members of a besieged ethnic collectivity; they were not rights bearers as women and their rights were not violated as women. From Mackinnon's point of view this is not a matter of semantics but one of supreme ethical and political importance, because in failing to understand violations of women's rights as grounded in the fact that they are women, international law perpetuates a situation in which women's rights are particularly vulnerable.

It is difficult to be sure of the extent to which rape was used deliberately as a weapon of warfare in the Bosnian wars. This is partly because the evidence is inevitably piecemeal and loaded with significance for propaganda for all sides. It is also because rape has always been recognized as part of warfare but not as a weapon of warfare, and to see it as such requires a paradigm shift of understanding. Traditionally, rape is something which soldiers (men) do – regrettable perhaps, a crime perhaps, but not to be seen as a war crime or crime against humanity. In the same way, within the state, rape is a regrettable, criminal thing that men do but it is not understood as being on a par with a racist attack. Two features of the rape of women in the Bosnian war shifted this commonplace perspective on rape as something which just happens, particularly in war situations: firstly, rape appeared to be being organized systematically; secondly, rape was linked to enforced pregnancy presented as the victory of the ethnically superior male over the ethnically inferior woman and, by extension, her male compatriots. In her book *Rape Warfare*, Allen has detailed some of the evidence presented from survivors of rape/death camps.[34] One of the things which is most obvious from Allen's account is the way that the systematic rape and impregnation of women was understood primarily in terms of its effect on the male enemy population. This worked in two main ways. Firstly, women were regarded as the possessions of husbands and fathers, thus sexual domination of women was a way of humiliating and depriving those husbands and fathers; the women's own humiliation and deprivation, let alone their pain, was instrumental to a broader purpose. Secondly, women were identified as the passive vessels that carried the future generation of the nation. The ethnic/national identity of the next generation was determined by the ethnicity/nationality of the father, therefore by impregnating enemy women, men were ensuring that the enemy people was not being reproduced and, more importantly, that their own ethnic/national inheritance would be transmitted.

The horror and absurdity of these ways of thinking and acting are shocking, but it is worth remembering that it is not long since in a modern liberal state like Britain, rape within marriage was not a recognized offence and the rights of British women to gain citizenship for their non-national husbands were different from those of men in the same situation. In Mackinnon's view, the systematic rape and forced impregnation of women in Bosnia was not a violation of the normal standards of human interaction enshrined in documents such as the UDHR. Instead, it was a particularly unpleasant example of the ways in which women are routinely counted as less than human. It did, however, provide an opportunity to rethink the notion of human rights to be more inclusive of women. When the international war crimes tribunal was set up, for the first time an explicit inclusion of rape as a crime against humanity (when committed in armed conflict against a civilian population) was made. In addition, rape and sexual assault could also be identified as crimes against humanity contributing towards genocide if committed with intent to destroy national, ethnic, racial, or religious groups. The inclusion of rape and sexual assault amongst crimes against humanity has been greeted as a legal watershed for humanitarian international law, and one which, by implication, represents a victory for the interests and rights of women – since the great majority of rape/sexual assault cases (though not all) uncovered by the war crimes tribunal were crimes committed against women. However, from Mackinnon's point of view, there remain acute problems with the ways in which international law has responded to the recognition of rape as a means of warfare.

What happens to women is either too particular to be universal or too universal to be particular, meaning either too human to be female or too female to be human.[35]

International law has not responded to rape as a crime against humanity with humanity understood as women. When rape is identified straightforwardly as a crime against humanity, along with torture and imprisonment of civilian populations, it is defined so that it is not specific to sex. Not rape of women but rape as the sexual penetration of either men or women is the category used. When rape is identified as linked to genocide, not rape of women but rape of members of a particular national, ethnic, racial, or religious group is recognized – a bizarre endorsement of the sick logic of the rape/death camps, since only if the rape of women is recognized as equivalent to the destruction of national, ethnic, racial, or religious groups does this equation make sense. Yet to assume this equivalence is to assume the peculiar possessed and passive role which women have been assigned in an absurd rhetoric of collective identity. On the one hand, women are humans capable of being sexually penetrated, on the other hand they are members of a collective, capable of being possessed and impregnated; but what is missed in all this is that it is only because women are women that they find themselves so oddly placed as humans or as members of a particular collectivity that systematic rape of women can count as an effective tool of genocide, not only to paramilitaries dosed in sexist and nationalistic propaganda but also to international lawyers and observers. Paradoxically, the explicit inclusion of rape as a crime against humanity in the specification of the jurisdiction of the Hague tribunal continues to perpetuate the marginalization and exclusion of women from the category of human.

Arguments such as those of Mackinnon are careful to stress that the idea of rights is of tremendous ethical importance, and that the growth of human rights discourses has provided vital resources for political resistance and legal protection of individuals within states and internationally. From a feminist point of view, it is clearly better to have rape recognized explicitly as a crime against humanity than for it to continue to be regarded as just another unfortunate side-effect of war. However, at the same time, Mackinnon sees the resources offered by generic understandings of human rights as being seriously inadequate, because they mask the differential realities of women's position and therefore effectively disempower their supposed beneficiaries. This argument is parallel to arguments developed in the context of feminist struggles over rights within the state: that in order for equality of right for women to be a reality, women need rights which are specific to them and which, when institutionalized, will help to deconstruct the patriarchal relations of power in which women are currently caught. At the heart of Mackinnon's point is an argument for the need to rethink the meaning of equality of right, a rethinking which she argues is implicit in feminist civil rights movements within states such as Canada and the USA, and which needs to be carried over into the international sphere:

Human rights locate equality in eliminating irrational differentiation; civil rights see equality as much in affirmative claims of cultural particularity, in ending oppression whether based on real differences or not, and in altering the mainstream to accommodate an uncompromised diversity.[36]

Because discourses of universal human rights assume humans are already the same in morally relevant respects, they do not grasp that rights are needed not because of sameness but because of difference. The profound shock of the Holocaust brought to the attention of liberal universalists the fact that members of ethnic, racial, or religious groups might need protecting because they are members of those groups, so that genocide becomes identified as the ultimate crime against humanity. But the differences of women's positions are so profoundly tied up with the institutional structure and common sense of the international community that feminists have had to struggle to enable the fact that women need rights because they are women, and that these might be different rights from those men need to have recognized. This struggle, however, continues to be underpinned by an ideal of equality of right, which Mackinnon identifies as emerging from the political practice of the women's movement:

This movement has produced a rich concept of equality as lack of hierarchy, not sameness. Its everywhere relative universality, its refusal to settle for anything less than a single standard of human dignity and entitlement, and its demand for elevation in that standard have left Aristotle in the dust.[37]

This quotation summarizes Mackinnon's ideal of how to think about human rights for women. This ideal retains the idea of a "single standard of human dignity and entitlement" which has always been central to rights-based thinking, but the meaning of this single standard is interpreted in terms which do not rely on the notion of a universal sameness to underpin the single standard. Mackinnon takes the ground of rights as being the actual power differentials between different groups (specifically, in this case, men and women), and the struggles of the disempowered to improve their subordinate position. Rights are therefore a political weapon as much as a moral ideal that can be used to alter the realities we inhabit. If this notion of rights is taken seriously, then human rights must be explicitly grounded in difference, and the subordination of women within family, nation, and international politics can become recognized, in all its various guises, as in itself a crime against humanity.

Conclusion

Ruddick and Mackinnon offer two different feminist responses to rethinking international ethics and politics. Both of these responses are premised on the rejection of mainstream approaches to thinking about international ethical issues. Ruddick opposes her ethic of maternal thinking to traditional just-war arguments, and Mackinnon differentiates her own notion of human rights from the dominant liberal ideal. In both cases, the experiences of women and of women's political movements and struggles are a major inspiration for the two theorists' work. The practical implications for international political norms of taking either Ruddick or Mackinnon seriously would be profound. Both thinkers take the role of grass-roots international actors, such as feminist campaigners at Greenham Common, Argentinian mothers, or those struggling for the recognition of women's rights as human rights, as exemplifying the kind of ethical engagement they would like to see more generally within the international sphere. However, the ways in which they envisage positive change are rather different. Ruddick's emphasis is on transforming the fundamental ethical presumptions embedded in state-centric just-war thinking, in which lives are, in the right circumstances, tradeable commodities. Her argument offers an ethic of virtue, and also a regulative ideal of a completely different kind of world for which we should be striving. Mackinnon's vision is in many ways more limited. She endorses an ideal of equality without sameness and difference without hierarchy, but in a context in which difference is actually hierarchy she acknowledges that there are fundamental conflicts of interest involved in the struggle for rights of subordinated groups. Mackinnon is quite clear that the institutionalization of women's rights as human rights will not be without cost to the men who currently benefit from the *status quo*. Although both theorists stress the importance of practice and the origin of norms and values in practice, often the practice of locally based groups, Mackinnon is more overtly interested than Ruddick in the possibility of international institutions, particularly international law, being reshaped and strengthened to protect and enhance women's interests.

In spite of the above differences, however, the arguments of Ruddick and Mackinnon share two significant features which, it is argued, represent the central promise of feminist interventions in thinking about international ethical questions. Firstly, as mentioned above, both thinkers combine a simultaneous recognition of particularity and universality in their ethical frameworks. Secondly, both thinkers recognize that international ethics and politics are inseparable in the sense that every ethics has political implications, whether acknowledged or not. The combination of particularity and universality derives for both thinkers from the ways in which in practice feminist activists have experienced the impossibility of basing their arguments either on the pure particularity of women's positions or on the universal sameness of women with men. Feminism as a movement has had to tack between these alternatives at different times and places, in the context of different struggles, and has been able to do so through the subordination of any particular ideological position to the pragmatic goal of furthering the interests and addressing the subordination of women. Feminist ethics reflects this fluidity and can make sense of it precisely because feminist ethics is premised on feminist politics. The fact of this premise renders feminist ethics more open and pragmatic than traditional ethical paradigms. It also, however, makes feminist ethicists sensitive to the political commitments underlying ethical paradigms that present themselves as apolitical. One of the main tasks of feminist ethics has been to make visible the masculine political agendas which can be concealed beneath languages of state or individual rights. The broader challenge which feminist ethics faces, however, is how to go beyond that critique to the construction of new political possibilities in the international sphere. In relation to this challenge, this chapter will conclude by suggesting that the feminist ethic of care and feminist rights-based thinking offer complementary strengths.

The strength of Ruddick's ethic of maternal thinking lies in the way in which it alters the ethical sensibilities and frame of reference of international actors. It accomplishes this by its insistence on the embeddedness of ethical judgement and prescription in relations of empathetic connection and responsibility. Maternal thinking requires ethical agents to use their imagination to put themselves in others' places, and to acknowledge and develop their own sense of responsibility for others. As such, maternal thinking is an extremely demanding ethic. However, to the extent that it can be achieved it has implications for the ways in which politics, whether in the context of movements of resistance against oppression or in the context of conflict resolution, should be carried out. The emphasis in such an ethic of care is on listening rather than speaking, and on cultivating moral sensibility rather than providing moral agents with ready-made principles for conduct. Strategies must be non-violent, not only in the sense of not physically violent but in the sense of not excluding/marginalizing the voices and concerns of any relevant actors within a particular situation. The ethic of maternal thinking is inclusive and interactive; solutions to dilemmas cannot be clear in advance and they will inevitably involve compromise and mutual adjustment. This means that, in spite of its idealistic character in terms of what is demanded of the moral agent, the ethic of maternal thinking is in many ways more appropriate to the messiness and ambivalence of problems in international politics than more rule-based moral theories.

If the strength of maternal thinking is to offer a different vision of moral judgement and prescription for international politics, then the strength of feminist rights-based thinking lies in the way in which it connects feminist interpretations of contemporary international ethical life directly to a political project to restructure international law and institutions to reflect feminist concerns. Instead of a radically distinct alternative to established international ethical thinking, a feminist rights-based ethic utilizes resources already available within contemporary international common sense (see Chapter 6, Donnelly, in this volume) to make visible the abuses of human rights suffered by women because they are women. The result of this is more radical than it might at first seem, since it implies a redefinition of the meaning of human rights and opens up the possibility of reconstructing existing law and institutions along lines that will help to create a very different kind of world for both women and men.

Notes

1. Basu, A., 1995, "Introduction", in Basu, A., ed., *The Challenge of Local Feminisms: Women's Movements in Global Perspective*. Boulder: Westview Press, pp. 1–21.
2. Peterson, V. S. and Runyan, A. S., 1993, *Global Gender Issues*. Boulder: Westview Press; Steans, J., 1998, *Gender and International Relations: An Introduction*. Cambridge: Polity Press.
3. Basu, note 1 above, pp. 13–18.
4. Peterson, V. S., 1990, "Whose Rights? A Critique of the 'Givens' in Human Rights Discourse", *Alternatives*, Summer, pp. 303–344; Mackinnon, C., 1993, "Crimes of War, Crimes of Peace", in Shute, S. and Hurley, S., eds, *On Human Rights: The Oxford Amnesty Lectures 1993*. New York: Basic Books, pp. 83–109.

5. Harris, A. and King, Y., eds, 1989, *Rocking the Ship of State: Toward a Feminist Peace Politics*. Boulder: Westview Press; Warren, K. J. and Cady, D. L., eds, 1994, "Special Issue: Feminism and Peace", *Hypatia*, Vol. 9, No. 2, Spring.

6. Elshtain, J. B., 1987, *Women and War*. Brighton: Harvester Press.

7. Enloe, C., 1983, *Does Khaki Become You? The Militarisation of Women's Lives*. London: Pluto Press; Vickers, J., 1993, *Women and War*. London: Zed Books; Steans, note 2 above, pp. 81–103.

8. Ashworth, G., 1999, "The Silencing of Women", in Dunne, T. and Wheeler, N. J., eds, *Human Rights in Global Politics*. Cambridge: Cambridge University Press, pp. 259–276.

9. Peterson, note 4 above; Ashworth, note 8 above.

10. Ashworth, note 8 above, pp. 265–270.

11. Ruddick, S., 1990, *Maternal Thinking: Towards a Politics of Peace*. London: The Women's Press; Ruddick, S., 1993, "Notes Toward a Feminist Peace Politics", in Cooke, M. and Woollacott, A., eds, *Gendering War Talk*. Princeton: Princeton University Press, pp. 109–127; Mackinnon, note 4 above.

12. Gilligan, C., 1982, *In a Different Voice: Psychological Theory and Women's Development*. Cambridge, MA: Harvard University Press.

13. Kohlberg, L., 1981, *The Philosophy of Moral Development*. San Francisco: Harper and Row.

14. Benhabib, S., 1992, "The Generalized and the Concrete Other", in Frazer, E., Hornsby, J., and Lovibond, S., eds, *Ethics: A Feminist Reader*. Oxford: Blackwell, pp. 267–300, at p. 270.

15. Bubeck, D., 1998, "Ethic of Care and Feminist Ethics", *Women's Philosophy Review*, No. 18, Spring, pp. 22–50.

16. Ruddick, 1990, note 11 above.

17. *Ibid.*, p. 123.

18. Ruddick, 1993, note 11 above, p. 121.

19. Ruddick, 1990, note 11 above, p. 135.

20. Hartsock, N., 1983, "The Feminist Standpoint: Developing the Ground for a Specifically Feminist Historical Materialism", in Harding, S. and Hintikka, M., eds, *Discovering Reality*. Boston: D. Reidel, pp. 283–310.

21. Ruddick, 1990, note 11 above, p. 135.

22. *Ibid.*, pp. 141–159.

23. *Ibid.*, p. 150.

24. Ruddick, 1993, note 11 above, p. 123.

25. Benhabib, note 14 above.

26. Walker, R. B. J., 1988, *One World, Many Worlds: Struggles for a Just World Peace*. Boulder: Lynne Rienner.

27. Ruddick, 1993, note 11 above, p. 124.

28. Warner, D., 1991, *An Ethic of Responsibility in International Relations*. Boulder: Lynne Rienner.

29. Mackinnon, note 4 above.

30. *Ibid.*, p. 91.

31. Pateman, C., 1988, *The Sexual Contract*. Cambridge: Polity Press.

32. Peterson, note 4 above.

33. Mackinnon, note 4 above, pp. 85–86.

34. Allen, B., 1996, *Rape Warfare: The Hidden Genocide in Bosnia-Herzogovina and Croatia*. Minneapolis: University of Minnesota Press.

35. Mackinnon, note 4 above, p. 85.

36. *Ibid.*, p. 104.

37. *Ibid.*, p. 102.

9

Ethics and refugees

Mark Gibney

In the realm of international relations – where ethical concerns are seemingly few and far between, and ethical practices, perhaps, in even shorter supply[1] – the notion of refugee protection serves a unique and special function. Through the provisions of the Refugee Convention[2] and Protocol,[3] as well as various regional refugee charters, states have assumed a legal obligation to protect "others". States assume international and regional obligations almost as a matter of course. State practice, however, is oftentimes something altogether different. All one needs do is to see how many signatories to the Torture Convention commit torture to realize this distinction. But in the area of refugee protection the separation between both legal and moral obligations and actual state practice is not so easily discernible.

In a century that saw incredible levels of human tragedy, in many ways refugee protection stood out as a beacon of sanity and hope. But it would be a grave mistake simply to equate granting refugee status with the notion of acting ethically. This is not to deny the fact that in granting refugee status to individuals we are, in nearly every instance, acting in an ethical manner.[4] And by that is meant that we are doing what is "good" or "right" in assisting those who are in need of protection or safety. We can, however, be faulted on two scores. The first is the degree to which we (meaning the West) have acted ethically in this realm. The second is that we systematically miss the nature of the duty that we owe to certain refugees, forever seeing refugee admissions as mere acts of charity rather than as acts that at times might be demanded by principles of justice.

The first section of this chapter looks at how different our moral "universe" is depending on whether we are speaking of events within our own domestic sphere or those that occur beyond our own national borders. Not only does our morality seem to change dramatically depending on geographic location, but so does what we view as being an ethical issue. With respect to events in the international realm, what we do repeatedly is to recognize as "moral problems" only certain aspects of much larger ethical issues. Invariably, those segments of the ethical issues that we will take up are those things that are much easier for us to deal with, and also tend to make us look much more ethical than perhaps we really are. This practice of "framing" ethical issues in such a way that we ignore many of the more difficult and intractable aspects of much larger ethical phenomena is certainly true in the area of refugee protection. The challenge of this work is to set forth what these "other" ethical issues are, to explore why it is that we have not dealt with them adequately, and, finally, establish how it is that we might do so.

The second section begins this venture by focusing on the very problematic way in which the West has defined a "refugee". To state matters bluntly, current interpretations of the UN refugee definition have gone far in defeating the whole purpose of refugee admissions – which is to protect people. Notwithstanding this, most governments meet their legal obligations under international law in the sense that they do not purposely send individuals back to countries where they will be harmed. However, at the same time they have gone to great lengths to try to eliminate the possibility of being able to apply for refugee status. These "non-entrée" policies are the focus of the third section.

Of course, the mantra rationalizing these restrictive measures is that there is widespread abuse of the West's asylum policies. What are these serious charges based on? Little more than the refugee determinations that we make ourselves, and the fact that there has been a sharp decrease in the percentage of applicants who have been granted "convention" status. The fourth section presents a different kind of empirical evidence that seriously challenges this view. In point of fact, the data show rather conclusively that a large percentage of those applying for asylum in the West are from exactly the kinds of countries one would expect refugees to come from: countries that are ruled by brutal and repressive governments, and where large numbers of individuals are either harmed or seriously threatened.

According to the manner in which we view the world in the West, refugees are always the result of someone else's actions – or so it is convenient for us to think. What is completely and systematically ignored is the manner in which we "aid and assist" so many of those practices that have given rise to enormous levels of human suffering, and which, in turn, have prompted large-scale migrations. The fifth section of this chapter looks at how Western countries continue to use the notion of state sovereignty to protect themselves from the charge that they might bear any responsibility for the creation of refugee flows. Finally, the last section presents two principles upon which a truly ethical refugee policy could be based.

Ethical standards?

How we frame ethical issues in the international realm

Perhaps the biggest problem in ethical theory is not so much in terms of determining what is or is not ethical behaviour, but rather what is or is not an ethical issue in the first place. Ethical theory devotes far too little time and effort to considering the parameters of our so-called moral universe, and along with that far too little time and effort to examining how we go about "framing" or "packaging" ethical issues. As the author has argued more fully elsewhere,[5] there is a decided tendency selectively to pick and choose those aspects of ethical issues that we wish to look at (invariably those that are more manageable for us, as well as those that tend to make us look more ethical), but to ignore those aspects of a larger moral problem that we do not wish to look at. In short, rather than addressing anything close to the entirety of a particular ethical problem, it is quite common to break off very small segments and deal with these – and only these.

This convenient (but problematic) means of "addressing" ethical issues is particularly pronounced in the international realm, and for a variety of reasons. The first is the lingering idea that there is very little morality once we have crossed our own state's borders. Instead, the dominant reflexive attitude is simply to rationalize that we live in a Hobbesian universe, and that our domestic laws and morals are only applicable at home. The writer has yet to see the issue raised any better than by Lea Brilmayer: "Is there any way to explain why an action suddenly becomes legitimate when it is undertaken outside one's territory? Would support for death squads in El Salvador be any different from support for death squads in Miami?"[6]

The second reason why there is a much greater tendency to package ethical issues in the international realm is that "foreign" problems seem (and in most cases are) far more intractable and overwhelming than "domestic" problems. Within the USA, for example, there have been discussions in policy circles and elsewhere concerning the prospects of making AIDS medicine available to all those afflicted with the disease, notwithstanding the hefty cost. Whether these measures ever get fully implemented or not remains to be seen. What is important, at least for present purposes, is that this is how the ethical and policy issues have been framed domestically. Contrast this with the AIDS situation world-wide. We cannot even begin to conceive of any kind of effort – national or international – that would provide medicine to any number of the tens of millions of individuals currently infected with this disease. This simply is not a moral issue for us. What *have been* considered to be moral issues in this realm are such things as the question whether individuals who are participants in AIDS tests in the third world should ever be provided with a placebo or not, and along with that, whether the testing practices commonly employed in the West should also be used in developing countries. *These* are moral issues that we can better deal with. Here we can talk in terms with which we are familiar, such as "informed consent", a patient's "right to know", and so forth. Without a doubt these are moral issues. But so is the question whether there is any kind of duty to provide AIDS medicine to any of those who are infected. But this larger ethical issue is too overwhelming, too expensive (or thought to be), and essentially too far removed from our everyday morality.[7] And because we cannot (or will not) think in those terms, this never becomes a moral issue for us.

The final reason offered as to why there is such a tendency to package ethical issues in the international realm is the simple fact that we have the ability to do so. Try as we might, oftentimes there is no escaping most ethical issues in the domestic realm. Sooner or later we will be confronted by these problems in one manner or another. There are, of course, no assurances that we will ever fully address such issues, but the point is that it is difficult to escape having to face them. They will be, in one way or another, part of our moral consciousness. We might not deal with the problem of homelessness very well, to use just one example, but it is quite difficult to avoid the sleeping bodies that we have to step over on our way to work. Contrast this with ethical issues that arise in other countries. Here there are no bodies to step over. And we can change the channel[8] – literally – when there are images that might begin to prick at our moral consciences, leaving us to remain in the cool comfort of the ethical sphere of our own choosing.

How we frame refugee issues in particular

Because refugee protection sits on the border between two moral spheres – "ours" and "theirs" – the manner in which we package such issues is particularly noteworthy and interesting to examine. We invariably begin with the unquestioned assumption – announced as something rising to the level of a principle of international law – that nation-states enjoy absolute discretion in terms of entry.[9] This power to exclude on whatever terms we so choose is viewed as an inherent sovereign right. But what this ignores is the manner in which this "sovereign right" has been (and continues to be) violated. It ignores, for example, the relatively short period of time that this "principle" has been established. And it also ignores much of current state practice, particularly that of African countries, which are marked by enormous migrations of human populations.

But perhaps the most fatal flaw in all of this is that this "sovereign right" is one that *we* enjoy, but it is not clear that others have enjoyed it as well. For one thing, it ignores the veritable invasion of European settlers into virtually every corner of the globe from the fifteenth century to the twentieth. The British population is presently fearful of immigration from Commonwealth countries; the French of migration from francophone Africa, and so on. Funny how quickly we forget our own actions in the world. The effort here is not to drag up "ancient history", because, in a number of ways, this is exactly what we are speaking about. But there is a marked tendency to go to the opposite extreme. We wish to write on an ethical clean slate when it serves our purposes to do so. And quite often it does serve our purposes.

Finally, the notion of a "sovereign right" to control borders ignores the manner in which the sovereignty of other states (and it is always *other* states, and not ours) is essentially ignored at the present time – with impunity. We might wish to pretend that we are far removed from much of the mayhem in the third world that has given rise to enormous levels of human migration and suffering, but we are not. Instead, as a matter of course Western countries have armed and equipped one civil war after another.[10] They have also provided billions of dollars in foreign aid to the most corrupt and brutal dictatorships in the world.[11] The point is, the practices of other states are anything but the practices of other states. Instead, in varying degrees, they are also *our* practices as well.[12] But it is very convenient for us to ignore all this.

This, then, is essentially how we have framed the ethical issue of refugee protection. After it is assumed that a state has absolute control over its borders, after it is assumed that countries like ours have absolutely no connection whatsoever with the creation of refugee flows in the first place, and finally, after it is so readily and easily assumed that whatever absorptive capacity for refugees exists we have undoubtedly reached that juncture and gone beyond, at that point ethical issues involving refugee protection become relatively easy for us to deal with. This should be no surprise because we have set up the moral problem in exactly that fashion. What we have done is to chop away most of the ethical issues that are (or should be) inherent in a discussion of refugee protection, leaving only a few relatively inconsequential issues for our "ethical" discourse. And after all this, we do in fact come across as truly ethical beings. For example, most Western countries provide a plethora of administrative hearings for asylum seekers and, for the most part, these adhere to the highest standards of due process under our domestic law. Living conditions for asylum seekers, particularly against the standards of the countries refugees are fleeing from, are quite good. And as perhaps the final proof of just how ethical we are, we do not even return or deport all that many of those we have determined *not* to be refugees. Rather, we allow large numbers of non-refugees (or, to be more accurate, those *we* have determined as such) to stay in our countries on some kind of humanitarian basis, or simply through our own incompetent (but benevolent) systems because of our inability to deport many of those we have rejected. This, in sum, is what we have attempted to pass off as a discussion of the ethics of refugee policy.

Our inability (or perhaps our unwillingness) to assess our actions

Ethics demands standards by which to judge our actions. One of the problems with refugee protection, however, is that there never is any attempt to assess how well we are doing. The ready reply to this assertion is that it is complete and utter nonsense. The critic would be able to cite – chapter and verse – that there are X number of refugees in the world and Y number of internally displaced persons. The critic could also cite statistics on the number of individuals who have been granted humanitarian status, the number who have been repatriated in one form or another, and on and on.

But statistics do not make for analysis, and they certainly do not make for standards either. We know, for example, how many individuals have been given refugee protection, but no one has ever bothered to try to figure out how many individuals are in *need* of protection (or were, before they were killed) – refugee or otherwise. We know the number of internally displaced persons in the world, but very few have asked why it is that the internally displaced have not left their country of origin, and what some of the implications of this might be.[13] Finally, we do a lot of talking about "compassion fatigue" and the "absorptive capacity" to take in refugees, but in a country like the USA at least, there is never any attempt to compare the claims of refugees with those of other migrants, although this latter group is more than ten times larger than the number of refugees admitted each year.

We also make no real attempt to connect refugee protection with how we act in the world quite generally. Stark evidence of this divorce between refugee protection, on the one hand, and the conduct of foreign policy on the other was evident in a highly visible asylum case in the USA a few years back. The case involved a woman, Fauziya Kasinga, who feared facing female genital mutilation (FGM) if sent back to her home country of Togo. After years of litigation, the claim was finally approved (due in large part, it is believed, to the amount of publicity generated by the case). The problem, however, is that the matter pretty much ended there.[14] Notwithstanding the act of granting refugee status (which in itself is proof that we find some particular practice in another state abhorrent), statements made at that time by officials of Western embassies in countries where FGM was systematically carried out strongly indicated that the issue was not one that was to be taken up with government officials of host countries. Instead, these were seen as "cultural practices" that were outside the scope of diplomatic initiative and concern.[15]

How, then, do we assess our actions? Staying with the example of FGM for the moment, do we look at how well we have treated the claims of the handful of women who are somehow able to get to our countries? The high standards of due process that we afford them once they are (somehow) here? Or perhaps the fine legal representation that such claimants will receive in a country like the USA? And what about the fact that many of the claimants (perhaps all of them) will be successful? Should *this* be our standard of how well we are doing? If it is, we are in fact a very moral group of people indeed. Or should we look at the fact that only the minutest percentage of women who will face FGM will ever be able to get to our borders, or to the West more generally? But along with that, we will make almost no effort to attempt to prevent this practice in other countries, or to assist those who will face (or have suffered from) this practice. Should *this* be our standard instead? If it is, then perhaps we are not as ethical or as moral as we would like to pretend that we are.

What follows is an assessment of refugee protection from what the author considers to be a more complete ethical perspective. As noted at the outset, there is no question that the granting of refugee status is an ethical act. But an ethical act does not make for ethical policy or practice – or, for that matter, ethical people.

Who is – and who is not a refugee?

The war exclusion

Under the Refugee Convention a person is a "refugee" who:

owing to well-founded fear of being persecuted for reasons of race, religion, nationality, membership of a social group or political opinion, is outside the country of his nationality and is unable or, owing to such fear, is unwilling to avail himself

of the protection of that country; or who, not having a nationality and being outside the country of his former habitual residence ... is unable or, owing to such
fear, is unwilling to return to it.

The essence of granting refugee protection is to provide protection to
people. This fact would be evident to anyone. Anyone, it seems, except
international refugee lawyers. One reason why this claim is made is that it
is commonly and all too readily agreed upon in those circles that individuals "merely" seeking safety from the dangers and ravages of war
are *not* refugees under the convention definition. The problem with this,
of course, is that war causes enormous levels of human suffering: hundreds of thousands of civilians are either killed or wounded each year
during the course of conflicts; villages and homes are destroyed; disease
flourishes, and so on.

Refugee lawyers know all this, of course. Yet, with very rare exceptions, they continue to read the convention standard as omitting individuals fleeing war.[16] More than this, however, they readily rationalize and
defend this conclusion. Among those in the vanguard taking this position
is David Martin. In a article that has much to commend it,[17] Martin
argues for a much closer connection between refugee relief and the protection of human rights. The problem with Martin's approach, however, is
that it is internally inconsistent. In one breath he very persuasively argues
that refugee relief should be based on human rights principles. But in the
next breath he defends (in a very unconvincing manner) the convention's
exclusion of civilians caught in a war situation.[18]

The empirical record, of course, shows scant protection for individuals
fleeing situations of war. The problem, however, is that the empirical
record is completely irrelevant, or at least has been treated as such by
refugee lawyers. Upwards of 400,000 civilians were killed in civil conflicts
in Central America during the 1980s, to use just one small area of the
globe. This is empirical fact. Yet notwithstanding these incredible levels
of human suffering, someone like Martin could (and did) take the position that a "large majority" of refugee claims from Central America are
"manifestly unfounded", and should be treated as such.[19]

The point is that the number killed or wounded could be double this or
more, and apparently it would still not matter. In fact, one could conjure
up a situation where something close to the entire population of a country was killed in the course of fighting, and still the convention definition
could be read in such a way so that any asylum claims from this country
could be dismissed as "manifestly unfounded". But in many ways the
craziness of the war exclusion can best be shown after the fact, and in a
particular setting. Consider, then, Mark Danner's wonderful and disturbing book *The Massacre at El Mozote*.[20] This is a gruesome tale of the

slaughter of nearly the entire population in one village in El Salvador during the civil war in that country. Against the backdrop of the cruelties of the war quite generally, there was not much that distinguished this particular massacre from hundreds of others that were also carried out in this afflicted country. In fact, the only reason why El Mozote entered our moral universe at all in the first place is that for years officials of the US government vehemently denied that the massacre ever took place. Thus, El Mozote has also come to symbolize US duplicity and complicity. But that is not important for present purposes. What *is* important is this: not one of these people would have qualified as a "refugee". That is, while all certainly had a "well-founded fear of persecution", not one would have been able to show that this persecution was "on account of" one of the five enumerated factors. *All* they would have been able to show is that government troops would, from time to time, exterminate an entire village. What this means, then, is that if one of more of these villagers had managed to escape from the advancing government troops and had sought safety in another country, there would have been nothing unlawful in sending these people right back to El Mozote – and certain death. And one of the arguments made in this chapter is that any time a person is not protected against "certain death" we should question whether we are perverting the reason for having refugee protection in the first place.[21]

The two major regional refugee instruments – that of the Organization of African Unity[22] and the Cartegena Declaration[23] – have it right here. Both define "refugee" in a manner that specifically includes individuals fleeing from war situations and generalized violence. And because they do, these conventions are far more advanced, certainly from an ethical perspective, than the UN convention (or at least the common reading of that instrument).[24]

The singled-out requirement

Related to the war exception is the requirement that has been read into refugee law that an individual has to show that s/he has been "singled out" for persecution. According to this view, large-scale suffering and gross and systematic levels of human rights abuses in another country are not enough to ensure that an individual applicant receives refugee protection. In fact, rather than helping an asylum seeker, these things will actually work *against* the asylum application. The rationale (somehow) is that conditions are very bad in your country of origin, but they are bad for everybody. And because they are bad for everybody, unless the applicant can show that s/he is placed in some kind of special danger, a refusal to grant refugee status is not unwarranted.

Elsewhere the author has described this as the "perverse inverse" relationship between levels of human rights abuses and the granting of refugee status.[25] That is, the greater the level of human rights abuses the greater the risk of suffering persecution – but along with this, the less likelihood of being able to show that you (as opposed to everybody else) are being targeted. What is behind this policy, of course, is the fear of the slippery slope. That is, if we grant refugee status to one person from one of the world's hellholes we will, of logical necessity, have to provide it to every person in that country. These are real fears that the writer does not mean to underestimate or denigrate. But quite often the end result of this kind of "thinking" is that those who are in the most need of protection – especially individuals who live in countries where violence is of epidemic proportions – are the least likely to be recognized as refugees. And this goes directly contrary to the entire purpose of why we provide (or should provide) refugee protection in the first place.

The demand of state action

Another way of substantially decreasing those eligible for refugee protection is for the receiving country to demand that the persecution in question be carried out by the state. In theory such a requirement is justifiable enough. Private squabbles should not invoke refugee protection. However, purposely or not, this requirement misses a number of things. One is that it is not uncommon for state actors to pose as other than state actors. A good example of this would be the systematic murder of street children in Brazil by off-duty security officials. In addition, such a requirement also ignores the fact that in a number of countries state officials readily allow private vigilante groups to commit large-scale human rights abuses.

Finally, and most important of all, to innocent victims it matters little where violence emanates from. Pick up the newspaper any day and you will invariably see a story (it is so commonplace now that it will appear towards the back of the news) that an entire village of people had been slaughtered the previous day in Algeria. Life in Algeria is hell. But the view generally taken by the European countries is either that it is not known who is responsible for these actions, or, more likely, such violence should be blamed on fundamentalist opponents of the ruling government. As a result of this, states are somehow able to rationalize that Algerians are less than deserving of their protection.

The demand under US law to prove the persecutor's intent

Another means of defeating the purpose of refugee protection has been established by the US Supreme Court in the case of *INS v Elias-*

Zacarias.[26] The facts of the case are as follows. During the latter part of January 1987, 18-year-old Elias-Zacarias, a Guatemalan peasant, was approached at his home by two armed, uniformed guerrillas who wore handkerchiefs to hide their identities. The purpose of the "visit" was to convince Elias-Zacarias and his parents that they should join their guerrilla organization, which they refused to do. The guerrillas told them to rethink their position, and threatened to return. Elias-Zacarias was placed in an impossible position. He was fearful of government retaliation if he joined the guerrillas, and likewise he was fearful of being killed by the guerrillas if he did not join. Seeing no other options, he fled Guatemala at the end of March 1987.

The Immigration and Naturalization Service apprehended Elias-Zacarias in the USA in July 1987 on the grounds that he entered the country without inspection. In the deportation proceedings brought against him, Elias-Zacarias conceded his deportability, but requested asylum and withholding of deportation based on the attempted recruitment by the guerrillas. Elias-Zacarias's asylum claim was rejected by the immigration judge, a decision that was upheld by the Board of Immigration Appeals. These administrative determinations were overturned by the Court of Appeals for the Ninth Circuit on the basis that the acts of conscription by a non-governmental group constituted persecution on account of political opinion, and the court determined that Elias-Zacarias had a "well-founded fear" of such conscription.

The US Supreme Court overturned the Ninth Circuit's holding. Writing for the court's majority, Justice Scalia held that Elias-Zacarias's refusal to join the guerrillas was not necessarily an expression of a political opinion. Scalia surmised that there are a range of reasons why someone might not join a guerrilla organization – he mentioned the possibility of a fear of combat, a desire to remain with one's family and friends, and a desire to earn a better living in civilian life – and that Elias-Zacarias had failed to show a political motive for not joining. Furthermore, the court held, the mere desire not to take sides in a civil conflict does not in and of itself constitute a political opinion.

Beyond this, however, the court held that even if remaining neutral could be considered to be a "political opinion", a refugee claimant must also show that s/he has a "well-founded fear" of persecution: that the guerrillas will persecute him on the basis of this opinion, rather than because of his refusal to fight with them, or for some other reason. In other words, the claimant has to show why the persecutor is persecuting him. Perhaps conceding the near impossibility of this task, the court held that a claimant need not provide "direct proof of his persecutor's intent".[27] However, the court continued, "since the statute makes motive critical, he must provide *some* evidence of it, direct or circumstantial".[28]

Under this ruling, a person could be returned to "certain death", and still this action could be viewed as consonant with the refugee definition. That is, under the Supreme Court's ruling in *Elias-Zacarias*, even if there was an absolute certainty that a person would be tortured and/or killed back in her country of origin, there would be nothing unlawful (under domestic law or the court's interpretation of international law) in returning this person to such a fate if she could not offer some substantial proof for why the persecutor intended to harm her.

The deprivation of protection

A more recent ruling by the US Supreme Court fails the "certain death" standard in a different way.[29] Under both international law and domestic (US) law, a refugee can be denied protection if he has committed a "serious nonpolitical crime".[30] In interpreting this provision, the UNHCR *Handbook* states that "it is ... necessary to strike a balance between the nature of the offence presumed to have been committed by the applicant and the degree of persecution feared".[31] Or, in the words of Jim Hathaway: "The risks associated with exclusion must not outweigh the harm that would be done by returning a claimant to face prosecution or punishment."[32]

Yet it was exactly this kind of balancing that was rejected, first by the Board of Immigration Appeals and then by the US Supreme Court. As a consequence of the court's holding in *INS v Aguirre-Aguirre*, it is the Attorney General (and not the members of the judiciary) who is to determine what is (or is not) a "serious nonpolitical offense". More than this, however, if s/he so chooses, the Attorney General does *not* have to consider the severity of the persecution that would be faced by the claimant upon her return.[33]

Gross inconsistencies in state practice

Although we have been speaking quite generally of the practices of "the West", it is important to note the enormous variability in state practice within and between these countries in terms of who is considered to be a refugee and who is not. Refugee practice is structured so that individuals are prevented from filing asylum claims in a number of different states. Because of this, we cannot compare the results of asylum adjudication on particular individuals across countries. We can, however, come close to obtaining this kind of data by making other kinds of cross-national comparisons, and these results are very unsettling. In essence, the system is without rhyme or reason, leading one to the conclusion that asylum determinations are based almost exclusively on political considerations, and that legal and moral rationales carry very little weight.

In a study of West European asylum practice with a particular emphasis on the Netherlands, Daan Bronkhorst found that there were seismic differences in acceptance rates of asylum seekers from the same countries.[34] He writes:

there are no grounds to assume that ... Turkish asylum seekers in Germany are generally of a different type than Turkish asylum seekers in the Netherlands or Denmark. Yet the Netherlands have admitted a percentage six times higher than that in the FRG.[35]

In addition, Bronkhorst also found that the variance within West European countries is rather remarkable as well. He notes, for example, that in Denmark Somali asylum applicants had a much better rate of acceptance (at the time of his study) than did Turks, while in the Netherlands it was the other way around. In the UK, Ethiopians fared somewhat better than Iraqis, while in Germany, Ethiopians had only half the chance of Iraqis. Bronkhorst concludes:

What comes out ... is that various European governmental bodies responsible for refugee determinations do not seem to agree at all about which groups of asylum seekers contain a high percentage of "genuine" refugees, and which groups do not.[36]

A 1987 study by the US General Accounting Office which looked at the asylum claims of four groups of nationals – from Poland, Iran, Nicaragua, and El Salvador – found questionable differences in treatment for asylum applicants who were making the same sort of claim.[37] To use one example, asylum applicants from Nicaragua and El Salvador who claimed that they had been arrested, imprisoned, had their lives threatened, or were tortured had approval rates that were considerably lower than applicants from Iran and Poland making the same kinds of claims.

Internally displaced persons and the compartmentalization of law and morality

One of the more unique features about refugee flows is that this phenomenon tests the neat compartmentalization that we have created and maintained between "our" law and morality and "theirs". For the most part we are able to make nice distinctions between those things that fall within our domestic sphere – and are thus governed by one set of law and morality – and those that happen to fall within the international sphere – and thus are governed by a completely different set of rules and standards (or perhaps no rules and standards at all). However, refugees oftentimes come rudely knocking at our door, not only demanding admission from us, but that we apply many of our domestic standards to them, whether it be in terms of due process requirements in asylum hearings, or something even more fundamental: not to send them back to a horror that so many of us in the West could not even begin to imagine. In fact, the author would argue that one of the reasons why refugees and asylum seekers create so much tension in the West, far beyond what their numbers would warrant, is that the refugee phenomenon tends to blur for us what had previously been thought to be well-defined distinctions.

In contrast to this, the internally displaced populations in the world have created far less tension and turmoil for us in the West – and we have responded in a corresponding fashion. That is to say, for the most part, we have tried to ignore these people in any way we can. We have genuflected at the altar of state sovereignty;[38] we have pretended that we have made every possible effort to reach "these people" when we have not; and when these efforts have been exposed for what they really are, we have thrown this problem to the UNHCR, but with no governing legal standard and very little financial support.[39]

This is not to suggest that internally displaced persons are – or should be – treated exactly the same as refugees. But it is to recognize the utter desperation that these populations face;[40] it is also to recognize that the crossing of national borders can be a completely arbitrary phenomenon which is more often than not completely beyond the control of those fleeing; and finally, it is to recognize that the neat distinction we have drawn between "refugees" and "internally displaced people" has been far more for our own benefit than for the benefit of the dispossessed in the world.

Summary

To sum up this second section, while there is a common definition in the West of what constitutes a "refugee", state practice has literally been all over the board in terms of who is recognized as such and who is not. In addition, the definition has been interpreted in such a manner so as to exclude large numbers (perhaps a majority) of those who are desperately in need of protection. The convention definition has been commonly read so as to exclude nearly all individuals fleeing from war. Along with that, no matter how terrible the human rights situation is in another country, asylum claimants will not be successful in obtaining refugee status unless and until they can somehow show that they have been "singled out". And the USA has gone one better by demanding that the victim offer proof of why the persecutor is persecuting her. Also under American law, a refugee who has committed a serious non-political crime can be returned to her country of origin without considering either the probability or the severity of the persecution faced there. Violence from non-state actors does not warrant protection in most countries, while violence from state actors does – although it is oftentimes impossible to know which is which. Finally, and with a few notable exceptions,[41] we have relieved ourselves of a great responsibility by generally treating internally displaced populations as being outside our control and responsibility. As great and as severe as all these shortcomings have been, in many ways they speak better about us than our systematic efforts to keep refugees away in the first place. We now turn to these practices.

Non-entrée[42] policies

Despite the presentation thus far of what might seem rather damning evidence of state practice, most governments do in fact follow the legal demands of the *non-refoulement* principle. That is, governments do not purposely send refugees back to their country of origin if there is a good likelihood that they will be harmed or their freedom taken away. What has happened instead, however, is that states have gone to great lengths to prevent individuals from getting into the refugee "system" in the first place.

In a recent article on the ethics of refugee protection, Joseph Carens asked: "Why do we have so many asylum seekers?"[43] His question, of course, is in response to the unprecedented number of people claiming refugee status in the West. There is no question that these numbers – and more importantly, these people – are causing enormous discomfort (and worse) in the countries that they are fleeing to and apparently settling in. Still, given the enormous levels of human rights violations in the world, the more accurate question might be this: why aren't there *more* asylum seekers than there are at present? We will explore why this is.

When return does not mean "return" (USA)

In 1993 the US Supreme Court handed down a startling eight-to-one decision. In the case of *Sale v Haitians Center Council, Inc.*,[44] the court ruled that the *non-refoulement* provisions in American law were only applicable to a person who was within the territorial jurisdiction of the USA. The court arrived at this decision after a tortuous analysis of what the word "return" meant. The court held that a person could only be "returned" after he had arrived in another country; but a person's "return" would not be effected simply by turning his boat around on the high seas and bringing that person back to his country of origin.

The case elicited an enormous amount of criticism, as well as it should.[45] One problem is that the decision fails the "certain death" test, and is thus contrary to why we have a system of refugee protection in the first place. That is, under the court's holding, the US government could forcibly and personally hand over an individual back to her persecutors – here is the political dissident who escaped from your prison! – knowing full well that this person would be harmed or killed. Yet there would be nothing illegal about this practice (under US law or international law, or at least the Supreme Court's interpretation of this law), so long as the person had never reached American soil (and in the case of Haitians at least, we will do everything in our power to prevent this from ever taking place). How far (or how far out) can *Sale* be taken? Could coastguard ships run these precarious "boats" from Haiti aground, and let the consequences fall where they may? Would there be anything unlawful (we will leave morality aside) if US military and/or security personnel purposely shot and killed refugees they came upon – on the high seas or in another country?[46]

Visa requirements and carrier sanctions (Europe)

It is very easy to criticize the US Supreme Court's decision in *Sale*. However, as this section will attempt to show, in many ways the practices of other Western countries are no less objectionable and no less inhumane than the practices of the US government on the high seas, although certainly far less visible and dramatic. These double-barrel policies are, of course, the implementation of visa requirements against nationals of certain countries, and along with that the enactment of carrier sanctions against airlines that have been found (after the fact) to have transported passengers without valid passports and visas.

In a truly moral universe, there would be no visa requirements for nationals of countries experiencing gross and systematic levels of human rights abuses. The reason, quite simply, is that these are conditions under which some number of people will be in need of protection in another country. This, however, is not the moral universe in which we presently live. In fact, receiving countries do just the opposite as a matter of course. That is, it is quite common for them suddenly to require visas for nationals of other countries whenever human rights conditions become grave and there is even the slightest trickle of refugees fleeing from these lands. If the aim of the visa requirement was to try to ensure some kind of order to the outflow and/or perhaps offer some avenue for individuals to begin to apply for refugee status, one might be willing to accept such a policy. But order is not the aim; elimination of refugee claims is.

But the attempt to prevent refugee claims has gone beyond visa restrictions and carrier sanctions. States have now begun to apply their immigration laws extraterritorially, although in a manner that differs in form (but not result) from US practices on the high seas. One measure is that Western states have now begun to post their own immigration officers at their diplomatic missions in countries from which they want to reduce exit movements toward their borders. Although some of their work consists of traditional administrative activities, these immigration officers have also trained airline check-in staff at airports which might serve as exit points for passengers with false documents, or no documents at all.[47] The end result of this is that many would-be refugees are kept from ever having the opportunity of applying for that status because they are prevented from leaving their countries of origin in the first place.

"Safe" third country provisions

Most European states have now adopted "safe" third country policies. There are two aspects to this. The first and more common is that countries will bar asylum applicants if it is determined that they have travelled through "safe countries of asylum", or countries in which the asylum seeker either found protection or could reasonably have done so before arriving at her ultimate destination. The second use of this term is the notion of the "safe country of origin". The idea behind this policy is to provide expedited procedure to the submission of claims by nationals or residents of countries generally considered to be safe. And "safe" in this context means that neither the asylum seeker nor the group to which he or she belongs is in danger of persecution.

In theory, there is much to commend such policies. The quicker and more efficiently we ferret out the claims of those not in need of protection, the sooner we can attend to the claims of those in dire straits. In practice, however, both of these safe country notions have been disastrous for asylum seekers, and they show (once again) that establishing an orderly procedure is not really the intended goal of such practices but rather the elimination or severe reduction of asylum claims altogether.

In the author's view, the biggest flaw with the idea of "safe country of asylum" is that it has frequently been interpreted so that even a fleeting connection with a so-called "safe country" – transiting through a country is a common example – will be enough to bar a person completely from even presenting a claim for asylum. The Norwegian example used by Rosemary Byrne and Andrew Shacknove highlights the absurdity of these policies.[48] According to Norwegian law, all claimants who have travelled via a safe third country are automatically returned, while all direct-flight asylum seekers (no matter where they are coming from) are allowed a full examination of their claim. Thus, a French asylum seeker arriving directly from Paris will receive full consideration, whereas an applicant from Somalia who transited (however briefly) to Norway via Heathrow will be summarily denied access to any asylum procedure.

With respect to the notion of "safe country of origin", the major complaint lodged against the practice is who is to determine what is or is not a "safe country", and on what grounds.[49] In the early years of the 1990s Switzerland was one of the first countries to name "safe countries", and those that it listed certainly do not inspire an enormous amount of confidence in the procedure. The "safe" countries listed by the Swiss government included Algeria (since removed), Angola, Bulgaria, Hungary, India, Poland, Czechoslovakia, and Romania. One of the problems with this list is the enormous differences in the human rights practices of these countries. For example, the human rights situation in what was then Czechoslovakia was considerably better than that which existed in Angola. Along with this, a far more serious flaw is the fact that several of these so-called "safe" countries (particularly Angola and India) were experiencing extraordinarily high levels of human rights abuses.[50]

The only conclusion that one can draw from this is the fact that the act of designating a country as "safe" or not has essentially been a political one. This is not to suggest that it would be impossible to come up with a list that was based on objective criteria. Such data exist. What might also be considered is to come up with a list of "unsafe" countries. The usefulness of such a list is that individuals from countries where there are "gross and systematic" levels of human rights abuse could (and, the writer believes, should) enjoy a rebuttable presumption that they have a "well-founded fear" of persecution.[51]

Abuse of refugee protection?

USA

Taking a position against refugee protection is just about impossible to do. That is, no matter how valid the policy goals against the admission of refugees might seem in theory or even in practice – rising domestic unemployment, overcrowded schools, assimilation problems, and so forth – these arguments simply pale when they are compared with the life-and-death issues inherent in refugee protection. It is indeed difficult to argue against saving a person's life, or protecting a person from harm. But because we cannot defeat the principle of refugee protection, what we have done instead is to go after those claiming refugee status. In this way we do not jar the moral universe that we live in. We can still maintain, fervently perhaps, that we are in favour of protecting refugees. However –

and this is a big however – what we have also gone on to do is systematically question whether those applying for protection are in fact *bona fide* refugees.[52] This has given rise to the widespread charge of "asylum abuse" that is heard so often in both Europe and the USA. And to assuage our consciences, we can simply point to the drastically declining success rates for asylum seekers as proof positive of this abuse.

Declining acceptance rates provide us with one kind of empirical evidence about asylum abuse. But it is important to realize that we are making these determinations ourselves. To use a sports analogy, it is as if a baseball pitcher were also calling balls and strikes. In other work, the author has tried to provide another kind of empirical analysis to test whether these accusations of asylum abuse have any grounding.[53] What this previous work has done, quite simply, is to test to see the relationship between levels of human rights abuse and claims for asylum.

These empirical results should be of some interest (although as pointed out earlier, empirical evidence seems to have little standing in this area). In terms of the USA, during the decade of the 1980s upwards of 80 per cent of asylum applicants were from countries experiencing gross and systematic levels of human rights abuse. Although this number declined to some degree in 1990s, the overwhelming evidence is that violence plays a pivotal role in producing refugee applicants. The practised response is to say that it is economic deprivation that mainly drives individuals to our shores. While it is true that most asylum seekers coming to the USA are in fact from poor countries, these countries are also very violent. In fact, they are invariably among the most violent countries in the world. However, very few asylum seekers are from countries that are poor but not violent. The conclusion the author draws from these data – in fact, it is next to impossible to draw any other – is that there is an inexorable connection between violence and the application for refugee status. Or to put this another way, the vast majority of asylum seekers in the USA come from exactly the kinds of countries one would expect asylum seekers to be from.

Strangely enough, this same statement could not be said of the American overseas refugee admissions programme, which dwarfs the number who are provided asylum within the USA. Each year the US government admits somewhere between 75,000 to 100,000 "quota refugees". Some of these individuals are from overseas refugee camps, but many now come directly from their country of origin.[54] There are two noteworthy things about this programme. The first is that, until very recently, the countries that these "refugees" came from have been countries that experience only "mild" levels of human rights abuses. In fact, each year only a very small number of individuals will be from countries experiencing "gross and systematic" levels of human rights abuses.[55] The other phenomenon is that the "persecution" these "refugees" face is nowhere near the kind of persecution other refugees suffer from. And in fact, this liberal attitude to refugees from certain countries has now become enshrined into American law.[56] As a result, each year the USA will admit tens of thousand of individuals who will face nothing more serious than some form of discrimination in their country of origin, which invariably will be a country with only moderate levels of human rights abuse and repression – and somehow call these people refugees – but at the same time it will systematically deny this categorization for people who have a very good chance of being killed or harmed. How one can speak about the ethics of refugee protection in this kind of moral universe is simply beyond comprehension.

Western Europe

Accusations of asylum abuse are quite common in Western Europe as well. What politicians and people in those countries have been trying to do is convince themselves that the rising number of denials of convention status, and their "non-entrée" policies more broadly, are justified. Again, one simply does not argue against the imperative of granting refugee status to bona fide refugees. You will not hear anyone maintain this position. What you will hear – very loudly and in lockstep – is that most of those presently applying for asylum status are simply not refugees.

Yet, according to empirical analyses the author has carried out, between two-thirds (1993) and three-quarters (1996) of the third world asylum seekers in Western Europe have been from countries experiencing "gross and systematic" levels of human rights abuses.[57] We might not like the fact that these people are in "our" countries, and along with that, we might well try to argue that there are other countries where safety can be – and should be – given. But there is no gainsaying the fact that the countries where most asylum seekers come from are in fact extraordinarily violent. Mirroring the American experience, the vast majority of asylum seekers in Western Europe (or at least those from the third world) come from exactly the kinds of countries we would expect asylum seekers to come from: countries that are brutal and repressive in nature, and where large numbers of people are either killed or harmed. What is stunning is how this fact has somehow been interpreted as systematic asylum abuse.

Refugee flows and transnational state responsibility[58]

One of the great difficulties in criticizing the refugee policies of the West is that we have readily allowed ourselves to see our own refugee admissions as nothing more than charitable acts, not actions that might be based on any kind of duty or responsibility to any group of refugees.[59] The reason for this view is that we rest content in the idea that refugee flows are always the consequence of the actions of "others",[60] but they certainly are not the result of any actions that we have taken. Rather, we are merely left to pick up the pieces in our own benevolent way.

In perhaps the leading philosophical treatment of this subject, Michael Walzer has suggested otherwise. Walzer maintains that our actions in the world will, at times, "help" to create refugees, and it is to those refugees that we owe a special duty. He writes:

Toward some refugees, we might have obligations of the same sort that we have toward fellow nationals. This is obviously the case with regard to any group of people whom we have helped turn into refugees. The injury we have done them makes for an affinity between us: thus Vietnamese refugees had, in a moral sense, been effectively Americanized even before they arrived on these shores.[61]

In the author's view Walzer has mixed together two concepts that are certainly not the same – justice and affinity. Still, the larger point is what is most important: that a state which has "helped" to turn individuals into refugees has a duty to these particular refugees that is of the same sort as the obligations that exist to fellow nationals. Yet as one moves from the philosophical realm to the real world one would be hard pressed to find any sort of recognition or indication, or understanding even, of this notion of "helping" to turn individuals into refugees.

The real problem, it is argued, is in our underdeveloped notions of state sovereignty. In the domestic sphere state sovereignty has undergone a veritable sea change in the past half century. In essence a state can no longer take the position that the human rights violations that it carries out against its own people are an "internal" matter, beyond the purview of the international community. Instead, states are now held accountable (at least in theory) for the manner in which they treat those whom they govern.

However, state sovereignty continues to protect against some forms of state responsibility, only now it is far more likely that countries will invoke the sovereignty of *another* state in order to remove *themselves* from any and all responsibility in assisting an outlaw country. Under this approach, no matter how much military and security aid is given to a state that carries out gross violations of human rights – and no matter what levels of refugee flows ensue from these practices – it is not likely that the countries which have provided this aid will have violated any duty or obligation under international law. According to the judgement of the International Court of Justice in the case of *Nicaragua v United States*,[62] the issue comes down to a matter of "control". And the decision of the court would strongly indicate that, while there may be instances where a state is held responsible for its own actions in another state, there will be extraordinarily few instances where a state will be held responsible for its "indirect" actions (in other words, aiding and assisting) in another state. Thus, to use a real-world example, notwithstanding the fact that the USA provides upwards of 80 per cent of the weapons currently being used by the Turkish military,[63] and despite the fact that the US government has been fully aware of the extent of the gross levels of human rights violations that have been carried out with these weapons,[64] it would appear that the USA has done nothing "wrong", or at least nothing wrong according to international law as it stands at present.[65] And what this would also seem to mean is that the USA has absolutely no special duty to any refugees from Turkey or to any of the one million displaced persons in that country.

The point of all this is not merely to show the shortcomings of international law or the hypocrisy of Western states. Far more important is the fact that it is this perpetuation of the notion of transnational state responsibility (but really, non-responsibility) which allows us to see absolutely no connection whatsoever between our own actions and the creation of refugee flows in other parts of the world. The truth is, there is not a single major refugee flow in the world where there has not been substantial involvement by one or more of the Western countries. And yet, as far as the author is aware, there has never been an instance where any one of the Western countries has ever acknowledged even the semblance of responsibility for the human suffering that has taken place in another country. Instead, the reigning attitude is that refugee flows are always caused by the actions of "others". Let us close this section by asking, once again, how it is possible to speak about an "ethics" of refugee policy in this kind of moral universe?

Two principles upon which an ethical refugee policy could be based

It is, of course, much easier to point to the shortcomings in current refugee practice than it would be to try to construct a full-blown ethical refugee policy. Still, at least two principles have emerged from this discussion. As trite and obvious as it might seem, the first principle is that it is important to understand why we have refugee protection in the first place: to save lives and offer protection to vulnerable people. Seldom can (or will) our actions in the world be so directly and so immediately translated into doing "good". Yet as we have seen here, all too often we have lost sight of the quintessential purpose of refugee protection. We have not done this because we are necessarily "bad" people. Rather, we live in a world that is commonly seen as ever more crowded, ever poorer, and ever more dangerous. And some of the refuse from so much of this – refugees – in turn poses a direct threat to our own way of life. But the threat posed by refugees is not simply to our livelihood in a material sense, but to our morality as well. On one level we fully recognize the strength of the claims that refugees possess, but on another level we understand that we are not up to the task of meeting the moral challenge that refugees pose. Because of this it has become easier for us simply to try to avoid having to "deal" with refugees as much as possible.[66] As a result, we have defined away many of those in need of protection, and along with that, we have made great efforts to prevent refugees from ever being able to confront us directly – or our morality.

The second principle that has emerged here is that those of us in the West have given ourselves licence to pretend that while we are a part of the refugee solution (although we grossly overestimate how much of the solution we represent), we are certainly not a part of the refugee problem. As strange as it will undoubtedly seem to future generations, we presently live in a world where states can (and do) fall all over one another to sell all sorts of military weapons to those who will eventually use these weapons to engage in genocide and other forms of gross human rights violations – what immediately comes to mind is the massive re-arming of Burundi and Rwanda that is currently under way[67] – but these same states will share none of the blame or responsibility (at least legal responsibility) for the "aid and assistance" that they provide. But the author will leave it to the reader to ask about the moral universe that we live in.

Notes

1. Marshall Cohen has stated this rather succinctly: "To an alarming degree the history of international relations is a history of selfishness and brutality." And this is the opening line of a piece on ethics in international affairs! Cohen, M., 1985, "Moral Skepticism and International Relations", in Beitz, C., Cohen, M., Scanlon, T., and Simmons, A. J., eds, *International Ethics*. Princeton: Princeton University Press.
2. 189 UNTS 2545, entered into force on 22 April 1954.
3. 606 UNTS 8791, entered into force on 4 October 1967.
4. One exception would be providing protection to so-called "refugee warriors", who invariably bring violence and brutality with them.
5. Gibney, M., 1999, "Missing the Forest for the Trees", *The Humanist*, May/June.
6. Brilmayer, L., 1989, *Justifying International Acts*. Ithaca: Cornell University Press, p. 28.
7. A common expression in ethical theory is that "ought implies can". And to some extent this is what we are seeing here. The point, however, is that the author is absolutely convinced that we "can" be doing much more than we are doing presently to alleviate or prevent human suffering.

8. See generally Moeller, S. D., 1999, *Compassion Fatigue: How the Media Sell Diseases, Famine, and War and Death*. New York: Routledge.

9. This is not to say that the author endorses "open borders", as Joseph Carens has in much of his work. In fact, in many ways the writer supports the opposite policy. Countries should maintain strict control over entry, but they should also establish – and follow – priorities for admission that are based on principles of justice and need.

10. The Human Rights Watch Arms Project has published a number of vital studies documenting the arms selling that goes on in some of the most volatile areas in the world. Among those reports are: "Stoking the Fires: Military Assistance and Arms Trafficking in Burundi", 1997; "Rwanda/Zaire: Rearming With Impunity: International Support for the Perpetrators of the Rwandan Genocide", 1995; "Angola: Between War and Peace: Arms Trade and Human Rights Abuses Since the Lusaka Protocol", 1996.

11. See generally Herman, E. S., 1991, "The United States Versus Human Rights in the Third World", *Harvard Human Rights Journal*, No. 4, pp. 85–104; Jochnick, C. B. and Zimmer, J., 1991, "The Day of the Dictator: Zaire's Mobutu and United States Foreign Policy", *Harvard Human Rights Journal*, No. 4, pp. 139–151.

12. Michael Walzer's book *Just and Unjust Wars* has spawned an enormous amount of attention and debate on the question of humanitarian intervention. See Walzer's piece "The Rights of Political Communities", David Luban's response "Just War and Human Rights", Walzer's counter "The Moral Standing of States: A Response to Four Critics", and finally, Luban's "The Romance of the Nation-State", all of which were republished in *International Ethics*, note 1 above. What makes the debate so artificial, in the author's view, is that it completely leaves out how outside states "intervene" all the time in the affairs of other countries, through the selling of arms and weapons as well as by other means. Thus, to ask under what conditions military "intervention" is appropriate – when a host of other forms of intervention occur almost as a matter of course – is to miss completely how states interact with one another.

13. One of the rare exceptions to this rule has been the work of Roberta Cohen and Francis Deng. See generally Cohen, R. and Deng, F., 1998, *Masses in Flight: The Global Crisis of International Displacement*. Washington, DC: Brookings Institution Press; Cohen, R. and Deng, F., 1998, *The Forsaken People: Case Studies of the Internally Displaced*. Washington, DC: Brookings Institution Press.

14. This is not completely the case. In 1996, obviously in response to the *Kasinga* decision, Congress passed a law that made the practice of female genital mutilation illegal in the USA.

15. Dugger, C., 1996, "African Ritual Pain: Genital Cutting", *New York Times*, 5 October, p. A1. In her article Dugger quotes Thomas G. Hart, the spokesman for the US embassy in the Ivory Coast: "It's a matter principally for local society to determine the extent to which those practices are to be tolerated." The French government echoed this response as well. In the words of Emmanuel Gagniarre, the spokesman of the French embassy in Abidjan: "This is a marginal problem. It's important, but to feed people is probably more important. I don't think it can be an issue when negotiations take place on aid provided to African countries."

16. An exception to this rule would be the approximately one million ethnic Albanian refugees who fled from the Kosovo province during the war between NATO and Serbia. To the author's knowledge, no one has raised the question whether this collective group of individuals were *bona fide* refugees or not – and with good reason. These individuals were specifically targeted and persecuted because of their nation origin (and perhaps because of their religion as well). Because of this (but also because of the Western involvement in the conflict), this seems to be an easy case. But the issue raised is whether this situation differs so markedly from so many other civil conflicts in the world, particularly other ethnic conflicts.

17. Martin, D., 1990, "Reforming Asylum Adjudication: On Navigating the Coast of Bohemia", *University of Pennsylvania Law Review*, No. 138, pp. 1247–1381.

18. Even Joseph Carens, who generally lauds Martin's article, has some apparent trouble reconciling these two views. Carens writes:

Martin acknowledges that civilians caught in a civil war need relocation and yet are not covered by the convention definition because they are not targeted for persecution. Indeed, he regards this as the least well justified element in the convention definition. Suggesting that this provision may reflect the rough judgement that the needs of such victims may often be met by temporary relocation rather than permanent asylum (unlike the needs of targeted victims of persecution), he nevertheless admits that this may often not be true. In a note, he seems to lean toward an expansive interpretation of the convention definition that would, in effect, count civilian populations in war zones as targeted victims when the risk was sufficiently great.

Carens, J., 1997, "The Philosopher and the Policymaker: Two Perspectives on the Ethics of Immigration with Special Attention to the Problem of Restricting Asylum", in Hailbronner, K., Martin, D., and Motomura, H., eds, 1997, *Immigration Admissions: The Search for Workable Policies in Germany and the United States.* Oxford: Berghahn Books, p. 13.

19. Martin, note 17 above, p. 1367.

20. Danner, M., 1994, *The Massacre at El Mozote.* New York: Vintage Books.

21. In many respects this is where Martin and the present author differ. The writer tends to agree with him that temporary protection would be a preferred option rather than permanent settlement, although the author would go further and not limit this policy merely to individuals fleeing war, but to all refugees. But what Martin is speaking about is policy, while the present writer is talking about law (and to a lesser extent morality). Under his view there would be (and should be) nothing *illegal* about sending an individual fleeing the ravages of war back to his country of origin – even to certain death – as long as this person could not show that his persecution was according to one of the five enumerated factors, or if the person could not show s/he was being "singled out" for persecution. In the author's view, any result such as this calls into serious question the law itself, or, more likely, our interpretation of it.

22. The OAU Convention governing the specific aspects of refugee problems in Africa, UNTS 14,691, entered into force 20 June 1974, employs the same kind of language that the UN definition does, but also adds the following:

The term refugee shall also apply to every person who, owing to external aggression, occupation, foreign domination or events seriously disturbing public order in either part or the whole of his country of origin or nationality, is compelled to leave his place of habitual residence in order to seek refuge in anther place outside his country of origin or nationality.

23. The so-called "Cartegena Declaration", adopted by 10 Latin American states in 1984, employs the convention definition, and then this additional language:

... persons who have fled their country because their lives, safety, or freedom have been threatened by a generalized violence, foreign aggression, internal conflicts, massive violations of human rights or other circumstances which have seriously disturbed public order.

Annual Report of Inter-American Commission on Human Rights 1984–85, OEA/Ser.L/ II.66, doc. 10, rev. 1, Conclusion 3.

24. A different issue, but one that deserves some discussion, is the relationship between the Torture Convention and refugee protection. Under Article 3 of the Convention Against Torture and Other Cruel, Inhuman or Degrading Treatment or Punishment, adopted 10 December, 1984, GA Res. 39/46, UN GAOR, 39th Sess., Supp. No. 51, at 197, UN Doc. A/39/51 (1984), "[n]o State party shall expel, return (*refouler*) or extradite a person to another State where there are substantial grounds for believing that he would be in danger of danger of being subjected to torture". Unlike the refugee definition, the Torture Convention does not demand that the ill treatment be based "on account of" any factors. In addition, unlike the Refugee Convention, the Torture Convention does not have a provision whereby protection can be denied because of any act that the claimant might have committed in her country of origin. A final issue is whether the protections of the Torture Convention should be read literally; that is to say, would the claimant who would face "certain death" (but *not* be tortured or subjected to cruel, inhuman, or degrading treatment) be able to claim any protection?

25. Gibney, M., Dalton, V., and Vockell, M., 1992, "USA Refugee Policy: A Human Rights Analysis Update", *Journal of Refugee Studies*, No. 5, pp. 36–46.

26. 502 US 478 (1992).

27. 502 US at 483.

28. *Ibid.*, emphasis in original.

29. *Immigration and Naturalization Service v Aguirre-Aguirre*, decided 3 May 1999 (http://laws.findlaw.com/).

30. There are differences in wording, which may have some significance. Article 33, paragraph 2 of the Convention Relating to the Status of Refugees, 189 UNTS 150, entered into force 22 April 1954, reads:

The benefit of the present provision [*non-refoulement*] may not, however, be claimed by a refugee whom there are reasonable grounds for regarding as a danger to the security of the country in which he is, or who, having been convicted by a final judgement of a particularly serious crime, constitutes a danger to the community of that country.

Under American law, the Attorney General may not grant asylum or the withholding of deportation if she determines "there are serious reasons for believing that the alien has committed a serious nonpolitical crime outside the United States prior to the arrival of the alien in the United States". 8 USC Sec. 1158(b)(2)(A)(iii).

31. UNHCR, 1979, *Handbook on Procedures and Criteria for Determining Refugee Status.* Geneva: United Nations, para. 156.

32. Hathaway, J., 1991, *The Law of Refugee Status.* Toronto: Buttersworth, p. 224.

33. Note that under US law it is not necessary that the refugee claimant be considered as a present danger to the American community. Rather, the statute denies protection to an alien who, at any point in time prior to his arrival in the USA, has committed a serious non-political crime. Note also that this prohibition stands even if the claimant had fulfilled the terms of criminal sanctions for those actions.

34. Bronkhorst, D., 1991, "The 'Realism' of a European Asylum Policy: A Quantitative Approach", *Netherlands Quarterly of Human Rights*, No. 2, pp. 142–158.

35. *Ibid.*, p. 148.

36. *Ibid.* These same kinds of results have also been reported by Arboleda, E. and Hoy, I., 1993, "The Convention Refugee Definition in the West: Disharmony of Interpretation and Application", *International Journal of Refugee Law*, No. 5, pp. 66–90. For example, the same year that Germany accepted less than 1 per cent of Sri Lankan asylum seekers and Switzerland approximately 5 per cent, France granted convention status to 64 per cent and Canada to 96 per cent. For Lebanese applicants, in 1989 and 1990 Switzerland

and Germany accepted between 0 per cent and 2 per cent, while Canada admitted 89 per cent and 80 per cent over the same period of time. These enormous disparities exist in a wide range of countries. The authors express deep concern about this:

What is clear from the statistics are the alarming disparities in the application of the Convention refugee definition among Western states. These disparities mirror the lack of a shared interpretation and understanding of the definition itself, a confusion as to who merits international protection, and the frequently contradictory pull between States' perception of their own national interest and their international legal obligations. Viewed from the perspective of a refugee in need of protection, the situation is indeed disturbing. Moreover, the widely varied interpretations of the Convention refugee definition expose a lack of practical consensus that subverts the integrity of international refugee law, at both theoretical and practical levels. (p. 82)

37. US General Accounting Office, 1987, *Asylum: Uniform Application of Standards Uncertain – Few Denied Applicants Deported*. Washington, DC: USGAO, p. 22.
38. As Bill Frelick has argued, the international community has been all too willing to accede to the "sovereignty" arguments of the Russian Republic and allow the issue of Chechynan autonomy to be treated as a completely "internal affair". He describes the ultimate result of this policy this way: "Displaced civilians not only received no assistance; they were strafed and brutalized even as they fled to make their escape." Frelick, B., 1998, "Aliens in Their Own Land: Protection and Durable Solutions for Internally Displaced Persons", *World Refugee Survey 1998*. US Committee for Refugees, p. 30.
39. See generally Cohen and Deng, *Masses in Flight*, note 13 above. The authors note that at the end of 1996, the UNHCR deemed 4.85 million internally displaced persons (or about a quarter of the world's IDP population) to be "of concern" to the organization.
40. Cohen and Deng, *ibid.*, write:

Of the world's populations at risk, internally displaced persons tend to be among the most desperate ... The U.S. Center for Disease Control reports that death rates among the internally displaced have been as much as sixty times higher than those of non-displaced persons within the same country. In fact, the highest mortality rates ever recorded during humanitarian emergencies have involved internally displaced persons. (p. 2)

41. Undoubtedly the most impressive accomplishment of the international community with regard to the treatment of internally displaced people has been Operation Provide Comfort in Iraq.
42. The author believes that Jim Hathaway first used the term.
43. Carens, note 18 above.
44. 509 US 155 (1993).
45. The UN High Commissioner issued this response to the decision:

[T]he obligation not to return refugees to persecution arises irrespective of whether governments are acting within or outside their borders. UNHCR bases its position on the language and structure of the treaties and on the treaties' overriding humanitarian purpose, which is to protect especially vulnerable individuals from persecution. UNHCR's position is also based on the broader human rights of refugees to seek asylum from persecution as set out in the Universal Declaration of Human Rights.

UN High Commissioner for Refugee Responds to U.S. Supreme Court Decision in Sale v. Haitian Centers Council, 32 ILM 1215 (1993).

46. As ridiculous and inhumane as all this might sound, there is some disturbing precedent in this area. For example, in *United States v Verdugo-Urquidez*, 494 US 259 (1990), the Supreme Court held that US law enforcement agents were not bound by the provisions of the Fourth Amendment in searching the home of a foreign national in Mexico. Beyond this, in *United States v Alvarez-Machain*, 504 US 655 (1992), the court held that the USA was not in violation of either an extradition treaty or international law when US law enforcement agents forcibly kidnapped a Mexican national in Mexico. Finally, and perhaps most disturbing of all, in *Koohi v United States*, 976 F. 2d 1328 (9th Cir. 1992), the Ninth Circuit Court of Appeals dismissed a lawsuit brought by the families of passengers of Iran Air flight 655, a commercial airliner that was mistakenly shot down over the Persian Gulf by the USS *Vincennes*. The court held that the claims were barred by the "combatant activities" exception under the Federal Claims Tort Act, 28 USC Sec. 1346(b) (1994). More than this, however, the court held that the statute would mandate the same result – even if the warship had *purposely* shot down the civilian aircraft.
47. Vedsted-Hansen, J., 1998, "Responding to the Arrival of Asylum-Seekers: Control vs. Protection in Asylum Procedures", paper presented to Technical Symposium on International Migration and Development, The Hague, 29 June–3 July, p. 15.
48. Byrne, R. and Shacknove, A., 1996, "The Safe Country Notion in European Asylum Law", *Harvard Human Rights Journal*, No. 9, pp. 185–228.
49. Goodwin-Gill, G., 1992, "Safe Country? Says Who?", *International Journal of Refugee Law*, No. 4, pp. 248–250.
50. For example, the US State Department *Country Reports on Human Rights Practices for 1990* has the following description of human rights practices in Angola for 1989.

The civil war has resulted in widespread human rights abuses by both sides and many civilian casualties throughout the country. In 1989 the human rights group Africa Watch estimated the total number of civil war victims at 200,000 Angolans killed, more than 20,000 orphaned, and 20,000 to 50,000 Angolans left as amputees due to the widespread use of landmines by both sides.... Across-the-board abuses of human rights ranged from extensive violence against civilians and mistreatment of prisoners to arbitrary detentions, absence of fair trials, and restrictions on freedom of speech, press, association, the right of citizens to change their government, and worker rights. (p. 2)

The State Department report for India that year was not nearly as bad as this (what could be?), but one should seriously question how the country deserves the designation as "safe":

[S]ignificant areas of human rights abuse remain, many of them generated by severe social tensions related to violent ethnic, caste, communal, and secessionist politics and the authorities reactions thereto. The severity of abuses varies from state to state. In 1990 problem areas included: security force excesses against civilians, particularly in Kashmir during operations against militants; separatist terrorism in Punjab, including political murder and kidnapping, as well as extrajudicial actions (harassment and beatings) by the police; incommunicado detention for prolonged periods without charge under national security legislation; political killing on an increasingly wide scale; torture and deaths of suspects in police custody; inadequate although increased prosecution of police and security forces implicated in abuse of detainees, including custodial rape; uneven implementation of laws affecting women's rights; infrequent prosecution of dowry deaths (wife murder); the widespread exploitation of indentured, bonded, and child labor; and widespread intercaste and communal violence. (pp. 1425–1426)

51. The author can draw on personal experiences here. Each year he directs a project – the Political Terror Scale (PTS) – which codes more than 130 countries on the basis of their human rights record for the previous year. Countries are coded on a scale of 1 to 5, where 1 represents few, if any, human rights abuses, and 5 the highest levels of terror. The data come from the State Department Report and the Amnesty International Report. Although there are some differences between the two reports, the similarities are far more common. The PTS scores for 1980–1997 can be found at www.unca.edu/~mgibney.

Countries with an average PTS score of 4.0 or higher have been designated as experiencing "gross and systematic" levels of human rights abuses. This, the author would suggest, would be analogous to terming a country as "unsafe". Countries with an average PTS score (combining Amnesty and State Department scores together) of 4.0 or higher in 1997 were Afghanistan, Albania, Algeria, Angola, Burma (Myanmar) Burundi, Chad, China, Colombia, Congo (Congo-Brazzaville), Egypt, India, Iraq, Kenya, Rwanda, Serbia, Sierra Leone, Sri Lanka, Sudan, and Zaire (Congo).

52. As David Martin has pointed out, the very different manner in which asylum seekers now arrive has made it that much easier to question the claims being presented. Under the old system, individuals would first flee their country of origin and then reside for some period of time (perhaps a decade or more) in an austere refugee camp before resettlement came about (assuming that it ever did). While this process was quite harsh for those who were forced to live through it, it did serve a decidedly useful purpose for receiving countries: the privations that these individuals lived through provided us with a strong assurance of their claims. As Martin goes on to point out, the same thing is not true today in the era of "jet-set" refugees (although this greatly overestimates the number of asylum seekers who arrive by air, at least in the USA). In essence, asylum seekers are no longer given any kind of benefit of the doubt. In fact, quite the opposite is true: their claims are met with enormous levels of suspicion – by policy-makers and the public alike. Martin, D., 1986, "The New Asylum Seekers", in Martin, D., ed., *The New Asylum Seekers: Refugee Law in the 1980s*. Dordrecht: Martinus Nijhoff.

53. See generally Gibney, M., 1998, "A 'Well-Founded Fear' of Persecution", *Human Rights Quarterly*, No. 10, pp. 109–121; Gibney, M., "In Search of a American Refugee Policy", in Forsythe, D., ed., 2000, *The United States and Human Rights: Looking Outward and Inward*. Lincoln: University of Nebraska Press.

54. Susan Raufer estimates that more than 80 per cent of the refugees admitted to the USA through the overseas admission programme are handled within the refugee's country of origin. Raufer, S., 1995, "In Country Processing of Refugees", *Georgetown Immigration Law Journal*, No. 9, pp. 233–262.

55. There is, however, some indication of significant change in American refugee policy. For one thing, although ideological considerations continue to play the single most significant role in determining who gets admitted as a refugee, in recent years other goals and interests have been pursued. For example, since 1995 there has been a surge in the number of refugees from Bosnia. Also noteworthy is the fact that the projection for refugee admissions from Africa for fiscal year 1999 would bring in twice the number of refugees from that continent as were admitted just two short years previously.

56. When sizeable numbers of Russian applicants were denied refugee status in the late 1980s – the simple fact is that they were not being persecuted – Congress responded by passing what has become known as the Lautenberg Amendment, which requires the Attorney General to establish categories of people from the Soviet Union, Viet Nam, Laos, and Cambodia "who share common characteristics that would identify them as targets of persecution". Under this amendment, a member of a category group could establish a well-founded fear of persecution merely by "asserting such fear and asserting

a credible basis for concern about the possibility of such persecution". To be sure, this standard is decidedly more liberal than the refugee definition itself.

57. Gibney, M., 1998, "Certain Violence, Uncertain Protection", paper presented at the conference "New Asylum Regimes in the World", University of Warwick, February 1998; Gibney, M., "The Myth of Asylum Abuse in Western Europe, Canada and the United States", in Tomasi, L., ed., 1999, *In Defense of the Alien, Vol. XXI*. Staten Island: Center for Migration Studies.

58. For an extended treatment of the issue of transnational state responsibility and the manner in which it is treated in various fields of international law, see Gibney, M., Tomasevski, K., and Vedsted-Hansen, J., 1999, "Transnational State Responsibility for Violations of Human Rights", *Harvard Human Rights Journal*, No. 12, pp. 269–295.

59. It is true, of course, that the *non-refoulement* provisions in international law prohibit states from sending a refugee back to a country where she would face persecution. Yet this is different from saying that the receiving state shares any of the responsibility for the refugee's plight in the first place.

60. And some proposals have been set forth to begin to make refugee-producing countries "pay" for producing refugee flows. See, for example, Garvey, J., 1986, "The New Asylum Seekers: Addressing Their Origin", in Martin, note 52 above. To the author's knowledge, no one has ever suggested that Western countries which help to perpetuate this violence and thereby help turn individuals into refugees should similarly "pay" for their actions.

61. Walzer, M., 1983, *Spheres of Justice: A Defense of Pluralism and Equality*. New York: Basic Books, p. 49.

62. *Military and Paramilitary Activities (Nicaragua v. United States)* 1986 ICJ 14 (27 June). This case is the only time that the ICJ has directly addressed the issue of state responsibility for military/security operations in another country. Nicaragua claimed that the USA had violated international law through a series of actions in that country and the ICJ agreed. However, Nicaragua failed to convince the court to hold the USA responsible for violations of international law committed by the Contras, a revolutionary military organization that had received substantial amounts of assistance and training from the US government.

The Court does not consider that the assistance given by the United States to the *contras* warrants the conclusion that these forces are subject to the United States to such an extent that any acts they have committed are imputable to that State. It takes the view that the *contras* remain responsible for their acts, and that the United States is not responsible for the acts of the *contras*, but for its own conduct vis-a-vis Nicaragua, including conduct related to the acts of the *contras*. (para. 116)

63. See generally, Tirman, J., 1997, *Spoils of War: The Human Costs of America's Arms Trade*. New York: Free Press; Human Rights Watch Arms Project, 1995, *Weapons Transfers and Violations of the Laws of War in Turkey*, New York: Human Rights Watch.

64. US Department of State, 1995, *Report on Allegations of Human Rights Abuses by the Turkish Military and on the Situation in Cyprus*. Washington, DC: Government Printing Office.

65. Given the approach currently being taken by the International Law Commission, it is not very likely that the law on transnational state responsibility will change substantially, at least not in the near future. The commentary accompanying Article 27 of the draft articles on state responsibility concerning "aid or assistance" rendered by one state to another demands an *intent* to bring about wrongdoing in this other state. To quote directly from the commentary itself:

As the article states, the aid or assistance in question must be rendered "for the commission of an internationally wrongful act", i.e., with the specific object of facilitating the commission of the principal internationally wrongful act in question. Accordingly, it is not sufficient that aid or assistance provided without such intention could be used by the recipient State for unlawful purposes, or that the State providing aid or assistance should be aware of the eventual possibility of such use. The aid or assistance must in fact be rendered with a view to its use in committing the principal internationally wrongful act. Nor is it sufficient that this intention be "presumed", as the article emphasizes, it must be "established".

2 YB Int'l L. Comm. 104.
66. And we also try to posture as being far more humanitarian than we really are. Consider the fact that while the war in Serbia produced more than a million refugees, the American "contribution" to sharing this burden was to take 20,000 refugees.
67. See generally, Human Rights Watch Arms Project, notes 10 and 63 above.

10

Does globalization have an ethical problem?

Ethan B. Kapstein

International economic theory demonstrates that the freeing of trade and capital flows leads to a more efficient allocation of the world's scarce resources, generating greater output and consumption than would be possible if countries adopted policies of self-sufficiency. As a quintessentially utilitarian doctrine, it also claims that openness makes for good policy, since more output and consumption is held to be better than less. This body of theory, however, is relatively silent on the question of how this wealth ought to be distributed both within and between countries.[1] It is the issue of how the gains from globalization are distributed within countries that is discussed in this chapter.

The argument that will be made is that, from a moral or ethical perspective, economic opening must be judged not only in terms of its contribution to national output, but also in terms of how it affects individuals and their life chances. If it can be shown, for example, that globalization or trade opening creates groups of uncompensated "losers", then its alleged contribution to social welfare may be challenged on normative grounds. Indeed, it will be suggested that there is a fundamental clash in economic theory between the utilitarian and liberal perspectives; that is, between a philosophy which promotes the greatest good for the greatest number and one which emphasizes individual well-being. In making this case the chapter will draw on both moral philosophy and the relevant economic literature.

It is hoped this chapter may be of interest not just to philosophers, but more broadly to those whose chief concern is with the political economy of globalization. With few exceptions, moral issues have not been treated systematically by international political economists, who have focused more on such issues as the domestic politics of protectionism or the international politics of hegemonic power. But power, as John Ruggie has reminded us, is shaped by moral purpose, and it is that purpose which may sustain particular international orders long after their power basis has changed.[2] Examining the moral order underlying the free trade regime may prove illuminating to those who seek an understanding of why popular movements against globalization have taken root in many countries in recent years.

The normative theory of free trade

While the utilitarian avoidance of distributive issues has enjoyed a strong intellectual hold over international economics, recent academic and policy debates over the impact of trade on labour markets suggest that this position is now under assault. The utilitarian framework is not only problematic from a theoretical perspective, but it also avoids some of the most difficult issues facing policy-makers, including the design of efficient and effective compensation packages for "losers". For that reason it is natural that scholars attracted to modern political economy, with its focus on the problem of how individuals pursue their interests, are taking a fresh look at the problem of distributive justice in the context of economic change. Relevant cases in this vein include not just globalization, but the transition from communist to post-communist "market" economies as well.

Trade would hardly raise a political eyebrow if the factors of production displaced by imports could make a frictionless transition to new and equally remunerative economic activities. But in reality trade-displaced workers may face unemployment when wages are rigid (as in Western Europe), or lower wages in the case of more flexible labour markets (as in the USA). That trade could have such an effect has long been part of economic theory.

According to the "factor price equalization" (FPE) theorem first developed by Paul Samuelson in the 1940s, two economies that adopt a policy of free trade will find (given certain strong assumptions) that the returns to the factors of production in each country will tend towards equalization at some intermediate point.[3] This work was built on an earlier theorem, developed by Samuelson and Wolfgang Stolper, asserting that if protection is used to raise the domestic price of goods, the return to the factor used intensively in its production will increase. It follows that if protection is abandoned, the prices and returns will decrease.

Given that free trade produces both winners and losers, how do we evaluate the net welfare benefits of liberalization to a society? That question has troubled economists for centuries, and it became the subject of heated debate in nineteenth-century Great Britain as that country struggled with the dismantling of the age-old Corn Laws which protected domestic agriculture from foreign competition.[4] In seeking to reconcile the ironic conflict between the increased wealth that free trade would bring the country as a whole and the reduced welfare it would cause rural labourers and landowners, John Stuart Mill posited the "compensation principle". As Douglas Irwin describes Mill's principle, "if compensation is paid to those whose incomes fall under free trade, no one would be worse off and everyone could potentially be better off. In this case, free trade would prove best not just for national wealth, but for national welfare as well."[5] That insight would prove especially valuable to the founder of modern welfare economics, Vilifredo Pareto.

Pareto, of course, argued that a policy change could only be justified when someone was made better off without anyone else becoming worse off, and he recognized that compensation would often be necessary in order to satisfy that result. But this "Pareto principle" is devilish to apply in practice, with few issues more challenging either theoretically or in policy terms than the design of compensation packages. This is certainly true in the case of free trade.

For example, while welfare gains from international trade can be achieved via lump-sum transfers to such losers as displaced workers, the problem, as Brecher and Choudri write, is that these "transfers ... require household-specific information ... This information is difficult to collect because households have an incentive to misrepresent their characteristics in order to obtain a larger transfer." To be sure, alternatives have been posited that do not require household-specific information (such as Dixit-Norman commodity taxes), but the underlying models normally assume a full-employment economy, and "do not address the important issue of compensating unemployed workers for jobs lost". Due to these complications, Brecher and Choudhri, among others, have asserted the "infeasability of Pareto gains from trade liberalization".[6]

Liberal – as opposed to utilitarian – social welfare theory, then, gives us surprisingly little reason to cheer free trade. In those cases where workers lose their jobs or see their wages fall owing to foreign competition, it may be hard to make the case that economic opening is Pareto-optimal, particularly given the difficulties associated with designing adequate compensation schemes; more on this problem in a later section. For that reason Brecher, in a classic article, reached the sober conclusion that "home levels of employment and welfare may be less with free trade than with no trade".[7]

On distributive justice

Economic theory tells us that opening a country to foreign trade may have distributive consequences for the domestic factors of production. But in what way does that constitute a moral problem, a problem of distributive justice?

As a body of theory, distributive justice concerns itself with the manner in which societies allocate scarce resources. That allocation is always a matter of policy choice. We could imagine some countries choosing an egalitarian principle of resource distribution, others adopting a market-based system, and still others following a proportionate scheme, as expressed by Marx's dictum, "to each according to his needs". As John Stuart Mill taught, the distribution of wealth and resources "is a matter of human institution only. The things once there, mankind, individually or collectively, can do with them as they like. They can place them at the disposal of whomsoever they please, on whatever terms. *The distribution of wealth, therefore, depends on the laws and customs of society"* (emphasis added).[8]

It has already been noted that international trade theory is a quintessentially utilitarian doctrine. Utilitarians advance the seemingly common-sense proposition that public policies should be guided by the simple rule of advancing the greatest good for the greatest number. This calculation, still widely used today in "cost-benefit analysis" (for example, the decision to build a new road or offer a tax credit), suggests that Policy 2 should be preferred over Policy 1 if Policy 2 produces the most overall "utility" or "happiness" for a given population (often defined in terms of wealth). Utilitarianism is thus a "consequentialist" philosophy; it argues that public policies should be chosen on the basis of their observable consequences for society, and not on the basis of any abstract "first principles" that must locate their ultimate source in God's will, natural law, or human intuition.

Unfortunately, utilitarianism is also perfectly compatible with wide-scale violations of individual rights in the interests of achieving the greatest good, a point noted by philosophers ranging from the liberal John Rawls to the libertarian Robert Nozick.[9] Take a simple example. Imagine that A, B, and C each earn $5 under Policy 1, for a total of $15. Under Policy 2 (let's call it a shift to free trade), A and B earn $3, but C now earns $12, for a total of $18. A utilitarian would urge us to adopt this policy change no matter the distributive consequences. (A more nuanced argument, such as that made famously by Nicholas Kaldor, would claim that since C *could* compensate A and B for their loss – say giving each of them $4 and keeping $10, so nobody is worse off but C is better off – it is the Pareto-superior policy.[10])

There are several reasons for attacking this utilitarian logic. One could argue, for example, that since A and B had legitimate property rights in their labour, policies which deprive them of the rents that normally accrued to them are unjust in the absence of compensation. But the contrary position could also be adopted: namely, that A and B were in fact "rent-seekers" who benefited from protection under Policy 1, and that the shift to Policy 2 is simply stripping them of that monopoly gain.

An alternative and powerful challenge to utilitarianism was developed by John Rawls in his monumental work, *A Theory of Justice*. The "justice as fairness" framework developed by Rawls has, it will be argued, tremendous relevance for debates over the distributive consequences of economic policy change, including the move towards a more open economy. Rawls's emphasis on the "least advantaged" among us is a powerful reminder that, were we on the losing end of change, we would probably want compensation of some sort to assist us in the adjustment process. It is this sort of argument that will be adopted here.

In making the case against utilitarianism, Rawls asserts that:

Offhand it hardly seems likely that persons who view themselves as equals, entitled to press their claims upon one another, would agree to a principle which may require lesser life prospects for some simply for the sake of a greater sum of advantages enjoyed by others. Since each desires to protect his interests ... no one has a reason to acquiesce in an enduring loss for himself in order to bring about a greater net balance of satisfaction ... a rational man would not accept a basic structure merely because it maximized the algebraic sum of advantages irrespective of his own basic rights and interests.[11]

One of the great strengths of the Rawlsian approach is its reliance on the economic framework, grounded on the assumption of rational, self-interested actors. The question at stake is the sort of institutions such actors would build, and whether such institutions conform to some reasonable notion of justice. For Rawls, the "primary subject of justice is the basic structure of society, or more exactly, the way in which the major social institutions distribute fundamental rights and duties and determine the division of advantages from social cooperation". These institutions, which include the political constitution and the principal social and economic institutions, "define men's rights and duties and influence their life prospects, what they can expect to be and how well they can hope to do". Rawls focuses on these deep structures because their effects on life chances "are so profound and present from the start".[12]

Thus, a societal structure that institutionalizes discrimination against certain individuals – that makes it more difficult or even impossible for certain people (perhaps because of race, creed, colour, or gender) to achieve the same goals as those who are in the favoured group – must be considered unjust. We should evaluate institutions in terms of the inequalities they engender – of income, of life chances, of expectations for holding office or achieving one's goals.

Now in choosing rules and institutions, it is likely that rational individuals, coming together as equals, would seek to establish a "level playing field" for their interaction. That is, they would wish to write rules and build institutions that do not favour one person over another, so that nobody would be unfairly advantaged at the start. In order to succeed at the task of social cooperation, the individuals would have to sit down together and put their own personalities, preferences, and interests aside. They must behave as if they were "representative" members of their community, making choices that they believe any rational individual would also adopt if he or she was in their place.

It is in this context that Rawls posits his famous "original position" in which individuals choose constitutional principles for the society in which they live behind a "veil of ignorance", in which they know nothing about their particular backgrounds or talents and act instead as if they were "representative" individuals. This setting "prevents anyone from being advantaged or disadvantaged by the contingencies of social class and fortune; and hence the bargaining problems which arise in everyday life from the possession of this knowledge do not affect the choice of principles".[13]

What principles of justice would one write from behind this veil of ignorance? Rawls posits two:

first, each person engaged in an institution or affected by it has an equal right to the most extensive basic liberty compatible with a similar liberty for others; and second, social and economic inequalities are to be arranged so that they are both (a) reasonably expected to be to everyone's advantage, and (b) attached to positions and offices (equally) open to all.[14]

The first principle is fairly straightforward; the second may be less obvious. Further, given its importance to this discussion of distributive justice, it warrants clarification and discussion.

Rawls's second principle, which he calls the "difference principle", is founded upon the idea that the problem of distributive justice concerns the "differences in (an individual's) life prospects" that arise owing to institutional and societal factors. Discrimination against women or minorities in hiring for certain jobs, or the decrease in life chances that may result because one is the child of a plumber rather than of a surgeon, would be examples of structural influences that place certain individuals in a disadvantaged position. For Rawls, these differences are just if "the advantages of the more fortunate promote the well-being of the least fortunate, that is, when a decrease in their advantages would make the least fortunate even worse off than they are. *The basic structure is perfectly just when the prospects of the least fortunate are as great as they can be*" (emphasis added).[15]

Now let us apply the Rawlsian framework to the issue at hand: the distributive consequences of economic policy change. Imagine, as suggested in the earlier example, that the shift from a policy of protection to a policy of openness results in a change in the distribution of income. Imagine further that unskilled workers find their incomes decline, while owners of capital find their incomes rise. As a result of free trade, income inequality has increased and new patterns of winners and losers have emerged.

What is wrong with that outcome? The Rawlsian view leads us to ask whether we, as self-interested actors, would approve such a policy *if we were unskilled workers.* The reason we would ask ourselves this rhetorical question, even if we were among the winners, is because economic policy change of a different kind could ultimately turn us or our children into losers, and so we have an interest in structuring institutions – buying insurance – in such a way as to account for that eventuality. We would thus probably adopt some compensatory scheme as the "price" we pay for economic opening; and indeed, many scholars have identified a strong relationship between economic openness and the adoption of welfare state policies, with such countries as Germany and Sweden providing notable examples.

Yet there are other types of institutions that are equally important in assisting losers, chiefly financial and economic institutions. These institutions are fundamental to promoting labour and social mobility. To the extent that a loser in Period 1 can get the financing and education needed to become a winner in Period 2, then s/he is more likely to accept economic change. The building of domestic institutions that help potential losers adjust to economic change should thus be seen as a fundamental complement to policies of greater openness.

Why should we care?

The empirical evidence to date suggests that opening a country to trade *does* have some distributive effects. According to the most recent studies, trade may be held responsible for 20–25 per cent of the observed increase in American wage inequality over the past 20 years.[16] Why should we care about this outcome? If we can assume that both investment bankers and janitors (not to mention university professors!) make rational choices about their education and careers, and have equally legitimate property rights in their labour, what is the justification for asserting that the income gap between them should be a matter of policy concern?

Four different types of arguments for policy intervention have been provided by the various authors addressing the distributive justice issue, based on *efficiency, equity, political considerations*, and *social tensions*.[17] This section will examine each of them, with a focus on equity-based arguments.

Almost all justifications for policy intervention begin with the supposition that a market failure has occurred which can be corrected by appropriate government action. In the case of policies for increasing efficiency, the assumption is that inefficiencies or failures in the labour and/or capital markets (such as the inability of unemployed workers to obtain bank loans for training programmes, a market failure which could be corrected by a programme of government loan guarantees) are such that trade-displaced workers are prevented from winning new jobs and thus becoming productive citizens. If a worker *could* obtain a new job upon completing a training programme, but can't pay for that programme due to a lack of personal funds or access to loans, then the government can smooth his or her adjustment path by providing a loan guarantee. The result would be to return the worker to the labour force more quickly, with the efficiency gains this entails. As Michael Mussa puts it, one can model such government actions "under the assumption that the economy is managed by a planner who maximizes the present discounted value of the economy's final output".[18]

This general line of argument, of course, is not trade specific; one could make identical points about displaced workers (or students forced to leave school for lack of funds) in general. But a major challenge to all those who would make such claims for government intervention is to demonstrate that state policy would actually be efficiency enhancing, and that is rarely done. In cost-benefit terms, government policies to compensate the losers may well result in a deadweight loss for the economy as a whole.

A second line of argument is grounded in the political economy of trade. Simply stated, trade adjustment assistance is a necessary pay-off in order to win the support of an important constituency, labour, in trade liberalization. The history of post-war American trade policy certainly supports this contention.

Labour's support for the 1962 Trade Expansion Act, which ushered in the modern era of trade liberalization with the "Kennedy Round" of multilateral tariff cuts, was indeed made conditional on adjustment assistance. As the president of the American Federation of Labor-Congress of Industrial Organizations (AFL-CIO), George Meany, told Congress:

... a trade adjustment assistance program is absolutely essential to a successful foreign trade policy, and, as we have said repeatedly, it is indispensable to our support of that policy. Trade adjustment assistance is based on the broad moral principle that if the Government adopts certain policies designed to promote the welfare and security of the Nation as a whole, it has an obligation to extend effective remedies to those who are penalized by those policies.[19]

Given that the USA is one of the few industrial countries to offer trade-specific adjustment assistance, Michael Aho and Thomas Bayard have concluded that "the political argument for government intervention is really the best argument ... The political argument is that certain interest groups have sufficient political power to block or delay socially beneficial changes unless they are generously compensated or otherwise assisted."[20]

The third line of argument is rooted in social dynamics: that growing inequality and unemployment will become a *cause* of political instability. As Dani Rodrik puts it, "the most serious challenge for the world economy in the years ahead lies ... in ensuring that international economic integration does not contribute to social *dis*integration" (emphasis in original).[21] In making this case, Rodrik uses the French strikes of October–December 1995 as his chief example. These strikes, mainly by public sector employees over their wages and benefits, were, according to Rodrik, driven by the Maastricht Treaty on European integration and its implications for the French welfare state. Given the treaty's "convergence criteria" that required European states to cut their fiscal deficits and lower their inflation and interest rates, governments were expected to make sharp cuts in social spending. On this basis, Rodrik asserts that "the strikes expressed a clear desire on the part of a sizable portion of the country not to sacrifice social protections to trade".[22]

What about equity-based arguments? The Rawlsian case was developed at length in an earlier section, but the reader is reminded here that Rawls's argument is grounded not in ethical reasoning but in *self-interest*. In the trade case, however, it could also be reasonably asserted from an equity standpoint that trade-displaced workers do not have any greater claim to taxpayer-sponsored assistance programmes than other workers, and indeed they may be owed *less*. The reason is that, to the extent workers in import-sensitive industries accrued a rent during the pre-free-trade era (since they were protected by trade barriers which pushed factor prices to artificially high levels), they have no claim on state funds now that those barriers – and, in turn, their rents – have been reduced.

Similar arguments can also be made against union members and other workers (for example, in the defence sector) who have accrued a rent at consumers' expense in time period one and then seek compensation for their subsequent job loss in period two.

In this context one recalls Rawls's argument: that the main reason why we build compensatory institutions which take account of the least advantaged is because we ourselves might someday be in that situation. Thus, the appropriate ethical question that follows concerns what sorts of programmes we would expect our societies to provide for those made "least advantaged" by trade opening. More likely than not, we would want programmes that help us respond to policy change.

Incidentally, there may also be good economic reasons to be concerned about rising inequality in the face of globalization, and one is its effect on long-run growth. A number of studies now suggest that rising levels of inequality may put a brake on growth, due to several possible causal pathways. One theory attempts to link rising inequality with popular demands for redistribution or "soak-the-rich" policies that in turn lead to capital flight, lower investment, and lower growth. An alternative theory, posited by Alberto Alesina among others, is that inequality is a *direct* cause of social instability, and thus lower investment and lower growth.[23] In either case, excessive inequality is likely to undermine social peace and economic development.

Compensating the losers

No matter what the rationale for government intervention, once the policy decision is taken to compensate displaced workers in some way, we will have an interest in designing programmes that provide them with the most assistance at the least cost. Naturally, the best outcome would be a seamless transition from job A to job B with no loss in income or benefits. But that rarely happens, even in an economy with tremendous job growth and low unemployment, as in the USA. Instead, the vast majority of workers will face some transitional period before they get a new job, and the question is what to do for them during that time.

A great debate on this issue continues to rage within the policy analysis community, with one important dividing line between those who focus on "welfare state"/social safety-net policies (such as income transfers) and those who focus on the construction of institutions that promote labour mobility (such as education and training). While a common-sense answer is that "some of both" are needed, the problem concerns how scarce resources should be allocated. The OECD, for example, is among those calling for greater emphasis on active policy measures.[24] However, since most welfare state programmes (for example, unemployment compensation) have now become entitlements, active measures become subject to annual budget appropriations and must compete for any available discretionary funds. That has made it more difficult to design and sustain programmes that may take several years to achieve success.

A useful review of existing programmes for trade-displaced workers in the American setting has recently been provided by Louis Jacobson. Jacobson has studied trade adjustment assistance (TAA) in more detail and over a longer period of time than anyone else on the American scene, and is a prominent player in programme design and evaluation. That makes his conclusion "that there is no inexpensive way to substantially reduce the large losses of high-tenure, dislocated workers" all the more disturbing.[25]

Jacobson reminds us that certain groups of workers have suffered tremendous income losses as a result of job displacement. Taking the case of industrial workers in Pennsylvania, for example, he argues that the "modal worker", who would have been a 37-year-old high-school graduate working in the steel industry, has suffered lifetime earnings losses averaging $80,000 following displacement. This supports the conclusion offered by labour economist Robert Hall: "The loss of a job can be a significant economic event."[26]

American workers who can show that their displacement was caused by imports have access to trade adjustment assistance, which provides unemployment compensation and educational/training benefits. TAA, which began in 1962, has been subject to considerable political controversy since the outset. As initially written, the legislation made it almost impossible for workers to prove that they had been trade displaced. Politically motivated changes during the Carter administration – driven largely by automobile workers facing Japanese auto imports – greatly increased programme spending. As a result, it was again scaled back during the Reagan administration.[27]

Even in the best of circumstances, these TAA programmes are temporary, and the question remains about the post-displacement experiences of unskilled workers. In order to encourage the transition to a new job, a great deal of emphasis has been placed in recent years – particularly by the Clinton administration and its first Secretary of Labor, Robert Reich – on training programmes. The underlying idea is that if workers somehow increased their store of human capital, becoming more highly skilled, it would be easier for them to find some of those new, well-paid jobs. Is that the case? How well have existing programmes done at moving workers from low-skilled to high-skilled status?

In fact, the latest available research casts considerable doubt on the value of training programmes. Careful screening of potential candidates is necessary to ensure successful programme completion, but this suggests, somewhat pessimistically, the strong correlation between success and prior educational background. In short, those who are more highly educated already are those most likely to profit from further education and training.[28]

What then can we do?[29] The answer depends, of course, on the problem we are seeking to fix; and in all cases economists will tend to prefer the most efficient solutions at hand. Thus, if the problem we are seeking to address is low wages, the answer would be higher wages via income transfers. In this vein some economists, notably Krugman, have focused largely on expansion of the earned income tax credit (EITC). He argues that "the incomes of low-wage workers need support ... The obvious answer is ... an income supplement."[30] Edmund Phelps, in contrast, advocates a wage subsidy, so that low-wage workers receive a "top-up" in their paychecks.[31] The USA, of course, has made significant use of the EITC, while Britain and other European countries are beginning to experiment with a modified version of the Phelps plan.

Yet a different programme of wage support has been advocated by a number of different economists, including Jacobson and analysts at the Brookings Institution. They suggest that the USA adopt "earnings insurance" so that displaced workers who find new jobs at lower pay receive additional income from some common fund. The programme would be designed in such a way that "most of the funds would go to workers with the largest losses, and workers would have strong incentive to earn as much as they can" in their new jobs. But the "problem with implementing earnings insurance" schemes, according to Jacobson, "is its high costs". His plan, for example, "would cost about $9 billion per year".[32]

Still another approach to displaced workers is to provide incentives for greater labour mobility. While the USA does permit moving expenses to be offset against income taxes, much more could be done to encourage interregional mobility. The logic here is that the human capital which workers have accumulated may be of value to employers in a different part of the country, and that this is a more efficient use of that individual's skills than attempting retraining into a new line of work. One reason why the government has not done more in this area is perhaps due to the fact that few congressmen have an incentive to develop programmes which encourage their constituents to leave. And this, of course, raises larger issues concerning the political economy of compensation schemes that few of the authors under review have probed in any detail.

With respect to the problem of unemployment as opposed to inequality, only Wood takes a stab at the problem. He suggests that "the government might use taxes and public expenditure to boost the relative demand for unskilled labor". Public works programmes, for example, represent one direct method for government to bring the unskilled into the workforce.[33] But such programmes must be designed in such a way so as not to replace existing (high-wage) workers with the unemployed.

Wood also says, and quite courageously in the European context, that "reducing unemployment might require a reduction in the real average wage".[34] Unlike their American counterparts, inequality has been less sharply felt by unskilled workers in Western Europe, largely due to a more supportive institutional environment. Indeed, it is said – probably too simplistically – that America has accepted greater inequality while Europe has accepted more unemployment. Wood makes clear that if Europeans wish to generate more jobs for the unskilled, they too may have to accept more flexible wages.

At a more fundamental level, many economists have also stressed the critical role that education – or the lack thereof – plays in future income. Indeed, studies of the relationship between education and inequality show a strong correlation. The World Bank reports that "policies that increase the education of the poor can have a dramatic impact on wage inequality".[35] What this confirms is the strong linkage between education and labour market outcomes. Such findings may be of little benefit to today's displaced workers, but adopting policies that ensure the ability of their children to get ahead is an important step to take.

Overall, the policy literature with respect to unemployment and income inequality leaves us with a fairly bleak picture. Those who lose their manufacturing jobs will probably suffer severe lifetime income losses, making it clear why insecurity among this group is on the rise. The emergence of new compensation schemes, like earnings insurance, has been blocked owing to problems with programme design, high cost, or existing political incentives. Proposals to "lower wages" may make good economic sense as a way of generating employment, but are unlikely to win much political support, particularly among Western Europe's social democratic regimes.

This suggests the unfortunate conclusion that it has proved very difficult to craft a set of policies capable of transforming today's losers into tomorrow's winners. Better education opportunities will certainly help the next generation of workers, but that provides little solace to those who are now displaced or labouring for low wages. Income transfers of the kinds proposed by Krugman and Phelps would help as a bridge, and indeed the earned income tax credit has already been expanded in the USA. The question of a "bridge to what?", however, remains unanswered.

Conclusions

The latest economic research on the relationship between economic openness and labour outcomes demonstrates that the growth of the 1990s' tide has failed to "lift all boats". Unskilled workers are struggling in the face of unemployment, job insecurity, and rising income inequality. Of all these developments, rising income inequality is of special concern to many scholars, due not only to its political implications for the free trade agenda, but also its possible economic consequence in terms of lower growth rates in future.

What are the implications of these findings for students working at the interface of philosophy and political economy? The literature reveals several important gaps that could usefully be filled by careful theoretical and empirical work. These contributions would help refine our understanding of the issues at stake in the globalization-labour debate.

First, as we have seen, there are important analytical gaps in social welfare analysis. Bridging the utilitarian and liberal perspectives remains a major challenge for political economy scholarship, with important implications for policy analysis as well. We have still not found a way to reconcile the view that economic openness is "good" for society with the design of adequate compensation schemes for losers and their families.

Second, the empirical finding of increasing income inequality in the USA and persistent unemployment in Western Europe raises important questions concerning the making of economic policy. Whose interests are reflected in public policy, and how has that constellation changed in recent decades? Are exporter interests trumping those of organized labour? What explains the differences in national labour adjustment strategies in the face of increasing economic integration? Comparative work that provides careful process tracing of the political economy of globalization, following the model of Peter Katzenstein's *Between Power and Plenty*, could shed needed light on the emerging pattern of winners and losers around the globe.[36]

Third, the openness-labour relationship reminds us of the role of political and economic institutions in influencing the life chances of all citizens, but especially the least advantaged. A just economy would be one in which all members of society can benefit from economic change as their talents permit. This means that change and opportunity must go together, via the capital markets and educational establishments. In countries that simply permit economic change to occur without the creation of such enabling institutions, resentment and backlash may be expected.

In sum, the ethics of globalization are a function of how its effects are channelled through social organizations, mainly nation-states and their associated institutions, to the individuals who constitute the ultimate moral unit. The author has argued that a Rawlsian approach, with its emphasis on the fate of the least advantaged, provides a useful analytical tool for examining questions of distributive justice within the context of economic openness. It reminds us that globalization can only be welfare enhancing when it promotes the life chances of *all* members of the international community. In this respect, we still have a long way to go.

Notes

1. For a classic statement of the utilitarian position with respect to trade theory, see Meade, J., 1955, *The Theory of International Economic Policy, Trade and Welfare.* Oxford: Oxford University Press, p. 5.
2. Ruggie, J. G., 1982, "International Regimes, Transactions and Change: Embedded Liberalism in the Postwar Economic Order", *International Organization*, Vol. 36, No. 2, Spring, pp. 195–231.
3. Cline, W., 1997, *Trade and Income Distribution.* Washington, DC: Institute for International Economics, pp. 40–41.
4. Crosby, T. L., 1977, *English Farmers and the Politics of Protection, 1815–1852.* Hassocks: Harvester Press.
5. Irwin, D., 1996, *Against the Tide: An Intellectual History of Free Trade.* Princeton: Princeton University Press, p. 183.
6. Brecher, R. A. and Choudhri, E., 1994, "Pareto Gains from Trade Reconsidered: Compensating for Jobs Lost", *Journal of International Economics*, Vol. 36, May, pp. 223–225.
7. Brecher, R. A., 1974, "Minimum Wage Rates and the Pure Theory of International Trade", *Quarterly Journal of Economics*, Vol. 88, February, pp. 98–116.
8. Mill, J. S., 1970, *Principles of Political Economy.* New York: Penguin, orig. 1848, book II, chap. 1, p. 350.
9. Nozick, R., 1974, *Anarchy, State, and Utopia.* New York: Basic Books.
10. For a useful review of the utilitarian literature see Acocella, N., 1998, *The Foundations of Economic Policy.* New York: Cambridge University Press, p. 34.
11. Rawls, J., 1971, *A Theory of Justice.* Cambridge, MA: Belknap Press, p. 14.
12. *Ibid.*, p. 7.
13. *Ibid.*, p. 321.
14. *Ibid.*, p. 60.
15. *Ibid.*, p. 328.
16. For a review of the evidence, see Kapstein, E. B., 2000, "Winners and Losers in the Global Economy", *International Organization*, Vol. 54, No. 2, Spring, pp. 359–384.
17. Collins, S. M., 1998, *Imports, Exports, and the American Worker.* Washington, DC: Brookings Institution, p. 36.
18. Mussa, M., 1982, "Government Policy and the Adjustment Process", in Bhagwati, J., ed., *Import Competition and Response.* Chicago: University of Chicago Press, p. 74.
19. Meany, G., 1962, "Statement of George Meany, US Congress, House of Representatives, Committee on Ways and Means. Trade Expansion Act of 1962", *Hearings before the Committee on Ways and Means.* 87th Congress, 2nd Session, 13 March, p. 1148.
20. Aho, M. and Bayard, T., 1984, "Costs and Benefits of Trade Adjustment Assistance", in

Baldwin, R. and Krueger, A., eds, *The Structure and Evolution of Recent U.S. Trade Policy*. Chicago: University of Chicago Press, p. 160.

21. Rodrik, D., 1997, *Has Globalization Gone Too Far?* Washington, DC: Institute for International Economics, p. 2.

22. *Ibid.*, p. 44.

23. For a review of this literature, see Kapstein, E. B., 1999, *Sharing the Wealth*. New York: W. W. Norton, pp. 112–123.

24. OECD, 1994, *The OECD Job Study*. Paris: OECD.

25. Jacobson, L., 1998, "Compensation Programs", in Collins, note 17 above, p. 475.

26. Hall, R. E., 1995, "Lost Jobs", in *Brookings Papers on Economic Activity*, 1. Washington, DC: Brookings Institution, p. 221.

27. Jacobson, note 25 above, p. 486.

28. *Ibid.*, pp. 505–506.

29. For a useful review of the options, see Lynch, L. M., 1997, *What Can We Do?: Remedies For Reducing Inequality*. New York: Council on Foreign Relations Study Group.

30. Krugman, P., 1997, "Workers and Economists I: First, Do No Harm", in *The New Shape of World Politics: Contending Paradigms in International Relations*. New York: Foreign Affairs/W. W. Norton, p. 210.

31. Phelps, E., 1997, *Rewarding Work*. Cambridge, MA: Harvard University Press.

32. Jacobson, note 25 above, p. 515.

33. Wood, A., 1994, *North-South Trade, Employment, and Inequality*. Oxford: Clarendon Press, pp. 368–369.

34. *Ibid.*, p. 386.

35. World Bank, 1995, *World Development Report*. New York. Oxford University Press, p. 42.

36. Katzenstein, P. J., ed., 1978, *Between Power and Plenty: Foreign Economic Policies of Advanced Industrial States*. Madison: University of Wisconsin Press.

11

Conclusion: The task(s) of international ethics

Nicholas Rengger

Ethical reflection on international politics has, it would seem, finally come in from the cold. Regarded as something of an Aunt Sally in most discussions of international relations during the Cold War, the last few years have made it obvious to all but the most hidebound (and antiquated) positivist that normative and ethical issues are irrevocably intertwined with all questions of world politics. The war in former Yugoslavia, the atrocities that occurred during it, the establishment of war crimes tribunals after it – all this amply displayed the centrality of normative questions, but then so have debates over global financial reform, the persistence, even increase, in the gap between rich and poor, the arrest and (possible) trial of the former Chilean president Pinochet, and many other events in recent years.

These events have naturally been mirrored by the growth of academic treatments of "international ethics" in general and specific aspects of it in particular, a trend to which this book is obviously a contribution. The previous chapters have covered a range of topics in international ethics, some familiar, some less so, and have amply shown the breadth as well as the depth that characterizes this growing discussion. In this concluding chapter, the author would like to reflect on these essays, offer some suggestions on what separates them and, more importantly, what links them, and, finally, suggest that there is an additional task for international ethics on top of the one all of the essays here concentrate on, which deserves consideration, not in *opposition* to the ways represented here, but as a complementary activity.

International ethics: Where are we now?

To start with, however, this chapter will offer a brief account of "where we are now" in international ethics, suggesting that there are three broad approaches to the subject available in the contemporary literature – approaches which, by the way, straddle a number of disciplinary boundaries (that is to say they are chiefly represented within philosophy, political science and international studies, law, and even, though rather more fitfully, economics and theology). For the purposes of this chapter these will be called the "traditional" approach, the "analytic" approach, and the "critical" approach. This obviously cuts across more usual ways of dividing up international ethics, perhaps the commonest of which is the division into "cosmopolitan" and "communitarian" approaches.[1] Without trying to argue the case in any detail here, it is simply suggested that, important and influential thought this division is, it does not quite encapsulate the parameters of the current debate in international ethics, and a tripartite division along the lines suggested above is more helpfully specific.

The traditional approach

This approach is probably the largest and certainly the most diverse. It ranges from some sceptical liberals (of differing sorts) to various forms of conservative and realist ethics. It also contains a large amount of what David Campbell calls "the increasingly familiar field of 'ethics and international affairs'" (see Chapter 5 in this volume). The paradigm case of this "field", Campbell suggests (and he is not alone in this), is many of the articles that appear in the journal of the same name published by the Carnegie Council for Ethics and International Affairs.[2] It is also probably true that this is the basic approach of many practitioners in international affairs who are concerned with ethical/normative questions. The general assumption that guides much writing in this area is the persistence – perhaps regrettable but real nonetheless – of the state and its power in world politics and the inference that is usually drawn from this, to wit that it is the moral behaviour *of states* that should be the main or at least the primary focus. The two books that would probably win most people's votes as obvious modern classics of "international ethics" both fall under this heading: Michael Walzer's *Just and Unjust Wars*[3] and Stanley Hoffmann's

Duties Beyond Borders.[4] Other leading scholars who would adopt variants of this approach include Mervyn Frost,[5] Michael Joseph Smith,[6] Joel Rosenthal,[7] Chris Brown,[8] Terry Nardin,[9] and rare (though happily increasing) non-Anglo-American entrants in the field, such as Luigi Bonanate.[10] The interests of all these writers are not the same, of course, and there are sharp differences of both method and substance between them. Nonetheless, they are recognizably engaged on a common activity, however much their versions of it might differ from one another.

The analytical approach

Over the last 30 or so years, however, a rather different emphasis has become increasingly important, though it overlaps a fair amount with the traditional approach. It has both benefited from and contributed to the growing power of analytical political philosophy since the publication of Rawls's seminal *A Theory of Justice* in 1971[11] (though Rawls himself, in his international ethics, is closer to a traditional view[12]). In general, it is much less attached to the basic structure of the states system than the traditional approach, and is thus often characterized by a thoroughgoing universalism of one sort or another. Major analytical international ethicists would include Charles Beitz,[13] Henry Shue,[14] Onora O'Neill,[15] Brian Barry,[16] Peter Singer,[17] Robert Goodin,[18] Thomas Pogge,[19] Martha Nussbaum,[20] Amartya Sen,[21] and increasingly David Crocker.[22] The political assumptions of analytical international ethics are broadly liberal as well as universalist in orientation (though some rather more than others) and it takes a variety of forms, most especially utilitarian (like Singer[23] and Goodin[24]) and deontological (like O'Neill,[25] Beitz,[26] and Pogge[27]), but also, more recently, a sub-naturalist human needs approach, known as the "capabilities" approach and associated especially with Sen[28] and Nussbaum.[29] The subjects that they have tended to focus on are continuations of the major concerns of liberal political philosophy more generally during the period, especially questions of justice and rights, and thus the key aspect of the analytical approach has been a focus on the development of *principles* of conduct and of institutional design and/or reform that can reflect, institutionalize, or embed such principles.

Critical approaches

Although the differences between the above two approaches have been emphasized, it is also worth pointing out that there is a good deal of overlap as well. Often the differences are as much a question of philosophical or theoretical style, or a difference of intellectual focus, as a difference of real substance. However, over the last few years a growing range of critical approaches have grown up in international studies in general, and these often have distinct ways of viewing "international ethics". Without wanting to deny the very real differences that exist between various critical approaches, one can suggest that one of two things (at least one) usually links them. The first is a difference of what we might call "background intellectual orientation" from the earlier two approaches. Specifically, approaches to ethics rooted in post-Husserlian European thought are extremely influential on many such writers (in this volume, David Campbell explicitly locates himself in this context). The second is a concern with a range of issues that tend to problematize the dominant assumptions of both the dominant trends in international ethics; to wit, the universalism of the analytic approaches and the statism (whether hard or soft) of the contextual approaches. Amongst the more prominent writers working in this area with a concern for international ethics would be Walker,[30] James Der Derian,[31] Jean Bethke Elshtain,[32] William Connolly,[33] Daniel Warner,[34] Michael Shapiro,[35] David Campbell,[36] Mick Dillon,[37] and, from a rather different perspective, Andrew Linklater,[38] plus many feminist writings on ethics both within and outside formal "international ethics" (as Kimberly Hutchings's chapter suggests). Some of these writers would, of course, have some overlaps with one or both of the other approaches. Perhaps most importantly here, Andrew Linklater's approach, drawing as it does on the recent discourse ethics of Habermas and advocating the emergence of a dialogic community, would seek to use all three traditions to develop an inclusive account of the ethical dilemmas governing contemporary world politics.[39] Notwithstanding this, however, most would be profoundly critical of the other two approaches to international ethics.

The current growth in "international ethics" is taking place in all three above approaches and – though more gradually – also as part of a dialogue between them. The critical approaches have in many respects started this, since by definition they need to debate to show what it is they are critical of, but it is increasingly being taken up by advocates of the other two approaches as well. This is a positive development, and again is one to which this book makes a contribution.

What contribution?

Which brings us, of course, to the question of what, exactly, the book argues: what contribution does it make? Obviously all the individual chapters contain new ideas – or alternatively, perhaps, traditional ideas expressed in new and challenging ways – so one answer to that question is to say that the "new issues" are to be found in the specifics of each chapter and, of course, up to a point that is true. All the essays contain new thinking, and even where the topics are not new (as with Pierre Hassner's meditation on one of the oldest ethical problems of all, violence), the treatment of them is fresh and invigorating.

Moreover, the three approaches outlined earlier are all represented (more or less) in the book. Oran Young's essay, for example, quite happily fits within the general rubric discussed here as "analytical", though it offers nods in the general direction of the traditional approach as well. Mark Gibney's thoughtful essay on refugees and Jack Donnelly's discussion of rights fit more into the traditional approach (though with nods in the direction of the analytical approach). David Campbell, meanwhile, offers a characteristically powerful and – if he will forgive the term – almost paradigmatic version of what is called here the "critical" approach.

Although the rest of the chapters are rather more difficult to "place", on the surface at least, one would have to say that the balance of this book as a whole leans towards a critical approach, since all the remaining chapters are "critical" in a broad sense – if less overtly "critical" than Campbell. This situation is also mirrored in the basic focus of the chapters. Those by Donnelly, Gibney, and Young are very much concerned with principles and institutions, those by Hassner, Hutchings, Toscano, and Kratochwil largely with contexts, norms, and the possibility of universality. That of Campbell contains a root-and-branch critique of traditional (and at least by implication, analytic) approaches.[40]

This last point brings us to a second way in which this book (as a whole) represents "new thinking in international ethics". One of the central issues addressed by the research project of which this volume is the culmination was the connection between discrete and specific aspects of international ethics and the *problematique* of universality/particularity. Most current writing in international ethics privileges *either* universality *or* cultural (or some other kind of) specificity, as the editors point out. This volume as a whole, however, seeks to move beyond this opposition, and in this sense at least seeks an openness in the discussion of international ethics that much of the current literature does not display. In particular, a number of the chapters in this volume (especially those by Hassner, Kratochwil, Campbell, Toscano, and Hutchings) foreground the question of universality *and* particularity. Without suggesting that all (or even any) of the contributors would agree with the way the author interprets this, it can be suggested that this view *itself* implies a certain ethical approach in contemporary world politics, and that this itself raises a "new issue" in international ethics not formally discussed in the book but implied by it.

This issue is simply how one understands the mechanics of practical reasoning in a multicultural and multi-perspectival world. The next section will briefly explore the ways in which this issue is foregrounded in the book, by teasing it out as a theme that links all of the chapters, though not always explicitly. The subsequent section will ask what this approach might generally imply, and suggest two possible ways of approaching it.

Cases, contexts, and dilemmas

To start by saying something about the three broadly "traditional" chapters, these are largely concerned with the ethical aspects of policy, process, and institutionalization in world politics, and all of them revolve around a central dilemma. In the case of Oran Young's thoughtful and detailed elaboration of environmental ethics and international society, the focus is on the networks of ethics found in the core documents of international environmentalism – the Stockholm Declaration on the Human Environment of 1972, the World Charter for Nature of 1982, the Rio Declaration of 1992, and the draft Earth Charter. The core principles to be found in these documents, Young says, form an embryonic international environmental ethics, but contained within it are two separable and potentially divergent ethics, a *biocentric* ethics of environmental protection and an *anthropocentric* ethics of sustainable development. In Young's view the latter is stronger in contemporary international society than the former, but it is seeking to relate these two together and recognizing the tensions which exist between them that he chiefly wishes to emphasize as a central task for those concerned about international environmental ethics in the future. For Gibney, the main problem in the discussion of refugees is the unwillingness of liberal states to recognize that, far from simply being the solution to the refugee problem, they are a large part of the problem. By selling arms to others they create the conditions which fuel most of the current wave of refugee crises, a point which amplifies Donnelly's closing remarks that even liberal democratic states, where in some sense the rights revolution has become most embedded, still have a long way to go. For Donnelly, the central thrust is to argue that the notion of human rights requires a certain kind of state – liberal, democratic, and oriented to welfare – but that this state is itself a state which seeks to strike a difficult balance between democratic participation, market efficiency, and internationally recognized human rights, a balance very difficult to strike effectively and one that is being put under increasing pressure as world politics evolves and changes.

In each of these chapters, then, the central dilemma is one of "striking a balance"; what balance should be struck, between what, and how? The focus is on the "principles" that we have evolved in international society and the difficulties of our keeping to them or arranging all our principles so that they cohere, but the real question is, so to speak, a "how to?" question rather than a "what?" question. The remaining chapters in the book, as already mentioned, appear on the surface very different. Yet one could suggest that they are fundamentally concerned with exactly the same issue, though they express it in different ways.

Take Pierre Hassner's absorbing contribution. Hassner argues, follow-ing in this case Leo Strauss, that the opposition between the universal and the particular is often seen as the "deepest" of ethical questions, the tension between one's own good and *the* good – if, indeed, a workable definition of the good for all is available (which, parenthetically, Strauss would probably privately have denied). In the context of discussing ethics and violence, Hassner suggests that the way through this tension in the context of violence is to break what he calls "the cycle or the dialectic of the bourgeois and the barbarian", of an "indirect, sanitized violence based on economics and technology and of a brutal, murderous, or sui-cidal one, based on the dehumanization of enemies", and that what this will require is ultimately "a rebirth of philosophy and a new birth of politics". Leaving aside for the moment either the likelihood or the character of such a new politics (*new* politics always have a worrying tendency to resemble older and more familiar ones, even if in disguise), Hassner is clearly gesturing towards a view of political ethics that is sep-arate from both the universalism of the analytic approach and the par-ticularism of the critical approach.

Both Roberto Toscano and Kimberly Hutchings seek to be rather more programmatic in this regard, but they too end up focusing on a dilemma. Toscano's thoughtful probing of the ethical possibilities of diplomacy concludes with a meditation on the importance both of a variation of Weber's ethic of responsibility and of going beyond it, towards a "pre-cautionary principle" which should result in "zero damage". This reminds the author, at least, of John Dunn's argument that what con-temporary political philosophy chiefly needs is a reworked conception of prudence,[41] and of course there is something to this. Yet one might say to Toscano, as the author has already said of Dunn,[42] that unless such a view is *also* yoked to a substantive conception which will enable us to make choices between goods or bads then it amounts to little more than a souped-up version of the old saw, "look before you leap". The dilemma here is what can help us develop a "precautionary principle" that does not make us cautious when we should be daring and vice versa. Hutch-ings, too, seeks to suggest that her particular focus, feminist ethics, can transcend the universality/particularity divide, but suggests that it does so by inserting a feminist ethic of care into the more usual rights-based ethics. Again, however, the question surely arises, *can* we do this (and if we can *how* might we do this) in a manner which allows the integrity of rights and the distinctive capacities of the ethics of care to be integrated?

David Campbell's characteristically powerful essay on Bosnia is, as was suggested above, very critical of the sorts of "appeal to principles" found in the chapters by Donnelly, Young, and Gibney. In their place he proposes a concern with the "ethical relation", where our "responsibility for the other" is the basis for reflection. Here surely, it might be thought, we move away from the focus on "dilemmas". Yet Campbell too ends up with a "dilemma" of sorts. By challenging the often-unquestioned assumptions about sovereignty that operate in the traditional discourses of "ethics and international affairs" (a challenge with which the author largely agrees in form, if not in content), he raises even more pressingly the question *how* do I decide what to do, who to help, when to act, and when to refrain from acting?

Of all the essays, it is Kratochwil who perhaps puts his finger on the key aspect of the problem. His argument is that we should pay much closer attention to the question of practical reasoning than either traditional scholarship in international relations or (modern) conceptions of ethics have done. And to do this, he suggests that we pay much closer attention to "law" than perhaps has been usual, as it provides us with a useful "first cut" at complex practical and moral choices in world politics, and also because its method of reasoning – casuitical, case based, and moving from facts to norms and back again – is peculiarly well suited to sorting out our ethical dilemmas in ways that the "tyranny of principles" (borrowing here a phrase of Stephen Toulmin[43]) is not.

This suggestion is a very important one. Kratochwil is quite correct, in the author's view, to emphasize the centrality of practical reasoning to ethical reflection, and quite correct also in suggesting that most dominant contemporary traditions of ethics – whether utilitarian/consequentialist, deontological, or post-structural – do not so foreground it. However, perhaps "law" is not the best place to begin the task of developing a practical reason for international ethics. A legal focus is, after all, only one way in which ethical "cases" might be discussed, and not always perhaps the best one. In many cases a largely legal focus might indeed *obscure* some of the central ways in which a case might need to be considered "ethically", which is not, of course to say that one should *ignore* the legal aspects of a case. In his penetrating study of the public policy processes involved in the *Thorp* decision in Britain, for example, William Walker has eloquently shown how an excessive focus on the legal aspects of the case blocked creative and casuitical ethical and policy choices that might have led to a possible way out of an otherwise seemingly intractable dilemma.[44]

The central problem, then – in all the chapters – is how we can reason in such a way as to give purchase on questions of praxis that force us to adopt neither a sapping and sterile "tyranny of principles" nor a sliding scale of "context is all" which makes ethical choice depend upon mere personal preference. This, the author would suggest, is the common thread which points up one of the central problems of contemporary international ethics: the need for a conception of practical reason which will enable us to judge, but hobble us neither with timebound universalisms nor sterile particularities.

Practical reason and/or cosmopolitan judgement

Practical reason, then, has emerged as a central issue in the book in all approaches to international ethics. There is not the space here, of course, to offer even a brief account of the various possible ways in which practical reason has been or might be understood. It is obvious that there would be many disagreements between the contributors to this book alone. To point to perhaps a very obvious one, Campbell's emphasis on the "ethical relation" to the other would clearly require and warrant a very different conception of practical reason (if he would even want to call it that) to that developed by Kratochwil. Although there is a sense wider than that shown in this volume of the importance of practical reason – even in the homeland of international studies[45] – the recognition is simply the beginning, not the end, of the journey. Rather than seek to summarize the complex and currently ongoing discussions about the appropriate character of practical reason and how to understand it, then, this penultimate section seeks to contrast two general approaches to the whole question of practical reason in international ethics, and suggest a reason why it is important that one is not allowed to swamp the other.

By way of an introduction, let us refer to an argument of Stephen Toulmin's.[46] For much of his career, Toulmin has argued for the centrality of a broadly Aristotelian conception of practical reason. The concern dates back to his now classic *The Place of Reason in Ethics* and *The Uses of Argument*, but is central to all his most recent work, which emphasizes the "rediscovery" of the importance of this in the modern, even post-modern, context. In his most recent treatment of all[47] he calls it "reasonableness". He points out that the whole notion of practical reason (on an Aristotelian understanding at least) issues not in principles or hypotheses but in actions, and that its hallmark is *reasonable* (and thus appropriate) action rather than simply *rational* (and thus perhaps inappropriate) action. "Reasonableness" is contextual, and can be sensitive to the specifics of any given case in a way that "rationality" – at least as

conventionally understood – cannot. Thus, human sciences which emphasize the rational *at the expense* of the reasonable (in his 1998 Tanner
lectures economics is singled out for special criticism here) are bound to
fail. This is a position which would clearly find some favour with many of
the contributors to this volume (even those closer to traditional and analytic approaches might not find it too objectionable), and it is unques-
tionably true that it is among the best ways of starting to think through
the question of practical reason in ethics generally. To this extent, the
"return to practical reason" evident in most of the contributions to
this book is an extremely important and valuable move in international
ethics, and should be one of the central areas of debate in the next few
years.

However, a prior question is surely to ask what, exactly, we are seeking
to do when we "do" international ethics. And here there is an interesting
parallelism in all the chapters in this book. *All* the approaches share the
view that they are primarily involved in what we might call action-guiding
activity. The agents might be different, the character of the actions would
certainly be different, the way the actions would be defended and justified
would be different, but the *point*, in a sense, is that "ethics" is action
guiding. Of course, it is also true that the *manner in which* it is action
guiding is different for different authors. Terry Nardin, in a well-known
book,[48] borrowed from Michael Oakeshott the idea that there might be
two modes of international association and therefore (though he does not
put it quite like this) two modes of international ethics, one oriented
around the idea of common purposes or goals and the other oriented
around the notion of a practical association governed by rules of accommodation. It is not that either is usually absent in world politics, rather
they coexist in a slightly uneasy tension one with another. Interestingly,
many "critical" theorists of international ethics and many analytic theorists would both argue that (different) versions of the purposive model
should be in the driving seat, whereas many traditionalists would favour
some version of the practical association model (as Nardin does himself).
However, the point here is that *both* models are predicated on the assumption that ethics is action guiding.

It is not, of course, wrong to suggest that ethics is action guiding. Indeed an ethic that was not action guiding in some sense would be a very
odd ethic indeed. However, the development (in whatever form) of
action-guiding ethical claims does not, the author suggests, *exhaust* the
requirements of international ethics. Rather it is a task that needs to be
complemented by a somewhat different approach.

This approach is not well recognized in contemporary international
ethics (indeed in ethics and political theory more generally), and where it

is recognized it is most commonly viewed with suspicion (at best). Here it will be termed a "cosmopolitan" approach, despite the risk that calling it that invites misunderstanding, since the advocates of liberal universalism such as Beitz, Pogge, and Nussbaum have all used that term to define their own views. This is not the place to seek to dispute their usage in detail (though dispute it the author certainly would), and it is simply asserted that *this* cosmopolitanism should not be confused with what is better termed "universalism" and to which the above-mentioned authors all subscribe. On this author's understanding, a cosmopolitan view would hold that human beings are of course ethical beings, but they are ethical beings *amongst other things*. Ethics (however understood) is indeed central to our self-understanding (this is why approaches in the human sciences that do not take cognizance of the irreducible normativity of human action can never offer properly meaningful accounts of human action), but the *character* of the ethical in human life and its relationship to politics is not best seen either in terms of "principles" or simply in terms of "practical reason", understood as Aristotle understood the practical syllogism (in other words, as action guiding). Rather it is an imperative to *place* ethics in human life and to understand its relation to other aspects of our existence. A truly "cosmopolitan" conception of ethics and politics then offers an understanding of the *place* of ethics, as well as contextually specific accounts of ethical action.

The problem is that *all* the dominant accounts of international ethics (and the author would also argue ethics and political theory in general) neither recognize nor allow space for such a conception. The demand that "ethics" – whether understood as the search for principles (an "ethical theory"), as the "ethical relation", or as some form of practical reason – be properly practical has evolved in such a way that a more detached "ethic" is almost read out of the equation completely. It should be added that, of course, this cosmopolitan view is also distinct from the view dominant in the anglophone ethical and philosophical traditions for much of the twentieth century that the real task of ethics is "meta-ethical": looking at the sort of thing ethics is, how we ground it, and so on. Its roots are much older (indeed, broadly Greek in origin), and its modern advocates, few though they have been, deeply critical of the notion of "meta-ethics".

On the author's reading, however, not only are the two tasks of international ethics complementary, but one could go further and suggest that in order properly to develop an action-guiding ethic, the cosmopolitan situating of ethics alongside other aspects of human evaluative commitments (political, aesthetic etc.) is *necessary*.

This last claim is certainly controversial, and it would take much more space than is available here even to sketch a defence for it. The author will just conclude by suggesting that it is only when we offer a rounded view of our evaluative commitments as human beings, and therefore stipulate what these commitments are to and when, that we can have a real sense of the weight we should place on ethical judgements *vis-à-vis* other kinds of judgements (for example aesthetic judgements), as well as being aware of the proper relation between such judgements. And it is only when we can do this that we can really understand what an "ethical" judgement might be in any given context (in this case, of course, an international context).

International ethics for a new century

The author would like, then, to close these concluding remarks with one final suggestion, though exhortation might be a better word. Amongst the "new issues" for international ethics in our new century is the job of relating the specific and often urgent contextual demands of normative judgement in an increasingly complex and multifaceted world to a sense of the place ethical judgements should have in the range of things we value as humans. Since ethical judgements as action guiding are necessarily context specific – which is not the same as saying that they are *relative only* to the specific context – such a task requires a cosmopolitical viewpoint (that is to say, one which does not prejudge any issue of value, obligation, or agency) which can *go hand in hand* with a recognition of the necessarily situated judgements we make in our day-to-day lives, whether in the private realm or the public one. For all the sensitivity to context and awareness of political specifics displayed by the contributions to this book, it is appropriate perhaps, at the end of it, to urge that the tasks of international ethics in the new century should not be limited to action guiding, even if, also appropriately, this task should take pride of place.

There will be some, the author does not doubt, who will suggest that such a task, even if necessary, is more properly left to philosophy. One could counter that this simply shows a failure to understand what is at stake in such a task. Without it, "international ethics" will, properly so called, be impossible. Without international ethics there can be no proper understanding of contemporary world politics. We cannot rely on others to perform the task for us – though we should certainly listen much harder than the social sciences have traditionally done to their conversations, even when conducted in languages we may initially find alien. However, the task of outlining a cosmopolitan view and relating it to the contextual complexities of twenty-first-century world politics is ours. We must not shirk it.

Notes

1. Brown, C., 1992, *International Relations Theory: New Normative Approaches*. Brighton: Harvester Press; Thompson, J., 1992, *Justice and Order in International Relations*. London: Routledge. I am not sure that Chris Brown would still divide up the field this way, either. In some of his recent work there are suggestions that he might not; see Brown, C., 2000, "Cultural Diversity and International Political Theory: From the Requirement to Mutual Respect", *Review of International Studies*, Vol. 26, No. 2, pp. 199–213.
2. Though the author thinks one should be careful of oversimplistically classifying an excellent journal, its audience, or those who write for it. For example, one recent issue (March 1999) contained five articles on one of the most important developing issues in contemporary international ethics (forgiveness, reconciliation, and restitution), hardly a common "traditional" theme, and previous issues have contained articles by a number of those who might be described as "critical" in their general approach. See, for example, Crawford, N., 1998, "Postmodern Ethical Conditions and a Critical Response", *Ethics and International Affairs*, No. 12, pp. 121–140.
3. Walzer, M., 1977 (2nd edn 1991), *Just and Unjust Wars*. Harmondsworth: Penguin.
4. Hoffman, S., 1981, *Duties Beyond Borders*. New York: Syracuse University Press. Though some might also opt for Shue, although this is clearly written in the analytical mode: Shue, H., 1980 (2nd edn 1996), *Basic Rights*. Princeton: Princeton University Press.
5. Frost, M., 1986, *Towards a Normative Theory of International Relations*. Cambridge: Cambridge University Press; Frost, M., 1996, *Ethics in International Relations: A Constitutive Theory*. Cambridge: Cambridge University Press.
6. Smith, M. J., 1997, 'Growing Up with *Just and Unjust Wars*: An Appreciation', *Ethics and International Affairs*, Vol. 11, pp. 3–18; Smith, M. J., 1998, 'Humanitarian Intervention: An Overview of the Ethical Issues', *Ethics and International Affairs*, Vol. 12, pp. 63–80.
7. Rosenthal, J., 1992, *Righteous Realists: Responsible Power in the Nuclear Age*. Baton Rouge: Louisiana State University Press; Rosenthal, J., 1998, *Ethics and International Relations*. Georgetown: Georgetown University Press.
8. Brown, 1992, note 1 above; Brown, C. (ed.), 1994, *Political Restructuring in Europe: Ethical Perspectives*. London: Routledge.
9. Nardin, T., 1983, *Law, Morality and the Relations of States*. Princeton: Princeton University Press; Nardin, T. and Mapel, D., eds, 1992, *Traditions of International Ethics*. Cambridge: Cambridge University Press; Nardin, T., 1998, *The Ethics of War and Peace*. Princeton: Princeton University Press.
10. Bonanate, L., 1995, *Ethics and International Politics*. Cambridge: Polity Press.
11. Rawls, J., 1971, *A Theory of Justice*. Cambridge, MA: Harvard University Press.
12. Rawls, J., 1994, "The Law of Peoples", in Shute, M. and Hurley, S. (eds) *On Human Rights*. London: Harper Collins; Rawls, J., 1999, *The Law of Peoples*. Cambridge, MA: Harvard University Press.
13. Beitz, C., 1979 (2nd edn 1999), *Political Theory and International Relations*. Princeton: Princeton University Press.
14. Shue, note 4 above.

15. O'Neill, O., 1986, *Faces of Hunger*. London: George Allen and Unwin; O'Neill, O., forthcoming, *Bounds of Justice*. Cambridge: Cambridge University Press.
16. Barry, B., 1991, *Democracy, Power and Justice*. Oxford: Clarendon Press.
17. Singer, P., 1993, *Practical Ethics*. Cambridge: Cambridge University Press.
18. Goodin, R. E., 1993, *Utilitarianism as a Public Philosophy*. Cambridge: Cambridge University Press.
19. Pogge, T., 1989, *Realizing Rawls*. Ithaca: Cornell University Press.
20. Nussbaum, M. and Sen, A. (eds), 1994, *The Quality of Life*. Oxford: Clarendon Press; Nussbaum, M., *et al*, 1996, *For Love of Country*. Boston: Beacon Press; Nussbaum, M., 1999, *Cultivating Humanity*. Cambridge, MA: Harvard University Press.
21. Sen, A., 1981, *Poverty and Famines*. Oxford: Clarendon Press.
22. Crocker, D., 1995, "Functioning and Capability: The Foundations of Sen's and Nussbaum's Development Ethic", in Nussbaum, M. and Glover, J., eds, *Women, Culture and Development*. Oxford: Clarendon Press; Crocker, D., 1999, "Reckoning with Past Wrongs: A Normative Framework", *Ethics and International Affairs*, Vol. 13, pp. 43–64.
23. Singer, note 17 above.
24. Goodin, note 18 above.
25. O'Neill, note 15 above.
26. Beitz, note 13 above.
27. Pogge, note 19 above.
28. Sen, note 21 above.
29. Nussbaum, note 20 above.
30. Walker, R. B. J., 1993, *Inside/Outside: International Relations as Political Theory*. Cambridge: Cambridge University Press.
31. Der Derian, J., 1997, "Post-Theory: The Eternal Return of Ethics in International Relations", in Doyle M. and Ikenberry G. J., eds, *New Thinking in International Relations Theory*. Boulder: Westview Press.
32. Elshtain, J. B., 1998, *New Wine in Old Bottles; Ethical Discourse and International Politics*. Notre Dame: University of Notre Dame Press.
33. Connolly, W. E., 1991, *Identity/Difference: Democratic Negotiations of Political Paradox*. Ithaca: Cornell University Press; Connolly, W. E., 1996, *The Ethos of Pluralization*. Minneapolis: University of Minnesota Press.
34. Warner, D., 1992, *An Ethic of Responsibility for International Relations*. Boulder: Lynne Rienner.
35. Shapiro, M., 1996, *Violent Cartographies: Mapping Cultures of War*. Minneapolis: University of Minnesota Press.
36. Campbell, D., 1998, *National Deconstruction: Violence, Identity and Justice in Bosnia*. Minneapolis: University of Minnesota Press; Campbell, D. and Shapiro, M., (eds), 1999, *Moral Spaces: Rethinking Ethics and World Politics*. Minneapolis: University of Minnesota Press.
37. Dillon, M., 1995, *Politics of Security*. London: Routledge.
38. Linklater, A., 1982 (2nd edn 1990), *Men and Citizens in the Theory of International Relations*. London: Macmillan; Linklater, A., 1997, *The Transformation of Political Community*. Cambridge: Polity Press.
39. Linklater, 1997, *ibid*.
40. It is worthwhile to note, though the author is unsure of its overall significance, that Campbell's chapter does not cite a single figure in what has here been termed the "analytical" tradition. Since he does cite Chris Brown's 1992 book (Brown, note 1 above), which does discuss them, as part of his general critique of conventional ethical theorizing, it is reasonable to assume that his intended critique applies to them as much as to the "ethics and IR" brigade he explicitly attacks. However, an attack on (for example)

Martha Nussbaum would have to be couched in very different terms to the one he launches, which is largely predicated on conventional approaches to ethics accepting the logic of sovereignty – which, agree with her or not, Nussbaum certainly does not.

41. Dunn, J., 1990, *Interpreting Political Responsibility*. Cambridge: Cambridge University Press.
42. Rengger, N., 1995, *Political Theory, Modernity and Postmodernity: Beyond Enlightenment and Critique*. Oxford: Blackwell; Rengger, N., 1995, "Trust, Prudence and History: John Dunn and the Tasks of Political Theory", *History of Political Thought*, Vol. XVI, No. 3, pp. 416–437.
43. Toulmin, S., 1992, *Cosmopolis: The Hidden Agenda of Modernity*. Chicago: University of Chicago Press.
44. Walker, W., 1999, *Nuclear Entrapment: Thorp and the Politics of Entrapment*. London: IPPR.
45. Alker, H., 1996, *Rediscoveries and Reformulations: Humanistic Methodologies in International Studies*. Cambridge: Cambridge University Press.
46. Jonson, A. and Toulmin, S., 1986, *The Abuse of Casuistry*. South Bend: University of Notre Dame Press; Toulmin, note 43 above; Toulmin, S., forthcoming, *The Rediscovery of Reasonableness*. Cambridge, MA: Harvard University Press.
47. Toulmin, forthcoming, *ibid*.
48. Nardin, 1983, note 9 above.

Contributors

David Campbell is professor of international politics and director of the Centre for Transnational Studies at the University of Newcastle, England. His most recent publications include *Moral Spaces: Rethinking Ethics and World Politics*, edited with Michael J. Shapiro (Minneapolis: University of Minnesota Press, 1999); *National Deconstruction: Violence, Identity and Justice in Bosnia* (Minneapolis: University of Minnesota Press, 1998); and *Writing Security: United States Foreign Policy and the Politics of Identity*, revised edition (Minneapolis: University of Minnesota Press, 1998).

Jean-Marc Coicaud is a senior fellow at the US Institute of Peace (Washington DC) while on leave from the Peace and Governance Program of the United Nations University (Tokyo), where he serves as a senior academic officer. He also teaches social and political philosophy at the New School University (New York). Formerly a fellow at Harvard University, he was a member of the Executive Office of the Secretary General of the United Nations (1992–96), where he served as speechwriter. He is the author of *L'introuvable démocratie autoritaire* (L'Harmattan, 1996), and *Legitimacy and Politics. A contribution to the study of political right and political responsibility* (Cambridge, 2001).

Jack Donnelly is the Andrew Mellon Professor at the Graduate School of International Studies, University of Denver. He has written extensively on international human rights issues, including the books *Universal Human Rights in Theory and Practice* and *International Human Rights*. His most recent book is *Realism and International Relations* (Cambridge, 2000).

279

Mark Gibney is the Belk Distinguished Professor at the University of North Carolina-Asheville. His interests include human rights, refugees, international law, and international ethics. He is the author and/or editor of *Judicial Protection of Human Rights: Myth or Reality?* (1999), *Open Borders? Closed Societies?: The Ethical and Political Issues* (1988) and *Strangers or Friends: Principles for a New Alien Admission Policy* (1986).

Pierre Hassner is a research associate and former research director at the Centre d'Etudes et de Recherches Internationales (CERI) in Paris. He also been a professor at the Institut d'Etudes Politiques, Paris, and a visiting professor at Harvard University. He is the author of *La violence et la paix* (Paris: ed. Du Seuil, 1995). He has also published many articles on political philosophy and international relations.

Kimberly Hutchings is a senior lecturer in politics at the University of Edinburgh. She works in the areas of international and feminist political theory. She has published *Kant, Critique and Politics* (Routledge, 1996); *International Political Theory: Re-thinking Ethics in a Global Era* (Sage, 1999) and *Cosmopolitan Citizenship* (co-edited with Roland Dannreuther, Macmillan, 1999).

Ethan B. Kapstein is Stassen Professor of International Peace at the Humphrey Institute and Department of Political Science, University of Minnesota, and currently is visiting professor of economics and politics at INSEAD, and a visiting fellow at the Institut Francais des Relations Internationales. He is the author of

many books and professional articles, most recently *Sharing the Wealth: Workers and the World Economy* (W. W. Norton, 1999).

Friedrich V. Kratochwil is Professor of International Politics at the Geschwister-Scholl-Institut of the University of Munich (Ludwig-Maximilians-Universität). He is author of *International Order and Foreign Policy* (Boulder: Westview Press, 1978) and *Rules, Norms and Decisions: On the Conditions of Practical and Legal Reasoning in International Relations and Domestic Society* (Cambridge: Cambridge University Press, 1989), as well as numerous articles. He has edited volumes on international law (together with Richard Falk and Saul Mendlovitz), international organization (together with Edward Mansfield), and most recently, with Yosef Lapid, *The Return of Culture and Identity in International Relations Theory* (Boulder: Lynne Reinner, 1996).

Roberto Toscano has degrees in law and in international relations. A career diplomat since 1969, he has served in Santiago, Moscow, Madrid, Washington, and Geneva, where he was deputy permanent representative at the Italian mission at the United Nations. He is presently head of policy planning in the Italian Ministry of Foreign Affairs. Author of a book on titled *Soviet Human Rights Policy and Perestroika* (Harvard University Press), he has published numerous essays and articles on international themes in Italy, the US, France, and Spain.

Nicholas Rengger is professor of political theory and international relations at St Andrews University in

Scotland. He is also currently the president of the international ethics section of the International Studies Association. He has interests in, and has published on, many aspects of political theory, intellectual history, international ethics, and world politics. His most recent book is *International Relations, Political Theory and the Problem of Order* (Routledge, 1999).

Daniel Warner is deputy to the director for external relations and special programmes at the Graduate Institute of International Studies, Geneva, and executive director of its Program for the Study of International Organization(s). He has written extensively on political issues including ethics, international organization and law, refugees, and responsibility. The author of *An Ethic of Responsibility in International Relations* (Boulder and London: Lynne Riener, 1991), and editor or co-editor of seven books, his writings have appeared in major academic journals.

Oran R. Young is professor of environmental studies and director of the Institute on International Environmental Governance at Dartmouth College. He is also a professor at the University of Tromsø. His most recent book is *Governance in World Affairs*.

Index